WOMEN WHO ROCK

To my mom—whose singing around
the house instilled love of music in
my heart—and to yours.

WOMEN WHO ROCK

BESSIE TO BEYONCÉ.

GIRL GROUPS TO RIOT GRRRL.

EDITED BY EVELYN McDONNELL

BLACK DOG
& LEVENTHAL
PUBLISHERS
NEW YORK

CONTENTS

WE'VE GOT THE BEAT

INTRODUCTION BY EVELYN McDONNELL

"In the beginning, there was rhythm." So shrieked teenaged Ari Up with full-throated joy over the herky-jerk of Viv Albertine's guitar, the dub lope of Tessa Pollitt's bass, and helter-skelter drums by Budgie (Soiuxsie Sioux's beau) in a 1980 song by English punk tarts the Slits. Rhythm—the repeated ordering of breaks and beats, of stops and starts, of motion and stillness, of life and death—gives popular music its pulse, its purpose. Rhythm is the pattern that propels us, onto the dance floor or maybe, with Martha Reeves and her Vandellas, into the street to dance. Grace Jones warned us about being slaves to the rhythm, or was she inviting us? Janet Jackson founded a Rhythm Nation. We can move to the rhythm, but also, crucially, we can move the rhythm. We are a rhythm movement.

Ari was a rhythm mover. With her bandmates, she created not just a new way of making music but of being in the world. A German waif plunked down into the cruel streets of Thatcher's London calling, the woman born Arianna Forster generated vocalizations with the wild abandon of an alien autodidact. She didn't just absorb the punk disruptions of such peers as Johnny Rotten; she propelled them, pulling notes like taffy—up and down, in and out—testing the bounds and elasticity of pitch, tone, volume. Ari cut her own path stylistically, too, with her ragged layers and spandex leggings. Sure, she sported that most dubious of dos: blond dreadlocks. But she wasn't so much from northern Europe as from

another planet, and eventually she decided to leave the colonizer for the colonies, reinventing herself as late-night dancehall groover Medusa in Jamaica. When I met her in New York in the nineties, she was a widow, a single mother, a legend, a character—and also someone just trying to figure out how to get by, to make her art and raise her children.

All the people in this book are rhythm movers: the musicians, the writers, the illustrators. They have not merely tried to fit into the grooves of popular music (or scholarship, or art) but have jumped the beat. They are musicians who inspire and compel us, the editors, writers, and illustrators of *Women Who Rock*. They also inspire other musicians—in fact, many of the contributors to these pages are musicians—by carving out sonic possibilities, by kicking down the doors through which their followers charge. They are pioneers more than settlers, explorers but not necessarily popularizers—mothers of invention. They are Sister Rosetta Tharpe, pulling the gospel out of a guitar. Selena, embodying the multiple cadences of border culture. Björk, dancing beside you in a virtual reality video then stepping inside you—or are you stepping inside her? Beyoncé, commanding, "World stop!" in a video alongside her bestie Nicki Minaj . . . then chuckling, "Carry on." Women who bend, break, and create code tend to be dismissed as weirdos, freaks, divas, or bitches. This book honors them as heroes, leaders, geniuses, and, in

Miami rapper Trina's phrase, da *baddest* bitches—as women who rock.

Early in the process of creating this book, my collaborators and I agreed that rather than attempt to be encyclopedic and all inclusive, summarizing the thousands of women who have made incredible, indelible music in the last century, we wanted to tell a narrative story by focusing on key select figures who were true game changers. From the beginning, we had the concept of "women who rock," which we knew was not a new phrase, and which we were fully aware was problematic even at the most basic semantic level—but which we also felt had a simple, direct power. Women. Who. Rock.

Women. We love women. That doesn't mean we hate men or overlook folks who fall somewhere in between the two poles of gender (from Big Mama Thornton to Joan Jett to Laura Jane Grace). But we also recognize the centuries of oppressive systems that have conscripted humans born with child-bearing hips (as PJ Harvey says) into hard domestic labor and barred their self-expression and public lives. Much of my work as a journalist, critic, and historian has been spent trying to describe and remedy the obstacles women musicians and writers face, and to celebrate the work they do despite—or perhaps because of—those obstacles. Carole King wrote some of the greatest pop songs of all time while she was a young mother in a bad relationship with her songwriting partner. A teenager named Alicia Armendariz found refuge from her violent father in LA's punk rock community and reinvented herself as Alice Bag. Janet Jackson broke away from binding family ties to assert control of her own career, music, image, and life.

We chose to make a book about women because there is strength in unity—divided, we fall. We're not arguing that these music makers are all formally or stylistically linked. This isn't a book about the genre "women's music" (though Alice Bag does salute June Millington and Olivia Records in the essay she penned) or even, necessarily, an embodiment of Hélène Cixous's call for *écriture feminine*, though I embrace her mandate in the essay "The Laugh of the Medusa": "Woman must write her self." *Women Who Rock* champions mold smashing and pattern disruption. It offers portraits of diversity, from Patsy Cline's country melancholy to Joni Mitchell's folk jazz to Missy Elliott's avant rap.

Who. Are you? This book honors identity. It unapologetically embraces exceptionalism. It's dedicated to the notion that while all people are created equal, some manage to excel. Yes, there were more than one hundred girl groups who collectively defined an era of pop, civil rights, and feminist history. But as storytellers, we understand the power of the individual human narrative that embodies the bigger cultural change, so we homed in on members of the Supremes, the Ronettes, the Crystals, and the Bluebelles. Call it great women history, if you want. We believe in the greatness of women.

Rock. Gender is not a genre in this book, and neither is rock. As I told the writers who helped choose whom to profile, we use *rock* as a verb, not a noun. We perceive it not as a static entity, defined by loud guitars and a 4/4 beat, but as an action that defies the containing force of a label—and that evokes a rich lineage of musical motions, from the lullaby swing of a cradle, to gospel's transformation of the soul, to the sexual call-and-response of rock and roll, full circle back to soul rocking your baby.

There were rough parameters that guided our choices. The subjects all created music after the advent of the commercial recording business—in other words, when popular music really came into its own as a performed, reproducible, sellable good. You could say that the book focuses on the rock era, the period beginning in the mid-1950s when hitherto segregated styles of music became entwined as rock and roll, and you would not be wrong. But I argue that we move the narrative arc forward and outward, into the pop era. (Or is it the mom-and-pop era?) After all, feminist and other scholars have for years critiqued "rockism": the hierarchizing of individualized styles of music, particularly those performed by white men, as more authentic than those styles that are created for broader commercial appeal, often via a collective process with women as its public face. Despite its title (and let's face it, *Women Who Pop* just doesn't work), this book fully embraces rockism's counter philosophy, poptimism, in that I believe the Supremes are just as important to musical history— let alone to history history—as Bob Dylan.

It has been twenty-one years since our clearest predecessor, *Trouble Girls: The Rolling Stone Book of Women in Rock*, was published. That's a generation or three in popular culture. In that esteemed volume, there's no TLC, no Dixie Chicks, no Lady Gaga, no Missy Elliott, no Taylor Swift, no Destiny's Child— let alone no Beyoncé! Women have ruled the popular music stage more than ever in the past five, even ten, years. It's well past time to canonize these game changers and to connect them to the noble lineage that made their advancements possible. Sometimes, I asked the musicians themselves to invoke their inspirations. Wendy Case of the great Detroit bands the Paybacks and Royal Sweets pays homage to Chrissie Hynde. Stephanie Phillips plays guitar and sings in the London punk band Big Joanie; she penned

eight entries in this book, including tributes to Poly Styrene, Aaliyah, and Amy Winehouse. Post-punk pioneer and pop survivor Adele Bertei enshrines volcanic diva Tori Amos.

Narrowing the list of subjects was a bitch. It was the absolute hardest part of this book (which overall was a joy and a thrill to put together). The selection process was both painstaking and arbitrary. I had a wish list. Then I consulted a dozen or so writers whose work I admired, experts in a variety of genres who represented different demographics: race, age, gender orientation, geography, and so on. I asked them to submit lists of ten musicians they would like to write about for this book. Their suggestions put the combined list of subjects well over two hundred, which forced me to make dozens of excruciating choices. Sometimes, that meant picking subjects who best represented an era, rather than, say, every worthy Riot Grrrl band, or OG rapper, or seventies singer-songwriter. The final 103 acts here are by no means my favorites—that would be a very different book—but they encompass a range that I think is both broad and deep.

There are excellent books about women and popular music written by single authors, including Ann Powers's *Good Booty* (Ann wrote about Joan Baez and Donna Summer for this book), Gillian G. Gaar's *She's a Rebel* (Gillian wrote several essays for us), and Lucy O'Brien's *She Bop*. We always envisioned *Women Who Rock* as presenting not just a plenitude of subjects but also of voices and visions— of literary and visual art as well as musical. Our original editorial team of about ten writers mushroomed for a variety of reasons, but mostly because there were so many women I wanted to work with, some of whom had space in their busy schedules for only one or two essays. I loved editing these talents. Peaches praising Sinéad O'Connor! Original Riot Grrrl Allison Wolfe talking to Girly Sound maker Liz Phair! Poet jessica Care moore's ode to Betty Davis! I believe some of these pieces—Jewly Hight on Dixie Chicks, Kandia Crazy Horse on Marianne Faithfull, Vivien Goldman on Angélique Kidjo—are *the* definitive takes on their subjects. Others make important arguments about pop's gender trouble, such as Daphne Brooks demanding to know why Nina Simone didn't earn a place in the Rock and Roll Hall of Fame decades ago, or Rebecca Haithcoat's testament to Janet Jackson as a model of self-determination.

Over and over in *Women Who Rock*, there are stories of women persisting—against all odds. Rape, bad contracts, sexual exploitation, addiction, anorexia, corrupt managers, suicide, domestic violence, prison, murder: These aren't extreme cases; they are recurring motifs. Women have put up with a lot of shit in order to sing their songs and make their records, to walk in this world and live the lives they choose. Too many of these tales end tragically. But perseverance, hope, family, love, change, stardom, talent, work, and revolution are also themes. One performance of one hymn may have sent two members of Pussy Riot to Russian gulags, but the spectacle of their trial shone a light on the repressive injustice of Vladimir Putin's regime and made them a global cause célèbre. Now they travel the world speaking out against prison systems and make videos that continue to engage and enrage.

The writers created portraits in words, each distinctive in its point of view but also illuminating. We wanted the artwork that accompanied these essays to be equally original. So rather than seek existing photographs, we commissioned artists to draw portraits in paint, ink, pencil, and digital color. These imaginative illustrations—Björk's head beside a planet,

Mavis Staples's afro curved into a Black Power fist, Fiona Apple shimmering in a pool of water—define *Women Who Rock* as much as the texts and their subjects do. If you're like me, you're probably wondering how you can simultaneously read this book and spread its pictures all over your wall.

"I wanna be your Joey Ramone, pictures of me on your bedroom door," the all-grrrl band Sleater-Kinney sing. If I had to give one single reason why this book exists, it's to pay it forward. I've been blessed in my career to have had access to many of the artists whose music has kept the blood pumping through my veins, some of whom are in this book as subjects, or writers, or artists (check out Grace Slick's self-portrait!). I feel personally heartsick that we didn't manage to include an entry on the Slits. Ari was by far one of the most interesting people I ever had the honor to know, but beneath her head of hair and kinetic energy beat a heart of gold. I'll never forget the time she called me from a thousand miles away on Valentine's Day; she was phoning all her girl friends, to let us know we were loved. It was one of the last times we talked; Ari Up died of cancer in 2010.

As human beings, we all search for models of how to be in the world, even if, like Oedipus, we also may want to replace those who made our existence possible. Just as Bessie Smith inspired Janis Joplin, who inspired Patti Smith, who inspired Tegan and Sara, I hope the rhythm movers in *Women Who Rock* inspire the next generation of wayward daughters to pick up a bass, or a microphone, or a sampler. Or a pen, or a laptop, or a paintbrush. Or maybe, even just to push the *Pause* button. Because as Ari also sang, "silence is a rhythm too."

World stop!

Now, carry on.

EDITOR'S NOTE

These essays are presented in chronological order based primarily on when the subjects first began their recording careers.

The playlists consist of tracks generally picked by the writers of the essays (June Millington picked her own Fanny favorites). Since this book covers a recording industry that moved from 78 rpm vinyl singles, to 45s, to albums, to CDs, to MP3s, to mixtapes, to online videos, figuring out what information to include in these lists and how to format them was tricky. We are simultaneously trying to provide a sense of historical record and provide a simple list of songs for you to find on your favorite streaming service or even to purchase. The dates indicate when a song was first made publicly available as a single, album track, download, or similar. The album titles (in italics) indicate either the long-playing record on which the song was first made available or a compilation on which it was eventually made available, sometimes decades after having been recorded or released as a single. In a few cases, the songs have never been released on albums or even as singles.

WOMEN WHO ROCK

BESSIE SMITH

DAPHNE A. BROOKS

ILLUSTRATION BY LINDSEY BAILEY

It's 1931 and we are riding high-water trouble with Bessie Smith and her ensemble of formidable seamen: Louis Metcalfe on cornet, Charlie Green on trombone, Clarence Williams on piano, and Floyd Casey on drums. Even before we hear the voice of the Empress, a tremulous muted horn announces that all is not calm out in these parts. Uncertainty hangs in the air as "Shipwreck Blues" opens with fits and starts before the band finds a pocket of smooth currents for our regal superstar to ride and make her entrance. This is the moment when our heroine executes the kind of undeniable authority that was, at that point in her career, synonymous with her name. She delivers crisp, clear-eyed orders to a "Captain" to whom she is not beholden, instructing him to "tell your men to get on board." We are made privy to the alluring force of her effortless control of this sonic space, the space of the blues that she dominated across the span of the 1920s. Bessie is past the peak of glamorous superstardom, but she sings with the conviction of an artist who knows that she has changed the game, having led a cultural revolution that would forever transform pop. We envision her on board that ship as though she were dressed for the jook, strewn in her trademark feathers and jewels. I like to picture her leading her mates, like Washington crossing the Delaware, holding it down at the mast while looking gravely out into the storm.

Smith is seemingly with the crew but not of the crew. She is our glamorous and seductively singular figure, a formidable contralto whose genius as a blues storyteller enabled her to spin gripping yarns and draw startling truths out of plaintive laments. So seasoned at this stage of her career, she embraces her role as the adventuress with delicious and winking imperiousness. She surveys the scenery of the song—an ecological universe of imminent catastrophe—while also doing her damnedest to work with the band and steer her vessel toward those extra helping hands that she spots on shore.

Clever euphemisms abound as they do in all good blues numbers. But lest we get too cozy with these sexual metaphors of ships riding into dock, our heroine flips the script in the second verse, turning inward. "I'm dreary in mind," she croons, "and I'm so worried in heart / Oh, the best of friends sho' has got to part." This was Smith's trademark move in classics like "Thinking Blues" and "In the House Blues," jams that revel in the complexities—the affective ambiguities—of a black woman's inner lifeworld. Growling, wrestling, fretting, mourning loss and rupture—this is Bessie Smith, our great pioneering vocalist of the modern century, the one who drove the blues into the center of the Roaring Twenties and dominated the race records industry during that high-rolling decade. As she would do

on her vast array of recordings—beginning with her debut on Columbia in 1923 and continuing through her last sessions with Okeh Records in 1933 and up to her untimely death—Smith builds indelible, hypnotic drama through impeccable timing and the profundity of her interpretative powers.

Smith's sound was drawn, in part, from the traumas of a childhood in which poverty, abandonment, and an abusive older sister shaped her polyphonous delivery. Bessie sang at the crossroads of protracted ache and steeliness. She began cultivating her skills at a young age, on the streets of Chattanooga, Tennessee, busking with her brother Andrew to survive orphanhood, picking up dance work and showbiz knowhow from brother Clarence, and finding a teacher, a rival, and possibly a lover in the form of Gertrude "Ma" Rainey, the country blues legend who paved the way for Smith to forge her own star charisma. Smith's storied relationship with Rainey is the stuff of contradiction, innuendo, "prove it on me" secrets, and ride-or-die gangsta lore. It's crucial to recognize the extent to which their collaboration and competition—beautifully rendered in Dee Rees's 2015 *Bessie* biopic—encapsulate the richness of all that so often gets left out of histories of the blues: in this community of artists who birthed the modern world of popular music, black women mentored black women, offering them secrets of the performing trade, business wisdom, and warnings. They also jockeyed for the limelight, stole one another's lovers, and battled for gigs and the adoration of fans.

Yet that period of apprenticeship when "Mother of the Blues" Rainey taught her pupil a thing or two about working the crowd and cultivating an aura on stage also reminds us of the secret history of those pioneers of the form who were experimenting,

rehearsing, and exercising their aesthetic aspirations alongside one another. Taking what she needed from Rainey, Smith struck out solo in 1913, working the tent show act on her own terms, building a devoted following with the intensity, wit, and luminous sex appeal of her stirring persona. Her sound accrued knowing sophistication on the road and under the big tent, out in the crowds where black migrant peoples who suffered myriad forms of displacement (from floods, economic exploitation, and white supremacist terror) pressed up close to each other and close to the stage, listening carefully to her rendering of their sorrow. She, in turn, learned how to convey the authenticity of a people's despair, to name the turmoil sonically and exorcise it for the masses.

Her Chitlin' Circuit celebrity reverberated along Southern and East Coast subcultural frequencies in those years before Mamie Smith's 1920 smash "Crazy Blues" broke the blues game wide open for black folks who'd been passed over as artists as well as consumers by a racist recording industry in the nascent days of the business. Bessie the lioness, Bessie the brawler, known for her rough-around-the-edges survival instincts and sounds, would have to wait until a Columbia deal came her way in 1923. When she finally stepped into the studios ready to take hold of Lovie Austin and Alberta Hunter's "Downhearted Blues," she knew some things about the appeal of blues grit that set her style apart from Hunter's vaudevillian floss and vamping. The performance that she belted into a conical horn and onto wax shifted the artistic weight of the recorded blues from its Tin Pan Alley theatricality (led by the likes of Hunter, Mamie Smith, and Ethel Waters) to a kind of erotic melancholia that was all Bessie's own. That big-label debut, backed by "Gulf Coast Blues," announced to the broader public the arrival of an assured artist who could express agony as forceful declaratives, as statements of simultaneous determination and aching undoing. Smith conveyed to the world her powerhouse ability to utterly dominate the twelve-bar blues form, to use a structure that relies on repetition and improvisational revision as a platform on which to consider a continuous stream of emotional vantage points and testimonials. This was singing that, as Hazel Carby, Angela Davis, and other black feminist scholars have shown, testified to and for the complex interiority of a generation just on the other side of emancipation and staring down the misery of Jim Crow. Smith was off and running on a different plane now, a live theater vernacular sensation turned record industry phenom who would go on to record 160 songs for Columbia and collaborate with fellow geniuses Louis Armstrong, Fletcher Henderson, and Coleman Hawkins, who were working out their own revolutionary blueprints in jazz.

What to call such a woman? The monikers given to her ("Queen of the Blues" before being quickly promoted to "Empress") set in motion the kind of diva tropes that have long been and remain a mainstay in pop culture. Bessie's own penchant for beaded headdresses and sumptuous garments solidified this labeling. Such terms seemingly aim to capture the regal energy and superlative achievements of women (particularly black women) operating at the height of their talents and above all the rest, sometimes at the risk of drifting into shallow hyperbole. But back in

Bessie's day, that title would have surely taken on a special meaning for the dispossessed, whose country denied them their citizenship, protection, and due process of law. It was these people—the ones whose ardent consumerism drove the "race records" industry—who championed a vocalist who promised to build an empire of black sonic alterity in which they could unmask themselves, their nightmares, their dreams. They elected her, this queer sister who unabashedly and fiercely loved women as well as men, to look out for and after them; to voice a compendium of social, sexual, and existential desires for them; and to guide them through the disaster called Jim Crow America.

Listen closely and we hear all this in those late recordings. The trills in "Shipwreck" are signs of a veteran musician ever so loose and savvy and playful enough at this moment in her artistry to dance around the melancholic conventions she had helped to make madly popular throughout the Harlem Renaissance twenties. Now a veteran of the form she'd reimagined, she digs in to the sly histrionics of her own storytelling abilities rather than depending on the conventions of heartbreak. She is not our Bessie longing for jelly on her roll or sugar in her bowl—which is not to say that erotics have nothing to do with the struggle at the heart of her performance. The Empress lets us know that this emergency, this impending disaster in which a woman finds herself with "friends" no more, demands a captain to "blow his whistle" and give his men the signal that service is necessary and urgent, because the only thing as ominous as the nautical perils ahead is a despondent and unsatisfied woman.

Blues is the source of Bessie's agency and infinite transformations. She uses her power to be both heroine in distress *and* storm system, "shipwrecked" protagonist and the conductor of an ensemble that oscillates between supplying the sounds of a superstorm as well as the steady vessel that will ride this rough water like a surfboard into port. Smith "rains" down on us in these final verses, sounding out a deluge at precisely the moment her lyrics suggest the tragedy of stasis.

Signature Bessie, indeed—but also a Bessie whom we might imagine as the sonic analogue to Romare Bearden's rendering of the Greek god Poseidon in his classic painting *Black Odyssey*. Or perhaps we might think of our "Shipwreck Blues" Bessie as an artist with the power to conjure her own sea god tale. Listen to how, for instance, on not just "Shipwreck Blues" but a song like the marvelously gothic "Blue Spirit Blues," she forges the crucial bridge between silent film and talkies, filling in the historical pauses in these advances in modernity by inventively collaborating with stride piano legend James P. Johnson to perform a fantastical dreamscape. Smith travels like Odysseus to the Realm of the Shades—led by the devil way down to that "red hot land of mean blue spirits" that "stick [their] fork" in her as she navigates an opaque path, *Game of Thrones*–style. We ride with her on this road strewn with "fairies and dragons spitting out blue flames" and "demons with their eyelashes dripping blood," and out of this odyssey we are made new by way of the demons she slays for us. The Greeks had their epics, but it's black folks who gave us the teachings and philosophies of the blues.

If Johnson's instrumental refrain on "Blue Spirit Blues" signals the clichés of vaudeville villainy and even early horror film cues for terror on the rise, he also collaborates in that final verse with Smith so as to forge an escape route out of the nightmare, kicking up the tempo as Smith's protagonist "run[s] so fast / till someone wake[s] her up." Like Odysseus, our heroine has traveled to the dark side and now returns to the land of the living, awakened, enlightened and bearing witness to a social death now seemingly relegated to the realm of sleep rather than the wake world. This Smith, the stuff of supernatural blues, defies the mythical tragedy of her demise on Route 61, the victim of a car crash somewhere between Memphis and Clarksdale, Mississippi, in 1937. While the lore of her passing fueled erroneous tales of white supremacist medical malpractice that lived on long after her legend began to fade (most notably in playwright Edward Albee's *The Death of Bessie Smith* from 1959), the sister who's got the "spirit" in this track sings her resilience across the great divide.

This, then, finally is the beauty of Bessie Smith's avant-garde poetics: we might think of her as making bold and unconventional use of narrative colors like our Afromodernist painter friend Bearden so as to compose a blackness capacious enough to evoke both despair and possibility, abjection and movement, selflessness and sensual solipsism, solo hopes, fears, and dreams as well as collective strategies for the future. With every spin of the 78, she takes us on a journey toward the home that is her own thrillingly mobile blues tonic. ■

SISTER ROSETTA THARPE

STEPHANIE PHILLIPS

ILLUSTRATION BY WINNIE T. FRICK

There is an illustration, widely circulated on the Internet, of Sister Rosetta Tharpe. It shows the gospel belter and guitar shredder looking fierce, while above her blaze the words: "Never forget that rock and roll was invented by a queer black woman." The meme conveys a swatch of Tumblr pastel pinks and punk attitude, reflecting a new generation's endless quest for visuals of marginalized people and greater appreciation for female artists.

But images offer reductive pedestals that disconnect us from the complexities of our predecessors' character and halt us from imagining ourselves in their shoes. To fully understand Tharpe, we need to delve beyond the image to the woman that created the foundations of rock and roll as we know it. Known as the godmother of rock and roll, during her heyday in the thirties and forties Sister Rosetta Tharpe blended the oratory style of her gospel upbringing with the throbbing pulse of the Chicago blues. It's a style that led to Tharpe becoming one of gospel's first national stars and one of the few female guitarists to enjoy fame.

Tharpe was born Rosetta Nubin on March 20, 1915, to cotton pickers Katie Bell Nubin and Willis Atkins, who were both singers. Her mother was a fierce Christian who left Rosetta's father when Rosetta was six years old and headed north to travel around the country, preaching the word of God. A child prodigy, Rosetta began singing and playing guitar to accompany her mother. She developed a ferocious following.

Watching footage of Tharpe's performances, it's hard to work out what hits you first. It could be the brassy tone of her belting vibrato vocals, that preached with the love and determination of a woman trying to lead her congregation. Maybe it's her unique guitar style. Rather than play her instrument rhythmically, Tharpe decorated her songs with melodic responses to her vocals and musical intonations, effectively playing an early form of rock and roll lead guitar even before she started playing electric guitar. Or it could be her stage presence, which was loud, proud, and defiant. At a time when African Americans were marginalized in every way, Tharpe's performances provided a relief for those who wanted to have fun for one night and bask in the knowledge that there was a better life waiting for them.

By the time she was nineteen and living in Chicago, Tharpe already had a legion of fans in the gospel community and was taking in the color and style of the city's blues and jazz scene. In an attempt to secure her daughter's future, Rosetta's mother married her off to preacher Tommy Tharpe. The marriage didn't last long but it did give Rosetta a new stage name and a reason to take her mother to New York to start a new career working in clubs. The gigs eventually led to Tharpe's crossover fame as a secular performer at the Cotton Club, working with Cab Calloway and Lucky Millinder.

In 1941 Tharpe signed a deal with Millinder to sing in his band, stating that she would play upbeat versions of spiritual songs. Her guitar work was not featured during these years, and Tharpe mellowed her vocal style to match that of other female big band singers. It wasn't too long before Tharpe was singing secular material, such as "Rock Me" and "I Want a Tall Skinny Papa," and gaining both success and notoriety for it. The bawdy undertones of her work with Millinder and further strays into the world of blues riled some of her early conservative fans. According to Tharpe's friend and confidante Roxie Moore, Tharpe was frustrated by the material she was given to sing and eventually walked out on Millinder and his band.

After Millinder, Tharpe returned to her gospel roots and enjoyed mainstream success after her 1945 hit "Strange Things Happening Every Day" became the first gospel record to cross over to *Billboard*'s Harlem Hit Parade Top 10. She spent most of the 1940s on the road, honing the guitar style and onstage performance she became known for. Her command of the guitar was entirely unique and her melodic approach to R&B was unheard of at the time. Although there were many black female guitarists around during Tharpe's career, including Memphis Minnie and Bea Booze, Tharpe enjoyed mainstream fame, a rare feat.

Tharpe married several times in her life while also having numerous affairs with both men and

women. Her most notable relationship was with singer and pianist Marie Knight, whom she met in 1946. Tharpe and Knight collaborated together on several songs including the hit "Up above My Head" and toured together. The sight of two single women traveling together in the late forties may have a raised a few eyebrows.

During the late 1940s to '50s Tharpe's popularity dwindled as more fans flocked to see rising gospel star Mahalia Jackson. Despite this, over the next decade Tharpe's influence on popular culture became more noticeable. Her foot-stomping performances and music were loved by Elvis Presley, Chuck Berry, Bob Dylan, Johnny Cash, Tina Turner, Aretha Franklin, Karen Carpenter, and many more.

During the height of the blues explosion in England in 1964, Tharpe went on a UK tour. While she was there she played a memorable gig in a railway station in Chorlton-cum-Hardy near Manchester. Dylan has publicly pondered how many bands were influenced by the then middle-aged Tharpe dressed in her finest, playing the smoothest rock and roll those young English kids would have ever seen.

Tharpe continued to play in her later years but stopped after she suffered from a stroke in 1970 and had her leg amputated due to diabetes complications. On October 9, 1973, at the age of fifty-eight, Tharpe passed away after another stroke.

Though Tharpe died at a young age, her legacy continues to live on through a wide array of new musicians, including the UK indie band Noisettes. A resurgence in popularity is bringing Tharpe's unique talents as a gospel belter and guitar shredder to fresh ears. The publication of Gayle Wald's 2008 biography *Shout, Sister, Shout! The Untold Story of Rock-and-Roll Trailblazer Sister Rosetta Tharpe* brought Tharpe back into public consciousness, as did a 2017 stage adaptation of Wald's book. In 2018, Tharpe was inducted into the Rock and Roll Hall of Fame.

When many music lovers picture the original rock-and-roll star, they see Elvis or Chuck Berry, but those men were actually channeling the fierce, infectious energy of a queer black woman. We as artists, writers, and lovers of music should take from this the knowledge that whatever the next style is, it will probably come from a black woman, too. ■

MAHALIA JACKSON

JANA MARTIN

ILLUSTRATION BY JULIE WINEGARD

There is the vocal power of gospel and there is the transcendent spirit of gospel; some gospel singers have been filled with one more than the other. But Mahalia Jackson, queen of the genre, brought both to the world: a supercharged heavenly force of a voice channeling the mystery and glory of the Holy Ghost. She was an out-and-out star who introduced white audiences to the soulful intensity of the black church. Wearing a jewel-collared dress, she'd hop and swing the word *holy* into an escalating climb of bent notes and conjure up a conscience: it was said that white audiences understood the heartless cruelty of Jim Crow when they heard Jackson sing. In her musicianship was a kind of narrative that touched the bone.

In the 1960s Jackson became a figurehead of the civil rights movement, layering solace onto its torment and frustration. She was a friend of Dr. Martin Luther King Jr. and, like King, grew up at the intersection of the sacred and the profane. She, too, was steeped in the do-right passion of the church and felt, similarly to King, that she had been called to this work. When King died, she sang his favorite hymn, "Take My Hand, Precious Lord" at his funeral. The song was originally inspired by ferocious loss—the great gospel composer Thomas Dorsey wrote it in a grieving frenzy as he confronted the sudden death of his wife and baby. It's a song about losing everything

and begging for redemption from above—and at that funeral, broken hearts rose on the apex of Jackson's transcendent notes.

Mahala Jackson (the *i* came later) was born in 1911 in a shack in New Orleans, soon shining in the children's choir of her Baptist church. Hers was an astonishing, undeniable talent. As a young teenager she left New Orleans to seek her fortune in Chicago, and her true tutelage began: she absorbed and remembered music like a brilliant sponge, drawing on influences all around her. She borrowed from the personas of Bessie Smith, Ma Rainey, and other blues queens, though without the jelly or backdoor men. Her percussive, jerky style of moving and singing reflected the drum-accompanied gospel of her local sanctified church—a historically African American house of worship that celebrates the infusion of the Holy Spirit into the soul. In Jackson that spirit was so strong it also seemed entirely unlearned—as if it came out whole. But Jackson was in fact a deliberate, obsessive student of her craft. She cultivated her rich contralto voice into remarkable dynamics, peppering her phrasing with blues inflections and shaping notes into wails, moans, and whispers with nearly gloves-off abandon. Still, she insisted on singing only righteous songs—a stubborn refutation of many a manager's instinct. That insistence on keeping it clean helped forge a kind of steel halo around herself that made her even more mythic

on stage: Mahalia Jackson, earthbound as she was, seemed moved only by the angels.

Early on, she held grindingly menial and then begrudgingly practical jobs: cotton picker, wash-woman, nursemaid. She went to beauty school and opened a salon and a flower shop. Initially she sang

with the Johnson Brothers, one of the first profes-sional gospel groups, gaining some notoriety for her uninhibited physical style of singing and scandal-izing some of the more conservative Midwestern preachers for moving to the music onstage in such a Southern way. She sang solo with a pianist in the

1930s, recorded for Decca in 1937 as their first gospel artist, and began "demonstrating" songs for Dorsey. She traveled the gospel circuit, appearing in cities like Birmingham, Alabama, and Buffalo, New York, giving a charismatic shot in the arm to the staid gospel performing style of the time.

She struggled and was nearly dropped by her new label, Apollo Records, but then had a stroke of luck with "Move On Up a Little Higher" by W. Herbert Brewster. The single (produced by Art Freeman, Apollo's savvy A&R director) made gospel history, selling an unprecedented 1 million copies: stores couldn't keep the record on the shelves. Suddenly that sleepy church music was hot, and Jackson was a celebrity. She appeared on television, guested on radio shows, had her own weekly show on CBS—another groundbreaker, as spirituals like this had never been heard on the radio—had another smash hit in 1954, "A Rusty Old Halo," and appeared on *The Ed Sullivan Show*. And like many artists pulled along by fame's odd go-where-it-will motor, she wound up a darling of the jazz and intellectual set, who would carefully go through her recordings for their Ellingtonian references (as Ralph Ellison noted) and musical boldness. She was now far too high-priced for the very community she'd risen within. Instead of black churches, she sang at the Newport Jazz Festival (1958). She sang for John F. Kennedy. She sang for Martin Luther King Jr. She toured Europe, still astonishing everyone.

By 1971, Jackson was tired. She performed her final concert in 1971 in Germany, clearly diminished, steamrollered by a nasty divorce, her health in question, her mighty presence onstage just a little smaller. But she was still the queen. She shut her eyes and lifted up her head, and that thick, soaring voice made its way around the notes with its preternatural ease and facility. Back in the US, she made her appearances. In an interview on *20/20* she was both sweet church lady—"God made me in his image, and I must first treat him right"—and diva: her presence in that chair was that of an unabashed public figure. But she also seemed, to those that knew her, more than a little unwell. She brought down the house on *The Johnny Cash Show*, singing a version of "Amazing Grace" that was sheer virtuosity. When she intones, "I can see," it's an oceanic procession of notes and air, and the entire television studio seems to holds its breath, finally exhaling on her "Hallelujah."

There's a searing edge to Mahalia Jackson's voice when it finally breaks over a high note that can't be unremembered. Even in fuzzy digitized old clips, her performances are eerily moving, like an artifact of a higher power, a rarely seen, musically impeccable genius testifying—well before the age of digital tuning and teleprompters. She showed her descendants from both the pop and gospel worlds—Whitney Houston, Aretha Franklin, and, through them, a new generation of heartfelt vocal gymnasts: Lady Gaga, Sia, Amy Winehouse—how it's done. Just turn to the Holy Ghost and let its song rip right through your soul. ■

PLAYLIST

"Move On Up a Little Higher, parts 1 and 2 (Alternate Take)," 1947, *Complete Mahalia Jackson: Intégrale Vol. 1: 1937–1946*

"Move On Up a Little Higher, parts 1 and 2 (Master)," 1947, *Complete Mahalia Jackson: Intégrale Vol. 1: 1937–1946*

"Take My Hand, Precious Lord," 1956, *Bless This House* (with the Fall-Jones Ensemble)

"Elijah Rock," 1962, *Recorded Live in Europe during Her Latest Concert Tour*

"Amazing Grace," 1979, *Mahalia Jackson*

"How I Got Over," 1995, *The Best of Mahalia Jackson*

WILLIE MAE
"BIG MAMA" THORNTON

GILLIAN G. GAAR

ILLUSTRATION BY ANNE MUNTGES

I n the beginning, it was her song—written for her, in fact. On August 13, 1952, two young songwriters were summoned by musician-bandleader Johnny Otis to a recording session at Radio Recorders studio in Los Angeles. Otis told the songwriting team of Jerry Leiber and Mike Stoller that Peacock Records owner Don Robey needed a hit for one of his artists, Willie Mae "Big Mama" Thornton. They came up with "Hound Dog," a gruff, growling blues about a shiftless gigolo. Released in February 1953, it topped *Billboard*'s rhythm and blues chart for seven weeks.

That should've tied Thornton to a key spot in the development of rock and roll, a signpost on the way from "Rocket 88" to "Maybellene." But the racial mores of the time turned Thornton's accomplishment into a footnote. When Elvis Presley recorded the song in 1956, he based his version on Freddie Bell and the Bellboys' sped-up arrangement. Presley also had the muscle of a major label behind him, as well as something an African American performer was rarely granted at the time: nationwide television exposure. His "Hound Dog" topped the pop, R&B, and country charts, selling over 4 million copies. Leiber might have noted in his memoir *Hound Dog*

(jointly written with Stoller), that "Elvis played with the song; Big Mama nailed it," but it was Presley who walked away with the glory.

Binnie Willie Mae Thornton was born on December 11, 1926, in Ariton, Alabama; the family later moved to Troy City, forty-three miles southeast of Montgomery. Her father was a Baptist minister, and Thornton learned to sing in church, where her mother was in the choir. Willie Mae also was fond of the blues, crediting Bessie Smith, Memphis Minnie, and Big Maceo Merriweather with helping her develop her own style—what she described to journalist Ralph Gleason as "old down home singing, with the feeling." She also taught herself to play the harmonica and drums.

After her mother died when she was thirteen, Thornton dropped out of school to go to work. Her performing career began inadvertently, when she filled in for an inebriated singer while working as a cleaner at a tavern. Another unexpected boost came after she moved to Montgomery and got a job working on a garbage truck. One day, while she was riding on the truck and singing to help pass the time, her voice caught the ear of vocalist Mary Smith McClain—aka Diamond Teeth Mary, in

town with Sammy Green's Hot Harlem Revue. She urged Thornton to enter a contest being held before the Revue's show that night at the Pekin Theater. Thornton not only won first prize, she landed a spot in the Revue. She was fourteen years old.

Thornton moved to Atlanta, where the Revue was based, and performed with them for the next eight years. Billed as the "New Bessie Smith," she also danced, did comedic routines, and played harmonica and drums. She was tall and had a penchant for wearing men's clothes, which caused people to speculate about her sexuality. She was known to have had a son, who was taken into foster care; she rarely spoke of him. Johnny Otis was among those who said he never knew her to have a romantic attachment to anyone—male or female.

Thornton relocated to Houston in 1948. She released her first single, "All Right Baby," in 1950, cruising through a lyric of playful innuendo (her baby's a jockey, who "knows how to ride"). She was then signed by Don Robey, recording for him for the rest of the decade. But initially none of her singles made an impression on the charts.

That was about to change. In 1952, she began touring with Otis's Rhythm and Blues Caravan. Leiber and Stoller were inspired by Thornton's attitude: "She looked like the biggest, bad-ass, saltiest chick you would ever see," Stoller recalled for *Rolling Stone*. The duo who was to become one of the first great songwriting teams of the rock era penned one of their most memorable tunes for Big Mama. With

PLAYLIST

"Hound Dog," 1952, *The Original Hound Dog*

"They Call Me Big Mama," 1953, *The Essential Recordings*

"Big Mama's Bumble Bee Blues," 1966, *Big Mama Thornton with the Muddy Waters Blues Band 1966*

"Ball and Chain," 1969, *Stronger than Dirt*

"Willie Mae's Trouble," 1969, *The Original Hound Dog*

"Summertime," 1969, *Stronger than Dirt*

"Born Under a Bad Sign," 1969, *Stronger than Dirt*

"Hound Dog," they wanted to write a song that, as Stoller put it, said "Go fuck yourself" without being explicit. It didn't have to be; Thornton's contempt for her would-be suitor is apparent from the way she snarls the first line. Her swaggering, don't-mess-with-me disdain becomes playful during the song's instrumental break, when she issues a few spoken word commands: "Now wag your tail . . . get it!" Get it, you good for nothing, she seems to say, before I kick you to the curb like you deserve.

Thornton played the Apollo Theater for the first time later that year, where her performance garnered rapturous applause. "Hound Dog" was released soon after. *Billboard* called it "a wild slicing loaded with excitement," while a Peacock Records ad proclaimed, "This is a HIT, HIT, HIT." But what should've been a launch pad to greater success became Thornton's commercial high point. She'd never have another substantial chart hit again.

For a time, Thornton rode high on the success of "Hound Dog." She released more records and began recording her own compositions, like "They Call Me Big Mama." She joined Johnny Ace in crooning their love for each other on his single "Yes Baby." She left Robey and settled in San Francisco, where she recorded another original, "Ball and Chain." It became the song that brought her the most recognition after "Hound Dog," when Janis Joplin, who heard Thornton singing the song in Bay Area clubs, recorded it herself.

The blues revival of the 1960s put Thornton in demand as a live performer. She played the Monterey Jazz Festival and the Newport Folk Festival. She toured Europe with the American Folk Blues Festival. She shared bills with Jefferson Airplane and the Grateful Dead in the psychedelic ballrooms of San Francisco and with B.B. King at Carnegie Hall. And there were more records; 1969's *Stronger than Dirt* album has powerful versions of "Summertime" and "Born under a Bad Sign," and new versions of "Hound Dog" and "Ball and Chain," the songs that she was staking as *her* legacy, white versions be damned.

But all those years on the road took their toll. Big Mama cut back on her favorite Old Grand-Dad bourbon only to switch it for gin and milk. She lost weight as her health declined, but she kept working—she had to. A few weeks after a show at the I-Beam in San Francisco she died in an LA boarding house on July 25, 1984. She was fifty-seven years old. She'd asked Johnny Otis, now a minister, to oversee the funeral arrangements, and she was laid to rest at Inglewood Park Cemetery.

The year she died, Big Mama Thornton was inducted into the Blues Hall of Fame. Years later, she received another honor that might have made her smile. Inspired by the Rock 'n' Roll Camp for Girls founded in 2001 in Portland, Oregon, a similar organization was established in New York City in 2004: the Willie Mae Rock Camp for Girls. ■

WANDA JACKSON

GILLIAN G. GAAR

ILLUSTRATION BY ANNE MUNTGES

In 1954, a teenaged Wanda Jackson turned a major career breakthrough into a pivotal moment of self-assertion. The emerging singer with the individualist streak was invited to play the *Grand Ole Opry*, country music's reigning radio program. In the 1950s, country and western singers had a specified look: a Western shirt, cowboy boots and hat, a full skirt if you were a woman, and lots of fringe. Being small in stature, Jackson felt hampered by such a getup: "I decided all those clothes were covering up my assets," she explained in an interview with this author. She slowly began instituting her own style. The hat disappeared. Then the boots. But she didn't mind fringe, draping the tight dresses that she favored (designed by Jackson and made by her mother) with a silky trimming that readily shook when she walked or simply patted her foot—just to get a little action going.

When Wanda showed up at the Opry in one of her fringe-laden dresses with rhinestone spaghetti straps, she was told her outfit wasn't going to fly on "country's most famous stage." Ernest Tubb himself said she had to cover her bare shoulders. Reluctantly, she put on a fringed leather jacket, and swore she'd never grace the Opry stage again.

There were plenty of male music rebels in the 1950s: Gene Vincent slouching and leering in his black leather suit; Little Richard, rock and roll's own Liberace; Elvis Presley and his dangerously swiveling pelvis. Women were out there rocking and rolling as well. But guitarist Lady Bo, in Bo Diddley's band, and Memphis musician and record label owner Cordell Jackson didn't get the same exposure as Chuck Berry, or Jerry Lee Lewis, or Carl Perkins.

Then came Jackson. The Queen of Rockabilly boldly threw off the constraints of how women should sound and look, crossing over from country to pop and giving women a rock and roll rebel of their own.

Wanda Lavonne Jackson was born on October 20, 1937, in Maud, Oklahoma. The family moved to California when Jackson was six years old, the same year that her father, who played guitar and fiddle, put a guitar into her hands and taught her how to play. Soon she was able to accompany him, singing songs from a songbook her mother had compiled. Country music—Hank Williams, Jimmie Rodgers, Hank Thompson—was her biggest influence.

In 1949, the Jacksons returned to Oklahoma, settling in Oklahoma City. Wanda began singing in the "talent spot" portion of a country music show on local radio station KLPR, eventually getting her own fifteen-minute program, later expanded to half an hour. It was one of the show's listeners, who was also one of Jackson's inspirations, who would help the then fourteen-year-old transform what was largely a hobby into a career.

One day after her radio show, Hank Thompson,

who headed up the Western swing band Hank Thompson and His Brazos Valley Boys, called Jackson and offered her a spot performing with him that Saturday at Oklahoma City's Trianon Ballroom. After clearing the engagement with her mother, Jackson agreed; it was the first of many times she'd share the stage with Thompson's band when they played the area.

It was Thompson who helped her land her first contract with Decca Records. On her first hit, the 1954 single "You Can't Have My Love," she playfully traded barbs with Billy Gray, a member of the Brazos Valley Boys. It reached number eight in the country charts, leading to her *Grand Ole Opry* appearance.

Her look might not have suited the Opry, but she found no shortage of other places to perform. And there were more than changes in fashion looming on the horizon. On July 20, 1955, Jackson was in her dressing room at the Cape Arena Building in Cape Girardeau, Missouri, when she heard shouting and screaming coming from the auditorium. To her surprise, it turned out to be the excitement generated by that nice-looking young man she'd met earlier in the day: Elvis Presley was tearing up the stage, taking country and R&B to places they'd never been before, sending the audience into a frenzy. Decades later, Jackson could still recall just how thrilling the baby-faced rocker was once the initial shock had worn off: "He was fresh, and new, and young, energetic—it was a whole new era being born."

Jackson would soon help usher in this era. She dated Presley whenever they shared a bill, and he convinced her she could sing in this daring new style herself. The country girl hesitated, then dove right in. Country remained her first love, but the next few years saw Jackson recording a sizzling series of rockabilly and rock and roll numbers—the songs that would eventually come to define her legacy.

In contrast to her smooth country music voice, Jackson had an appealing throaty growl when she sang rock and roll. That raw tone gave an additional edge to such songs as her remarkable covers of Little Richard's ravers "Long Tall Sally," "Slippin' and Slidin'," and "Rip It Up." "Fujiyama Mama" was originally recorded by Annisteen Allen, but Jackson made it her own, gleefully detailing her ability to down sake and smoke dynamite while comparing herself favorably to the atomic bomb. She even gave Elvis a run for his money with her version of "Let's Have a Party," a crossover hit that landed Jackson in the pop Top 40.

By the mid-1960s, Jackson returned to country music full time, and later took up gospel. The rockabilly revival of the early eighties led to the rediscovery of Jackson's wilder side, and a new appreciation of her work as a musical, and sartorial, pioneer.

She's still out there, making music; on 2011's aptly named *The Party Ain't Over* (produced by Jack White), she tackles Amy Winehouse's "You Know I'm No Good" with panache. She sings with the same joy you can find in a clip of Jackson on the show *Town Hall Party* in 1958, where she jokes about singing a "beautiful love song" then bursts into "Hard Headed Woman." The fringe on her two-piece ensemble shakes as she sways her hips and dances around the microphone. There's no jacket covering her bare shoulders this time. Wanda Jackson's doing it her way. ■

PLAYLIST

"Money, Honey," 1958, *Wanda Jackson*

"Let's Have a Party," 1958, *Wanda Jackson*

"Fujiyama Mama," 1960, *Rockin' with Wanda!*

"Mean, Mean Man," 1960, *Rockin' with Wanda!*

"Hard Headed Woman," 1961, *Queen of Rockabilly*

"Riot in Cell Block #9," 1961, *Queen of Rockabilly*

"You Know That I'm No Good," 2011, *The Party Ain't Over*

PATSY CLINE

HOLLY GEORGE-WARREN

ILLUSTRATION BY JULIE WINEGARD

"I *don't want to get rich . . . just live good!*" Patsy Cline's life was so plagued by difficulties, she couldn't dream much bigger than that. After quitting school in eighth grade to help support her family, she earned a few dollars singing the country and western music she loved. In the process, she developed a full-throated sound that tapped into every hurt she'd ever suffered. Country music's first torch singer, Cline created a body of work with such emotional honesty that it resonates with audiences six decades later.

Cline had few role models: since the 1920s, female solo artists infrequently appeared on the Grand Ole Opry or signed record contracts. A rare C&W smash by a woman occurred in 1935, three years after Cline's birth, when Patsy Montana sold a half million copies of "I Wanna Be a Cowboy's Sweetheart." Not until 1952, when Kitty Wells hit number one with "It Wasn't God Who Made Honky-Tonk Angels," did a recording career seem even remotely possible to a fearless girl with a remarkable voice and a brash attitude. The following year, Virginia Patterson Hensley changed her name to Patsy Cline, signed with 4 Star Records, and began her ascent. A decade later, after 102 recordings, hundreds of spine-tingling performances, and a handful of hits, she died in a plane crash at age thirty. During her short life, Cline's music was first embraced by country audiences, and

then, thanks to *that* voice swathed in strings, she crossed over to the pop charts. Her success paved the way for a new generation of female artists like Loretta Lynn, Tammy Wynette, and Dolly Parton. And she gave us "Walkin' after Midnight," "I Fall to Pieces," "Crazy," "She's Got You," and "Sweet Dreams"—American music standards.

Patsy Cline channeled her life's tragedies into songs of heartache and melancholy. She was born in rural Virginia in 1932, a week after the marriage of her sixteen-year-old mother, Hilda, to her forty-two-year-old father, Sam. The family struggled after the birth of two more children, with Sam, a blacksmith by trade, chronically unemployed. When he became a maintenance man at Washington and Lee University, their eldest child—who went by Ginny—heard live music for the first time, as big bands fronted by female singers performed on campus. She joined the church choir and listened to Opry broadcasts featuring sassy singing cowgirl Texas Ruby accompanied by her husband, Curly Fox.

By the time Ginny reached her teens, the family had moved nineteen times. The last relocation occurred when Hilda took her three children to set up housekeeping as a single parent in Winchester, Virginia; it is likely Ginny had been molested by her father. In Winchester, Hilda worked as a seamstress, while Ginny took jobs as a janitor at the Greyhound station, a worker at a chicken-packing plant, and a soda jerk at Gaunt's Drugstore. But music remained her focus: at fourteen, she was auditioning for talent shows dressed in cowgirl outfits sewn by her mother, with matching boots and hat. One Saturday morning, she and Hilda stopped by Winchester's radio station, WINC, and Ginny asked DJ Joltin' Jim McCoy if she could sing on his Saturday morning C&W show. He was bowled over by her mature voice and spunk. By late 1949, she was a regular on the program, backed by Jim McCoy and the Melody Playboys. She appeared with local entertainer Bill Peer, who became her manager and told her to pick a stage name: "Patsy" was short for "Patterson" and a nod to Montana. The following year, in 1953, she added "Cline" when, at twenty, she married local businessman Gerald Cline, eight years her senior.

After Peer paid for her first demo tape, opportunity knocked. Her unique delivery—using breaking notes, growls, and slides—along with her sumptuous voice impressed Bill McCall, owner of California-based indie label 4 Star. In 1953, he signed her. Though Cline was overjoyed, she soon discovered her contract gave her a mere 2.34% royalty rate, about half of what most (male) artists received, and she was required to record material for which McCall owned the publishing. The upside was that she could record in Nashville at the recently opened studio of producer Owen Bradley, who had produced Kitty Wells; 4 Star also licensed the release of Patsy's records to Wells's label, Decca. Their first session, on June 1, 1955, yielded a Wells-style divorce number, "A Church, a Courtroom, Then Goodbye." The single flopped, but her increasingly larger audiences loved her onstage charisma and homespun charm. Unlike most country singers, the sultry Cline swayed and moved to the music. Her opening number was the engaging "Come On In (Make Yourself at Home)"; she cracked jokes and talked to her audience as if they were family.

Also a natural on TV, Cline became a regular on regional country music programs. She recorded a diversity of material, ranging from mournful ballads to up-tempo pop, syrupy weepers, and rockabilly barn burners—all with that Patsy Cline flair—but none caught fire commercially. After more than a year of flops, in January 1957, she appeared on the popular CBS program *Arthur Godfrey's Talent Scouts*. A producer advised her to ditch the buckarette garb for a more polished image. Before a live New York audience, she nearly broke the clap-o-meter with her bluesy "Walkin' after Midnight," winning first place. The single shot up the charts, peaking at number two on the C&W survey and number twelve on the Hit Parade. For the first time, thanks to national television, a female country artist gained the kind of exposure that led to pop music stardom.

It would be two years, though, before she scored another hit. She'd divorced Cline and moved to Nashville with her new husband, Charlie Dick, with whom she'd have two children. When her 4 Star contract expired, she signed with Decca, where Bradley was vice president of A&R. Now, she could record material by some of Music City's young bucks, like Willie

PLAYLIST

"A Church, a Courtroom, Then Goodbye," 1955, *The Patsy Cline Collection*

"Honky Tonk Merry Go Round," 1955, *The Patsy Cline Collection*

"Walkin' after Midnight," 1957, *Patsy Cline*

"Three Cigarettes in an Ashtray," 1957, *Patsy Cline*

"Gotta Lot of Rhythm in My Soul," 1959, *The Patsy Cline Collection*

"I Fall to Pieces," 1961, *Patsy Cline Showcase*

"Crazy," 1961, *Patsy Cline Showcase*

"She's Got You," 1962, *Sentimentally Yours*

"Sweet Dreams (of You)," 1963, *The Patsy Cline Collection*

"Faded Love," 1963, *The Patsy Cline Collection*

Nelson, Harlan Howard, and Hank Cochran. Bradley had moved into a more lush production style known as the Nashville Sound, and in late 1960 she cut Cochran/Howard's torchy "I Fall to Pieces." Her gut-wrenching delivery encapsulated all the heartbreak she'd experienced in her life. By the summer of 1961, the record was climbing up the country and pop charts. But in mid-June, she was nearly killed in a car accident—crashing through the windshield, slashing open her face, breaking her wrist, and dislocating her hip. First in a wheelchair and then on crutches, she returned to the stage and the studio just as "I Fall to Pieces" hit number one C&W and number twelve pop; it is one of her most enduring performances.

"After 'I Fall to Pieces,'" she told an audience, "I was in a really bad car wreck. I don't know what's gonna happen with this new record! It's called 'Crazy'!" In the fall of 1961, the Nelson tune became her biggest smash yet, with Cline's majestic voice wrapped in velvety strings. She toured relentlessly, including a rare country music concert at Carnegie Hall ("it's fabulous but it ain't as big as the Opry"), a month-long residency in Las Vegas, and top billing at the Hollywood Bowl. She became the first female country star to headline her own tour. It all came to an end way too soon, when Cline died on March 5, 1963, flying home from a benefit concert in a Comanche four-seater that crashed in rural Tennessee.

Before she died, Patsy Cline released seven chart singles and three albums. Just weeks before her death, she recorded the elegiac "Sweet Dreams" and "Faded Love," among other devastating tracks that became posthumous hits. She has inspired several generations of artists, from Loretta Lynn to k.d. lang, from Emmylou Harris to Rhiannon Giddens. Today, the brand-new Patsy Cline Museum in Nashville, filled with her show clothes and home furnishings, her salt and pepper shaker collections, and her leopard-print bathing suit, helps us "know" the woman who worked so hard to "live good." She liked to kick back with a cocktail, and she rushed home from gigs to be a mom to her kids. But her recordings are the incomparable riches Patsy Cline left us: the soundtrack to heartache that will haunt us forever. ■

NINA SIMONE

DAPHNE A. BROOKS

ILLUSTRATION BY LINDSEY BAILEY

Forget everything you think you know about blackness, feminism, pop music, and political radicalism when you discuss Nina Simone. She was celebrated as the High Priestess of Soul, but her aspiration was to be a classical concert pianist. One of her biggest hits, "My Baby Just Cares for Me," was a jazz standard that initially appeared on her 1958 debut album, *Little Girl Blue*, and received the most attention when Chanel No. 5 chose the track to hawk its fragrance in a 1987 television ad. Yet in her 1991 autobiography *I Put a Spell on You*, Simone wrote (with "sorry [not sorry]" middle-fingers-in-the-air swagger) that "calling me a jazz singer was a way of ignoring my musical background because I didn't fit into white ideas of what a black performer should be." Nina Simone was Afropunk royalty before we had a word for it.

Mass culture was never the place where our Nina (as she is often referred to by the denizens who continue to adore her) held major sway. But if we understand the music that defined and dominated mid- to late-twentieth-century pop culture as entailing revolution, artistic rule breaking, mastery of musicianship, spectacularly defiant performances, and sonic disturbances that seduce, rivet, and hypnotize, then we might just as well call Nina Simone rock and roll. Throughout her long and stormy career, one with remarkable highs and excruciatingly painful lows,

Nina, dear Nina, manifested that singular spark of aesthetic genius, experimental bravery, and high-voltage danger so characteristic of the numerous dude icons inducted into the Rock and Roll Hall of Fame. Simone was magnetic and eccentric, unpredictable and impossible to pigeonhole with regard to her sound as well as her persona. And like the countless men who, up until 2018, populated Cleveland's museum of legends without Nina hanging alongside them in that stardust-and-glitter room where it happens, she was also largely an artistic loner whose profound originality spurred her on as she forged her own path. But, as we burrow deeper into a millennium of catastrophe, and with King's "fierce urgency of now" once more taking hold of our social and cultural scenes, she returns to us, seizing hold of our collective consciousness. The prodigiousness of her sound demands that tastemakers and gatekeepers get woke and steer clear of misunderstanding her (as she would famously warn in one of the many songs she made her own). In this long overdue season of Nina, the time is ripe to pay tribute to her daring, boundary-crossing vision; and continue to do justice to her massive still-I-rise legacy.

The North Carolina–born, New York City–bound woman who would come barreling out of the Atlantic City supper club circuit in the late 1950s and onto the national scene was arguably something that the jazz universe, let alone the rest of the pop world, had never before encountered. A classically trained black female pianist with a penchant for Bach fugues, Simone made it clear from her earliest recordings that she knew her way around a Billie Holiday classic like "I Loves You Porgy" (itself a strikingly angst-ridden reading of Gershwin) as well as cocktail club melodrama (the Peggy Lee hit "Don't Smoke in Bed"). But she was just as inclined to drop folk hymns ("He's Got the Whole World in His Hands"), pop standards ("For All We Know"), and Broadway showstoppers ("You'll Never Walk Alone," "Love Me or Leave Me"). And then there were her mischievous original gems like the instrumental "African Mailman" that showcased her robust arsenal of talents on the keys while also gesturing toward the kinds of black Atlantic world sounds that would grow more prominent in her work in the years to come. She'd been rehearsing that diverse repertoire in nightclubs, biding her time and paying the bills while holding on to dreams of winning admission to study piano at the Curtis Institute in Philadelphia. Rejection from that elite school turned a raised-in-the-church child prodigy, Southern sister outsider named Eunice Waymon into a powerhouse performer who went by the stage moniker Nina Simone.

Our Nina, the woman armed with a basement-heavy contralto that flirted with androgyny. The woman who was prone in her early years to staging exhaustingly virtuosic marathon sets that stretched into the night and found her engaging in what would become her notoriously fastidious brand of showmanship, improvising her way onto plane after plane of new sonic discoveries. The woman who, as the 1960s black freedom struggle swiftly unfolded alongside her, quickly turned her attention to scoring the sounds of black radicalism and resistance, writing raw, in-your-face songs about Southern white terrorism and Northern white liberal hypocrisy and apathy ("Mississippi Goddam") and black feminist anthems that told tales of gross historical injury ("Four Women"). The woman who talked politics with dear friend James Baldwin, read Lenin and Marx with gone-too-soon BFF Lorraine Hansberry, and wrote black love and power elegies for the fallen ("To Be Young, Gifted, and Black," "Why? [The King of Love Is Dead]"). The woman who turned Brecht and Weill avant-garde theater classics ("Pirate Jenny") into cold-as-ice African American battle cries, and the woman who covered her fellow enigmatic pathbreaker Bob Dylan ("Just Like a Woman," "Just Like Tom Thumb's Blues," "The Times They Are-a-Changin'," "The Ballad of Hollis Brown," "I Shall Be Released") more frequently than many of her contemporaries. She shared with that shapeshifting trickster a passion for mining the truths of "old weird America," as Greil Marcus has famously described Dylan's masterful excavation of folk arcana. But her archival forays also stretched beyond America's past into the African diaspora ("See-Line Woman," "22nd Century") and cycled notably through France (Jacques Brel's "Ne Me Quitte Pas"), forecasting and then reflecting the fruits of her expatriate journeys and relocations in the wake of the civil rights and Black Power movements. And if, as one of her

PLAYLIST

"I Loves You Porgy, 1958, *Little Girl Blue*

"My Baby Just Cares for Me," 1958, *Little Girl Blue*

"African Mailman," 1959, *Nina Simone and Her Friends*

"Mississippi Goddam," 1964, *Nina Simone in Concert*

"Feeling Good," 1965, *I Put a Spell on You*

"Four Women," 1966, *Wild Is the Wind*

"I Wish I Knew How It Would Feel to Be Free," 1967, *Silk and Soul*

"Why? (The King of Love Is Dead)," 1968, *'Nuff Said!*

"I Shall Be Released," 1969, *To Love Somebody*

"22nd Century," recorded 1972, released 1998 on *The Very Best Of Nina Simone, 1967–1972: Sugar In My Bowl*

twenty-first-century, genre-defying descendants, Janelle Monáe, insists, "we were rock 'n' roll," Nina was one of the artists who surely planted that flag. She was the woman who invented and curated her own sonic palette, her own increasingly strange and beautiful, Brian Wilson–ish cosmos wide enough to include earnest readings of canonical rock figures (the Beatles, the Animals, and Prince) as well as wry renditions of Top 40 mainstays like Hall and Oates (all of whom beat her into the Rock Hall).

Although domestic violence in the sixties (at the hands of her second husband, Andy Stroud) and mental illness in the 1970s (perhaps brought on, in part, by the traumas and weariness of activist insurgency) would nearly incapacitate her for periods of time, her intense, focused dedication to the live set—delivering, for instance, stunning and now legendary recorded shows at Montreux, Switzerland, and Fort Dix, New Jersey—provides lasting proof of her ferocious artistry.

Yet it is the power and impact of her still-growing influence that demonstrates the undeniable. Witness the onslaught of biographies and scholarly articles (in this thing we now call "Nina Simone studies"), art exhibits and murals, documentary films, (ill-advised) biopic projects, T-shirts, statues and memorial sites, tribute concerts and albums. Witness the numerous MCs who sample her indelible voice to drop "a taste of power" into the mix and the countless pop stars of our present moment—from Lauryn and Meshell, Alicia and Mary to Kanye, Jay-Z, and Queen Bey—who look to her as a patron saint of black liberation music, and the everlasting truth of Nina should be loud and clear. While the Rock Hall has finally bowed to her clarion call, it's the young ones cueing her up on the frontlines in our current age of peril who remain the true keepers of her flame, stalwart and as resolute as the High Priestess herself, that nothing be left misunderstood. ■

ODETTA

KANDIA CRAZY HORSE

ILLUSTRATION BY WINNIE T. FRICK

Ladies of the Canyon. The phrase summons up images of willowy blondes in retronuevo Victorian dresses, baking bread for their cosmic cowboy "old men" in late 1960s Los Angeles. But the title should rightly be applied to Odetta, who was an early presence in the Topanga Canyon folk and proto-hippie scene, where she lived with her mother, Miz Flora.

Odetta typified a black Southern child of her time. Born Odetta Holmes in Birmingham, Alabama, on December 31, 1930, she was reared by her mother, Flora Sanders, in the Deep South during the Great Depression and later with her stepfather, Zadock Felious, in Los Angeles. Odetta showed early musical interest by belting out kitchen table blues numbers and banging on the family piano until her kin's nerves were rattled. An elementary school teacher took notice of her singing voice, which led to formal training. Her eventual stellar career was partly the result of her LA voice coach Paul Reese encouraging Odetta to stop attempting to emulate the classical singer Marian Anderson—hero to Odetta and her mother—and become a folksinger instead. In 1954, the release of her debut solo album, *The Tin Angel*, minted Odetta as a single-monikered diva. She started creating music that would be referred to as "the soundtrack of the civil rights movement," a life journey that would see her crowned with the National Medal of Arts in 1999 by President Bill Clinton.

When asked about her early sonic foundation, she replied that central to it was her father's adoration of the *Grand Ole Opry*, which was beamed into their home. Odetta was a country girl, a 'Bama, with an epic contralto and a *sage femme* homespun mother who befriended her slightly freakish scene friends, like one Elliot Charles Adnopoz, whom she rechristened for the counterculture, saying: "Honey, that boy was the ramblingest boy I have ever met." Performing at the organic canyon outpost Norah Kathleen's Bake Shop, at the Ash Grove, and in San Francisco's folk clubs such as the Tin Angel, Odetta superimposed her big, black self on the abiding twentieth-century iconography of the California siren queen. Her effect initially had its limits; as she said: "My feeling has been, and I've said this for years, that if I was white, looked like a dog, and had only a fraction of what I have going on I would've been out there!"

Part of Odetta's existence was dedicated to responding to the wounds of being raised under Jim Crow laws. She lent her star power and voice to the struggle for black liberation. Rosa Parks favored her music and Dr. Martin Luther King Jr. in 1961 dubbed Odetta "the Queen of American folk music." Odetta hit with Harry Belafonte, dueting on "There's a Hole in My Bucket" and sang her "Freedom

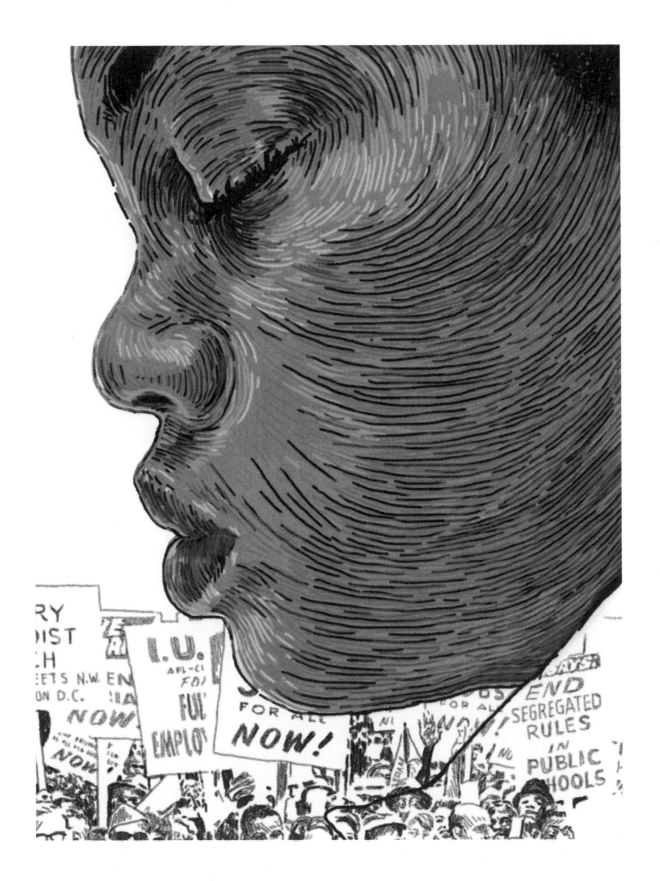

Trilogy"—"Oh Freedom," "Come and Go with Me," "I'm on My Way"—at the historic 1963 March on Washington. Her performance signaled a new form of black pride and new possibilities in the entertainment field for her cohort of black progressives seeking to transform their position in American life.

Even Bob Dylan, who has had a complicated relationship with black vernacular culture and a storied relationship to iconic black women, including Mavis Staples, civil rights activist Dorie Ladner, and superstar sessioneer Clydie King, considers Odetta's role in his self-fashioning. As Dylan's sonic mother, Odetta is as important to his construction of an iconic persona and to late modern music as Woody Guthrie. Dylan learned all the songs on her 1956 album *Odetta Sings Ballads and Blues*. "The first thing that turned me on to folk singing was Odetta," he told *Playboy* in 1978. "I heard a record of hers in a record store, back when you could listen to records right there in the store. Right then and there, I went out and traded my electric guitar and amplifier for an acoustical guitar, a flat-top Gibson. [About Odetta there was] just something vital and personal."

Odetta also had a profound impact on her peers of the folk revival and afterward, including Harry Belafonte, Joan Baez, Bernice Johnson Reagon, Dorris Henderson, Janis Joplin, Taj Mahal, Carly Simon, Joan Armatrading, and Tracy Chapman. Tom Chapin declared, "She had a voice that was totally unique. When she spoke a word or sang a song, it was like Mother Earth speaking."

No female artist with a repertoire focused on work songs, blues, folk, and protest music had recorded or toured in solo format prior to Odetta; there's a reason the *New York Times* proclaimed her

"Mother Goddess of Folk/Blues" at the end of the last millennium. Armed with her guitar, named Baby, her readings of "Amazing Grace," "This Little Light of Mine," and "He's Got the Whole World in His Hands" became world-spanning classics. She illuminated alternate black histories at her appearances, relating stories of the Southern experience, and swung between accompanying herself and using band arrangements on such releases as *Odetta and the Blues* (1962) and her eponymous 1967 album. Odetta kissed Dylan back across the racial divide by recording the second-ever collection of his songs in 1965, *Odetta Sings Dylan*. The album is notable for containing some of the best interpretations of his songs this side of Richie Havens, including a riveting "Masters of War" and the then obscure "Baby, I'm in the Mood for You." However, she was not content merely being an icon of the most radical sphere of the 1950s and early 1960s. She overcame not just in the revolutionary streets and on wax but internally, conquering her avowed self-hatred by identifying with the protagonists of "Prison Song" and "John Henry," using their stories to mediate her anger at an unjust society with its deep strictures on black female agency.

One of the final glowing achievements of Odetta's career was being invited to sing at the first inauguration of President Barack Obama. Sadly, it was not to be. She died from heart failure on December 2, 2008. Still, her message of love, hope, and social change remains as her legacy, continuing to heal us all. ∎

PLAYLIST

Spiritual Trilogy: "Oh, Freedom," "Come and Go with Me," "I'm on My Way," *Odetta Sings Ballads and Blues* (1956)

"Take This Hammer," 1957, *At the Gate of Horn*

"Sometimes I Feel Like a Motherless Child," 1960, *Odetta at Carnegie Hall*

"This Little Light of Mine," 1963, *Odetta Sings Folk Songs*

"Baby, I'm in the Mood for You," 1965, *Odetta Sings Dylan*

JOAN BAEZ

ANN POWERS

ILLUSTRATION BY WINNIE T. FRICK

In junior high, Joan Baez joined the choir at her Redlands, California, school. She believed that something powerful was rumbling inside her being; in her diary that year, she wrote: "I am not a saint. I am a noise." But she hadn't yet been able to shape the noise correctly. All she could manage was the plain, flat tone of a young girl. How could she convey her essence, the power that would startle people and make them notice her? Baez did it methodically and with utter confidence, as she would do so many things throughout her groundbreaking, generation-shaping career. Doing exercises in the shower, rubbing her fingers against her throat, she forced a vibrato. Eventually she could maintain it. "By the end of the summer," she wrote years later, in her autobiography, "I was a singer."

This anecdote reveals the blend of brass and perfectionism that made Baez the signature artist of the 1960s folk revival and the primary role model for countless young women negotiating the tricky waters of the counterculture. Joan was raised in a cosmopolitan, academic family—her physicist father was born in Mexico, her mother in Scotland, and her sister, Mimi Fariña, later also became a beloved figure in the folk revival. She moved from New York to California to Boston in her youth and gained the self-assurance of someone accustomed to making space for herself. Brown-skinned like her father, she encountered racism while in school, an experience that, along with her family's Quakerism, fed her sense of social justice. Her 1959 debut at the Newport Folk Festival brought her instant renown: she was a pristine oracle in a scratchy ethnic sweater, immediately labeled a new Madonna by young fans building ideals from the ashes of the Cold War–besieged New Left. The clarion call of her singing communicated a unique blend of authority, innocence, and willfulness—exactly what her bookish, earnest listeners needed as they ventured forth from coffeehouses, where they talked about politics, to marches, where they enacted them. She used the authority she projected to champion a new generation of socially conscious songwriters, from Phil Ochs to Richard Farina to her occasional lover and partner in iconicity, Bob Dylan. Though she rarely wrote songs herself, when she did they further cemented her position as a truth teller: her confessional views of politicized bohemia on 1970's "I Live One Day at a Time" and 1975's "Diamonds and Rust" are key examples of the feminist critique of the left that began to emerge in that decade.

Throughout the 1960s, Baez embodied the activist power and the pop potential of folk music. She was there, in front, at the March on Washington, singing next to her friend Martin Luther King Jr. She refused to pay taxes in protest against the Vietnam War and

was jailed twice. She journeyed to Hanoi, where she landed in the middle of a US-led air strike. Later, after the counterculture became less movement-oriented and more about identity and lifestyle, she became a kind of international ambassador of the Left, befriending Poland's Lech Walesa and the Czech Republic's Václav Havel, touring in Latin America to draw attention to civil rights violations there, and appearing like an anti-fascist fairy godmother at the 1985 blockbuster charity concert Live Aid. In the twenty-first century she's continued to speak out about climate change, against war, and for human rights; she performed at the Women's March in San Francisco after Donald Trump's inauguration; and, when inducted into the Rock and Roll Hall of Fame in 2017, called for more activism: "We the people must speak truth to power, and be ready to make sacrifices," she said.

PLAYLIST

"A Hard Rain's a-Gonna Fall," 1965, *Farewell, Angelina*

"Gracias a la Vida," 1974, *Gracias a la Vida*

"Diamonds and Rust," 1975, *Diamonds and Rust*

"Recently," 1988, *Recently*

"House of the Rising Sun," 2016, *75th Birthday Celebration*

Baez's legacy as a rabble-rouser is so strong that sometimes it overshadows her music. But her voice has always been the agent of her power. Her early recordings, collections of traditional folk ballads, remain startling in their immediacy; her readings of much-thumbed texts like "Silver Dagger" and "The House of the Rising Sun" repopulate them with subversive female energy, exposing the violence at the heart of this repertoire, peril that often beset women in service of men's rule. Though often praised for its purity, it's the rage within Baez's delivery that's most striking in her first few albums; it confronts the listener, cuts into her preconceptions. Taking in her remarkable performances, it's easy to imagine that

Baez's voice was one of the sources of the "wild mercury sound" that Dylan cultivated in his own music: the return of what history had drowned in its rivers, a feminine force pushing its way back to the surface.

In those days Baez also had to push against the phenomenon that Dylan was becoming, though she benefited from it and, in many ways, enabled it. She was his mentor, introducing him to her vast audiences, championing his genius even when it began to overshadow her own. When he began to shy away from both her companionship and the folk style that she represented, he was cruel about it—something for which he publicly apologized only after another forty years went by. The pair continued a relationship that remains mysterious to outsiders, performing together during Dylan's 1975 Rolling Thunder Revue tour, which featured Joan sometimes dressing up in Bobby drag onstage. Often cast within the Dylan drama as his muse and, eventually, his millstone, Baez was really a prime collaborator who helped him devise a public image that he'd tap into for the rest of his life. In the mid-1960s, he aggressively worked to diminish her importance in his life, to cast her as a spiritual parent he'd outgrown. She continued to acknowledge his greatness as an artist: "Whether or not he decides to join forces with the human race, he's a genius," she told a reporter in 1969. Baez got the sweetest kind of revenge through her music, becoming one of Dylan's greatest interpreters. Her 1968 album *Any Day Now*, recorded in Dylan's then favorite musical town of Nashville, rivals his own melding of country and cool.

Baez accommodated the confessional mood of the soft-rock 1970s with some excellent work: the title song of her beloved album *Diamonds and Rust*, which is about her time with Dylan, is one of the greatest examples of autobiographical writing the rock era has produced. (Also worth hearing: "Recently," her 1987 rejoinder to ex-husband David Harris, a perfect dissection of countercultural love's tendency to fracture in divorce.) But her primary gift to popular music remains her expansion of the idea of folk to accommodate contemporary singer-songwriters from many different corners. The 1980s saw her lending her still powerful voice to songs by U2 and Peter Gabriel; in the 1990s she mentored younger songwriters like Mary Chapin Carpenter and Indigo Girls, who remain her occasional tour-mates. Most recently she's cultivated a kinship with Americana artists like Steve Earle, who produced her 2008 album *Day after Tomorrow*.

The Baby Boom generation that Baez helped compel to action, and which in turn brought her stardom and real political influence, did change the world. But to some, its ideals seem outdated. Joan Baez was propelled to stardom by a folk revival and a student movement that made real efforts toward integration,

but remained white-dominated and found places for women that were only rarely up front. (Baez herself retired to housewifery for a couple of years when married to antiwar activist Harris.) Baez continued her work beyond the political moment that so well suited her, changing both her sound and her activist approach as she grew more enlightened. At seventy-seven, she can still rouse a crowd with her voice, which remains rich and versatile. She is the quintes-sential Baby Boomer in the best ways: in her passion for dreaming; in her belief that art can create com-munity and cross, if not erase, boundaries; and in her commitment to taking that belief into the streets. Or, if the times demand it, to the internet. In 2017, for the first time in twenty-five years, Baez released a song she herself wrote. It was a protest song, naturally, this time inspired by Donald Trump. "Nasty Man" went viral, garnering more than 3 million views. "I'm not agitating enough people," she said when asked why she wrote the song. Spoken like a woman who'd rather be a noise than a saint. ■

CAROLE KING

GILLIAN G. GAAR

ILLUSTRATION BY LINDSEY BAILEY

"Will You Love Me Tomorrow?" was Carole King's first big hit as a songwriter, one of her signature songs. Two different versions, recorded a decade apart, illustrate the era-spanning impact King had as a songwriter and then as a singer-songwriter. The original version, released in 1960 by the Shirelles, is upbeat and winsome, a song of adolescent yearning written while King, though married and a new mother, was still in her teens. Ten years later, when she was a divorced single mom trying to find her musical direction, she recorded the song herself for her breakthrough album *Tapestry*. Slowing the tempo, she drew out the song's underlying sadness and fear of heartbreak. The original "Will You Love Me Tomorrow" was rooted in innocence; King's version was the result of hard-won experience.

As a young woman herself, King helped define the girl-group era of early rock, writing melodies that were rich with romance and desire. She later crafted the definitive album of the 1970s singer-songwriter genre, expressing the genuine emotions of natural women everywhere. Her compositions have become standards, endlessly played and covered, moving the earth under the feet of successive generations of music fans and revived in 2016 for the Broadway musical *Beautiful*.

Carol Joan Klein was born on February 9, 1942, in Manhattan and grew up in Brooklyn. She recalled first putting her hands on a piano keyboard as soon as she was tall enough to reach it, crafting her own songs at the age of three. She absorbed the music playing around the house: classical, show tunes, and standards by George Gershwin, Cole Porter, and Irving Berlin. In April 1955, at a concert at the Brooklyn Paramount, she sat mesmerized by the music of doo-wop vocalists the Moonglows, LaVern Baker's bold rhythm and blues, and B.B. King's guitar licks. In subsequent months she'd see the cream of this new crop of entertainers, the rock and roll stars: Little Richard, Jerry Lee Lewis, Chuck Berry, Fats Domino. The music was "heaven sent," she wrote in her memoir, *A Natural Woman*. She wanted to be a part of that world.

King formed a doo-wop group with her classmates, the Cosines, a name taken from a trigonometry book (even King admitted it was a "dreadful" choice). But she knew that to get beyond the realm of high school parties, you needed a record deal. King found ABC-Paramount Records in the phone book and called them up, landing an audition and then a deal. Soon after, her first single, "Baby Sittin'," was released, credited to her new name: Carole King.

King acknowledged it was little more than a silly

pop song, but it was a start. She soon met another aspiring songwriter, Gerry Goffin, at Queens College. He wrote lyrics, and she wrote music, so they teamed up professionally and personally, getting married in 1959. Their friend, singer and songwriter Neil Sedaka, brought them to the Aldon Music publishing company, and the Goffin-King team (Gerry's name naturally came first) set to work in their cubicle at 1650 Broadway, writing alongside other songwriters all hoping to score the next hit.

For Goffin-King, "Will You Love Me Tomorrow" proved to be the magic moment. Though people would later compliment King for the words, the lyrics were all Goffin's, a poetic recasting of the question "Will you still respect me in the morning?" It was a daring theme for a pop song, but the Shirelles were initially unimpressed; it sounded too white, "country-western," as singer Beverly Lee told author Sheila Weller. King's sweeping string arrangement won them over. "Tomorrow" wasn't only the first number one for Goffin-King; it also marked the first time an all-female African American group topped the pop charts.

The song launched the "girl group" era, as songs sung by teens to other teens—and girls to other girls—dominated the charts and airwaves. Goffin-King wrote a string of girl group classics with King's irresistible hooks and toe-tapping melodies: "One Fine Day," "The Loco-Motion," "Chains," "Don't Say Nothin' Bad (About My Baby)." Their songs weren't all centered on teen dreams; "Pleasant Valley Sunday" depicted the sterility of suburbia, and the redemptive power of love in "(You Make Me Feel Like) A Natural Woman" was addressed from a completely adult perspective.

Goffin-King managed to ride out the British Invasion; UK bands like the Beatles, the Animals, and Herman's Hermits, inspired by the girl groups, worshipped the writing team and covered their songs. But by the end of the decade, King was in Los Angeles. Her marriage was over due to Goffin's infidelity, drug use, and struggles with bipolar disorder. She continued writing and was encouraged to sing more herself (she'd had a Top 20 hit with the wistful "It Might as Well Rain until September" in 1962). After recording an album with a group of friends credited to her band, the City, she finally went solo.

Her first album, *Writer* (1970), was mostly Goffin-King compositions. But on *Tapestry*, King wrote lyrics as well as the music. The piano-based melodies helped emphasize King's vocals, revealing that the starry-eyed romanticism of her earlier work was now grounded in a new maturity. She sounds regretful, but not defeated, about a relationship's end in "It's Too Late." In "Beautiful," the positive self-affirmation of the chorus matches the melancholy tone of the verses, which reflect on a world marred by sadness. The pulsating desire in "I Feel the Earth Move" is evident in both her bold piano playing and her forceful vocal. King never felt her voice measured up to the prowess of an Aretha Franklin or Barbra Streisand, but she had a distinctive warmth of her own, and nowhere is this more evident than on "You've Got a Friend," a ballad with gospel underpinnings. It's the sound of a woman comfortable in her own skin.

When *Tapestry* was released in February 1971,

PLAYLIST

"It Might as Well Rain until September," 1960, *The Essential Carole King*

"I Feel the Earth Move," 1971, *Tapestry*

"It's Too Late," 1971, *Tapestry*

"You've Got a Friend," 1971, *Tapestry*

"Been to Canaan," 1972, *Rhymes and Reasons*

"Jazzman," 1974, *Wrap Around Joy*

"Really Rosie," 1975, *Really Rosie*

"One Fine Day," 1980, *Pearls: Songs of Goffin and King*

it exploded, selling 3 million copies by the end of the year; for a time it was the biggest-selling album in history (with over 25 million copies sold to date). The album, and King, won four Grammys (five if you count the Grammy for James Taylor's version of "You've Got a Friend").

In an era soon awash with acoustic and piano-based songs and earnestly delivered self-reflective lyrics, King suddenly epitomized the new singer-songwriter. But King had always said she wanted to be successful, not famous. She didn't show up for the Grammy awards in 1972, choosing to stay at home with her newborn daughter. And her reluctance to embrace fame led her to retreat to rural Idaho for a number of years.

There were further hits ("Jazzman," "Sweet Seasons"). There was also *Beautiful: The Carole King Musical*, an award-winning, somewhat sanitized show about King's life up to *Tapestry*. But there was never another *Tapestry*. Wisely, King knew the difficulties inherent in trying to create another blockbuster and never tried. Instead, she continued writing songs she hoped would touch the listener's heart and soul, secure in the knowledge that she'd already created an impressive catalog of music that does exactly that. ■

CELIA CRUZ

MICHELLE THREADGOULD

ILLUSTRATION BY LINDSEY BAILEY

A glorious personification of Afro-Latindad, the Cuban exile and legendary salsa singer Celia Cruz took the stage at the Latin Grammys in 2002 wearing a sky-high white and blue wig, feather cape, a sequined floor-length mermaid dress, and her signature four-inch heels. She had recently been diagnosed with cancer, a fact that she kept hidden under her huge smile and hearty laugh as she salsaed across the stage.

That year, at age seventy-seven, she took home a Grammy for Best Salsa Album, for *La Negra Tiene Tumbao*, which featured one of her most celebrated singles, the title track, which loosely translates to: *that black woman has swagger*. The song fuses salsa, rap, and African drumming and proved that after six decades of making music in her island birthplace and her exile home, the Cuban luminary never lost her swagger. She was still known for shaking her hips and peppering every song with a healthy amount of *Azucar! Azucar!*

Celebrating the sweetness rather than the bitterness of life was Cruz's greatest calling.

Born in the working-class barrio of Santos Suárez, in Havana, Cuba, on October 21, 1925, Úrsula Hilaria Celia de la Caridad Cruz Alfonso was named by her mother after Santa Cecilia, the patron saint of music. Her modest house was home to as many as fourteen family members and relatives

during different periods of Cuba's war efforts and economic collapse, when food and jobs were scarce. Cruz was very close to her *tía* (auntie) and mother, both of whom had strong singing voices and shared her love of Cuban music.

During the late thirties and forties, Havana became a cultural epicenter for the musical form *danzón*, which would create artistic offshoots like *danzón-mambo* (mambo) and cha-cha-chá, and later evolve into salsa and Latin jazz. *Danzón* blended Creole and African dance and drumming with European-style strings and compositions. Singers like Paulina Álvarez, the Empress of the Danzonete (a form of *danzón* with vocals), were played across the radio and performed live with orchestras at Havana's largest venues, influencing Cruz's performance style.

At the age of thirteen, Cruz's cousin, Serafín, entered her into a radio talent show called *Los Reyes de la Conga* (the Kings of the Conga) to sing, live on air. Celia won the contest, and for the next ten years while she studied and went to a teachers college, she competed on radio shows to help provide financially for her family. Eventually, in her early twenties, Cruz worked full-time on the radio and performed regularly at Havana's most popular nightclubs, like the Tropicana, making a name for herself with her low, husky voice. She was also famed

for her call-and-response improvisations and inter-pretations of classic Cuban songs. She wore elegant white dresses and drew energy by cha-chaing, clapping wildly, and flashing her electric smile for her audience.

In 1950, Celia Cruz joined Cuba's most successful orchestra, the Sonora Matancera, where she would meet her future husband, Pedro Knight, the group's trumpet player. However, the public didn't initially embrace her. The orchestra's previous singer, the Puerto Rican Myrta Silva, had been a light-skinned, curvaceous, and sensual performer—while Cruz was slim, black, and more friendly, charismatic, and giddy than sensual. The public called her "ugly," a manifestation of the effects of colonialism and racism in Cuba. In spite of her detractors, Cruz performed with the band for nearly twenty years in sold-out venues across the world, recorded seventy-four albums, and transformed herself into "La Guarachera de Cuba"—the queen of *guaracha*, a *conjunto* style of up-tempo big band music.

History changed Cruz's relationship to Cuba forever. After Fidel Castro toppled General Fulgencio Batista's corrupt military dictatorship and Batista fled the country in 1959, Cruz felt creatively stifled in Cuba. As opposition radio stations, newspapers, and television stations were taken over by the state and became vehicles for communist propaganda, Cruz's distaste for Castro grew. Then, on two separate occasions when she sang with the Sonora Matancera, Castro requested to meet Cruz and that she perform his favorite song, "Burundanga." She refused and walked offstage without greeting Castro after both sets.

Because tensions were high between Cruz and the Cuban government, the director of Sonora Matancera felt that the band had limited options and risked being blacklisted for not vocally supporting communism. On July 15, 1960, the orchestra boarded a plane to Mexico without realizing that they would be stripped of their Cuban citizenship and barred from returning to Cuba. The director broke the news to the group once they were in flight, and Cruz felt an intense sense of loss, as she left behind her mother, who had cancer.

While she was in exile, Cruz's parents died, and she wasn't allowed to return to Cuba for their funerals. Her music was banned in an attempt to erase her from Cuba's history books. As someone who was famous for saying, "amo a mi país" (I love my country), being unable to return to her homeland especially stung Cruz.

But her music was played in secret and in underground nightclubs across the country. Meanwhile, even through these personal tragedies, Cruz remained strong and went on to reinvent herself in the US. After marrying Knight in 1962, Cruz chose to leave the Sonora Matancera in 1965 to pursue her solo career.

Cruz began collaborating with musicians who would totally redefine the genre of salsa in the seventies and eighties, like the Puerto Rican percussionist Tito Puente, and the salsa innovators Johnny Pacheco and Willie Colón. She also became involved in the Fania All-Stars, and signed with Fania Records, the Latin equivalent of Motown. Cruz recorded six albums with Pacheco, and her

PLAYLIST

"Burundanga," 1953, *Celia Cruz y la Sonora Matancera*

"Tumba (La Incomparable)," 1958, *La Incomparable Celia (with La Sonora Matancera)*

"Oye Mi Rumba," 1965, *Sabor y Ritmo de Pueblos*

"Quimbara," 1974, *Celia y Johnny*

"Canto a la Habana," 1974, *Celia y Johnny*

"La Vida Es un Carnaval," 1998, *Mi Vida Es Cantar*

"Yo Viviré," 2000, *Siempre Viviré*

"La Negra Tiene Tumbao," 2001, *La Negra Tiene Tumbao*

album *Celia y Johnny* (1974) went gold. The recording featured "Canto a la Habana," a song many Cuban exiles felt represented their longing for their homeland.

During this time, Cruz also developed her flamboyant style of dress, which was an homage to her barrio of Santos Suárez in Cuba and the neighborhood's *comparasas*, or amateur musicians who performed yearly at Carnaval. The *comparasas* would parade through the streets of Havana in elaborate feathered costumes in conga lines and dance. The joy of Carnaval was an aspect of Cuban culture that Cruz deeply missed. Throughout her career, Cruz wore towering, brightly colored wigs; fur jackets; and dresses with elaborate trains, sequins, and feathers. Her hit song "La Vida Es un Carnaval" (1998) paid tribute to the spirit of living life as if it were a Carnaval celebration.

In the nineties Cruz was invited to the US naval base in Guantánamo Bay to perform for Cuban employees on Cuban-American Friendship Day. It was Cruz's first trip back to Cuba in thirty years. The Cuban American photographer C. M. Guerrero told the *Miami Herald* that as he was talking to her, "All of a sudden, Celia leaned down, reached under the fence and used her bare hands to dig up soil from the Cuban side, filling a Styrofoam cup. 'I finally feel at peace holding this soil,' she said."

Though she would never return to Cuba, Cruz never stopped dreaming of her homeland. That Cuban soil was one of her most prized possessions, which she requested to be buried with her when she died.

Throughout the nineties and the early aughts, Cruz continued making music and collaborating and influencing members of the "next Latin wave," including Marc Anthony, Gloria Estefan, Jennifer Lopez, and Ricky Martin. She was nominated for twelve Latin Grammys, winning a total of seven awards and making appearances on the MTV Video Music Awards and Spanish-language television shows. Cruz was also invited to perform at the White House in front of President George H. W. Bush and President Bill Clinton, and she received honorary doctorates from Yale and the University of Miami.

One of her crowning moments was the release of her second-to-last album, *La Negra Tiene Tumbao* (2001), which charted across Latin America. In her popular music video for the titular song, Cruz danced with energy unimaginable for someone in her seventies, in a whirlwind of costume changes. She reveled in knowing that she would always perform and embody salsa on her terms.

Cruz's final album, *Regalo del Alma*, was recorded in 2002, after Cruz was diagnosed with brain cancer, and released in 2003. The album would be her last gift to her fans. She passed away just a few months later, in July 2003. Thirty thousand people attended her funeral held in New York, and Miami and Union City, New Jersey, named streets after her to honor her legacy.

Fifteen years after her death, you can still hear Cruz's music in Latin dance clubs; on the streets of Miami, New York, and San Francisco; and worldwide. Cuba lifted its ban on her music in 2014. Celia inspired generations of music lovers to live with *tumbao* and to carry a piece of their homeland with them wherever they go. ■

TINA TURNER

KATHERINE TURMAN

ILLUSTRATION BY ANNE MUNTGES

One fraught night in Dallas, Texas, with a Mobil card and thirty-six cents in hand, Tina Turner began the second half of her career—and life. It was July 2, 1976. After sixteen years, the performing powerhouse, thirty-seven, had escaped the heavy hand—literally and figuratively—of Ike Turner, the man who turned her, Svengali-like, from Anna Mae Bullock into the vocal force propelling such Ike and Tina hits as "Proud Mary" and "River Deep—Mountain High."

For Turner, bruised and battered both physically and emotionally, leaving Ike—and her entire life—seemed like the end, but it was in fact a new beginning. Starting in the eighties, as a solo vocalist, incendiary performer, and actress, Turner turned into arguably the world's most successful female rock/R&B artist, selling more than 180 million albums worldwide. Ballads like 1984's "What's Love Got to Do with It" (also the title of the award-winning film based on her *I, Tina* autobiography) and the *Mad Max* soundtrack single "We Don't Need Another Hero" are the proud products of a self-made woman. Her movie roles as the dramatic, cape-wearing Acid Queen in the Who's 1975 musical *Tommy* and as the powerful, Amazon-like Aunty Entity in 1985's *Mad Max beyond Thunderdome* further solidified Turner as an entertainment icon. She was, as her 1989 hit single put it, "simply the best."

At five-foot-three, Turner possesses a giant talent, endless legs, leonine hair, and a voice—raspy, sexy, powerful—that's intimate when a song calls for it, but rollicking and beautifully bawdy on bluesy rock tunes. In Ike and Tina's signature version of "Proud Mary," Tina speaks, sultry-voiced, telling the listener they might want to hear something "nice and easy." But, "You see, we never ever do nothing nice, easy. We always do it nice and rough." The song begins slow, sweet, and near-acapella, her bell-clear voice harmonizing with Ike's baritone and female backing vocals. Then two minutes and thirty-four seconds into the song, "rough" is invoked; Tina's voice—piercing, powerful—is pure rock and roll with a rasp on the high end. Her demeanor, onstage and off, possesses that duality: polished with a hint of raunchiness, her persona grateful and graceful. She attributes much of her personal power, serenity, and sense of karmic justice to Nichiren Shōshū Buddhism, which she began following in the early seventies.

Her survivor's saga began on November 26, 1939, as World War II was beginning. Born in Nutbush, Tennessee—a locale immortalized in her biggest self-penned song, 1973's "Nutbush City Limits"—her early life was not unhappy, but neither was it stable or nurturing. Her parents, Zelma and Floyd Bullock, along with older sister Alline, lived in a shotgun shack. Papa Bullock was a Baptist deacon, and Anna

Mae first began singing in church. Though the family wasn't especially poor, Anna Mae picked cotton as a kid and, in the mid-fifties, cleaned house for a white family named the Hendersons, who treated her with respect. In her 1987 bestseller *I, Tina*, she says of the Hendersons' marriage, "I wanted that kind of affection and caring and commitment."

In a scenario that would later play out in her own life, after years of strife, Turner's mother left her father—and their two daughters. Anna Mae was eleven. Bouncing between her grandmother and relatives, as a young teen she proved social and athletic. At sixteen, after her grandmother's death, she moved in with her mother and sister in St. Louis. Anna Mae began to explore the live music clubs of East St. Louis with Alline, encountering charismatic guitarist and bandleader Ike Turner at the Manhattan Club with his influential R&B/blues lineup Kings of Rhythm. In 1951, Turner's recording of "Rocket 88," a swinging boogie-woogie shuffle written by Kings member Jackie Brenston, was considered by some the first rock record. Riding high, with women galore, Ike didn't pay Anna Mae much notice—until one night, during a break between sets, she grabbed a mic meant for someone else, and her powerful singing floored him. Joining the band onstage for jazz/pop standards like "Since I Fell for You," the skinny teen with the huge voice was an instant hit with both fans and the band.

She joined the Rhythm Kings in 1960, at first in a "sibling relationship" with Ike. After their 1962 wedding in Tijuana, Mexico, the woman now dubbed Tina Turner embarked on more than a decade of backbreaking on-the-road and recording work with emotional ups and downs. Their sets—R&B, blues, and rock amalgamations—featured many covers but incendiary interpretations, including the Beatles'

"Twist and Shout" and the Otis Redding gem "I've Been Loving You Too Long," executed with pain and pathos. The Ike and Tina Turner Revue, as they were known in the late sixties, rose to superstar ranks, thanks in no small part to her rousing voice and sexy stage performances. They appeared on *The Ed Sullivan Show* in 1969, earned seven Grammy nominations (winning in 1971 for "Proud Mary"), opened for the Rolling Stones, and released an astounding twenty-three albums between 1961 and 1974.

Ike and Tina enjoyed huge success by any standards, but life with a drug-addled, controlling husband drove the stoic singer to a suicide attempt in 1968. Still, it was eight more years until she reached her breaking point. After Tina left Ike, it took a few years for her to rebuild, both personally and professionally.

After three years as a struggling solo artist during the disco era, Turner met manager Roger Davies, who would guide her to new career heights. Working with English producers and recording overseas, Europe and the UK became Turner's strongest markets. Her hits there included "Ball of Confusion" (1981) and, two years later, a stellar cover of Al Green's "Let's Stay Together."

But it was 1984's *Private Dancer* album, her fourth solo outing since 1974, that blew her career into the stratosphere. In nine songs and forty-four minutes, songs including the megahit "What's Love Got to Do with It" harnessed Turner's raw power into pop ballads and jazzy R&B gems. From a dramatic, cinematic rework of David Bowie's

PLAYLIST

"River Deep—Mountain High," 1966, *River Deep—Mountain High* (with Ike Turner)

"Acid Queen," 1975, *Acid Queen*

"Private Dancer," 1984, *Private Dancer*

"Better Be Good to Me," 1984, *Private Dancer*

"Nutbush City Limits," 1988, *Tina Live in Europe*

"The Best," 1989, *Foreign Affair*

"1984" to the spare, sensual, mid-tempo sway of the album's storytelling title track, penned by Dire Straits' Mark Knopfler, Turner owned every note she sang, reimagining her career along with the songs. *Private Dancer* sold more than 20 million worldwide and remains the best-selling record of her fifty-year career. Turner was forty-five and becoming one of the world's most recognizable singers on her own terms.

The mid-eighties saw her modernized but not tamed, and Turner's live shows over the next sixteen years covered decades of classic hits, her energy and likability as off the charts as her albums, which hit every few years, notably *Break Every Rule* (1986) and *Foreign Affair* (1989). Her romantic life blossomed as well. In 1986, Turner began dating German music executive Erwin Bach, and in 2013, the pair married in Switzerland.

The film *What's Love Got to Do with It* (1993), a major hit starring Angela Bassett as Tina and Laurence Fishburne as Ike, spawned a soundtrack that featured what would be Turner's last Top 10 US single, the melancholic, memorable "I Don't Wanna Fight." From the outside, Turner appeared ageless. But she effectively retired from live performances in 2009, bidding farewell with a forty-city fiftieth anniversary tour that earned more than $47.7 million. As a solo artist, with nine studio albums, forty-six music videos, and sixty-eight singles, Turner's appeal crosses race, age, and language barriers. Ongoing projects include a Broadway musical. The poised, private, and self-possessed former Anna Mae Bullock manifested what she dreamed of, her fame, fortune, voice, and respect soaring far beyond Nutbush's city limits. ■

ARETHA FRANKLIN

CARYN ROSE

ILLUSTRATION BY JULIE WINEGARD

The indisputable Queen of Soul, the almighty Aretha Franklin has had hits across four decades, singing soul, gospel, jazz, R&B, funk, pop, rock, opera, show tunes, and standards of the American songbook. She has had more than twenty number-one singles, has won eighteen Grammy awards as well as the Grammy Lifetime Achievement Award, was the first woman to be inducted into the Rock and Roll Hall of Fame, was the youngest artist to be accorded the Kennedy Center Honors, and received the Presidential Medal of Freedom. She performed for queens, popes, and presidents, and sang at the funerals of Dr. Martin Luther King Jr. and Mahalia Jackson. She made Barack Obama cry over her show-stopping performance of one of her all-time greatest records, "(You Make Me Feel Like) A Natural Woman," at the 2015 Kennedy Center Honors. The breadth of her accomplishments makes it seem inadequate to simply declare her the greatest singer of our time. She is Lady Soul; she is blues personified; she sings the gospel from a place so deep an unbeliever will feel the presence of the divine.

If Aretha—and she is the original one-named diva—takes a liking to someone else's song, watch out, because she will turn it inside-out and make it her own. Just ask Otis Redding: the first time he heard her version of his "Respect," he told Jerry Wexler, with a big smile on his face, "This girl has taken that song from me. Ain't no longer my song. From now on, it belongs to her." Sarah Vaughan refused to sing "Skylark" after Aretha got her hands on it.

Aretha would also place herself firmly on the right side of history as a leader of social change, loaning her tremendous talent to promote justice. She firmly stood up for civil rights, answering the call from the Southern Christian Leadership Conference whenever they asked, or stepping up to play benefits for African American causes ranging from the families of the victims of the Attica prison riots or assisting Jesse Jackson in bootstrapping his Operation PUSH, an organization to help improve the economic status of African Americans in Chicago. Aretha was raised in an environment where there was no difference between moral justice and social justice; her father, the activist/minister/singer C. L. Franklin, connected racial equality and economic parity from the pulpit early on.

While she was born in Memphis, she moved north, first to Buffalo, then to Detroit—the place she still calls home—with her family as her father advanced his ministry. Rev. Franklin was comfortable behind the pulpit as well as in the media, hosting his own radio show in Memphis and Buffalo. In Detroit, C. L. Franklin began making records

and touring the gospel circuit. B.B. King referred to him as "the bluesman's preacher" because Rev. Franklin didn't see a divide between church music and secular music; "it all comes from God," he used to say. Aretha's gift manifested itself at an early age, even for a city like Detroit, where serious music talent flourished in abundance. She became part of Rev. Franklin's service and his traveling ministry, on the road at the age of twelve. So she never had to make the choice that agonized so many other artists about whether she was going to stay in the church or seek commercial success. The Rev. Franklin was her de facto manager in the early days, and both of them looked to the careers of artists like Nat King Cole and Sam Cooke, who successfully crossed over into the mainstream from gospel. For the Franklins, *père et fille*, the goal was to sing it all; there was no material Aretha couldn't handle.

Only Aretha Franklin could release five albums under legendary talent scout John Hammond at Columbia Records and have them be a minor note in her career. The lack of success for her Columbia material wasn't due to lack of quality, but rather to the fact that she had not yet developed a singular musical vision. When that contract ended, she moved to Atlantic Records under the aegis of the legendary Jerry Wexler, and within a few weeks of entering the studio along with the Muscle Shoals Rhythm Section, she had her first million-selling, crossover hit with "I Never Loved a Man (The Way I Love You)." Two months later, her "Respect" went to number one on both the pop and R&B charts, and it would become the hallmark of her repertoire. "Respect," as well as "Think," which would come shortly thereafter, became anthems of black pride and power, as well as feminist equality. Her voice is enormous and ferocious and will not be denied.

While Otis smoothly, ardently pled, Aretha did not ask: she set the terms of engagement. With "Respect," Wexler was originally concerned that Franklin would be able to deliver a rendition sufficiently different than the original; not only did Aretha flip around the arrangement, adding a strong, hypnotic rhythm and cadence, which adds to the song's urgency, but her voice crackles with electricity, full of endless power and promise.

The Atlantic era remains Franklin's strongest. In addition to her pop records, it includes *Amazing Grace* (1972), a stunning live gospel album recorded with the Rev. James Cleveland and the Southern California Community Choir that is both the biggest-selling album of Franklin's entire career and the biggest-selling black gospel album ever. In coming back to the church, Aretha brought all of her talents, bringing in Carole King, George Harrison, and Marvin Gaye alongside gospel warhorses. The same year, she recorded a live album at the Fillmore West, where she won over the flower children completely. "It wasn't that the hippies just liked her," said Billy Preston, who played piano in that band. "They went out of their minds."

In 1976, Franklin went to work with Curtis Mayfield on *Sparkle*, a jewel of hot buttered soul that should be a classic of the era, as much of a concept album as Marvin Gaye's *What's Going On*. It is

PLAYLIST

"Respect," 1967, *I Never Loved a Man the Way I Love You*

"I Never Loved a Man (The Way I Love You)," 1967, *I Never Loved a Man the Way I Love You*

"Do Right Woman, Do Right Man," 1967, *I Never Loved a Man the Way I Love You*

"Chain of Fools," 1968, *Lady Soul*

"(You Make Me Feel Like) A Natural Woman," 1968, *Lady Soul*

"Think," 1968, *Aretha Now*

"Rock Steady," 1972, *Young, Gifted, and Black*

"Freeway of Love," 1985, *Who's Zoomin' Who*

"Sisters Are Doin' It for Themselves," 1985, *Who's Zoomin' Who*

"Jumpin' Jack Flash," 1986, *Aretha [1986]*

a record like nothing Aretha had done before, or since, and was the next logical step of her career, solid thematically and musically from end to end. *Sparkle* should have been the beginning of Aretha's next act. Sadly, she did not deliver on that promise.

Just when the industry was ready to count her out, Aretha came back in the eighties, starting with her delightful cameo in *The Blues Brothers* movie, performing "Think." She signed with Clive Davis and Arista records, and Davis helped match her with the right producers, beginning with Luther Vandross on 1982's *Jump to It*, which would provide her first gold record since *Sparkle*. Like she did back in her Columbia days, in the eighties, Aretha wanted *hits*. That goal was achieved with 1985's *Who's Zoomin' Who*. The joyous "Freeway of Love" was her biggest hit since "Respect," and her duet with Annie Lennox of Eurythmics, "Sisters Are Doin' It for Themselves," put her behind an equally feminist anthem. *Aretha* (1986) served up a funky, modern, and deeply soulful cover of "Jumpin' Jack Flash" for the movie of the same name, at Keith Richards's personal request.

The enormity of Franklin's talent may have best been exemplified at the 1998 Grammy Awards. Franklin, there to perform "Think," was asked to pinch-hit for Luciano Pavarotti, who was supposed to sing "Nessun Dorma." She had learned the aria for a private benefit concert that took place a week before, but this was a different arrangement, with a sixty-five-piece orchestra and a twenty-voice choir, and on live television. Aretha asked two questions—was the arrangement in her key (no) and was there a tape (yes)—before agreeing to do it, with less than half an hour to prepare. "She wasn't afraid of the aria," said Jerry Wexler, which is a severe understatement. She interpreted Puccini as Aretha Franklin, and the result was nothing short of magnificent. It was broad, deep and colorful, full of pathos and triumph and exultation, and her voice, while not perfect, more than stood up to the performance of one of grand opera's greatest arias.

Even in 2015, performing something as mundane as the National Anthem before a Detroit Lions football game, Aretha would demonstrate that she was still a force to be reckoned with. Wearing a full-length fur coat and a Detroit Lions knit cap, she sat down at a grand piano positioned at the fifty-yard line and played her way through a soulful meditation of "The Star-Spangled Banner," which went on for over four minutes, before ending with fireworks and a standing ovation. If the NFL wanted a brisk, standard version of the anthem, they should have called someone else, and not the woman *Rolling Stone* named the "#1 Greatest Singer of All Time." Amen. ∎

DANCING IN THE STREETS

If the iconic image of the first era of rock stars was a guitar-wielding guy (and despite the successes of Sister Rosetta Tharpe, Wanda Jackson, and Lady Bo, men dominated 1950s rock and roll), then the second wave belonged to women in tight dresses and bouffants gathered around a microphone. Inspired by doo-wop, and following the path blazed by the Andrews Sisters in the 1940s, girls in high schools across America banded together in vocal groups during the late 1950s to mid-1960s. They sang songs in tight harmonies about how teenage crushes on bad boys allowed rebel girls to make their first breaks with family and tradition, about the ensuing heartache that hurt so good, about parties, and loneliness, and, as the sixties progressed into a decade of upheaval, about dancing in the streets.

Most of these women were black. Rock and roll was birthed in the 1950s through a merger of African and Anglo traditions, as artists like Ray Charles and Chuck Berry wrote country songs and Elvis Presley answered record maker Sam Phillips's wish for a white man who sang like a black man. But it was often the white artists who had the pop hits while black artists were segregated to the Rhythm & Blues charts. Some historians describe the period between the death of Buddy Holly in 1959 and the British Invasion in 1964 as a fallow time for rock and roll. That's white men's history. In fact, the real social revolution occurred during those years, when all of a sudden, everyone on *American Bandstand* was doing the twist and boogaloo to music by girl groups and Motown acts. The Beatles began as a group of English lads either explicitly covering or trying to imitate black American artists. Ronnie Spector and her Ronettes were their muse and their passion. John Lennon, the Rolling Stones, Bob Dylan: they all wanted to be her baby.

The Shirelles, the Supremes, the Crystals, the Blossoms, Patti LaBelle and the Bluebelles, Martha and the Vandellas, the Marvelettes, the Shangri-Las: hundreds of all-female vocal ensembles charted during the 1960s. Women were combining their talents, empowering each other, and making themselves heard. But they still battled exploitation, appropriation, and abuse, often at the hands of white Svengali-like figures—for example, Phil Spector. Brilliant talents such as Darlene Love were robbed of their own agency, their names kept off the records they sang, their identities anonymized in groups where sometimes the members were interchangeable, unnamed, or even nonexistent. Beginning with Diana Ross, the supreme Supreme, girl group members did increasingly assert themselves into the spotlight. By the end of the 1960s, it was the powerhouse front woman—Aretha, Janis, Grace, Mavis—who personified and promoted the new sexual revolution. They traded the harmonies, lovelorn lyrics, and "sh-bop" choruses of the girl groups for mighty wails and demands for respect. But the flip side of the focus on individual artistry was the bust-up of musical sororities, of the proto–second wave consciousness-raising cells that were the girl groups, feminists in black eyeliner and unified voices.

DARLENE LOVE

GILLIAN G. GAAR

ILLUSTRATION BY WINNIE T. FRICK

Darlene Love's biggest hit was "He's a Rebel." On the girl group classic, Love eulogizes the wonder of loving the "bad" boy who will "never ever be any good." Her rich, warm voice provides a relatable point of entry against producer Phil Spector's trademark "wall of sound," a thick instrumental backing punctuated by handclaps and honking saxes. The song was an irresistible confection, and topped the charts for two weeks in 1962, a time when black women like Love sang the soundtrack of the burgeoning civil rights era but white men like Spector got all the credit.

You won't find Love's name on the recording of "He's a Rebel." The song is credited to the Crystals, a group Love was not even a member of. Adding insult to injury, despite Spector's promise that the next song he produced for Love would be released under her own name, he again credited "He's Sure the Boy I Love" (1963) to the Crystals.

It was another blow for the woman who was on her way to becoming the biggest unknown singer in rock. Even when she was ostensibly the lead singer, Love was pushed into the background. Still, she found ways to maneuver. "When you're a singer on the side," she wrote in her 1998 memoir *My Name Is Love: The Darlene Love Story*, "sometimes you have the best view."

She was born Darlene Wright on July 26, 1941, in Los Angeles, where she grew up, aside from a few years in Texas. Love was raised in a religious family, attending the church where her father preached, and learned about music by listening to her mother's Marian Anderson records. It was a strict household; when she brought home a friend's copy of Hank Ballard and the Midnighters' racy "Work with Me Annie," her mother denounced it as "filth" and smashed it to pieces.

Unsurprisingly, the first place Love began to sing was in church. She was soon singing beyond the church's walls: at the Hollywood Bowl, when the choir won a contest to open for Nat King Cole, and making her radio debut when the choir director picked her to sing on a program broadcast from the Music Mart, a Christian bookstore. Her first appearance on record came not long after, in 1957, when she provided backing vocals on the single "Aye Senorita" by a local pop group, the Echoes.

Doo-wop and early rock and roll were changing the way Americans heard each other. Via the seemingly benign sorority of vocal groups, women's voices were about to take over the airwaves. While still in high school, Darlene was asked to join a female vocal group, the Blossoms. After overcoming her parents' opposition, she eagerly accepted. The Blossoms' own releases were unsuccessful, but they provided backing vocals on numerous hit records for a wide

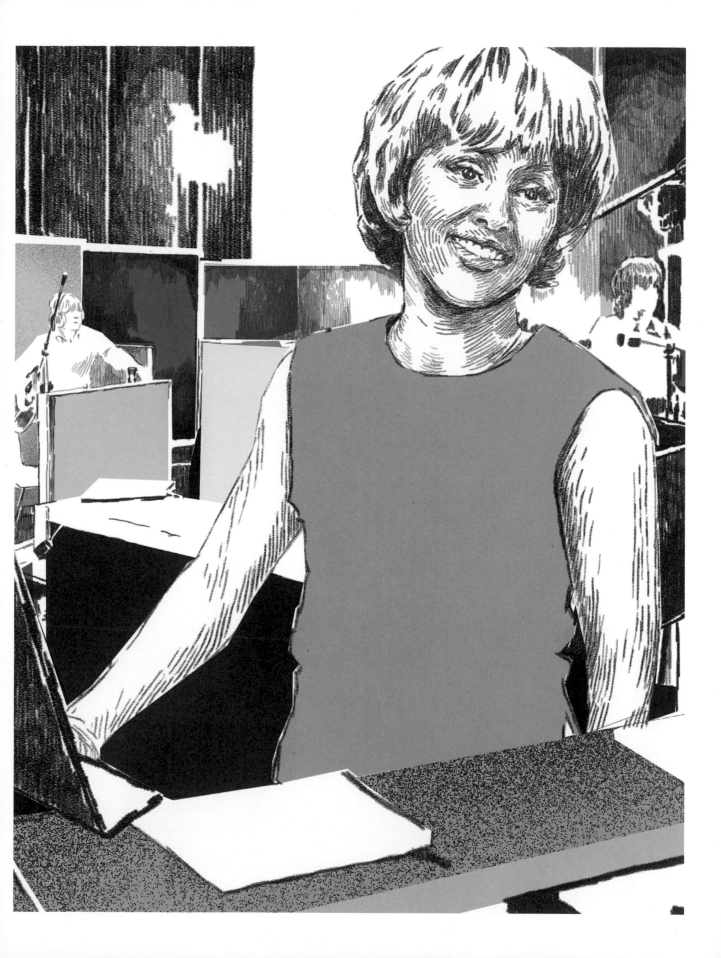

variety of artists, illustrating their versatility: Sam Cooke ("Everybody Likes to Cha Cha Cha"), Shelley Fabares ("Johnny Angel"), the Beach Boys ("In My Room"), and Bobby "Boris" Pickett ("Monster Mash"), among many others. Love's career twenty feet from stardom had begun.

Recording "He's a Rebel" for Phil Spector seemed like just another gig for Love, who was only two years younger than the budding impresario. Spector had written his first hit record when he was nineteen ("To Know Her Is to Love Her"), and was building a reputation as an exacting and domineering producer. He'd heard "Rebel," written by Gene Pitney, in New York City, but wanted to record it with Los Angeles musicians, rushing to get the song completed before a rival version by Vikki Carr was released. He attributed the record to the Crystals, a New York group with whom he had worked, because they were a hit act, and Love was an unknown quantity. The producer felt that since the public rarely even knew the names of a group's members, it didn't matter who was actually singing. They were cogs; he was the machine.

Love was used to backing singers receiving no credit; at the time, scant mention was made of anyone besides the stars who appeared on a record. Until the advent of the Supremes, individual members of girl groups were rarely identified by name. But never before had her vocals been attributed to someone else entirely. It set the stage for enduring conflict in Love's relationship with her producer. She wound up being one of the few who would stand up to Spector.

Her next chart success came as a member of a group of session singers that Spector named Bob B. Soxx and the Blue Jeans. She finally stepped out under her own name on the album *A Christmas Gift for You from Philles Records*, as Darlene Love (a name contrived by Spector; it was taken from the name of gospel singer Dorothy Love Coates). Her versions of "White Christmas" and "Winter Wonderland" were lively and fun, but it was her heartfelt rendition of "Christmas (Baby Please Come Home)"—the only original track on the album—that would become her signature song. Love was up to the challenge of striking the right note in a song that wasn't dipped in holiday cheer, easily navigating its high emotional quotient without falling into despair. And when you think she can't ramp up the intensity any further, she digs deep inside to soar even higher, begging "please . . . please," in a climactic call-and-response with her own backing singers.

Meanwhile, the Blossoms were in demand. They were in the house band on the rock music variety TV show *Shindig*, against the network's objections of having an African American group as regular performers. They appeared on Elvis Presley's acclaimed 1968 comeback TV special, *Elvis*, and did live work with the Righteous Brothers, Nancy Sinatra, and Dionne Warwick. There was never a shortage of session work. Yet they remained largely unknown by name, few recognizing the similarity of the backing voices that appeared on records by the likes of Ike and Tina Turner, Dusty Springfield, and Cheech and Chong, among others. When the group received an NAACP Image Award

PLAYLIST

"He's a Rebel," 1962, *The Sound of Love: The Very Best of Darlene Love*

"Christmas (Baby Please Come Home)," 1963, *A Christmas Gift for You from Phil Spector*

"Not Too Young to Get Married," 1963, *The Sound of Love*

"A Fine, Fine Boy," 1963, *The Sound of Love*

"River Deep, Mountain High," 1985, *Leader of the Pack*

"He's Sure the Boy I Love," 2014, on Bette Midler's *It's the Girls!*

"Forbidden Nights," 2015, *Introducing Darlene Love*

in 1971, Love noted it was "the only real recognition we'd received in our career."

Tired of standing in the shadows, Love wanted to make her name as a singer in her own right. She signed with Philadelphia International Records in 1973, only to be dismayed to learn that her contract had been sold to her nemesis—Phil Spector. While recording the song "Lord, If You're a Woman," their relationship came to the breaking point. Love dismissed the song as "tripe," but nonetheless turned in a strong, soulful performance. But she quickly tired of what she viewed as Spector's dismissive attitude toward her during the session. Maybe the lyric, which has a woman begging for the strength to leave an abusive man, made an impression. She walked out and never worked with Spector again. Later she'd successfully sue him for nonpayment of royalties.

Love was now free, but lean years lay ahead. When she couldn't land a record deal and session work dried up, she could only find work as a housecleaner. It's a common showbiz story: a once high-flyer dragged back down to earth. But this was also the moment when Love's underlying resilience began to come through, as she fought to revive her career. She found work on cruise lines, appeared in the 1984 stage musical *Leader of the Pack* (based on the life of songwriter Ellie Greenwich, who'd worked with Love in the 1960s), and landed a recurring role in the *Lethal Weapon* film series, as Danny Glover's wife. In 1986, she started a tradition of her own, singing "Christmas (Baby Please Come Home)" on *Late Show with David Letterman*—the first of twenty-nine annual appearances. Darlene Love was center stage at last.

There was growing acknowledgment of the key role she'd played in creating the soundtrack of a generation. In 1993, she starred in a long-running one-woman revue based on her life, *Portrait of a Singer*. Twenty years later, Love was featured in the Oscar-winning documentary *20 Feet from Stardom*, about the struggles of backing singers, who contribute so much to the songs that move us but too often remain unrecognized.

The film captures the most triumphant moment of Love's career, the night she was inducted into the Rock and Roll Hall of Fame in 2011. She summarizes her determination to the filmmakers: "Every time you get up you might fall down. But you've got to get back up again." ■

RONNIE SPECTOR

STEPHANIE PHILLIPS

ILLUSTRATION BY LINDSEY BAILEY

Voice of a generation is a title that few could live up to, but Ronnie Spector fits the bill. As the lead singer of one of the 1960s' most influential girl groups, the Ronettes, Spector sang hits that redefined popular music. Their signature style—bouffant hairdos teamed with wiggle dresses and thick eyeliner—is still emulated today, most recently by British singer Amy Winehouse. Under the management of legendary producer Phil Spector, the Ronettes had a Top Ten hit in "Be My Baby," a song that captured a key ingredient of the rock-and-roll era: puppy love.

For a few short years the Ronettes were global icons. They toured with the Beatles in the US and had numerous Top Ten hits. On their UK tour a band named the Rolling Stones opened for them. At the peak of their success, twenty-four-year-old Ronnie Bennett married Phil Spector, imagining that a fairytale life of love, success, and happiness would follow. Sadly, Ronnie's career foundered as Phil refused to release the Ronettes' records. She was kept a virtual prisoner in their Los Angeles mansion for the majority of her marriage until she managed to break out of the house. Since then she has tried desperately to reach the same levels of stardom she had at the peak of her career, perhaps unaware how much she has already influenced pop culture.

Spector was born Veronica Bennett in New York City in 1943 to an African American mother and Irish American father. She was raised in Spanish Harlem with her future bandmates, older sister Estelle Bennett and cousin Nedra Talley. An average Saturday night for the family involved entertaining each other with songs and routines at their grandmother's home. It was these family parties that inspired a teenage Ronnie to form the first incarnation of the Ronettes.

First known as the Darling Sisters, the act played wherever they could get a gig until they were introduced to Colpix Records producer Stu Phillips in 1961. The girls renamed themselves Ronnie and the Relatives and recorded four songs that failed to chart. Their big break came when they were mistaken for dancers outside the chic New York club the Peppermint Lounge and earned themselves a regular job dancing to popular songs and occasionally singing.

It was during this time that the Ronettes perfected their signature look. Most girl groups at the time, such as the Shirelles or the Chantels, wore demure dresses that screamed respectability and wouldn't look out of place at church. It was a modest style that could help groups that were predominantly made up of women of color cross over to middle America. The Ronettes also wanted to look feminine, but they were working-class girls from Spanish Harlem and were influenced by the women in their multicultural neighborhood. So they copied their look. Armed with cans of Aqua Net hairspray to hold their skyscraping bouffant hairdos and heavy eyeliner and mascara, the girls perfected working-class femininity. Ronnie, with her bubbly personality and smoldering looks, acted as a cultural reference point for bad girls all over the world. The Ronettes were in fact so young they weren't let out of their families' sight for long enough to misbehave, but nevertheless, the image stuck.

Disappointed with their lack of success at Colpix, Bennett took the initiative to call the already famous Spector to arrange a meeting. In Ronnie, Phil found his muse. At their audition, as Ronnie began to sing Frankie Lymon's "Why Do Fools Fall in Love," Phil jumped up and shouted "That's the voice I've been looking for!" The Ronettes terminated their contract with Colpix and signed with Phil's label, Philles. After a few songs that, written for them, were given to other bands (a regular occurrence at Philles), the Ronettes eventually struck gold with the pop classic "Be My Baby" (1963). Written by Phil Spector, Jeff Barry, and Ellie Greenwich, the song was a Top Ten hit. Opening with one of the most memorable drum fills in rock and roll, "Be My Baby" is a strikingly direct request for love from a young woman, unusual for the time. The song defined Spector's Wall of Sound approach as strings, horns, and guitars burst through the speakers, fighting for attention. Ronnie's voice takes center stage, capturing the innocence of youth in the excitement of her singing.

At the age of twenty, Spector was the lead singer of a band with a Top Ten hit and was loved and admired by many. She had her share of romances and dated both John Lennon and Keith Richards. In her book *Be My Baby: How I Survived Mascara, Miniskirts,* *and Madness*, Ronnie writes: "By the fall of 1963 our lives were turned upside down. All the things I ever dreamed about were finally coming true."

While later releases charted relatively high, the Ronettes couldn't match the groundbreaking sensation that was "Be My Baby." The group's success hinged largely on Ronnie, who was the face of the band and often the only member singing on their records. She had an imperfect warble that rustled and shrieked with excitement. It's apparent both from video footage from the sixties and from Spector's performances today that she was born to perform.

The Ronettes' records set the standard for pop genius, one that artists have been trying to recreate ever since. Brian Wilson reportedly was so enamored with "Be My Baby" that he listened to it every day trying to work out the root of its perfection. Bruce Springsteen based many of his early records on the Ronettes' girl group era sound. Ronnie's bad-girl image and gravelly vocals even earned her fans in the punk scene, including both Johnny Thunders and the Misfits. Joey Ramone called her one of his favorite singers.

Ronnie was a star, and after a handful of singles and an album, the Ronettes were positioned to rise even higher—until Phil Spector got in the way. Phil was enamored with Ronnie, and by 1966 he refused to release any of the Ronettes' records. It is rumored that his insecurities about his relationship with Ronnie and his worry that she would outgrow him led him to hold on to their material.

PLAYLIST

"Be My Baby," 1964, *Presenting the Fabulous Ronettes Featuring Veronica*

"Do I Love You," 1964, *Presenting the Fabulous Ronettes Featuring Veronica*

"Walking in the Rain," 1964, *Presenting the Fabulous Ronettes Featuring Veronica*

"Baby, I Love You," 1964, *Presenting the Fabulous Ronettes Featuring Veronica*

"(The Best Part of) Breaking Up," 1964, *Presenting the Fabulous Ronettes Featuring Veronica*

Frustration with their lack of hits and inability to release new songs led the Ronettes to break up in 1967. Ronnie married Phil a year later, beginning seven years of hell. By her accounts, she was kept a near prisoner in their California mansion. She was so terrified of Phil's bizarre antics that she began drinking to ease the pain and found that her visits to rehab were more enthralling than her everyday life. During this time Phil brought Ronnie into the studio to record "You Came, You Saw, You Conquered" (1969). Most radio stations had moved on from the early sixties girl group sound, and the record flopped.

By the time she left Phil it was the mid-seventies, and she kept her married name as her stage name. Despite the fact that she was adored by rock stars, Ronnie's attempts to restart her career were received as the work of an oldies act. Nevertheless Ronnie continued trying to reform the Ronettes with different members, releasing solo albums and enjoying a resurgence in popularity as a vocalist on Eddie Money's hit song "Take Me Home Tonight" (1986). Referencing her biggest hit, Ronnie responds to Money's lyric "Just like Ronnie sang" with "Be my little baby."

Reading interviews with Spector and seeing her perform live, I get a sense that she feels as if she was never allowed the career she thought she deserved. Like many of our greatest icons, Ronnie probably doesn't know the true impact of her work or the fact that her influence will only continue to grow. Her music has been adored by everyone from the Ramones to Amy Winehouse. In 2007, the Ronettes were inducted into the Rock and Roll Hall of Fame. Hopefully it was the proof that Ronnie needed to realize her work and talents were loved and appreciated. ■

DIANA ROSS

CARYN ROSE

ILLUSTRATION BY LINDSEY BAILEY

Everyone knows Diana Ross because her hits were *hits*. Her career encompasses decades of excellence and an ability to sing pretty much anything from country and western to show-tunes. Her songs sold millions because they were timeless and memorable and could not have been sung by anyone but her. The sixties canon usually shoves Motown over in a corner for not being serious music, ignoring the fact that Diana Ross and the Supremes chased the likes of the almighty Beatles and the Beach Boys up and down the charts throughout the decade, and that the latter groups themselves idolized the music coming out of Detroit.

The string of number-one singles racked up by Diana Ross and the Supremes is worth a page in a history book: "Where Did Our Love Go," "Come See about Me," "Stop! In the Name of Love," "Back in My Arms Again," "I Hear a Symphony," "You Can't Hurry Love," "You Keep Me Hangin' On"—there would be eleven in total, all sublime, perfect pieces of pop, delivered by three women with phenomenal poise and grace. Sure, they had Holland-Dozier-Holland writing for them, but that was just it: H-D-H wrote specifically for Diana's voice (as well as Florence Ballard's and Mary Wilson's) and once they found the formula that worked—accidentally dropping the key down a bit—the sky was the limit.

Berry Gordy, founder of Motown, is owed credit

for seeing the potential in Diane Ernestine Earle Ross, native daughter of the Motor City, but Diana was the one who originally got the Primettes—the quartet that preceded the Supremes—in the door of Hitsville, USA, for their first audition. And she was the one who devised the stubborn yet ultimately effective strategy of coming back and sitting in the lobby every day until someone needed backup singers for a session. The other Supremes—founder Ballard and Wilson—were strong performers with beautiful instruments, but Diana's voice and presence made Gordy believe she could be a star. Diana, on the other hand, already knew that.

In an era of girl groups, the Supremes stood out because of the consummate songwriting, the stellar Motown house band, and their trademark gorgeous vocal blend: the combination of the precision of Wilson and Ballard's backing vocals layered behind the delicate yet reverberant tone of Ross's voice in front, silvery and soothing, backed by firepower. Ross sang with strength, grace, and boldness; there was gravitas in that sultry soprano.

It's easy to disregard the influence of a pop group on history or culture, especially in the sixties, when the ground was shifting out from under everything. But it would be a mistake to underestimate the impact that three very young, poised, talented, elegantly attired African American women had by

being constantly in the spotlight. The Supremes appeared on *The Ed Sullivan Show*, the epicenter of mainstream American culture of the time, eleven times. Oprah Winfrey, when Diana was a guest on her show, explained, "In a culture when there were no black people on television . . . there was nobody who looked like you . . . [Ross] represented possibility, and hope . . . it was life-changing for me." Even the Rev. Ralph Abernathy of the Southern Christian Leadership Conference would tell Ross at the height of the civil rights movement: "Just continue to be great. Every time the white man sees you on television or in concert and becomes a fan, you are being of assistance."

Gordy's belief in Ross was relentless, and he put all of Motown's resources behind Diana and the Supremes—including his own personal attention to Diana. The two had a tumultuous yet productive relationship, Gordy aiming her career toward the solo stardom they both wanted for her. Unfortunately, he neglected the other members of the group, despite their talent and the fact that fans loved all three of the Supremes, not just Diana. In their rush to get Ross the solo career they envisioned, both Gordy and Ross pushed the group—now Diana Ross and the Supremes—to an undignified end. The Supremes were left out of recording sessions. Then Ballard was fired; Wilson continued with two replacements before moving into a solo career with moderate success. All—including Diana—would end up suing Motown for income they felt they deserved. The impact of the group's rise and fall in popular culture would prove itself out a decade later when *Dreamgirls*, based partially on the Supremes, came to Broadway.

Ross badly wanted to succeed in film, but her reliance on, and desire to be independent from, Gordy would hamper that ambition. Neither of them knew anything about Hollywood, and although Diana was talented enough, the results were inconsistent. Her portrayal of Billie Holiday in *Lady Sings the Blues* (1972) garnered her an Academy Award nomination, and the soundtrack went to number one on the *Billboard* album charts. But *Mahogany* is best remembered for its gorgeous theme song ("Do You Know Where You're Going To?") and for the costumes that Ross personally designed. Her final attempt at movie stardom was her role as Dorothy in *The Wiz*. Gordy was against the idea, and he was right: Ross's performance was awkward and lackluster.

Ross had a few strong releases in the early post-Supremes era— "Touch Me in the Morning" is silk-sheet soulful, and her cover of "Ain't No Mountain High Enough" is sheer triumph. The beginnings of disco would propel Ross back to the top. "Love Hangover" (1976) is a flat-out get-down dance-floor boogie cut that went to number one on the pop, soul, and club charts. The track's success allowed her to break the record for most number-one hits by a female vocalist, which she would hold until 1988. Counting Ross's twelve number-one hits with the Supremes, and then her two number-ones in the eighties—the Chic-produced "Upside Down" and "I'm Coming

PLAYLIST

WITH THE SUPREMES:

"Where Did Our Love Go,"
1964, *Where Did Our
Love Go*

"Stop! In the Name of Love,"
1965, *More Hits by the
Supremes*

"Back in My Arms Again,"
1965, *More Hits by the
Supremes*

"You Keep Me Hangin' On,"
1966, *The Supremes Sing
Motown*

"Reflections," 1967,
Reflections

"Someday We'll Be
Together," 1969, *Cream of
the Crop*

SOLO:

"Ain't No Mountain High
Enough," 1970, *Diana Ross*

"Touch Me in the Morning,"
1973, *Touch Me in the
Morning*

"Love Hangover," 1976,
Diana Ross

"I'm Coming Out," 1980,
Diana

Out"—she has had eighteen number-one hits, a number topped only by Mariah Carey in the mid-aughts. She was a 2007 recipient of the Kennedy Center Honors and in 2016 was awarded the Presidential Medal of Freedom. The fact that Diana Ross has never won a Grammy (except for the consolation prize of the Lifetime Achievement Award), despite being nominated no less than twelve times, is utterly ridiculous.

Ross made her final break with Motown, and with Gordy's role as mentor and creative svengali, at the beginning of the eighties. She was, unbelievably, struggling financially, and at the age of thirty-seven, with two number-one hits, wanted to leverage her success. Motown wouldn't meet her financial demands—Gordy didn't believe that she would leave the fold—and so she was on the market at the very moment she teamed up with Lionel Richie on the sweetly saccharine ballad "Endless Love." The record went to number one and stayed there for months, becoming one of the major hits of the decade

and the biggest (and final) success of Ross's career. Ross then signed a seven-album deal with RCA to the tune of $20 million, achieving yet another milestone that would be ignored by the mainstream, who instead focused its attention on Diana's request to be referred to as "Miss Ross," her emotional relationship with the other Supremes, or her quest for perfectionism, which resulted in a steady turnover of staff. If she'd been a white man, all of the above behavior would have been lauded as charming idiosyncrasies.

Ross's true legacy is larger and more eternal than gossip or tabloid fodder: her string of hits, her unmistakable voice, and her presence as a strong, multitalented woman of color in mainstream media. Ultimately, it's the magic of her voice crackling out of a car radio as you drive down the road on a beautiful summer day, the memories evoked by the hits she sang, and the universal emotions she captured across multiple eras for which she will rightly be remembered. The rest is noise—*sound and fury, signifying nothing*; Ross's performances remain everything. ∎

DUSTY SPRINGFIELD

STEPHANIE PHILLIPS

ILLUSTRATION BY ANNE MUNTGES

Standing under the spotlight center stage. Her dramatic false eyelashes point toward the floor. Head down, she collects her thoughts just as the band starts to play. Her head rises, the band pauses for just a second as she sings the opening line: "When I said I needed you." Standing on stage at her own TV show (simply titled *Dusty*) in her trademark towering blond wig, thick black eyeliner, and glamorous evening gown, belting out her hit song "You Don't Have to Say You Love Me," Mary O'Brien was no longer a mousy middle-class girl from the home counties. Mary reinvented herself as Dusty Springfield: queen of blue-eyed soul.

The term *blue-eyed soul*, a label for white artists who either can or try to evoke the heart and soul of black music, can quickly veer from a term of endearment to a charge of cultural appropriation, depending on the eye of the beholder. While Springfield was a white, middle-class woman who profited from black American sounds, her connection to R&B was strong. Dusty supported and promoted Motown acts particularly. She was friends with Martha Reeves, covered many of Motown's greatest hits, and invited the label's artists over to play their first televised UK gig, giving them crucial exposure at a time they had not yet crossed over in the UK. Rather than outright copy the music she loved, Dusty played to her strengths, creating a tender version of R&B that added to rather than stole from the genre.

Springfield's upbringing was at first glance typically British and middle class. She was born Mary Isobel Catherine Bernadette O'Brien in West Hampstead in 1939 and raised just outside London in a comfortable suburb. Beneath the surface was a dysfunction that stemmed from her parents' frustrations with each other. Arguments would break out, often leading to food fights, a behavior that Dusty would repeat throughout her life.

As a child she was thought of as a tomboy and earned the nickname Dusty because she played football in the street with the local kids. The one strain of normality that kept Dusty and her family together was their love of music. Her father listened to old jazz records and classical music, and Dusty's brother performed in the band the Springfields with her. Dusty got her first taste of music making at the age of twelve when she recorded Irving Berlin's song "When the Midnight Choo Choo Leaves for Alabam" at a local record shop.

After she left school, Dusty joined the all-girl group the Lana Sisters, where she learned how to harmonize. She performed live with the group across the UK and US. She left in 1960 to form the Springfields with her brother Tom Springfield (real name Dion O'Brien) and Tim Feild. The folk-pop trio enjoyed success in the UK with hits such as "Break-away" and "Bambino," and were even given their own fifteen-minute special on the BBC.

In 1963 the group was at the height of its success, but Dusty felt there was something missing in her career. She had grown tired of the folk revivalist act and wanted to focus on something new and youthful. On her way to record a new album with the Spring-fields in Nashville, Dusty stopped off in New York to take in the atmosphere. Walking through the city streets, she passed a record store that happened to be blaring the latest hit, "Tell Him" by the Exciters. The upbeat R&B record burst through the speakers, offering up lead singer Brenda Reid's arresting vocals and excitable relationship instructions. Instantly Dusty knew that was the kind of music she wanted to make.

It didn't take long for her dream to come true, as weeks after she left the Springfields, her debut solo single "I Only Want to Be with You" was released in November 1963. Filled to the brim with horns and strings, the upbeat number was a tribute to Phil Spector's production style and set Springfield up for a career as both an R&B interpreter and one of Britain's finest songstresses. Her first album, *A Girl Called Dusty* (1964), was packed full of her favorite pop hits, including Motown covers. The album is also notable for starting her working relationship with Carole King, Burt Bacharach, and Hal David.

Springfield's contemporaries were fellow British pop stars such as Cilla Black and Sandie Shaw until she recorded the Bacharach/David classic "I Just Don't Know What to Do with Myself," a hit that quickly defined what we expected from Dusty. It was a dramatic number that allowed her to use her husky vocals to drag out the bottomless despair evoked in the lyrics. Onstage she would accentuate the drama of the song by casting her hands into the air and dramatically covering her face. It was a move to be replicated by drag queens everywhere when they took on imitating the diva.

Motown was still in Dusty's heart, and she decided that the British public needed to find out about her fascination. In 1965, on a special edition of *Ready, Steady, Go!*, a British music show, Springfield introduced a selection of R&B favorites, including the Supremes, the Miracles, Stevie Wonder, Martha and the Vandellas, and the Temptations. Britain in the sixties was still a reserved place, so it was fitting that a well-spoken girl from a middle-class family was the vessel through which British audiences could learn about African American music. Her prominent position in pop culture allowed her to bring "the Sound of Young America" to a wider audience and perhaps also lay the ground for that particularly British genre, Northern Soul.

After a lull in her career and a change in popular tastes, Springfield had fallen out of favor with the general public. Deciding to take fate into her own hands, she fought back against the changing music scene and signed to Atlantic Records to make a R&B record, hoping the home of Aretha Franklin would change her direction. To record her next album Dusty ventured to Memphis, a city that had long been a hotbed of R&B and blues artists such as Memphis Minnie, B.B. King, and Elvis Presley. Working with producers Jerry Wexler, Tom Dowd, and Arif Mardin, who worked with her hero Franklin, Dusty was initially too intimidated to record. The producers brought

PLAYLIST

"I Just Don't Know What to Do with Myself," 1964, *Dusty*

"Wishin' and Hopin'," 1964, *A Girl Called Dusty*

"I Only Want to Be with You," 1964, *Stay Awhile/I Only Want to Be with You*

"You Don't Have to Say You Love Me," 1966, *You Don't Have to Say You Love Me*

"Son of a Preacher Man," 1968, *Dusty in Memphis*

the high-energy, brass-filled Motown sound Dusty had yearned for while she herself resisted temptation to copy her heroes, preferring to remain understated and effortlessly seductive. The resulting album was *Dusty in Memphis* (1969), featuring songs written by the Brill Building's finest and considered to be one of the greatest albums of all time by *Rolling Stone*, among others. Sadly, critical success did not turn into commercial success for Dusty at the time, though the album, particularly the song "Son of a Preacher Man," has become a classic, included in such cultural landmarks as Quentin Tarantino's *Pulp Fiction*.

Despite her success, Springfield was still the same troubled girl she always was. Her tendency to hurl plates around was at first viewed as a fun quirk but soon developed into a concern. Dusty was insecure about her looks and what her fans thought of her. She imagined they would desert her if they found out she was a lesbian. In the entertainment business in the sixties, the fear of being outed and losing your career could be all-consuming. Though she spoke very briefly about the rumors about her sexuality once or twice and was known to have girlfriends, Dusty never really came to terms with her sexuality.

On top of this, her decline in popularity throughout the seventies and eighties, and addictions to drugs and alcohol, led to a deterioration in her mental health and further dampened her career. Springfield moved to the US in 1970, removing herself from the public eye altogether. In the seventies she turned down offers to record "Killing Me Softly," "Don't Go Breaking My Heart," and "Nobody Does It Better," the theme for *The Spy Who Loved Me* (1977), all of which were huge hits for the singers that later recorded them. Dusty had an unexpected career revival in the late eighties after she was invited to be a guest vocalist on the Pet Shop Boys' single "What Have I Done to Deserve This?" (1987). The electro pop hit reached number two on the UK charts, reigniting Dusty's career and once again proving she could become a master of any genre.

In 1994, Springfield was diagnosed with breast cancer. Though treatment seemed to be successful, the cancer came back in 1996 and she died in 1999. Two weeks later, Elton John inducted her into the Rock and Roll Hall of Fame. Dusty could perform a plethora of styles and make them hers. She was a flawed diva but could lay bare a river of emotion just for the listener to drink in. Few have come close to her status as the queen of blue-eyed soul. Dusty's legacy lives today and can be seen in pop diva Adele, with her careful interpretations of soul, meticulously teased blond bob, and striking false eyelashes. Whether she will have any other contenders to her crown depends on whether other white soul singers can compete with her ability to lift up the voices and work of black artists while staying true to who they really are. She's a hard act to follow. ∎

MARIANNE FAITHFULL

KANDIA CRAZY HORSE

ILLUSTRATION BY ANNE MUNTGES

Marianne Faithfull is a British folk-pop singer-songwriter and actress whose career first flowered in 1964. During the course of her early fame and four-year romance with Mick Jagger, Faithfull became a major sixties fashion icon and rock royalty, alongside her best friend and fellow Rolling Stones paramour Anita Pallenberg. The Stones' infamous 1967 drug bust bolstered the band's reputation as cultural outlaws but all but destroyed Faithfull's career and part of herself—"When you lose your reputation at 19, you lose everything," she said. By 1969, she had embarked on a heroin addiction that would overshadow the next decade of her existence until her stunning creative comeback with the landmark feminist, punk-inspired *Broken English* (1979), her seventh studio album.

Faithfull was born in London in 1946. By rights her title is Baroness von Sacher-Masoch; she's the descendant of the Austrian-Hungarian Leopold von Sacher-Masoch, from whom we get the term *masochism*. As Faithfull has opined, "I don't think I had any choice but to be decadent." Yet the era's sex kitten image was imposed on her from without; the former convent schoolgirl has said that she scarcely fulfilled the "sex" part of her generation's "sex, drugs, and rock and roll" mantra, having to rely on drugs and alcohol to deal with intimacy. Still, as an actress

who appeared in *I'll Never Forget What's'isname* (1967), *Dope* (1968), and *The Girl on a Motorcycle* (1968), she was credited with being the first person to say "fuck" in a mainstream movie. She wed pop artist John Dunbar and became a mother early, after being discovered by Rolling Stones manager Andrew Loog Oldham and subsequently recording his clients' first song, "As Tears Go By." She made headlines for being arrested wearing only a bearskin rug at the 1967 raid at Keith Richards's estate. She was trying to become a New Woman somewhere in the eye of the heady turbulence of free love, women's liberation, and the aesthetic experimentation of the 1960s, questing after mysteries at Stonehenge and in North Africa, becoming a face of the age fit to rival Brigitte Bardot, Jane Fonda, and Edie Sedgwick. At the height of the sixties, Swinging London came close to changing the very face of the world, and the beautiful blond Faithfull was as an exemplar of this cultural hegemony, a gilded young spirit of the last days of empire.

All too soon, Faithfull would be making the transition from the public's favored English Rose to homeless junkie to feminist powerhouse. Yet before and after releasing the first version of "Sister Morphine" (written with Jagger and Richards and later recorded by the Stones) as a single in 1969, she released a great folk-rock record and a fine

country-rock album, *North Country Maid* and *Rich Kid Blues*, respectively, both produced by Mike Leander. On *Maid* (1966), her fourth studio album, Marianne undertakes a blend of traditional folk standards, including "Scarborough Fair," alongside contributions from the Young Turk folk-rockers of her London scene—Bert Jansch's "Green Are Your Eyes" and Donovan's "Sunny Goodge Street." The sitar on the lovely "Wild Mountain Thyme" captures the high purity of her voice in its sunset.

On the other hand, *Rich Kid Blues* was cut in 1971 once Faithfull had lost custody of her son, Nicholas, to ex-husband Dunbar, attempted suicide, and fallen deeply into heroin's grip as a homeless addict on the streets of Soho. This is where Leander found her and attempted to help revive her career, although the album would not see the light of day until 1985. Very high throughout the recording process, Faithfull has a voice that is both frail and sensual, beginning to show the weathering that's been the hallmark of her latter-day career. And yet *Rich Kid* contains some fine performances, such as the country standard "Long Black Veil," a searing, pedal steel-drenched cover of George Harrison's "Beware of Darkness," and the heartbreaking inclusion of "Corinna, Corinna" about the daughter Faithfull and Jagger lost to miscarriage.

The ensuing decade was marked by trauma. Faithfull surfaced from underground here and there, once to duet with David Bowie on television in a nun's habit singing Sonny and Cher's "I Got You Babe." Backed by Joe Cocker's former Grease Band, she recorded *Dreamin' My Dreams*, an interesting 1975 country and western album featuring songs by Waylon Jennings ("This Time"); his wife, Jessi Colter ("I'm Not Lisa"); the ever reliable Jackie DeShannon

("Vanilla O'Lay"); and the title track, which topped the charts in Ireland.

Then Faithfull made an unforeseeable transition, with a now wraithlike voice. In the second half of the seventies, the British Invaders and California "easy rock" royalty were mostly appalled and disgusted by punk. But punk provided partial salvation for Marianne as she settled into a Chelsea squat with Vibrators bassist Ben Brierly and counted Sex Pistol Johnny Rotten as a guest at their wedding. Together, the couple would fashion *Broken English*, the album that would cement Faithfull's artistic reputation forever and provide a compelling example of a female supernova repurposing rock's anarchic spirit. Amid the jagged guitars and almost sinister synths, even Shel Silverstein's tale of suburban anomie "The Ballad of Lucy Jordan" became an empowering anthem.

Marianne was still experiencing the needle and the damage done; witness her disastrous-but-riveting *Saturday Night Live* appearance to promote the album. But Faithfull's singing throughout *Broken English*, whether she was snarling lines like, "Every time I see your dick / I see her cunt in my bed" (from the unforgettable "Why'd Ya Do It?," initially penned by the English poet and painter Heathcote Williams for Tina Turner) or sounding more ancient than Albion in voicing the Great Mother on "Witches' Song," proved there was merit in her having transcended her convent girl incarnation. This success marked a permanent turn in her universe, enabling her to creatively summon the interests in Lotte Lenya, Cole Porter, classical music, and the Brecht-Weill canon

PLAYLIST

"As Tears Go By," 1964, *Strange Weather*

"Why D'ya Do It," 1979, *Broken English*

"Broken English," 1979, *Broken English*

"Sister Morphine," 1990, *Blazing Away*

"Sliding through Life on Charm," 2003, *Kissin' Time*

that she had received from her parents. Between such high points of interpretation as *Strange Weather* (1987) and *Easy Come Easy Go* (2008), she earned respect for her unique aesthetic from younger would-be mavericks such as Nick Cave, Pulp's Jarvis Cocker, Beck, Antony Hegarty (Anohni), PJ Harvey, and Smashing Pumpkins' Billy Corgan; she even dueted with Metallica on "The Memory Remains." While carving this niche over eleven albums, including standouts *20th Century Blues* (1997) and *Kissin' Time* (2002), Faithfull also engaged with her storied past in the memoirs *Faithfull: An Autobiography; Memories, Dreams, and Reflections*; and *Marianne Faithfull: A Life on Record*.

With the UK's Second Summer of Love in the 1990s, Marianne Faithfull again become the blond glittery dream girl of the movement's boy bands.

Aspiring It Girls Patsy Kensit and Kate Moss vampirized her style and life beats. In episodes from 1996 through 2001, Faithfull played God to Pallenberg's Devil on the comedy *Absolutely Fabulous*. For her part, Faithfull was bored by the constant dredging up of four years of her life in the Rolling Stones' bubble and came swinging out of the sixties declaring that feminism was the best thing to arise from the decade. No less a legendary wild woman than the Witch of Positano, Vali Myers, said of her: "Marianne Faithful turned up one day with her boyfriend to see some of my work. I thought, who is this scrawny little guy, so I said to him, 'What is it you do Micky?' How would I know who the bloody hell Mick Jagger was?—I wasn't interested in Mick Jagger, I was always into Marianne. She was a real fighter." Rebellion has, indeed, kept Marianne Faithfull alive. ■

GRACE SLICK

KATHERINE TURMAN

SELF-PORTRAIT BY GRACE SLICK

When the Summer of Love blossomed in 1967, Grace Slick was twenty-eight and the reigning psych-rock queen of San Francisco. The Jefferson Airplane frontwoman wrote her psychedelic paean, the indelible counter-culture anthem "White Rabbit." Its hookah-smoking caterpillar and anthropomorphized chess players were such iconic images that Slick utilized them forty years later as key figures in her second notable creative career: painting.

Grace Slick is a broad in the best sense of the term. Bawdy, independent, bold, beautiful, smart, and unrepentant, she is a mother and muse whose liberal activism continues into her late seventies, twenty years past her retirement from music.

However, she wasn't to hippiedom born. Grace Wing was birthed in Highland Park, Illinois, on October 30, 1939. Her dad worked in investment banking; her mother was a *Mayflower* descendent. Grace attended Castilleja School, a private all-girls school in Palo Alto, California, and then Finch College, a now-defunct private women's college on New York City's Upper East Side. She returned to the Bay Area, where in 1961 she married aspiring filmmaker-musician Gerald "Jerry" Slick, taking his suitably rock-star surname. Grace began to write music, and inspired by the Beatles—and also local act Jefferson Airplane—Grace co-founded her first band, the

Great Society. There were three Slicks in the band: Grace, her drummer husband, and her brother-in-law, guitarist Darby. Grace's powerful, versatile contralto—on some songs, sounding like a lovely droning sitar—paired with her confident stage presence overshadowed the group's glorified garage rock.

When Signe Toly Anderson left Jefferson Airplane, bassist Jack Casady asked Slick to join and sing alongside Marty Balin, her future frenemy. Thrilled,

she accepted, marking the end of the Great Society and the beginning of the end of her marriage. On October 16, 1966, Grace debuted with the Airplane. Nine months later, she found herself a star as the lead singer for the Airplane's two Top Ten hits, "White Rabbit" and the equally iconic "Somebody to Love," penned by Darby Slick. It was 1967, and her recorded debut with the band, *Surrealistic Pillow*, shone with seventeen songs and nearly an hour of music. "White Rabbit" kicks off with a portentous marching beat,

PLAYLIST

WITH JEFFERSON AIRPLANE:

"Somebody to Love," 1967, *Surrealistic Pillow*

"White Rabbit," 1967, *Surrealistic Pillow*

"Crown of Creation," 1968, *Crown of Creation*

WITH PAUL KANTNER AND JEFFERSON STARSHIP:

"A Child Is Coming," 1970, *Blows against the Empire*

WITH PAUL KANTNER AND DAVID FREIBERG:

"Ballad of the Chrome Nun," 1973, *Baron von Tollbooth and the Chrome Nun*

WITH STARSHIP:

"We Built This City," 1985, *Knee Deep in the Hoopla*

her mysterious, mellifluous vocals telling a story of drug experimentation. The song was intended as a "what did you expect?" to parents who raised their kids on "Alice in Wonderland" and trippy fairy tales, then worried about their drug use. As Slick told the *Wall Street Journal* in 2016: "Looking back, I think 'White Rabbit' is a very good song . . . My only complaint is that the lyrics could have been stronger. If I had done it right, more people would have been annoyed."

Provocation rather than annoyance is what Grace did—and does—best, though she succeeded at both. In 1968, Slick and the band performed "Crown of Creation" on TV's *The Smothers Brothers Comedy Hour*. She was in blackface and ended the song by raising her black-gloved left hand in a Black Panther fist salute. In today's climate, the cultural inappropriateness would have caused a glaring backlash. In the sixties, however, most took it as she intended: a rock star using her platform to show solidarity with the Black Panther movement. She was also the first person to say "motherfucker" on live TV during a performance of "We Can Be Together" on *The Dick Cavett Show*, as part of a lyric that referenced the New York anarchist affinity group Up Against the Wall Motherfucker. Then, in 1969, she was refused entrance to the White House when she brought political activist Abbie Hoffman as her date and it was discovered that the pair planned to spike President Richard Nixon's tea with LSD.

Still, mainstream love graced the Airplane. In 1968, the band was on the cover of *Life* magazine with the title: "Music That's Hooked the Vibrating World: The New Rock." They played all the big festivals: Monterey Jazz, Monterey Pop, Woodstock, and Altamont. Grace's heavy fringe of bangs and "don't fuck with me" stare were her calling cards. Her subversive, smart lyrics, and bold, sometimes drink-and-drug-influenced actions became her hallmark.

"Feed your head," as the Dormouse advises in "White Rabbit," is generally interpreted as a call to drug dabbling, and Slick's phrase became one of the sixties' rallying cries, which still resonate to this day. Grace practiced what she preached, and powders, booze, and psychedelics fueled her life on and offstage. She was in car accidents, kicked off a TV show, and caused an audience to riot when she was too wasted to perform. In her 1998 book, *Somebody to Love? A Rock-and-Roll Memoir*, she looks wryly back, noting: "without alcohol I'd be richer by two million dollars that went to pay lawyer's fees."

As her success rose, so did her excess in the drug and sex realms. The birth control pill wasn't widely available to unmarried women until 1972, but Slick was liberated and liberal. She began living with Airplane guitarist Paul Kantner in 1969, and he fathered her only child. China Wing Kantner was born in 1971, and a year later, Jefferson Airplane officially ended its run.

Kantner, Slick, and other bandmates carried on with the name-updated Jefferson Starship, as Grace concurrently began a solo career. Her 1974 solo record debuted another creative talent: Grace drew all the artwork for the album. Motherhood didn't mellow Grace: the album was provocatively titled *Manhole*, but it failed to deliver a big punch.

By 1976, she'd wed Skip Johnson, a Jefferson Starship lighting designer, a union that lasted until 1994. Her partying continued, between stints of sobriety, which was addressed in her 1980 album *Dreams*, where, in "Do It the Hard Way," she sings: "They all knew she was bound to go down 'way before she fell . . . But there's just no way to tell her."

During the 1980s, while Slick was the only former Jefferson Airplane member in the band now named Starship, the band scored huge hits with "We Built This City," "Sara," and "Nothing's Gonna Stop Us Now."

As a first-generation female rock star, Grace Slick had few role models for the experience of "growing old" in public. In a 1998 VH1 interview, she said: "All rock-and-rollers over the age of fifty look stupid and should retire." So she did. And stuck to it. Slick let her hair go its natural white, her personality as vivid and unapologetic as ever.

Retired but never retiring, since 2000 she's had dozens of gallery shows and sold her paintings. Her best-selling works reference her music: versions of the white rabbit and Alice, as well as portraits of musical peers, including Jim Morrison and Pete Townshend. In 2016, she gave the middle finger (literally, in a photo) to restaurant giant Chick-fil-A, whose CEO had made anti-LGBTQ statements. Slick allowed them to use "Nothing's Gonna Stop Us Now" in a commercial and then donated the profits to Lambda Legal to support the LGBTQ community. In an op-ed piece for *Forbes*, she explained that she came from the era "when musicians took a stand, when the message of songs was 'feed your head,' not 'feed your wallet.'" For fifty years, Slick's message has remained as solid and strong as the songs she's written and sung: nothing's going to stop her now. Or ever. ∎

LAURA NYRO

KANDIA CRAZY HORSE

ILLUSTRATION BY WINNIE T. FRICK

"At the edge where I live . . . home sweet home, America," sang Laura Nyro in the Navajo documentary theme song "Broken Rainbow." The New York City–born and –bred singer-songwriter could easily have been singing of herself. Despite the wide recognition of her incandescent musical talent in the 1960s and '70s, fame somehow eluded her in her own time. Nyro's vignettes of her beloved city became hits for pop stars and had as indelible an emotional pull as the songs of her contemporary and follower Carole King, but they seem to have come from a soul who was on the outside looking in.

This failure to thrive remains a mystery of the ages since Nyro had an auspicious beginning. After releasing her debut album *More than a New Discovery* on Folkways in 1967 and gaining the loving and protective patronage of then rising music mogul David Geffen, she made the leap to the majors on Columbia Records. Nyro mightily impressed boss Clive Davis to the point that her labelmate Janis Joplin was jealous. She had "Eli's Comin'" with its spectral, minor-key intro covered by Three Dog Night, played Carnegie Hall, and *Rolling Stone* called her second album, *Eli and the Thirteenth Confession* (1968), "the work of a brilliant, young talent." She also seems to have effortlessly been given the laurels of black cool for which many young white postwar artists yearned.

Patti LaBelle praised the blackness of the "Bronx Brontë" with whom her all-girl band Labelle recorded the 1971 masterpiece *Gonna Take a Miracle*. And still, Nyro was apparently always at the edges of normalcy or not at one with the times. Her former High School of Music and Art schoolmate and fellow 1960s New York musical prodigy Janis Ian reckoned that she shared a fashion sense with Morticia Addams in her long black dresses with trailing dark locks and ruby red lipstick. Yet perhaps in Laura Nyro's case, black is what she wore because black was how she *felt*.

Or, maybe, her blackness was immanent in her true name. Nyro was born Laura Nigro in the Bronx in 1947, the daughter of Gilda Mirsky, a Russian-Polish Jewish bookkeeper, and Louis Nigro, an Italian piano tuner and jazz trumpeter. As a child, young Laura absorbed her father's universe of sound, sang along at community gatherings in the Catskills, and kept journals delineating future imagined albums. She grew up to be a true original, selling her early song "And When I Die" to folk-boom trio Peter, Paul, and Mary for $5,000, and making her first extended live stand at San Francisco's Hungry I at eighteen. Nyro's precocious talent then blossomed on the emphatically titled *More than a New Discovery*, displaying her patented blend of Tin Pan Alley and Brill Building pop, Ravel, Debussy, rock, Stephen

Foster–isms adorned with sassafras and moonshine, gospel, Broadway, twang, jazz, and folk. The black street music of her borough of New York City never left the mix, either. Her voice mimicked the horns of her father and other jazz players, swooping through her sensual, confessional themes and sometimes pushing her sound through the stratosphere. "When I was about 14 or 15, I guess, John Coltrane and Miles Davis was happening," said Nyro. "The music was just so great. Doo-wop and soul music. And even folk music was really happening. There was such a great cross-section of music that you could tune into."

Despite such wide-ranging ears, the type of meteoric superstardom visited upon Joplin was not her lot; Nyro was too much of a maverick in the preamble to Women's Lib and unwilling to capitulate to the starmaker machinery her peers engaged with. She would go on to eschew the pop mainstream in the last days of her career by playing with female musicians and creating work predominantly aligned with the peace, women's, and ecological movements. Still, Nyro must have taken heart in the clearly acknowledged soul debt paid her by the elite of black pop. Just watch Roberta Flack in her orange and hot pink caftan in 1971 emoting her way through Nyro's hymn "Save the Country" under a cloud of kinks on LA's KCET. The 5th Dimension's stature as a hit machine seemed to rely on Nyro's prodigious output. Black vocal clique the Blossoms performed "Stoney End." When Bones Howe set out to produce Diana Ross as a "black Barbra Streisand" for her solo debut on Motown, Ross covered Nyro's "Stoney End" and "Time and Love"—a year before Streisand attempted to make her career-turning "rock" albums including the same tunes. *Hair* starlet and Janelle Monáe foremother Melba Moore took on "Captain Saint Lucifer" for her solo turn *I Got Love*, while jazz singer Carmen McRae did "Goodbye Joe," and, fascinatingly, Ronnie Dyson essayed "Emmie"—viewed by some as an early lesbian-themed touchstone in mainstream pop. And the Alvin Ailey American Dance Theater centered the second movement of its iconic Judith Jamison spotlight dance Cry with "Been on a Train" from *Christmas and the Beads of Sweat*, an album that was Nyro's penultimate masterpiece, which bid farewell to flower power and all that.

The supposed eccentricities that caused Nyro to be revered as a hippie gypsy goddess while simultaneously being deemed too other for the then current rock mainstream, and that led her to audition *Eli and the Thirteenth Confession* for Clive Davis in the gloom of her Manhattan flat lit only by the television, clearly did not diminish the embrace of her genius. She supposedly infamously flopped at the 1967 Monterey Pop Festival, to which she brought her cultural mulatto urban persona and black female background singers. But thirty years later, *Monterey Pop* documentarian D. A. Pennebaker and festival organizer Lou Adler debunked Nyro's flop, having unearthed footage of audience members declaring her set "Beautiful!" Sadly, she passed from ovarian cancer at forty-nine before she could visit the premises where they were working to restore the film.

Among the world of musicians, Nyro made a lasting impact on Lady of the Canyon folk-rock queen bee Joni Mitchell (hear Nyro's 1975 "Sexy

PLAYLIST

"Eli's Comin'," 1968, *Eli and the Thirteenth Confession*

"Woman's Blues," 1968, *Eli and the Thirteenth Confession*

"Stoned Soul Picnic," 1968, *Eli and the Thirteenth Confession*

"It's Gonna Take a Miracle" 1971, *Gonna Take a Miracle* (with Labelle)

"Sexy Mama," 1976, *Smile*

was moved to become a player in the emerging singer-songwriter movement of LA by the vision of Nyro transcendent on her piano stool. Nyro possessed enough goddess power to convince Todd Rundgren that he had to write songs in her image. Like the disenfranchised black artists who identified with her, Nyro must have somehow reveled in what glory could be found in the shadows on the edge.

"Can you surrey?"—when Laura Nyro queried this in her much-revered "Stoned Soul Picnic," she was riding a burst of country-rock creation in the late 1960s and early '70s. Associated in most minds with the white ethnic world of a now lost midcentury New York City, Nyro was also an apt student of Stephen Foster's Dixie songbook, and a swath of her work demonstrates mastery of Americana beyond her hermetic narratives of a woman's sensibility. Yet her last great work after her classic trio of albums, including *New York Tendaberry* (1969), was a glorious revisiting of the songs she used to hear and sing in the Bronx beneath the elevated subway: *Gonna Take a Miracle*. And she highlighted her heart's mesh with Africana by recording the 1971 opus with not only Labelle—recently transfigured from their bouffants-and-cocktail frocks days as Patti LaBelle and the Bluebelles—but Philadelphia Sound producers Kenny Gamble and Leon Huff

Mama" side-by-side with *Court and Spark*–era Joni), Bob Dylan, Sir Elton John, Barry Manilow, Rickie Lee Jones, Phoebe Snow, Cyndi Lauper, Suzanne Vega, and British shoegazers Lush, whose debut, *Spooky*, featured the homage "Laura." Carole King

at the dawning of their decade-long run of dominance in the last golden era of black music. This collection of what Nyro deemed "teenage heartbeat songs" was capped by a take on the Royalettes' "It's Gonna Take a Miracle," a triumphant manifesto of a woman's fierce fidelity about a decade before Deniece Williams revised it as a Quiet Storm smash. Forged at a time when the Black Power movement was characterized by virulent homophobia and a mistrust of white-identified Women's Lib, and when doo-wop as a genre was passé, Labelle recording with the bisexual feminist Nyro made an indelible statement of stoned soul solidarity. For the duration of ten tracks at least, Laura Nyro was indeed a black girl in a white girl's body, living boldly at the edge of America's Great Divide. ■

JANIS JOPLIN

ALI GITLOW

ILLUSTRATION BY LINDSEY BAILEY

Janis Joplin's illustrious life as a misfit began, as so many people's do, when she was a teenager. Living with her family in small town Port Arthur, Texas, she quickly realized she wasn't like the other girls in high school. She had cystic acne, scraggly hair, and a raspy voice, plus was a bit pudgy. Also, she thought blacks and whites should be integrated—a radical political belief to hold in the late 1950s American South. "I was always outrageous. I got treated very badly in Texas," she once said. When a friend let her borrow some old blues records, young Janis was irreparably smitten. She would practice crooning just like Bessie Smith, Lead Belly, and Big Mama Thornton, finding in their expressions of otherness a match for her own. The voice she developed as a result was rooted in the blues, but also wholly distinctive: a raw, powerful, unmistakable wail. However, Joplin didn't just try to be a white girl singing like black folks. Her identification with these musical influences was so strong that, shortly before her tragic death at age twenty-seven, she helped pay for a headstone for Smith's grave that reads "The Greatest Blues Singer in the World Will Never Stop Singing." In some ways, she was writing her own epitaph.

Joplin studied at the University of Texas in Austin, where she performed with folk trio the Waller Creek Boys. In 1963, she quit school to move to San Francisco, joining the burgeoning countercultural hippie revolution. Amongst the freaks of Haight-Ashbury, she found her tribe. She grew into her own skin, developing a personal style that included billowy dresses and blouses with flared arms, beaded necklaces, open sandals, fur hats, and rose-tinted glasses. Her first recordings were created the following year with Jorma Kaukonen, who would go on to become Jefferson Airplane's guitarist. Dubbed *The Typewriter Tape*, the demo featured six tracks including "Trouble in Mind" and "Kansas City Blues"; it was only released as a bootleg years later. Most of these tunes were covers; Joplin preferred to take others' songs of love, heartache, and loss and make them all her own, using an impassioned tone and impeccable sense of timing. She could tackle it all, too, from blues to country, gospel to soul, and unrelenting rock and roll.

Temptation swirled all around. Joplin's casual dalliances with drugs got more serious, and after developing addictions to methamphetamine and alcohol, she returned home to Port Arthur in an effort to get on the straight and narrow path. She went back to college, started dressing more formally, and even got engaged for a brief period. However, she was lured back to San Francisco in 1966 when the psych rock band Big Brother and the Holding Company needed a singer. Things really took off when the

group played the Monterey Pop Festival in the summer of 1967. Performing songs off their self-titled debut album, such as "Ball and Chain" and "Down on Me," Joplin manifested raging, unbridled emotion in human female form. The actor Juliette Lewis aptly summarized this approach in the 2015 documentary *Janis: Little Girl Blue*: "You might as well be slashing yourself onstage and opening your skin."

As quick as a flash Joplin and Big Brother became stars, touring the US, appearing on *The Dick Cavett Show*, and working on their first major-label studio album. Sporting a cover drawn by the underground comic book artist R. Crumb, *Cheap Thrills*, released by Columbia in 1968, included Joplin mainstays "Piece of My Heart," "Summertime," and "I Need a Man to Love," on which she was able to fully showcase the complexities of her range. She was a magnet for adolescents interested in expanding their consciousness and a perfect antidote to stuffy societal and cultural norms. Compared to the popular doe-eyed female singers and girl groups of the day, she was a wild child. Though she enjoyed this new-found attention, her lifelong battle with feeling like an outcast caused her to search for approval in relationships and sex with both men and women, as well as drinking and drugs. "I think there were two Janises," Cavett revealed on ABC's *20/20 Downtown* program

about her life. "There was the high school girl who desperately wanted acceptance, and the character she created—which was the tough-talking, tough-drugging, drinking, rock-and-roll star."

The spotlight isn't usually big enough to accommodate multiple egos at once. And so, after mounting tensions, Joplin decided to leave Big Brother in late 1968. She formed a new backup group, the Kozmic Blues Band, with whom she recorded the LP *I Got Dem Ol' Kozmic Blues Again Mama!* and toured Europe in 1969. In August of that year, Joplin and the band played at Woodstock, gracing the stage at two a.m. It was quite a sight: she was visibly hopped up on heroin, rambling to the audience before launching into "Kozmic Blues," "Try (Just a Little Bit Harder)," and "Work Me, Lord" off the new record, her voice occasionally cracking.

At the end of 1969 Kozmic Blues Band split up. Joplin went on vacation to Brazil, where she met fellow American tourist David Niehaus. Their intense courtship helped her get clean. When she returned home, Joplin formed Full Tilt Boogie Band and they began recording the album *Pearl*. She began drinking and drugging again, and as a result, her relationship with Niehaus came to a somber end—though she went on to think of him as her great lost love. She quickly moved on to singer-songwriter Kris Kristofferson (plus covered his tragic ballad "Me and Bobby McGee") and, soon after, shacked up with a twenty-one-year-old college student and coke dealer named Seth Morgan, to whom she became engaged. Though Joplin had a home of her own in Larkspur, she moved into the Landmark Motor Hotel in Hollywood so she could be closer to the studio. When ex–Big Brother drummer Dave Getz visited her there, the two ominously discussed mutual friends' drug-related deaths. In *Janis: Little Girl Blue*, he describes how she told him, "My people are pioneer stock. They came across the country . . . they're tough. I've got those genes and nothing's gonna happen to me."

On October 4, 1970, Janis Joplin died of a heroin overdose—just sixteen days after Jimi Hendrix. Ironically, she was scheduled to record vocals for "Buried Alive in the Blues" that same day. *Pearl* was released the following year, featuring songs like "Cry Baby," "Get It While You Can," and "Mercedes Benz" (the last tune she ever recorded). Since then, she has been lionized as the first true female rock icon, a trailblazer for women musicians, and a perpetual testament to the validity of alternative lifestyles. She

is one of the top-selling American musicians of all time and has earned a Grammy Lifetime Achievement Award, a star on the Hollywood Walk of Fame, and a spot in the Rock and Roll Hall of Fame. At the latter induction ceremony in 1995, her attorney and friend Robert Gordon said: "Janis never went through the motions. She gave every bit of herself in every way in every aspect of her life."

It's such a shame Joplin isn't around to see the world she helped create. Scores of budding weirdos who've come of age in her wake have benefited from a society where female musicians have a chance to succeed not by following any preconceived molds or norms, but on their own terms. Now, maybe she wouldn't feel so alone. ■

CAROL KAYE

KATHERINE TURMAN

ILLUSTRATION BY WINNIE T. FRICK

The Beach Boys' "California Girls," Nancy Sinatra's "These Boots Are Made for Walkin'," and Barbra Streisand's "The Way We Were" are iconic songs with one thing in common: Carol Kaye. The versatile musician is unarguably the premiere female session bassist in history, playing on an estimated ten thousand recordings during a fifty-year career. Her instantly memorable walking bass line in Sonny and Cher's "The Beat Goes On" was instrumental for both the song and her own creative spark. In the studio, she elaborated on the bass part as originally written, and the huge impact of the finished product make Kaye realize how crucial a bass line could be. Her funky, plucky, slick bass parts, played, always, with a pick, lifted up Mel Tormé's "Games People Play." Ironically, she'd intentionally overplayed in the studio, as she didn't think that particular take would be used in the final song.

Session players and singers—who perform in individual recording sessions or as backing bands on tour, rather than being a permanent member of a group—are, by dint of the job description, usually unsung. They rarely give interviews about their musical work for other artists. Sometimes they're even uncredited, which was often the case in the sixties, when the illusion of a band playing its own instruments was important. It's a calling that not all musicians are suited for: long hours, multiple sessions a day, lots of practice, little recognition. While many revered session players are allowed to create and improvise their own parts, other sessions call for a by-the-book rendering of the song as written. What a session musician needs, besides stellar musicianship and sight-reading skills, is the ability to move easily between genres and styles, while respecting and adapting to the creatively demanding personalities and peccadillos of musicians and producers. Grace under pressure, as the musical requests often come fast and furious, is key. Kaye, whose credits run the gamut from Frank Zappa's progressive, jazzy time signatures to Glen Campbell's heart-wrenching pop-country tunes, has those traits and more. She is the most acclaimed of a historic and growing assortment of women who choose to apply their formidable skills as behind-the-scenes laborers rather than spotlighted stars.

Born in 1935, Kaye began playing guitar in her early teens. A seeming prodigy, she became a professional musician as well as teacher, playing bebop guitar in LA nightclubs with some of the best jazz artists in the late fifties. At twenty-two, she did her first session, on guitar, with Sam Cooke. A few years later, when a player failed to show for a session at Capitol Records in Hollywood, she was asked to fill in on bass. In her heart and by training, Kaye was a jazz guitarist, but, as she told Carl Wiser of Songfacts.com, "When somebody didn't show up they put the bass in my lap and I thought, Okay, if I

play bass then I don't have to carry in five or six different guitars, 12-strings and all that stuff."

Kaye's most prolific period was in the sixties and seventies. She was often a go-to for the creative mind and layered sounds of Brian Wilson, including on the legendary *Pet Sounds* album. As the only female member of the Wrecking Crew, an elite group of LA-based studio musicians who coalesced around producer Phil Spector, her playing helped his Wall of Sound productions gain their breadth and bottom end. Her guitar legacy encompasses the Righteous Brothers' "You've Lost That Lovin' Feeling," "La Bamba" by Ritchie Valens, twelve-string guitar work on the Crystals' "And Then He Kissed Me," and dozens of other classics by the top names of the day. Kaye is generous in sharing her knowledge and, starting in 1969, wrote the first of many instructional books, *How to Play the Electric Bass*, delving into her secrets for paradiddle tough licks and offering breakdowns of music reading. Online, she offers complex instruction and lengthy personal responses to fan and musician questions.

If Kaye is part of an elite club, following in her fretsteps is a cadre of respected, talented women from exceedingly varied backgrounds. Instrumentalists who've made—and continue to make—huge contributions to music behind the scenes include the second-generation studio musician and guitarist-vocalist Wendy Melvoin, best known as a member of Prince's band and Wendy and Lisa. The daughter of Wrecking Crew pianist-arranger Mike Melvoin, Wendy has done studio work with Madonna, Neil Finn, and Rob Thomas, while consistently writing for TV and film, winning an Emmy in 2010 for the *Nurse Jackie* title song.

Bobbye Jean Hall Porter is a multi-instrumentalist percussionist whose skills move easily among rock, soul, blues, and jazz. Her playing can be heard on twenty-two *Billboard* Top 10 hits, and such classics as Janis Joplin's "Me and Bobby McGee," Tom Petty's "Don't Come around Here No More," and Bill Withers's "Ain't No Sunshine." She also worked on Pink Floyd's *The Wall*, and, unlike many session players, the Detroit native tours often, hitting the road with such notables as Stevie Nicks and Bob Dylan.

Bassist Gail Ann Dorsey is equally prolific on stage and in the studio. Growing up on music from Rufus and Chaka Khan to Queen, she became David Bowie's bassist in 1995, playing with him until his death. Dorsey told Andy Green of *Rolling Stone* that Bowie was "this incredible mentor. I feel so privileged to have had this opportunity to learn about music and being professional and stretching and doing things that I didn't think I could do." Pre-Bowie, she recorded and toured with Tears for Fears, and performed and tracked with such top-tier names as Lenny Kravitz, Bryan Ferry, Indigo Girls, Gwen Stefani, and Ani DiFranco. She has also released three solo albums on which she played guitar and bass and sang.

Numerous other women are working hard and coming up in the session world, including guitarist Kat Dyson, who in the studio and on the road has plied her trade with Prince, Cyndi Lauper, George Clinton and the P-Funk AllStars, Céline Dion, Ziggy Marley, and Dave Stewart of Eurythmics, as well as composing for film and TV.

PLAYLIST

CAROL KAYE:

"La Bamba," 1959, on Ritchie Valens's *Ritchie Valens*

"These Boots Are Made for Walkin'," 1966, on Nancy Sinatra's *Boots*

"The Beat Goes On," 1967, on Sonny and Cher's *In Case You're in Love*

"Games People Play," 1969, on Mel Tormé's *A Time for Us*

GAIL ANN DORSEY:

"I'm Afraid of Americans," 1997, on David Bowie's *Earthling*

Starting guitar at eight and later attending Hollywood's Musician's Institute, nimble-fingered virtuoso Jennifer Batten was Michael Jackson's onstage foil for three world tours from 1987 to 1997, and from 1999 to 2001 she toured and recorded with Jeff Beck. She has released three studio albums since 1992 and authored two books on music. Playing styles ranging from metal to worldbeat, she tours on her own and supporting other musicians, while releasing instructional DVDs and teaching musical self-empowerment courses.

If the number of female session musicians pales greatly in comparison to their male counterparts, by most accounts, they are no less revered. Kaye, featured prominently in the 2008 documentary *Wrecking Crew*, clearly earned the respect of her usually all-male session mates and producers during the burgeoning decades of Women's Lib. While a session player may have all the work and none of the seeming glamour of their onstage counterparts, they are as proud of their contributions, even when acknowledged by the industry rather than the fans. They play for the joy of music, not the lure of the spotlight. There are slowly increasing numbers of women with top-notch technical skills and musical chops whose valuable contributions help put—and keep—singers on their musical pedestals. Fortunately, most female players pay it forward when it comes to knowledge and connections.

Beyoncé put female musicians front and center when she put together a ten-piece, all-female touring band, naming them Suga Mama after a track on her *B'Day* album. Bey's empowerment goal? "I had the idea to have a lot of women on stage playing instruments so hopefully young girls can see that and it'll inspire them to play instruments." Goal achieved, as Suga Mama saxophonist Kat Rodriguez explained to *Elle* magazine: "The women that played with Bey on the [2016] Formation tour are like 10 years younger than [the original lineup], so when they were looking at her 10 years ago, they were looking at us. It's amazing to see that we are part of that cycle and that it impacted so many people." The beat, indeed, goes on. ■

CHER

LUCRETIA TYE JASMINE

ILLUSTRATION BY WINNIE T. FRICK

When the young pop singer Cher met fashion designer Bob Mackie in 1967, she admired one of his gowns, telling him that one day she would wear his dazzling designs. And so she did, on the TV shows that bore her name during the 1970s. *The Sonny and Cher Comedy Hour* (1971–1974) established the California native as a star of many talents: singer, actor, comedian, businesswoman. On the piano she sprawled, bold and bawdy and singing at the top of her lungs, wearing red and not much of it. Sex was a joke, but she was not the butt of it, as girls and women usually were (and are). Cher made life and sexual expression seem fun. Her comedy hour featured guest musicians, including Fanny, one of the first all-female rock-and-roll bands, and Tina Turner, another musical legend whose successful career began with a controlling man but also flourished solo.

Cher, in big earrings and big hair and singing 1971's "Gypsys, Tramps, and Thieves," made theater of social issues and status. Backed by the little-known but highly sought Wrecking Crew for 1973's "Half-Breed," Cher in feathers and casually astride a horse sang about being insulted for her skin color and mixed race. Fabulous sets made the songs come true for a few minutes as Cher performed stories about girls and women in relationships and exiting them, dark ladies who danced and laughed as they lit the candles one by one, fortune-tellers and outlaws, outcasts and the condemned. Cher's crooked teeth presented a new beauty, her low voice venturing forth unembarrassed and strong and in narrative control, the music bright and jangly and emphatic. Cher's contralto singing voice, the lyrics she sings, and her elaborate self-presentation signal a trust in one's own experiences.

Cher forthrightly stated that she didn't feel pretty growing up. She looked different than the prevailing standard of beauty: blond, blue-eyed, pale. Born Cherilyn Sarkisian in El Centro, California, on May 20, 1946, to an absent father and a young mom who married eight times, their poverty felt shameful to Cher. She spent time in an orphanage. At other times, life was lush, her upbringing filled with dancers, performers, and actors. Her ancestry includes Armenian, English, and Cherokee.

She dropped out of high school at sixteen, determined to be rich and famous, beginning her singing career as back-up, performing on the Ronettes' "Be My Baby" and the Righteous Brothers' "You've Lost That Lovin' Feeling." She moved in with an older musician, Sonny Bono, and tried to hide the fact from her mom, but that secret didn't last long; in 1965, with Sonny, a teenaged Cher sang "I Got You, Babe," one of the biggest-selling pop rock hits of the 1960s.

Cher initially sang by looking only at her singing and marital partner, who helped bring her to stardom and made sure the money she made went to him. She ultimately figured out how to extricate herself from bad contracts, negotiate good contracts, and sing to the audience.

The élan of Sonny and Cher's 1967 song "The Beat Goes On" was prescient, signaling Cher's impressive staying power. Long before Madonna, Cher strategized reinvention. Early fans tired of the duo, whose optimism and furry clothing seemed naïve in the sophisticated and heartbroken days that closed the 1960s, but Cher kept her sense of humor—and her business sense. Joking around in between songs during sparsely attended concerts, playfully insulting Sonny, her jokes became the basis for their comedy show.

Cher has embraced and enhanced the exoticism of her "half-breed" looks, sometimes surgically, with her often bared and hypnotizingly flat stomach, her sheet of hair that Heart singer Ann Wilson describes as black satin, her nose with a bump, and her dark coloring and high cheekbones. She dresses with the showbiz panache of glitter and body-baring glitz, commanding the stage.

A sneak preview audience laughed when they first saw Cher's name credited on the silver screen for her co-starring role in 1983's *Silkwood*, directed by Mike Nichols with a screenplay by Nora Ephron, but Cher silenced them with her talent. *Come Back to the 5 & Dime, Jimmy Dean, Jimmy Dean* (1982), directed by Robert Altman, *Mask* (1985), directed by Peter Bogdanovich, and *Moonstruck* (1987), directed by Norman Jewison, convinced most Hollywood heavy-hitters of Cher's serious consequence. But not movie star Jack Nicholson, who didn't want her for the role in 1987's *The Witches of Eastwick* because he didn't see her as attractive enough. She got the part—and an Oscar the next year, for *Moonstruck* (the same year Jack was nominated for another film, but didn't win). In 1996, she starred in and also directed a segment of *If These Walls Could Talk*, a film about reproductive freedom. *Burlesque* (2010), directed by Steven Antin and co-starring pop star Christina Aguilera, showed Cher firmly holding her own in the twenty-first century. Get back, Jack.

A perfume, exercise tapes, a rock band, and a Gothic-themed mail-order line evidence Cher's continued drive and business interests. People mocked her once again, this time for her infomercials. But she never lets anything stop her. Accordingly, Cher honors physical challenges and individual rights, contributing her name, time, talents, and/or money to vulnerable children, soldiers and veterans, Habitat for Humanity, AIDS organizations, and the LGBTQ communities. Cher, with her uniquely named sons, Chaz and Elijah Blue, stands at the helm of self-determination. She honestly discusses her struggles as a mom, including her difficulty accepting the gender transition of her firstborn, who was born a girl named Chastity and who became a man named Chaz.

Cher starred in the first video allegedly banned

PLAYLIST

WITH SONNY AND CHER:

"I Got You Babe," 1965, *Look at Us*

"The Beat Goes On," 1967, *In Case You're in Love*

SOLO:

"Bang Bang (My Baby Shot Me Down)," 1966, *The Sonny Side of Cher*

"Gypsys, Tramps, and Thieves," 1971, *Chér*, later renamed *Gypsys, Tramps, and Thieves*

"Half-Breed," 1973, *Half-Breed*

"Dark Lady," 1974, *Dark Lady*

"Take Me Home," 1979, *Take Me Home*

"If I Could Turn Back Time," 1989, *Heart of Stone*

"Walking in Memphis," 1995, *It's a Man's World*

"Believe," 1998, *Believe*

"You Haven't Seen the Last of Me," 2011, *Burlesque: Original Motion Picture Soundtrack*

by MTV, for the 1989 hit "If I Could Turn Back Time." Filmed aboard a US Navy ship, that aquatic bastion of masculinity, one scantily dressed and tattooed woman among many sailors in full dress, Cher turns what could be a dangerously pornographic situation into a fun-loving celebration of singing, sexuality, and dancing, outlandishly harnessing that powerful energy.

On the radio, on screen, on stage, and in magazines, her voice and image as familiar as her laugh, Cher articulates celebration and management of the pageantry of life. The spectacle of Cher is a stage show, a lived experience she works hard to control. Alliances with moguls such as former husband Sonny (who owned 95 percent of Cher Enterprises while a lawyer owned the remaining 5 percent, limiting her to working only with Sonny), David Geffen (her lover as she disengaged herself from the contract with Sonny), and designer Mackie (who worked with her from 1971 to 2014) demonstrate her evolution and ambition. When she divorced Sonny, she cited "involuntary servitude." When she owed thousands (and thousands) of dollars to the hotel where she lived, she charged David Letterman's show the amount she owed for a guest appearance, and after Letterman balked, he paid. Cher takes charge of her plot quest.

She is the only artist with a number-one single on a *Billboard* chart in each decade from the 1960s to the 2010s. With 1998's "Believe," Cher became the oldest female artist to have a US number-one song in the rock era, at the age of fifty-two. She regularly tours, with Las Vegas a popular venue. Numerous beguiling costume changes, a dizzying documentary about her life, glittering dancers, and a trapeze act all contribute to Cher's onstage extravaganza. She duets with Sonny once again by performing alongside cinema-sized archival footage of him. Soon there will be a Broadway musical about her life. Her 2010 hit "You Haven't Seen the Last of Me" makes a promise she keeps. "This is far from over," she belts out.

One of five actor-singers to have a US number-one single and an Academy Award, Cher's numerous awards for her singing and acting also include a Grammy, an Emmy, three Golden Globes, the Icon Award . . . and a Razzie. Cher, oft partnered and oft the subject of ridicule, long demonstrates her relentless work ethic, sense of humor, bewigged spectacularity, and ability to withstand and transcend critics, including her own self-criticism. In the *Behind the Music* episode about her, she observes: "Someone once said that after a nuclear holocaust the only thing left will be Cher and cockroaches. I think that's funny, because you know, I'm a survivor." ■

DOLLY PARTON

LUCRETIA TYE JASMINE

ILLUSTRATION BY JULIE WINEGARD

Dolly Parton's life is a quintessentially American rags-to-riches story, with its country-pop soundtrack and self-governing glory. A songwriter, multi-instrumentalist, singer, and actor, Parton also runs her own companies. Emerging alongside the Women's Liberation movement in the 1960s, she has become an icon of entrepreneurial spirit. The stories she writes, the stories she sings, and the stories she stars in intermingle in a chorus of celebration, like a gospel preaching creative and sexual freedom and unity, diversity, and equality. With over 100 million records sold worldwide, twenty-five number-one songs on the *Billboard* Country charts, and forty-one Top 10 country albums, Dolly has achieved more honors than any other female country performer. She may seem to be a Backwoods Barbie, as she called her 2008 album, but she possesses the poise, voice, and authority of a politician.

Dolly Rebecca Parton, born January 19, 1946, in Sevier County, Tennessee, grew up in a one-room log cabin, the fourth of twelve children. When Dolly was born, her farmer father and homemaker mom paid the doctor with a sack of cornmeal. Church and a homemade guitar introduced her to music as a child.

Of all her songs, Parton has said her favorite is 1971's "Coat of Many Colors," about a coat her mom made for her when they were too poor to buy a new one. The lyrics promote Christian values and do-it-yourself resourcefulness: "I recall a box of rags that someone gave us . . . Momma sewed the rags together / Sewing every piece with love." While her mom sews, she tells Dolly a story from the Bible, about Joseph and his coat of many colors. Her mom blesses her garment with a kiss. The song also shows the narrator's ego strength as she matter-of-factly confronts schoolmates who mock her colorful coat. With a narrative storytelling power inherited from her mom, Parton explains to her schoolmates that the coat was made with love, making her richer than anyone.

Parton's duets with Grand Ole Opry legend Porter Wagoner established her on the country music scene. During 1966–1967, she joined his traveling show as well as his weekly TV show, *The Porter Wagoner Show*. They released several albums and many hit singles. She wrote 1973's "I Will Always Love You" as a way to end their seven-year partnership. Porter reportedly said it was the prettiest song he ever heard, and that she could leave if she let him produce the song. Whitney Houston's 1992 rendition brought the already twice chart-topping single astounding popularity. Dolly, upon first hearing Whitney's version on the car radio, almost veered off the road from the power of it. She has said, "Well, a lot of people say

that's Whitney's song, and I always say, 'That's fine, she can have the credit, I just want my cash.'"

Parton's lyrics show that she has faith in the decisions she makes, and that she believes she has a right to make them, too. Her 1968 song "Just Because I'm a Woman" augurs second-wave feminism with its discussion of female sexual freedom within patriarchal double standards. Dolly reportedly wrote the tune in response to her husband questioning her sexual history. 1974's "Love Is Like a Butterfly" is considered her signature song; the freedom-loving butterfly became her logo.

Wedding country, pop, and bluegrass, Parton works with a variety of artists and styles. Her 1977 song "Here You Come Again," written by Brill Building icons Cynthia Weil and Barry Mann; 1980's "Starting Over Again," written by disco queen Donna Summer; her duet with Kenny Rogers on 1983's "Islands in the Stream," written by disco kings the Bee Gees; and *Trio* (1987), a collaborative album with Emmylou Harris and Linda Ronstadt, showcase the many sides of Dolly.

Parton demonstrated the multiple facets of her talent with her acting debut in Colin Higgins's 1980 movie about sexism in the workplace, *9 to 5*, co-starring feminists and activists Lily Tomlin and Jane Fonda. Her theme song for the film was a crossover hit, its expression of working-class heroism popular in both the country and pop arenas. As the hooker with a heart of gold

in Higgins's 1982 film *The Best Little Whorehouse in Texas*, Parton played the part that had inspired her stage look: when Dolly was growing up in Sevierville, she admired the gaudy glamour of a local sex worker.

She has appeared in thirty-four films and TV shows, building respect from critics and expanding her audience over time. On *Cher . . . Special* in 1978, she sang a segue into George Harrison's 1970 song "My Sweet Lord." Dolly appeared all in white, and Cher (in purple) ascended steps to reach Dolly's outstretched hand. In a 1990 episode of *Designing Women*, Dolly again appears as an angel, a guardian celebrity who reassures, gives guidance in dreams and visitations, carries the dying to the afterlife, offers comfort, and promises soft ascension. In the 2011 film by Tara Johns, *The Year Dolly Parton Was My Mom*, viewers never see Dolly in the flesh. Her voice becomes an otherworldly three-dimensional character, embodied by her lyrics, songs, and egalitarian beliefs. As a radio interview plays, Parton can be heard declaring that what's important is to be yourself, whatever your color or gender or sexual orientation. No wonder fans have nicknamed her "The Dolly Lama."

A persona obviously constructed with care, Parton appears at once angelic and exaggerated. Her strength of will can be seen in her own self-presentation. Her surgically enhanced breasts suggest her determination as well as a culture's obsession with size. Bridges in Mobile, Alabama, and Memphis, Tennessee, are nicknamed after her because they resemble her bosom. Scientists named a cloned sheep Dolly because the host was a mammary gland.

Parton has received plenty of recognition for her lifetime career. The Oscars, the Grammys, *Ms.*

Magazine, BMI, the US Library of Congress, the National Medal of Arts, the Kennedy Center Honors, the Academy of Country Music Awards, the Country Music Association Awards, and the American Music Awards have all honored Dolly, sometimes more than once. The Grand Ole Opry, the Nashville Songwriters Hall of Fame, the Country Music Hall of Fame, and the Songwriters Hall of Fame have all inducted Parton. In Sevierville, there is a bronze statue of the guitar-wielding prodigal daughter.

Parton has supported the American Red Cross, HIV/AIDS-related charities, the environment, and People for the Ethical Treatment of Animals. Dollywood is her Smoky Mountains theme park that also houses the Southern Gospel Museum and Hall of Fame and distributes scholarships to high school students and free books to children.

On stages and in interviews, Parton has said she never plans to retire. With her longtime marriage to Carl Dean and significant business partnerships, she handles the men and media in her life with a never-ending work ethic and effective charm. Dolly disarms with humor and forthrightness; her delicate vibrato, sure bravado, and rhinestone-covered guitar sparkle and persuade.

It might be difficult to discern the woman beneath the artifice: the big blond wigs, the heavy makeup, the cosmetic surgery. But Dolly's narrative power is clear. Her extravaganza of self-expression, a story she writes, resounds like a hit song. ∎

MAVIS STAPLES

GAYLE WALD

ILLUSTRATION BY LINDSEY BAILEY

Mavis Staples's remarkably durable and wide-ranging career has been defined by an unshakable belief in the inspiriting power of music, whether to console a wounded spirit or galvanize an entire political movement. Through her work with the Staple Singers, a family group including her siblings Cleotha, Pervis, and Yvonne and led by her father, the indomitable Roebuck "Pops," she was one of the defining musical voices of the civil rights movement. As a solo artist since the late 1950s, she has produced genre-spanning work while teaming up with an impressive roster of peers and admirers, including Curtis Mayfield, Prince, David Byrne, Ry Cooder, the Band's Levon Helm, and her mentor, Mahalia Jackson. It was through one of these collaborations, with fellow Chicagoan Jeff Tweedy, frontman of the rock band Wilco, that Staples won a 2011 Grammy in the Americana category for *You Are Not Alone*, a collection of old and new material. In 2013, hip-hop trailblazer Lauryn Hill inducted the Staple Singers into the Rock and Roll Hall of Fame, calling the family "great gospel warriors" and citing Mavis Staples as an enduring example of a woman who perfected the art of being simultaneously righteous and fly.

Mavis Staples is a lifelong resident of the Windy City, born in 1939 on Chicago's historically African American South Side. Through her father and mother, Oceola Ware Staples, children of the Great Migration, she inherited the rich musical culture of rural Mississippi. Like gospel music itself, the Staple Singers (Pops dropped the "s" in the family surname for their professional moniker) were formed in the cultural crucible of the urban North, even as the South was audible in Pops's trademark tremolo blues guitar and the Staples siblings' spacious and straightforward approach to harmony and vocal delivery. Mavis stood out from her siblings at a young age. Although petite, she had a vocal register that could dip down "in the basement" with the boys, to tenor or even bass territory, as well as a grown-up timbre that combined grit and grace. Like all the Staples kids, she received musical training from the church (her family belonged to Chicago's Trinity United Church of Christ, a congregation later made famous as the church of Michelle and Barack Obama) and from various Golden Age gospel vocalists, including the Soul Stirrers, Mahalia Jackson, and the Gay Sisters, whose music was permitted in a household that frowned on more secular recordings. But it was Pops Staples who most shaped Mavis's emotionally open approach to vocalizing. "You be sincere and sing from your heart," he told his children. "What comes from the heart reaches the heart."

The Staple Singers came to public attention in the mid-1950s through now classic recordings of traditional Christian hymns including "Will the Circle Be Unbroken" and "Uncloudy Day," the latter of which features an early haunting solo by Mavis. By the early 1960s, through Pops's developing friendship with Martin Luther King Jr., the group had become closely associated with the civil rights movement. In an interview with poet Elizabeth Alexander, Mavis remembered that while the Staple Singers were on tour in Montgomery, Alabama, her father, who had heard King on the radio, took the family to hear the young preacher speak. "If he can preach it, we can sing it," Pops declared, presaging the group's turn to more overtly political "freedom" songs, music that voiced African American determination for collective liberation. From 1963 on, such "marching music" became a central part of the Staple Singers' repertoire; highlights include "Freedom Highway," inspired by the 1965 Selma-to-Montgomery march, and "Why? (Am I Treated So Bad)," an homage to the nine black children who integrated Central High School in Little Rock, Arkansas, in 1957. During this formative period of the Staple Singers' career, Mavis and her family traveled through the country by automobile, risking their own safety in locales hostile to black civil rights "agitators" even as they used their talents to encourage and embolden others.

The musical and moral authority of the Staple Singers' freedom songs attracted the attention of impresario George Wein, who invited the group to perform at the 1963 Newport Folk Festival. There they mingled with white folk revivalists, including a thoroughly smitten Bob Dylan, who asked Pops for Mavis's hand. (She ultimately turned him down, although remained friendly with the singer and paid homage to him with covers of "Masters of War" and "A Hard Rain's a-Gonna Fall"). Yet if Newport provided a source of bona fides with the folk world, it was the group's late 1960s work with the Memphis-based Stax label, which specialized in fusing the sensibilities of gospel, soul, and rock, that propelled the Staple Singers onto the *Billboard* charts. Songs like "Respect Yourself" (number two R&B, number twelve pop) and "I'll Take You There" (number one R&B and pop), from the album *Be Altitude: Respect Yourself*, featured Mavis's self-assured and yet unflashy vocals and spoke to the new black consciousness, even as they powered bodies on the dance floor. Suddenly, the Staple Singers were playing for the artists and intellectuals on *Soul!*, entertaining the kids on *Soul Train*, singing to Ghanaian audiences at the legendary 1971 Soul to Soul concert in Accra, and taking the stage at Wattstax, shortly after their Chicago friend Jesse Jackson led a crowd of over 110,000 people in Black Power chants of "I am somebody!"

When the Staple Singers' touring career began to lose steam in the late 1970s, Mavis increasingly stepped out on her own, having established herself as the Singers' virtuoso. In the 1980s and '90s she recorded two solo albums for Stax; collaborated with Prince, who released two Mavis Staples albums, including the critically praised *The Voice* (1993) on his Paisley Park label; and released a Mahalia Jackson tribute album, *Spirituals and Gospel*, with the keyboardist Lucky Peterson. Her most enduring solo work has emerged, perhaps not unexpectedly, in the wake of

PLAYLIST

WITH THE STAPLE SINGERS:

"Uncloudy Day," 1961, *Swing Low Sweet Chariot*

"Freedom Highway," 1965, *Freedom Highway*

"Will the Circle Be Unbroken," 1965, *Freedom Highway*

"Respect Yourself," 1972, *Be Altitude: Respect Yourself*

"I'll Take You There," 1972, *Be Altitude: Respect Yourself*

SOLO:

"You Are Not Alone," 2010, *You Are Not Alone*

"Only the Lord Knows," 2010, on *You Are Not Alone*

the devastating death of Pops Staples—the powerful figure with whom she had performed for half a century. The need to reinvent herself in the age of digital downloads and internet self-branding led first to *Have a Little Faith*, her aptly named LP on the Alligator label, and then ultimately to two fruitful collaborations with white male artists. With Ry Cooder she put out a studio album, *We'll Never Turn Back*, which revisits some of the Staple Singers' freedom songs, and *Hope at the Hideout*, a live album recorded at the tiny West Side Chicago club in summer 2007, when Barack Obama was in the midst of a historic presidential campaign. (The album was released on election day.) One of the people in Hideout that night was Jeff Tweedy, who would work with Staples on *You Are Not Alone* (2010) and *One True Vine* (2013).

Staples's post-millennial work as an authoritative interpreter of twentieth-century black music, from gospel to soul to rock, has led her to play before audiences of young adults who were children in 2005, when seeming government indifference led to the suffering or deaths of thousands of black New Orleans residents after the devastation of Hurricane Katrina. These young people have worked backward from her collaborations with the likes of Tweedy and Arcade Fire to discover in the Staple Singers' catalog the record of an earlier, and no less vital, moment of the black freedom struggle. Staples's career is marked by its remarkable longevity, a rarity among women in the music industry and a testament to her courage and fortitude as a performer. It is likewise defined by her remarkable ability to direct her talent in new musical directions while staying committed to a vision of music's restorative and transformative potential. Wherever and whenever God's children are being mistreated, there is Mavis Staples's voice, infusing her listeners with the energy and confidence to heal the world. ■

LADIES OF THE CANYON

Laurel Canyon is a picturesque neighborhood of bungalows and bougainvillea nestled in the Hollywood hills, between the San Fernando suburbs and urban Los Angeles. In the late sixties, it became Southern California's ultimate hippie enclave, a bucolic gathering place for a who's who of musicians and artists, including Carole King, Odetta, Linda Ronstadt, Joni Mitchell, and the Mamas and the Papas. Mitchell immortalized her neighbors on the 1970 folk-rock masterpiece *Ladies of the Canyon*. In the title track the Canadian émigré paints portraits of three women—an artist, a baker, and a musician—in secondhand coats and gypsy shawls, "cats and babies 'round her feet." Other cities had their own boho hotspots during this tumultuous decade, including New York's Greenwich Village (where Joan Baez met Bob Dylan) and San Francisco's Haight-Ashbury, which housed the two women who defined the age's grooviness with their sartorial sass and big voices: Grace Slick and Janis Joplin. But Ladies of the Canyon became a catchphrase for bohemiennes everywhere, a sobriquet for the hippie chicks whose afros and long locks had replaced the bouffants and beehives of the first half of the decade.

The collectivist era of the girl group and the garage band had been eclipsed by the individualist rise of the rock star: a sort of Romantic Promethean hero, deliverer of truth to humankind. The singer-songwriter, not the producer, was now at the center of popular music; it was a great time for women to sing their minds. The floodgates opened for a slew of artists inspired by Baez (who was the Queen of Folk long before she took Dylan under her wing), as well as by the protest songs of Odetta, Mary Travers, and Nina Simone. The late sixties and early seventies were a sort of golden age for gold dust women: Laura Nyro, Emmylou Harris, Minnie Riperton, Janis Ian, Buffy Sainte-Marie, Judee Sill, Carole King, Carly Simon, Stevie Nicks, and Linda Ronstadt. The deeply talented Mitchell was the queen of the troubadours; Aretha Franklin, the queen of soul.

Many musicians, though not all, were drawn to the recording studios of Los Angeles and the generally looser vibe of the West Coast. Free love and women's liberation were crucial but not always complementary doctrines of this counterculture. People "shacked up" together in sometimes communal living situations, bands sharing houses and switching partners. In their wondrous assemblages of feather boas, velvet frocks, and hot pants and dedicated to the anti-Puritan pursuit of the pleasure principle, groupies embodied the free spirit of the times. But many ladies were not content to simply nurture their male cohorts or serve as muses. Girlfriends picked up guitars, or keyboards, or microphones. A gang of groupies formed the GTO's. Betty Davis introduced her husband Miles to Jimi Hendrix, then split to record her own albums of space funk. The photographer Linda Eastman went on the road with her husband Paul McCartney, setting wing to a thousand coed bands of the alt-rock future. In 1972 Australian-American artist Helen Reddy scored a number-one hit with a song whose feminist declaration was unabashed and said it all: "I Am Woman."

JONI MITCHELL

JANA MARTIN

ILLUSTRATION BY ANNE MUNTGES

Joni Mitchell is often described as some kind of brilliant contradiction: a winsome folkie who invented an incredibly complex guitar tuning; a confirmed dulcimer-and-soprano folk artist who composes cerebral jazz; the famed author of *the* seminal song about Woodstock, circa 1967, who wasn't there.

Mitchell is all of those things and more. She's a confirmed musical genius who would prefer other people stay confused rather than trap her in their oversimplifications. She's beat a few hasty (and angry) retreats from the music industry, yet her music is instantly recognizable and a vital part of pop music's canonical songbook. And she has always insisted that she's really just a painter whose career was, as she famously said, "detailed by circumstance." Mitchell had a radio-friendly voice that embodied a generation, then chafed against the pop harness and headed toward more experimental horizons. She came at her music from an artist's point of view.

Her origin story has a kind of sixties mythos: the stubborn child of no-nonsense parents in Saskatoon, Canada, she had early talent for piano but refused to play for ten years after a teacher criticized her for playing by ear. She began singing and performing when she was stricken by polio and confined to a hospital. Her trademark stubbornness drove her to write her own songs when Canada's folk

clubs wouldn't book her singing covers. She left the Toronto folk scene for the US and became a bona fide hitmaker: when Judy Collins recorded Mitchell's "Both Sides Now" it rocketed to number eight on the US pop singles charts in two months. But the song also immediately galvanized a trope that Mitchell, as well as Collins and others, would fight the rest of their careers: the open-eyed pretty girlfriend in a miniskirt, philosophizing about the illusion of love yet ever ready to be swept off her feet again.

David Crosby (of Crosby, Stills, Nash, and Young) saw her playing in a club in Florida and convinced her to come to California, where her star ascended fast, with three albums in rapid succession: *Joni Mitchell/Song to a Seagull* (1968), produced by Crosby (with Stephen Stills on bass); *Clouds* (1969), which won Mitchell a Grammy for Best Folk Performance; then *Ladies of the Canyon* (1970), which firmly affixed her star in the pop-folk pantheon. But she was already wriggling out of those confines. It's a particular Mitchellian kind of irony that the hit that FM radio loved the most was also a damning environmental indictment of American sprawl, "Big Yellow Taxi." "They paved paradise, put up a parking lot," she sang, and cynical as it was, it was also an infectious hook, sung by girls in summer camp and teenagers clustered around the radio. And it's still a hook, covered by Counting Crows (2009) and sampled by Janet Jackson featuring Q-Tip (1997), Kelly Rowland featuring Wiz Khalifa (2013), and the electronica giants Aphex Twin (2015), among others.

Charting was never Mitchell's goal, but her songs stick like glue, an uncanny combination of inventiveness—those elusive guitar tunings, for one—and knife-sharp poetry: "you are in my blood like holy wine," she sings on "A Case of You," from *Blue* (1971). Nor did she want to be the blond and high-cheekboned scribe of jaded romanticism, but Mitchell is extraordinarily good at writing—and singing—songs about love: the folly of it, the allure of it, the open road that healed it, the push and pull of it. Her voice conveys gorgeous soprano hope and alto introspection.

She had plenty of experience. As a young unwed mother out of options in Toronto, she put up her baby for adoption, and her raw grief, as she has noted, triggered her to start writing deeper songs. (She and her daughter reunited years later.) Though she arrived in the US married (to fellow folkie Chuck Mitchell), she soon shed the marriage and would go on to be involved with many folk and folk-rock poster heartthrobs: Leonard Cohen, long-time lover Graham Nash, James Taylor, Jackson Browne, Sam Shepard (the purported catalyst for her breakup with her then drummer and partner John Guerin). Many made an appearance, acid or appreciative, in her songs—often explained, in time, by Mitchell herself, who has always insisted on the right to narrate her own adventures. Nash inspired "Case of You." Shepard was the subject of no regrets in "Coyote," and Guerin had her musing in the desert and thinking of the lost aviatrix Amelia Earhart on "Amelia," and singing about heartbreak in the poignant "Blue Hotel Room," all on the incredible

Hejira, Mitchell's eighth album. Many of the lyrics on that 1976 album have a self-confessional glow—love's pain salved by the open road. It was a renegade idea at the time, a woman striking out for the highways, independent and craving her own company. But what really makes that album stand out is something else entirely. And that, again, is what marks Mitchell as the giant she is.

Hejira was a firm musical departure (signaled with *Court and Spark* in 1974) that marked the end of the pop-folk Mitchell. Weary of bass players who chained themselves firmly to the root note of a chord, she sought a far more exploratory sound, and found it in the playing of Jaco Pastorius, whose fretless work freed the low end to craft its own melodies. Intensely creative and harmonically and rhythmically sophisticated, the album was not only influenced by jazz, it *was* jazz—though some critics refused to give Mitchell the benefit of the label. No matter: she was done with pop, her miniskirt replaced by a composer's beret and a cape. And despite radio's rejection, the album went gold and reached number thirteen on the *Billboard* 200 chart.

Mitchell turned to jazz with a sure exuberance that drew on her own prodigious skill and training: just as she would say she was a painter who'd taken a left turn, she was also a serious musician who'd taken a folk-pop detour. After the lavishly clever *Don Juan's Reckless Daughter* (1977) she recorded with jazz giant Charles Mingus (*Mingus*, 1979) and

PLAYLIST

"Both Sides Now," 1969, *Clouds*

"Big Yellow Taxi," 1970, *Ladies of the Canyon*

"Woodstock," 1970, *Ladies of the Canyon*

"A Case of You," 1971, *Blue*

"You Turn Me On I'm a Radio," 1972, *For the Roses*

"Help Me," 1974, *Court and Spark*

"Coyote," 1976, *Hejira*

"Paprika Plains," 1977, *Don Juan's Restless Daughter*

"God Must Be a Boogie Man," 1979, *Mingus*

"Sunny Sunday," 1994, *Turbulent Indigo*

then worked with a whole series of collaborators in the 1980s—Thomas Dolby, Wendy and Lisa, Tom Petty, Don Henley from the Eagles. She kept making albums, one after the other, commercially successful or not. In 1994, she released the gorgeous *Turbulent Indigo*, which won a Grammy for Best Pop Album. Every time she seemed poised to slow down, she didn't.

It's true, also, that like a number of musical geniuses, she seemed to become more and more disillusioned and critical of the music industry, dispensing barbs with her trademark husky voice, often a cigarette in hand. Her voice shifted in the 1980s, triggered either by age or mysterious causes, but the change served to help cleave the mature musician from her iconic, girl-in-a-calico-dress past. She suffered from a debilitating and chronic skin condition, had a terrifying stroke, and rumor had it that she was felled for good, voiceless, inanimate. She's not.

As of this writing she's probably telling someone another tale from her remarkable, prodigious, hyperproductive life, tolerating one documentary filmmaker or another (for a short while at least), helping herself to another cigarette, explaining away reports of an old insult—such as the time she called Bob Dylan a "plagiarist" in 2010. She has sold more than 10 million copies of her albums, and her songs are still turning up in new ways: she's name checked by performers from Madonna to Corinne Bailey Rae and James Blake to Chaka Khan and Prince—who sampled "Help Me" for his "The Ballad of Dorothy Parker." Kanye West took a snippet of "River" for "Crazy." Taylor Swift wants to play her in a biopic, though Mitchell has cynically put the kibosh on that endeavor. Whatever route you take to Joni Mitchell, it sticks. Most likely, we'll call her the Mozart of pop music. But that won't entirely be accurate, and we'll know it as soon as we say it. ∎

THE GTO'S

LUCRETIA TYE JASMINE

ILLUSTRATION BY WINNIE T. FRICK

Groupies, young adult women who emerged on the cusp of second-wave feminism as the avante-garde of the sexual revolution, navigated old-fashioned double standards with daring independence. They were colorful cohorts to the new counterculture royalty—the rock star—following their idols from hotel to hotel on tours, grooming them, inspiring them, supporting them, and, yes, having sex with them. Lillian Roxon, author of the *Rock Encyclopedia* (1969), defined groupies as "fans who have dared to break the barriers between the audience and the performer." Roxon said the word *groupie* surfaced in 1965–1966 along with easy access to local bands.

Groupies, who were mostly women, quickly became almost as famous as the men—and they were almost entirely all men—with whom they consorted. *Rolling Stone* magazine dedicated an entire issue to groupies and published the book *Groupies and Other Girls: A Rolling Stone Special Report*. The 1970 documentary *Groupies* interviewed groupies about their lives. In 1973, *Star* magazine debuted, with a regular comic panel about groupies and centerfolds of rock stars. The GTO's, known as a groupie group, figured prominently in the reporting, embodying the spirit of the times.

The GTO's, or Girls Together Outrageously, were friends whose en masse dancing in outlandish attire at concerts, clubs, and on the street generated word-of-mouth publicity. Musicians sought them out and absorbed their style. GTO's members Miss Christine and Miss Pamela (as they called themselves) suggested or designed the iconic appearances of many male superstars: Alice Cooper's makeup, Rod Stewart's blond shocktop, Gene Simmons's top knot, Paul Stanley's star, Gram Parsons's jacket. "I be all the people I want to be / And find all the treasures I want to find," sings GTO Miss Mercy, in "The Ghost Chained to the Past, Present, and Future (Shock Treatment)," a song from the band's one and only album, *Permanent Damage* (1969).

GTO Miss Sparky describes how the band formed: "GTO's were founded by FZ [Frank Zappa] as performance artists and local color for performing on stage with them . . . not man hunters. . . the musicians were friends and fabulous men. . . " GTO Miss Pamela adds, "We didn't join anything, we were already together, just dancing." Making original music merged with unique self-presentation and open-minded philosophies. Musician and record-producer Zappa believed the GTO's could be rich, famous, and culturally radicalizing. He and his wife, Gail Zappa, a former groupie herself, lived in a Laurel Canyon log cabin, where the band coalesced around several mainstay members. Zappa's assistant, the writer Pauline Butcher Bird, managed the band.

Zappa paid the GTO's for their work as musicians until 1971, but when some of the members were busted for drugs at the Landmark Motor Hotel in Hollywood, Zappa lost faith.

The legendary GTO's 1968 performance at the Shrine Auditorium in Los Angeles showcased the band as fun-loving performers with an interest in artistic experimentation, an experimentation they also lived. They were a performance art rock group known to dress up in diapers. The show at the Shrine, billed with Wild Man Fischer, Alice Cooper, and the Mothers of Invention, featured their zany dancing and singing along with skits that included snow falling and DJ Rodney Bingenheimer dressed as Santa Claus, with Miss Pamela perched on his lap, announcing her wish list.

The GTO's believed in sexual self-determination and liberation, including sex outside of marriage, with partners of choice, and with birth control. Miss Pamela told me she "popped the pill on the Sunset Strip." One of the first songs they sang as a group, "Getting to Know You," a 1951 Rodgers and Hammerstein song from the musical *The King and I*, gleefully announces the band members as subjects who take action rather than objects who are acted upon. The GTO's lived their lives notoriously: the amount of drugs they took, the numerous places they lived and traveled, the many rock stars they bedded/ didn't bed but influenced, the freaky clothes they wore. Their groupie feminism was an assertion of experimentalism in love, sex, self-presentation, and music, a challenge to hierarchy and status quo. Miss Pamela said, "I wanted to ignite people's imaginations and make life a playground." The GTO's demonstrated self-empowerment and artistic license even as some acted out self-destruction.

The GTO's collaborated on *Permanent Damage*, writing their own lyrics and co-writing some of the music. *Permanent Damage* thwarts narrative pleasure with jarring segues and name-calling. Their music, a theatrics of sound, makes songs out of spoken word, recitation, conversations, interviews, and diary reading. Their a capella singing, conversational and warm, also sounds vaguely terrifying with its repeated group chanting. Several respected musicians and artists (including Jeff Beck, artist Cynthia Plaster Caster, who plaster-casts the genitals of rock stars, and Rod Stewart) can be heard on the album.

The lyrics are baffling and at times disturbing. The cultural observations they express can morph into prejudice, and their sexual exploration can segue into sexual opportunism, such as in the songs, "Who's Jim Sox?," "Wouldn't It Be Sad If There Were No Cones?," and "Love on an Eleven Year Old Level." But Miss Mercy's "The Ghost Chained to the Past, Present, and Future (Shock Treatment)," her "I Have a Paintbrush in My Hand to Color a Triangle (Mercy's Tune)," Miss Christine's "TV Lives," and Miss Pamela's playful and insistent "I'm in Love with the Ooo-Ooo Man" keep playing in your mind even after the song ends.

The GTO's had seven main members.

Miss Christine, born in San Pedro, California, nannied for the Zappas' children. Zappa's 1969 album, *Hot Rats*, features her on the cover. After

PLAYLIST

"Who's Jim Sox?," all songs 1969, *Permanent Damage*

"Wouldn't It Be Sad If There Were No Cones?"

"TV Lives"

"Rodney"

"I Have a Paintbrush in My Hand to Color a Triangle (Mercy's Tune)"

"The Original GTO's"

"The Ghost Chained to the Past, Present, and Future (Shock Treatment)"

"Love on an Eleven Year Old Level"

"Miss Pamela's First Conversation with the Plaster Casters of Chicago"

"I'm in Love with the Ooo-Ooo Man"

spending at least a year in a spine-straightening cast, Miss Christine died in 1972.

Miss Cynderella, born in Los Angeles, the youngest GTO at seventeen, met the GTO's through Miss Mercy. Songwriter John Cale wrote 1977's "Guts" about her. She died in 1997.

Miss Lucy, born in Puerto Rico, acted in several of Zappa's films, playing a groupie in 1971's *200 Motels*. Miss Lucy, unhappy with the commercial ambition of the GTO's as they made the album, quit the band. She died from AIDS in 1991.

Miss Mercy, born in Los Angeles, gave the album its name: *Permanent Damage*. She said, "I crawled inside the radio and never came out again." Her memoir is due out in 2018.

Miss Pamela, born in Reseda, California, nannied the Zappas' children. Author of several books, including 1987's bestselling *I'm With the Band: Confessions of a Groupie*, she provides the best line on the GTO's album: "I was a virgin the last time he was in town."

Miss Sandra, born in San Pedro, California, lived in the Zappa household. Miss Sandra's liner-note portrait shows her with a big star painted on her pregnant belly. She died from cancer in 1991.

Miss Sparky provided vocals and sound effects for Zappa's 1976 album *Zoot Allures*. An artist, she is intensely private, rarely giving interviews.

As the GTO's navigated their own presence in society, second-wave feminism and civil rights set the stage for a sexual and racial liberation that would announce itself most loudly in the music arena; the term *rock and roll* began as a term for sex, representing rebellion, freedom, and fun. Indeed, white Miss Mercy married black musician Shuggie Otis, giving birth to a son they named Lucky.

It's true that rock stars sometimes abused groupies, and that many groupies were underage. It's true that groupies, in their sexual freedom that tried to equal men's, were often discarded like Band-Aids. Which is why the GTO's are so crucial. In this sparkling passage of music history, it seemed as though women could equal men in freedom of purpose and power. So rock stars took center stage. Groupies worshipped at the altar. The GTO's, for one album and at least one esteemed show, were both. ■

YOKO ONO

GILLIAN G. GAAR

ILLUSTRATION BY JULIE WINEGARD

On the night of December 8, 1980, Yoko Ono was in the studio with John Lennon, working on her new song, "Walking on Thin Ice." A taut, edgy number, Ono's haunting, enigmatic lyrics carried a hint of foreboding, underscored by Lennon's searing guitar work. An excited Lennon told his wife, "Yoko, this is your first number one!"

Later that night, as the couple returned to the Manhattan apartment building in which they lived, John was shot, putting an end to the most famous and infamous marriage in rock history. His death, just at the moment that the couple was emerging from years of creative and romantic turmoil into a public renaissance, left his widow with the daunting task of preserving the Beatles' legacy—and ensuring her own, as a formalistically radical but deeply humanistic musical and visual artist who would ultimately find herself vindicated against the haters and naysayers.

Her marriage brought Yoko notoriety, but it also eclipsed what was already an extraordinary life and career. Yoko Ono was born in Tokyo on February 18, 1933. Her father, a banker, moved the family to San Francisco and New York when she was a child, but they returned to Japan as the threat of war escalated. When the bombing became too intense in Tokyo, Ono's mother took the children to live in the countryside; their money soon ran out, and they were forced to forage for food. After the war, the family was reunited and Ono's father returned to banking, eventually finding another position in the US. In 1953, the family relocated to Scarsdale, New York, and Ono enrolled at Sarah Lawrence College. She had taken piano lessons as a child, but when she told her father she wanted to be a composer, he discouraged her, telling her that women were better at interpreting music than creating it. She nonetheless continued studying music, developing an interest in modern composers like Arnold Schoenberg and John Cage.

In 1956, Yoko dropped out of college and moved with her husband, composer Toshi Ichiyanagi, to Manhattan. The two became caught up in the city's bohemian art scene, and in 1960 Ono began hosting events at the couple's loft—"happenings," which featured experimental poetry, music, and dance. Ono, later dubbed "the high priestess of the happening," performed as well. In "Pea Piece," she threw legumes into the audience while whirling her long hair. Her 1964 book *Grapefruit* contained what she called "instructional poems," with cryptic suggestions like drawing a map to get lost. Her works also invited the audience's participation, as in "Painting to Be Stepped On." A more striking statement was made in "Cut Piece" (first performed in 1964), in which Ono sat silently on stage, a pair of scissors in front of her, and asked the audience to cut off a piece

of her clothing. It was both a dare and a provocation, posing the question to performer and observer alike: how far are you willing to go?

By 1966, she was living in London with her second husband, Tony Cox, and their child, Kyoko. She met Lennon when he came to one of her art exhibits, later sending him a copy of *Grapefruit*. Lennon was intrigued by her idiosyncratic work, and in 1968 they began a relationship, marrying the following year. The two created art projects together, including a series of albums that baffled and outraged the public. *Unfinished Music No. 1: Two Virgins* (1968), for example, provoked scandal due to its cover of the couple in the nude, and puzzlement at the *musique concrete* on the record itself: a half hour of birdsong, random notes played on guitar and piano, Ono's warbling, and Lennon cracking jokes.

Ono's musical career began in earnest with *Yoko Ono/Plastic Ono Band* (1970). The music was potent, explosive, and riveting, with Ono's ululating vocals perfectly matched by Lennon's lacerating guitar. But in a rock era that was post–Velvet Underground and pre–Patti Smith—before punk, post-punk, New Wave, and No Wave—Ono's sound creations shocked. No one was making music like this. No woman in rock had ever sounded so extreme.

The subsequent albums *Fly* (1971), *Approximately Infinite Universe* (1973), and *Feeling the Space* (1973) had a broader musical palette. Already misogynistically hated for supposedly breaking up the Beatles, Ono's music prompted people to send her pictures of her albums stuffed into trash cans and racist hate mail. But there was more to Ono's music than harsh extremity. An element of wry humor was apparent in song titles like "I Felt Like Smashing My Face in a Clear Glass Window." "Midsummer New

York" was a slice of rock-and-roll parody (she later said she was emulating Elvis Presley). "Yang Yang" offered a scathing depiction of an executive whose life revolves around his telephone, set to a straightforward rock beat. "Woman Power" was a stirring feminist anthem. "Mrs. Lennon" provided a gentle, if surreal, look at married life.

In 1971, the couple relocated to New York City, in part to escape the racism Ono faced in Britain, and to try to relocate her daughter. (Though Ono was awarded custody of Kyoko, Cox had taken the child, returned to the US, and then vanished; Ono wouldn't see her daughter for another thirty years). After a highly publicized separation and reconciliation in the mid-1970s, Ono and Lennon put their artistic activities on hold. Ono gave birth to a son, Sean, and took over the family's business affairs. *Double Fantasy*, released in November 1980, announced the couple's return to music. Ono's songs in particular were right in step with contemporary musical fashion as heard in New York's downtown clubs. Though now regarded as a portrait of a loving relationship, a number of the album's lyrics reveal otherwise; this was a marriage with its fraught periods, too. And the last song on the album, Ono's "Hard Times Are Over," comes with a qualification; they're only over "for a while."

Ono's response to Lennon's murder on the night the couple was working on "Walking on Thin Ice"

PLAYLIST

"Why," 1970, Yoko Ono/ Plastic Ono Band

"Midsummer New York," 1971, *Fly*

"Mrs. Lennon," 1971, *Fly*

"We're All Water," 1972, on John Lennon and Yoko Ono with Elephant's Memory's *Some Time in New York City*

"Yang Yang," 1972, *Approximately Infinite Universe*

"Death of Samantha," 1973, *Approximately Infinite Universe*

"Woman Power," 1973, *Feeling the Space*

"Walking on Thin Ice," 1981, *Walking on Thin Ice*

"Warzone," 1995, *Rising*

"Waiting for the D Train," 2009, *Between My Head and the Sky*

was the unsettling *Season of Glass* (1981). There were unsurprisingly songs of grief, like "Goodbye Sadness" and "Even When You're Far Away." But it was also an album of anger. The stark cover shot of Lennon's bloodstained glasses was, in its way, as shocking as the nudity on the cover of *Unfinished Music No. 1*. And other songs made the tragedy explicit as well. "No, No, No" opened with the sound of four gunshots, followed by Ono's scream. And in a spoken word passage in "I Don't Know Why," Ono finally unleashed her rage against her detractors: "You *bastards*! Hate us, hate me! We had *everything*!"

Two albums of more pop-oriented material followed, then Ono put her music aside again. She returned in 1995 with one of her strongest albums, *Rising*, recorded with her son, Sean. She drew on her experiences living through World War II in the bracing "Warzone" and torturous "I'm Dying," counterbalancing that intensity with the teasing funk of "Wouldnit" and the reflective "Will I," which tries to crack the mystery of death. For the first time, her connection with John Lennon was not the focus of the album's reviews. For a new generation, that was old news; instead, Ono was welcomed as a peer. Her songs were remixed by Cibo Matto, Tricky, and Thurston Moore. When she toured, she was joined on stage by members of Soundgarden and the Melvins. In the twenty-first century, remixes of Ono's work found a home on the dance charts. Twenty-three years after his studio prediction, Lennon turned out to be right, when a remix of "Walking on Thin Ice" topped *Billboard*'s dance chart in 2003, a moment of sweet vindication. It was the first of thirteen number ones she'd have on that chart, as Ono found her audience in clubs populated by gays, women, and people of color—folks used to being dismissed as outsiders by the dominant culture. Performing over backing tracks at all-night dance parties probably wasn't where Ono expected to find herself, but transformation has always been a key element of her work. "Revelations," the closing number on *Rising*, recasts anger as energy, sorrow as vulnerability, jealousy as empathy. For Ono, changing the negative into a positive has meant more than simply being optimistic. It's been her very means of survival. ■

PATTI LABELLE

THEO KOGAN

ILLUSTRATION BY WINNIE T. FRICK

You hear people talk about musicians and how well they play instruments, and most likely in rock and soul they would be talking about guitar, bass, drums, keyboard, or horns—you get the drift. Patti LaBelle's voice is an instrument. She has honed this instrument with supreme devotion and elite athletic precision so that her use of it seems effortless, yet it is quite obviously at the top of its class. LaBelle's golden pipes at times sound more like a mechanical instrument than a biological one. She makes gospel sound like opera and vice versa. Her vocal range is vast; she can shift from glass-shattering high notes to deep, soulful gut-wrenching growls. The woman who began in a 1960s girl group and in 2017 released her first jazz album simply cannot be denied as owner of one of the biggest, most powerful voices of the last half century.

Take a look at LaBelle in the 1970s funk/soul/rock group that bore her last name (albeit with a lowercase b): Labelle were three African American women (Nona Hendryx, Sarah Dash, and LaBelle) with killer voices in glam-rock goddess-from-outerspace costumes complete with six-inch platform boots. They looked like three otherworldy superheroes. Their trio of voices slid with perfection from belts and howls into precision harmonized vibrato on frantic, fast, disco-driven funk songs and groovy grind-your-hips soul jams ("Lady Marmalade," anyone?).

Live, Patti engages with her audience with love and interest, accepting flowers, bringing people on stage, giving hugs. She was a supporter of gay rights way before it was cool and helped make AIDS awareness a promoted issue in the late 1980s. I hadn't delved deep into LaBelle until I met my drag queen mothers in NYC. I went to see her in the 1990s with a few of my drag friends at a theater, where she was singing classic standards as well as some originals. The players consisted of Patti and a pianist. I was blown away. Her show business expertise, stage presence, and purity of feeling conveyed through song came across blissfully. The way she connected with her fans was heart-rending. It was an extraordinary show.

Patti LaBelle was born May 24, 1944, in Philadelphia as Patricia Louise Holt. She changed her name to LaBelle, French for "the beauty," as a sort of a fuck-you to the world that told her she wasn't pretty. Her career has spanned many genres, from the Ordettes in 1959, who then became 1960s girl group the Bluebelles (aka Patti LaBelle and the Blue Belles),

PLAYLIST

WITH LABELLE:

"You've Got a Friend," 1971, *Labelle*

"Moon Shadow," 1972, *Moon Shadow*

"Lady Marmalade," 1974, *Nightbirds*

"Space Children," 1974, *Nightbirds*

"You Turn Me On," 1974, *Nightbirds*

"Get You Somebody New," 1976, *Chameleon*

SOLO:

"Eyes in the Back of My Head," 1978, *Tasty*

"Wild Is the Wind," 2017, *Bel Hommage*

which susequently became Labelle after a member change (Cindy Birdsong left in 1967 to sing with the Supremes) and at the prodding of their manager Vicki Wickham, a behind-the-scenes tour de force herself. (Wickham also changed music history by producing the *Ready, Steady, Go!* TV series and managing Dusty Springfield.) Labelle was a rock-and-roll moondream of soul, pop, glam, and funk. They were the first African American group of any kind to perform at the Metropolitan Opera House and the first African American group to be on the cover of *Rolling Stone* magazine. They smashed those ceilings down! Breaking barriers left and right, their three voices were infallible and orchestral together, a power trio to be reckoned with. Three black women in space-age costumes with voices from beyond our stratosphere and so much soul, they regularly performed at the Apollo Theater. Labelle went their separate ways in 1976 but did reunite many years later.

Patti began her solo career the following year with her eponymous debut album. She has continued to sing, record albums, and reinvent herself repeatedly. With soul singer Al Green, Patti hit Broadway for the first time in *Your Arms Too Short to Box with God* (1995). She signed with MCA Records and found pop success with two hits from the *Beverly Hills Cop* soundtrack: "New Attitude" and "Stir It Up." Her duet with Michael McDonald on "On My Own" went to the top of the pop chart. She has won two Grammys and sold over 50 million albums worldwide.

LaBelle is a woman alive with abundant talents. She is a true diva (I am not one to throw the word around lightly). Yet she is also someone I'd want to sidle up to and ask if I could help her bake something. She began writing books in the 1990s and now has six cookbooks, some of which are best sellers. She's also written best-selling books about her own life. She owns a dinner theater in Philadelphia called Chez LaBelle and launched a line of sauces called Patti LaBelle Good Life. Her love of cooking and sharing weaves through all she does. Patti is an entrepreneur on many fronts. She has a put out a line of lipsticks and nail polishes, and has launched two perfumes. She acted in the film *Beverly Hills Cop* as well as in the TV show *A Different World*, and more recently was on the cult TV show *American Horror Story* and *Dancing with the Stars*.

Patti is consistently able to open our hearts and bring us to tears, from the Blue Belles' rendition of Burt Bacharach's "Always Something There to Remind Me" to her 2017 album *Bel Hommage*, with a cover of David Bowie's "Wild Is the Wind." She has diabetes, and she lost all of her sisters to cancer. She has five kids, two of whom she adopted after her sisters' deaths. She must know grief a bit too well.

Perhaps best experienced in concert, where she truly gives her all to the crowd, LaBelle's voice is unmistakable: emotive like a magical winding tree with both elation and torment. She is funny, fearless, and a do-gooder to boot—she really does give a shit.

She's loyal to her former bandmates and has performed and recorded reunion albums with the Blue Belles and Labelle. One of Labelle's biggest hits, "Lady Marmalade," a song about a prostitute in New Orleans that brought French pillow talk into bedrooms around the world, will continue to be one of the most hip-shakin' songs ever in rock and soul music until the end of time. ■

LINDA RONSTADT

KANDIA CRAZY HORSE

ILLUSTRATION BY LINDSEY BAILEY

As the 1970s Queen of Rock, the Mexican American singer Linda Ronstadt provided a beacon of diversity for young listeners marked as Other in our society. For this Afro-Native author and musician being raised in a Chicano *barrio* in the early 1970s, she was the most visible and successful of an elite cadre of red-brown women in the entertainment field. Artists such as Buffy Sainte-Marie, Rita Coolidge, and Cher made it possible for us to project ourselves into such a rarefied subculture as the folk and rock scene of Los Angeles's Laurel Canyon. Ronstadt was truly a part of that vanguard, having moved to the West Coast from her native Arizona at seventeen and made early folk-rock impact as a member of the Stone Poneys. She had a sweet, girl-next-door quality and understated sexuality. Yet she was completely in step with her countercultural generation of artists as a pioneer of the country-rock sound, swinging at shows in her signature stripey Betsey Johnson dress. Ronstadt appeared to seamlessly reconcile the "far out" imaginary of the times with the traditional-leaning country sound of her earliest solo output.

In later years, Ronstadt told a rock critic that she had never been a country singer. Yet, drawing on the sounds she'd heard in her living room prior to age ten, Ronstadt effectively helped construct the next generation of California country, following the earlier innovations of Buck Owens and Merle Haggard, with her great first three solo releases for Capitol Records: *Hand Sown . . . Home Grown* (1969), *Silk Purse* (1970), and *Linda Ronstadt* (1972). *Hand Sown . . . Home Grown* was arguably the third alt-country or Americana album made by a woman, after the 1968 masterpieces by Mississippi's Bobbie Gentry (*The Delta Sweete*) and Kentucky's Jackie DeShannon (*Laurel Canyon*). *Hand Sown* operates perfectly at the transition from LA folk-rock to the scene's turn-of-the-seventies embrace of twang and cherry-picked Nashville sound values. Ronstadt's voice literally sometimes transitions between the two valences mid-lyric as she essays classics by Greenwich Village folk icons like Fred Neil ("The Dolphins") and a take on John D. Loudermilk's "Break My Mind." Ronstadt makes her first pass at a song clearly central to her feminist self-fashioning: "Silver Threads and Golden Needles," the Jack Rhodes/Dick Reynolds tune first recorded by Wanda Jackson in 1956 and a 1962 hit for the Springfields. Linda would achieve a country number twenty with the second go-round, a more country-pop version from her 1973 *Don't Cry Now*. (Even this album's outtakes are fascinating, such as the Appalachia-meets-India track "It Won't Be Easy," which reimagines Ronstadt as a singer of the holler with sitar in lieu of autoharp or banjo.)

This trio of albums illuminates the artistic coming of age of Linda Maria Ronstadt, who was born in Tucson in 1946. They are the product of her rearing in a highly musical family wherein by age fourteen she'd formed a folk trio with her siblings. Together, they performed a wide variety of styles, including folk, bluegrass, country, and traditional Mexican mariachi and ranchera music. The big-eyed Latina in *chola*-meets-hippie hoop earrings on the cover of her eponymous 1972 album could belt with a rare power and strived to hold her own in the studio and on the road with her backing bands from the period: Swampwater and the outfit that coalesced at her habitual LA hangout the Troubadour and included future Eagles guitarist Glenn Frey and drummer Don Henley.

California rock ruled the world during this period, and Ronstadt was America's sweetheart—and actual sweetheart, for a time, of California governor Jerry Brown. After she enjoyed her true mass breakthrough with 1974's Grammy-winning *Heart Like a Wheel*, which featured the smashes "You're No Good" and (a cover of the Everly Brothers) "When Will I Be Loved," Ronstadt continued to be the astute song collector that had mixed honky-tonk like "I Fall to Pieces" and

"Crazy Arms" with the gems of her LA peers Neil Young, Eric Kaz, Warren Zevon, Jackson Browne, and Lowell George on her subsequent work. However, as with most of the decade's triumphal LA rock sound, her music began to be overproduced and lack the "hand-sown" charms of her first solo entries. This grandiosity reflected the times: the callowness of the

Me Decade and the proliferation of cocaine throughout the homes and studios of Ronstadt's milieu of cosmic canyon cowboys.

Ronstadt pushed back at being perceived as in thrall to her notable managers John Boylan and Peter Asher. She countered the weight of being deemed a rock queen bee by *Newsweek* and being oversexualized for the covers of *Rolling Stone* and *Time* by befriending her putative country-rock rival Emmylou Harris and paying homage to her country foremother Dolly Parton. The three women conceived of a joint project in 1977 and later collaborated on *Trio* (1987) and *Trio II* (1999). She paid homage to her Mexican heritage via the landmark albums *Canciones de Mi Padre* (1987) and *Mas Canciones* (1991) (she also ventured into Afro-Cuban sounds via Frenesí).

Rolling Stone may have dubbed Linda Ronstadt "Rock's Venus," but she was inducted into the Rock and Roll Hall of Fame in 2014 for having bested the boys of her scene at their own game. By the seventies' end, she had outsold many of them and become a superstar live draw. No other female artist had achieved five straight platinum LPs. Her accolades include eleven Grammys, an Emmy, and a National Medal of Arts. Ronstadt was silenced in the musical sphere by illness in 2012—as she told *AARP Magazine*: "No one can sing with Parkinson's disease, no matter how hard you try."

Aside from her gift as an interpreter and her ongoing crusading for social justice, the now retired Ronstadt should best be remembered for helping establish the country-rock genre. As *Country-Western Stars* magazine opined in 1970: "Rock people thought she was too gentle, folk people thought she was too pop, and pop people didn't quite understand where she was at, but country people really loved Linda." Linda Ronstadt never encountered a boundary she did not seek to cross. ∎

KAREN CARPENTER

LUCRETIA TYE JASMINE

ILLUSTRATION BY WINNIE T. FRICK

Karen Carpenter's contralto voice, a good-girl voice grown up—a good-girl grownup with her own ambitions and dreams—hits every note just so, like the way she played drums. It's a voice full of emotional depth and warm range, like a woman in a velvet gown. Her voice grown up, all velvety and womanly.

The singer of the 1970s soft-rock sibling duo the Carpenters, the woman who sang and embodied the lament "Superstar," was born in New Haven, Connecticut. As a child, Carpenter played with toy machine guns. She played baseball. She played the accordion, bass guitar, and flute. She collected Disney stuff. She marched in the marching band, beginning with the glockenspiel until she convinced the band director to let her play drums, at a time when high school drum lines excluded women. "I picked up a pair of sticks, and it was the most natural-feeling thing I've ever done," Karen states in Randy L. Schmidt's *Little Girl Blue: The Life of Karen Carpenter* (2010).

At thirteen, she moved with her family to the bedroom community of Downey, California, where her parents hoped her older brother Richard could better pursue his musical ambitions. Karen joined Richard's jazz trio, and in 1969 it was her voice that caught the ear of trumpeter Herb Alpert, the A of A&M Records. Together, Karen and Richard—the

Carpenters—became one of the most successful groups of the 1970s, their carefully orchestrated light pop songs capturing the veneer of Nixon's America (Karen and Richard were guests at his White House)—but Karen's low voice also mournful. The Carpenters, among the best-selling music artists ever, with plentiful albums, singles, television specials, and even a TV series, appealed to listeners with their musical structure of determined optimism and ominous chords.

In their early shows, Karen played drums while she sang. Richard, in the KCET documentary *Close to You* (1997), says his sister perceived herself primarily as a drummer. Her name emblazoned on the drums, the kit sparkled. *The Carpenters: Live in London* (2011), with footage from early performances, attests to those skills, and to her happiness behind the kit. But management thought her drums created a barrier to the audience, so she moved out in front of the instrument she loved so much and became the focal point for the band.

Her octave-shifting voice on "Looking for Love" (1966), a song written by her brother before they became the Carpenters, bespeaks her lustrous singing. Richard was the fastidious writer and arranger, but it was Karen the world wanted to hear sing. She laughingly wore her nickname, Lead Sister, on a T-shirt. The sister and brother were close, her vocals

and his piano-playing an exquisitely timed dialogue. They scored three number-one singles, five number twos, and twelve more that made the Top Ten, songs whose ubiquity continues today.

Roger Nichols and Paul Williams wrote "We've Only Just Begun" (1970) for a Hal Riney commercial for a bank. A weird and massively successful single for the Carpenters, as heartbreakingly laughable and hypnotic as the commercial itself, the lyrics portray marriage as salvation. But Karen's singing intimates the poignant impossibility of a fairy tale coming true, an optimistic articulation that sounds surprisingly possible through her unwavering voice, a voice Williams described as innocent and sensual.

She didn't like the song that became a gold record for them, "Superstar" (1971), written by Bonnie Bramlett and Leon Russell about a real-life groupie, until her brother rearranged it, and then it became one of her favorite songs to sing. Its multiple layers of disciplined longing, energetic with desire and in perfect arrangement, sound here and there those baleful chords that can be heard throughout the Carpenters' oeuvre. "Goodbye to Love" (1972), with its use of fuzz guitar, could be the first power ballad. Wrapped in soft choruses and electric guitar, her sophisticated tone conveys calm acceptance of loss. And too a calm acceptance of success: her "Top of the World" (1972) is something she believes in as she closes the song with an affirming smile in her voice. Karen sang close to the mic, giving her recordings and performances the feeling of intimacy.

Walking carefully across the stage with mic-whipping competence, or running happily from massive drum sets to microphones, Carpenter's professional authority mixed with a playfulness and humor live and on their many TV appearances. Rehearsed and polished, their well-mannered performances left little room for spontaneity; the band ceded to Karen's direction, and she to her brother's. The songs were perfect.

In the short-lived magazine for groupies, 1973's *Star*, Karen discusses being the only woman on the road with a band of men, and explains that her music comes before romantic liaisons. She also states: "People always call me because they think that being a chick drummer, I'm a Woman's Lib fanatic, and *I'm not*! . . . I'm not a successful *girl drummer*, I'm just a drummer that happens to be a *girl*." Just as comfortable in jeans and T-shirts as in gowns, she explains that the onstage gowns she wears are actually disguised pants for better drumming.

Just like her hidden garments, the Carpenters hid secrets. Richard developed a drug addiction, and Karen developed an eating disorder.

In 1967, a doctor prescribed a diet for Carpenter. In the interview with *Star*, an interview that begins with discussion of her weight, Karen says that she just got tired of being fat. Over the years, she starved, and binged and purged, taking excessive amounts of thyroid pills to speed up her metabolism and syrup of ipecac to instigate vomiting. In rehab, she crocheted the motto: "You win, I gain." It hung above her bed.

PLAYLIST

WITH THE CARPENTERS:

"Looking for Love," 1966, *The Essential Collection*

"(They Long to Be) Close to You," 1970, *Close to You*

"We've Only Just Begun," 1970, *Close to You*

"For All We Know, " 1971, *Carpenters*

"Superstar," 1971, *Carpenters*

"Rainy Days and Mondays," 1971, *Carpenters*

"A Song for You," 1972, *A Song for You*

"Goodbye to Love," 1972, *A Song for You*

"Top of the World," 1972, *A Song for You*

"Calling Occupants of Interplanetary Craft," 1977, *Passage*

SOLO:

"Last One Singin' the Blues," recorded 1979–1980, released 1996, *Karen Carpenter*

She felt too fat because a music critic described her as pudgy. Or chubby. Or chunky. Whatever, not skinny.

By the time she was twenty-five, she weighed eighty pounds. Her eating disorder was a way of talking, vomit a collapsing language, a pound of flesh. Spilling her guts.

In 1980, Karen performed duets with jazz great Ella Fitzgerald for the Carpenters' TV special. To her angry disappointment, her eponymous solo album from 1980 was shelved. It was released thirteen years after she died.

In 1983, on February 4, at 8:51 a.m., an emergency call brought the Downey Fire Department to Karen's parents' house, where she sometimes stayed the night. Carpenter was found naked and unconscious on the floor of a walk-in wardrobe. She weighed 108 pounds. She died from cardiac arrest.

Posthumously, the personification of adult contemporary music became a sort of cause célèbre of alternative culture—a symbol of the deadly machinations of show business. In Todd Haynes's short film about her short life, *Superstar: The Karen Carpenter Story* (1987), the actors are dolls. In Sonic Youth's "Tunic (Song for Karen)" (1990), she disappears inside a tunic. Feminist theorists posit that the more cultural and political space women take, the less physical space women are allowed to take.

Karen Carpenter playing drums, Karen in the center of a spotlight, singing at the microphone. Karen in a poster I never had on my wall. She wears a strange white dress, covered up from neck to ankle. Strange because it looks so frilly and prudish. Karen on the cover of *Rolling Stone* magazine, playful in a hat that covers her eyes. Karen starving herself to death. The media's obsession with Karen's physical appearance silenced her voice, and her drumming.

Among notable accolades for her drumming and singing, a memorial foundation in her name funds research on eating disorders.

In her elucidated reprise of "A Song for You" (1972), Karen Carpenter's voice emerges and recedes and emerges again, approaching like a ghost embodying herself. Girl on a diet, forever diet. Drummer girl with a voice of dark gold. ■

JUNE MILLINGTON

ALICE BAG

ILLUSTRATION BY LINDSEY BAILEY

I f you're a queer woman of color, you can have talent, blaze a trail, work for decades at your craft, and still be largely ignored by the mainstream media and general population. June Millington rocked just as hard as the boys, played better than most of the boys, and toured as relentlessly as the boys. Her band, Fanny, was the first all-female rock group to release a full-length studio album on a major label. They were ahead of the game, and the music industry didn't know how to package them. All-female bands were seen as novelty acts, so Fanny was unjustly relegated to the archives, their legacy nearly forgotten. But some of us refuse to forget. We choose instead to delve deeper into the life and legacy of one of Fanny's founding members, June Millington, a woman who opened the door for countless female musicians.

In the spring of 1948, June was born to Yolanda Limjoco, a beautiful, young Filipina socialite, and Lt. Commander John Millington, a US naval officer stationed in Manila. Barely four years had passed since allied forces had liberated the Philippines from the Japanese army, who had invaded the islands during World War II. Jack and Yola, as the two were known by friends and relatives, met on a blind date and bonded over their mutual love of music and dancing. They fell in love, and by 1947 they were married and forming a family of their own.

June Elizabeth Millington was the firstborn of Yola and Jack's seven children. The Millington family lived with June's affluent maternal grandfather and grandmother in a large home with cooks, maids, a chauffeur, and a swimming pool. Even at a young age, June was aware of the class differences in Filipino society.

June attended the American School, where she had difficulty making friends. Many of the students at the American School were white and lived on American military bases, and June, being of mixed race, began to feel the sting of discrimination. Through a variety of verbal and nonverbal cues, Millington got the message that the white, American children felt superior to Filipinos and to her. During those difficult years, music became her refuge. She learned to play the piano and ukulele, and on her thirteenth birthday, her mother gave her oldest daughter a gift that would change her life: her first acoustic guitar.

Following June's thirteenth birthday in 1961, her father announced that they were moving to the US. Jack went first to secure housing for his family, and a short while later Yola, June, and the

PLAYLIST

(SELECTED BY JUNE MILLINGTON)

ALL WITH FANNY:

"Badge," 1970, *Fanny*

"Bitter Wine," 1970, *Fanny*

"Place in the Country," 1971, *Charity Ball*

"Hey Bulldog," 1972, *Fanny Hill*

"Long Road Home," 1973, *Mothers Pride*

rest of her siblings boarded the USS *Cleveland* on a journey that lasted twenty-one days before reaching the shores of northern California. To pass the long, boring days at sea, June and her younger sister, Jean, serenaded the passengers and crew, singing the popular songs of the day while accompanying themselves on ukulele and guitar. This was her first taste of performing for strangers.

The Millington family settled in Sacramento, where June and Jean continued to play music together. It was the early 1960s, and June was listening to pop, rock, and Motown on the radio. It wasn't long before the acoustic guitar replaced the ukulele as her instrument of choice, and in junior high she began writing original songs. By 1962, June and Jean were performing some of that original material along with cover songs at their junior high school talent shows. The duo began playing at hootenannies, parties, and other functions.

In high school, the sisters met a kindred spirit: a girl named Kathie Terry who played drums. A trio was formed. The band's instrumentation at the time was two acoustic guitars and a drum set, until another guitarist, Cathy Carter, joined. It became apparent that one guitarist should probably switch to bass, so the girls flipped a coin and Jean became the bassist. Their new ensemble, the Svelts, performed mostly cover songs while June continued to write originals. They practiced and gigged constantly, gathering fans, skills, and

momentum. Without any prior experience, role models, or a blueprint, the Svelts did it all themselves.

New band members rotated in and out of the band. June and Jean remained a constant. Eventually, the Svelts morphed into Wild Honey, which included June and Jean Millington plus Alice de Buhr on drums. It was Wild Honey that first garnered the

interest of record industry executives during a show at the West Hollywood nightclub the Troubadour. Warner Bros. subsidiary Reprise Records offered the band a contract with the caveat that they had to change their name, since another Wild Honey already existed. It was 1969 and Fanny was born.

Just before going into the studio to record their eponymous debut LP, Fanny decided to invite Nicole (Nickey) Barclay to play keyboards. The band's first release, in 1970, was met with mixed commercial success. Fanny toured extensively in support of major rock acts of the early seventies, garnering fans along the way, including Barbra Streisand and David Bowie, who later described them as "one of the finest rock bands of their time."

In 1973, after four albums, June left Fanny. The band continued for one more album, with Jean on bass, Patti Quatro (formerly of the Pleasure Seekers) on guitar, and Brie Brandt on drums; that group recorded Fanny's biggest hit, "Butter Boy."

June moved to New York, where she purchased a farm and continued to work on music with other women. She became a pioneer in the women's music movement, which supported the voices of women, and particularly lesbian women. In 1977, she was featured on *Lesbian Concentrate: A Lesbianthology of Songs and Poems*, released on Olivia Records. Olivia was a company started in the early seventies by five enterprising women who wanted to create a space where women could produce music specifically for the feminist and lesbian market. The female-owned and -run label pioneered a genre that would be known as Women's Music and became a much-needed outlet for lesbian voices. The company provided opportunities for women in all aspects of the recording industry and offered business and technical as well as musical training. Later, June would start her own label, Fabulous Records, as a subsidiary of Olivia.

In the late 1980s, June and her longtime partner, Ann Hackler, founded the Institute for the Musical Arts (IMA). Located in Goshen, Massachusetts, the IMA's mission is to teach music, performance, and the power of rock and roll to girls. To this day, June and Ann mentor and support girls and young women who are interested in music and careers in the music industry.

As of the time of this writing in 2017, June has reunited with former members of the Svelts and Fanny to record a brand new album: *Fanny Walked the Earth*. It's a fitting title, a pronouncement that this band has left an indelible mark on the face of rock and rejects the erasure of their contributions. Now approaching her seventieth birthday, June Millington has never stopped rocking; she continues to write and play music. Her legacy grows through the inspiration she provides to musicians, especially women, people of color, and members of the LGBTQ community. ∎

BONNIE RAITT

MICHELLE THREADGOULD

ILLUSTRATION BY LINDSEY BAILEY

A Vietnam veteran down on his luck saw his wife in divorce court and told the Nashville publication the *Tennessean*, "You can't make a damn woman love you if she don't." That quote inspired Bonnie Raitt's greatest hit, "I Can't Make You Love Me," written by Mike Reid and Allen Shamblin, at a time when the rhythm-and-blues singer was over forty and had more than a twenty-year career under her guitar. Raitt may have seemed like an unlikely choice to sing "I Can't Make You Love Me," as she was known for using her slide guitar as a second voice, and not for sparse, bittersweet piano ballads. But she had experienced some hard luck of her own; she was recovering from alcoholism and had been dropped by her label, Warner Bros., a few years earlier. On "I Can't Make You Love Me," her voice combined soulful, tomboy toughness with an open heart, incredible pitch, and the ability to sing with the tenderness of her inspirations Otis Redding and Mary Wells.

In her hands, "I Can't Make You Love Me" became a feminist ballad, a song about loving someone who doesn't love you and not wanting to live the lie anymore. When she sang the words, "Just hold me close, don't patronize," you could feel her heartache, as she nailed what it's like to be strong and vulnerable and not want to "give up this fight."

Led by this hit single, her 1991 album *Luck of the Draw* would go on to sell over seven million records, produce three Top Ten hits including "Something to Talk About," and receive three Grammys. "I Can't Make You Love Me" would be reinterpreted and covered by George Michael, Prince, Adele, and Bon Iver, and remain one of the most beloved American ballads of all time.

Before that, for many years, Raitt doubted that she would ever "make it." There was a caustic narrative in the early seventies, still strong today, that if you haven't "made it" as an artist by your thirties, you're never going to. Even though Raitt had a loyal grassroots following and had been playing with rhythm and blues greats like John Lee Hooker, Buddy Guy, and Junior Wells for years—B.B. King described her as the "best damn slide guitar player working today"—she wasn't on the radio or making chart-topping singles.

Still, Raitt wouldn't give up this fight. "I think I'm a living embodiment of don't try to push me around or squash me," Raitt told *Billboard* in 2012.

Part of her fighter spirit came from being born to artistic activist parents. She was raised Quaker and brought up to believe that "there's that of God in everyone." That belief went on to define Raitt, and she became committed to fighting for human rights, social justice, and environmentalism. As a young girl, Raitt marched on Washington, and

later in life she was involved in antiwar movements, Occupy, and environmental causes from preventing the clearcutting of redwood trees to stopping the Dakota Access Pipeline.

Raitt is a woman who believes that if you see injustice, you should do something about it.

She was born in southern California on November 8, 1949. Her father, John Raitt, was a Broadway music star who encouraged his daughter to explore her love of music. She began playing guitar at the age of eight; as a young girl, Raitt listened to soul and rhythm and blues. Ray Charles was one of the first singers to make an impression on her, and in her teen years, when her family moved to New York, she became obsessed with Muddy Waters, Mississippi Fred McDowell, and the folky, forlorn Bentonia blues of Skip James.

Raitt played her own hybrid, bluesy-rock anthems at the blues clubs in Boston in her twenties, where she taught herself to play the slide guitar and caught the attention of Howlin' Wolf, Son House, and eventually Junior Wells's manager, Dick Waterman. She signed with Warner Bros. in the early seventies, and during that time experimented with different blues styles, from country-tinged covers of "Don't It Make You Want to Dance" to a gospel rendition of "Angel from Montgomery." Raitt found that she had an interest in combining folk, soul, blues, rock, pop, and country, and her nine albums during the seventies and eighties were a natural progression of this sound.

At the time, Raitt was an anomaly: a red-headed California girl with a passion for the grinding, rough-and-tough blues that had deep roots in the black community and the American South. But Raitt approached rhythm and blues with the humility of a student, studying the wailing of John Lee Hooker and the fingerstyle acoustic guitar ramblings of Lightnin' Hopkins. She practiced relentlessly, until she became known for her finger-picking, aggressive slide guitar, and fluency in genres ranging from spirituals to electric blues.

Raitt was a blues legend in her own right, touring with the Eagles, Little Feat, and Jackson Browne's band. Bonnie and the bands she played with could draw several thousand at a show, but she was not producing hits, and Warner Bros. dropped her, leaving her labelless for six difficult years. While she struggled with Warner Bros. to put out her album *Nine Lives*, which she had already fully recorded, Raitt set out to the California coastal community of Mendocino to take a break from touring and concentrate on her next album.

She wound up producing her first breakthrough album, *Nick of Time*, with the several songs that she wrote there, start to finish. "I was very clear-headed," she told *USA Today*. "My spirit was rejuvenated after the heartbreak of being dropped and having a romantic love affair fall apart in the mid-eighties." She had found a new home at Capitol Records and a sympathetic producer in Don Was. Her tenth album went to number one on the *Billboard* charts in 1989, went five times platinum, and won three Grammys, including Album of the Year.

Raitt proved that she was here to stay.

With the success of *Nick of Time*, *Luck of the Draw* (1991), and *Longing in Their Hearts* (1994)—all multiple Grammy winners—Raitt focused on giving back to the community of musicians that had helped her grow. She partnered with the Rhythm and Blues Foundation, raising money to help pioneering artists negotiate royalties and receive medical and financial assistance. She also created the Bonnie Raitt Guitar Project, providing guitars to underprivileged kids in underserved communities. And, she has spent the last two decades actively involved in philanthropy, while releasing a steadfast stream of albums from *Fundamental* to *Silver Lining* to her 2016 release, *Dig In Deep*.

Some think that the guitar is a man's game—those "thinkers" haven't seen Raitt play. In her late sixties, Raitt can still give 'em something to talk about, whether it's the funky jazz- and reggae-tinged tracks of *Slipstream* or her latest country-meets-blues songs about heartbreak. She's still the ruling queen of blues, and her electric slide playing is her proclamation that keeps us all free. ∎

BETTY DAVIS

JESSICA CARE MOORE

ILLUSTRATION BY JULIE WINEGARD

It was the mid-nineties and I was backstage after a concert at popular NYC live music venue Wetlands, when drummer Ahmir Thompson, aka Questlove from the Roots, told me I smiled with Betty Davis teeth. He then followed up with a very important question. "You know which Betty Davis I'm talking about, right?"

I was a poet on the black rock music and spoken word scene in New York City, in search of ways to push boundaries with language, instead of structure. Inspired by Alice Walker, who made a sojourn to central Florida to find and honor the unmarked grave of the Harlem Renaissance's Zora Neale Hurston, I was always digging up unsung, unknown feminine architects of history with hopes of telling their story.

So I began to research the music and life of the woman who shared my smile. I had to search past the popular white actress Bette Davis and the song that references her eyes to finally find pieces of this funk rock icon and her tremendous music offerings online. I was forced to go through her trumpeter husband, Miles Davis, from whom she would inherit her name. Such obscurity is the case for many pioneering women who

defy the social norms of their time and overwhelm the patriarchal entertainment industry with one monumental kick of a right leg in red stilettos.

My curiosity led me to the growl and black scream of Betty Davis, to her timeless fishnets and blown-out afro coils wrapped around a funk that was born straight from her gut, a sonic crash into my ears. Her guttural blues sped up was made of Pittsburgh blue-collar steel, and I wanted to find this magical music woman and tell everyone who had not already sampled her that she was responsible for unloosening the tie of jazz. That she was pivotal to what became known as jazz fusion, having introduced her friend Jimi Hendrix to Miles.

Who else can hold a note while singing 'bout chitlins, celebrating the sharing of lovers from San Francisco to Detroit, and shouting out John Lee Hooker as necessary blues in one heavy breath. Her veins deep as spirituals, Betty told our collective story straight, without fear, no chaser. No feminist movement to defend her, she spit out this wide-hipped music as defiant flame with Midwest grit, and a longing for truth. Authenticity was not sexy in the seventies if you were a tall Nubian killer of beauty. Mask for no one, she spun records and men on her fingers while singin' anti-love songs.

I wanted people to know the power and honesty of Black Betty.

More importantly, I wanted them to know she was still very much alive!

Born Betty Mabry in 1945 in North Carolina, she was raised outside of Pittsburgh. She penned her first song, "I'm Going to Bake That Cake of Love," at twelve years old. A child of John Lee Hooker, BB King, and others, the curious young songwriter and NYC Fashion Institute student would grow into a stunning, tall beauty, signed to the Wilhelmina Models agency. While she was successful as a young model, Betty had a music in her body she needed to share. As Betty Mabry, she recorded "Get Ready for Betty" b/w "I'm Gonna Get My Baby Back" in 1964 for DCP International. Her single "The Cellar" referenced the cool, artsy music and fashion scene she worked and socialized in. She penned the hit "Uptown (to Harlem)" for the Chamber Brothers in 1967. In 1968, when she was still involved with Hugh Masekela, she recorded several songs for Columbia Records, with Masekela doing the arrangements.

In 1968 she married Miles Davis, planting the seeds of his future musical explorations by introducing the trumpeter to psychedelic rock guitarist Hendrix and funk innovator Sly Stone. The Miles Davis record *Filles de Kilimanjaro* (1968) includes a song named after her, and her gorgeous photo adorns the album cover. Betty returned to Columbia's 52nd St. Studios to record a series of demo tracks, with Miles and Teo Macero producing. At least five songs were taped during those sessions, three of which were Mabry originals, two of which were covers of Cream and Creedence Clearwater Revival songs. Finally, in 2016 for the compilation *Betty Davis: The Columbia Years*, 1968–1969, these songs were released by Seattle's Light in the Attic Records.

Davis began unleashing her provocative energy

inside her music and through her high-boots and rebellious fashion choices. Despite critical acclaim, she received backlash from the new black middle class and conservative, racist white audiences who were only comfortable with male sexual domination through the likes of Mick Jagger or even her close friend Stone, and who could not handle the aggressive, sexual confidence of a black woman claiming her eminent power on and off stage. Her labels asked her to tone down her everything, and she always refused.

Davis was quoted in an early *Jet* magazine interview: "I'm very aggressive on stage and men usually don't like aggressive women. They usually like submissive women, or women that pretend to be submissive."

After the end of her short marriage with Davis, Betty moved to London to pursue her modeling career. She wrote music while in the UK and returned to the US around 1972 with the intention of recording songs with Santana. Instead, she recorded her own songs with a group of West Coast funk musicians. Her first record, *Betty Davis*, was released in 1973. She had two minor hits on the *Billboard* R&B chart: "If I'm in Luck I Might Get Picked Up" and "Shut Off the Lights." Davis released two more studio albums, *They Say I'm Different* (1974) and her major label debut on Island Records, *Nasty Gal* (1975).

Her music wasn't about commercial appeal; it was about defying the times. It was about a woman creating a space for women that did not exist. What Betty Davis became for us was a symbol of survival and early womanist politics through the arts. In nineties music scenes across the country, women artists were reclaiming their right to rock unapologetically on microphones. As a woman in a male-dominated poetry and music scene in Detroit and NYC, I would find my voice often in unison with the groundbreakers who experimented with sound outside of traditional rhythm and blues and hip-hop. Controlling our images and how we claimed our goddess stance on stage was just as important as *what* we were saying. We were the metaphorical daughters of Betty Davis. In 2004 I produced my first tribute concert to Betty Davis, Black WOMEN Rock! We packed the Variety Playhouse in Atlanta. Betty Davis called us, and she wanted us to know she was alive. The fact that Davis became a recluse for the second half of her life is the reason we must continue to create new spaces for black women to play, sing, write, and be celebrated in rock and roll, now. How did she outwit an early rock-and-roll death? How do we, her rock daughters, survive, feed our children, and continue to create in an industry that allows only one or two of us to hold court and shine at the same time? How do you balance being from the future in the past, Betty Davis?

A few years ago I received a handwritten card from Betty Davis thanking me for keeping her music alive. The reality is, we exist because she rocked for us—first. ∎

SUZI QUATRO

KATHERINE TURMAN

ILLUSTRATION BY ANNE MUNTGES

A 1966 photo of Susan Kay Quatro in her first band, the all-girl Pleasure Seekers, finds sixteen-year-old Suzi in spangly minidress and black vinyl boots, already owning a tough chick 'tude. Her shaggy dark hair and chin-up defiance were clearly beginning to crystalize into a confident, multifaceted talent that would take her beyond her family band. Suzi Quatro had little template to follow as a charismatic rock-and-roll frontwoman—save Elvis. Playing bass guitar and sporting a tomboy-next-door toughness, Quatro created the mold out of which sprung a line of iconic rock chicks, including Joan Jett, Chrissie Hynde, and KT Tunstall, whose 2007 *Drastic Fantastic* album photo pays direct homage to Quatro. Big in Japan, Europe, and elsewhere, ironically this pioneer became known at home not for her glam jams but for her art-imitating-life role of Leather Tuscadero on the sitcom *Happy Days*. She's the rocker who played a rocker on TV. Quatro released at least sixteen studio albums between 1973 and 2017, including a 1986 cast album for her starring role in the London production of *Annie Get Your Gun*. In 2014 *Suzi Quatro: The Girl from Detroit City*, a four-CD anthology with eighty-two songs and a fifty-four-page booklet, marked her fiftieth year in the music business.

While Quatro is a raison d'etre to some musicians—male and female—she mostly remains a cult figure for American music fans. Film music consultant Kevin Laffey surmises why: "I think American radio, et al., weren't ready for an independent, hard rock chick in leather, although her male equivalents were having hits in similar styles at the time—David Essex, T. Rex, Sweet, Gary Glitter, etc. Carol Kaye notwithstanding, women bass players in rock were rare if not non-existent before her."

Born in Detroit to an Italian dad and Hungarian mother, Quatro grew up in a deeply musical family. Little Suzi's first onstage appearance was with her dad's jazz band, the Art Quatro Trio, playing bongos. Her three sisters and brother all played instruments. She studied classical piano and percussion and by fourteen, in 1964, she'd started on bass. Self-taught, and with no real female role models, she admired James Jamerson, a prominent session bassist for Motown, and Elvis. Her 1957 Fender Precision bass allowed her to join sisters Patti, Nancy, and Arlene in the talented, darkly cool, garagey Pleasure Seekers. Suzi quickly became the frontwoman, and the

PLAYLIST

"Can the Can," 1973,
Suzi Quatro

"48 Crash," 1973,
Suzi Quatro

"Devil Gate Drive," 1974,
Quatro

"The Wild One, 1974,
Quatro

"Stumblin' In" 1978,"
If You Knew Suzi . . .

"Rock Hard," 1980,
Rock Hard

"Doin' What Comes
Naturally," 1986, *Annie
Get Your Gun*—*1986
London Cast*

"Back to the Drive," 2006,
Back to the Drive

"Strict Machine," 2011,
In the Spotlight

caught the attention of British producer–label head Mickie Most. Signing to Most's RAK Records and working with the songwriting and producing team of Nicky Chinn and Mike Chapman, renowned for their big-glam pop sound and irresistible sing-along choruses (Sweet's "Ballroom Blitz," Toni Basil's "Mickey"), Quatro relocated to the UK in 1971.

Quatro's 1973 self-titled solo album kicks off with her powerful wail on "48 Crash," where she addresses the aging of a boy toy, a "juvenile Romeo." It ends with the dramatic, even catchier "Can the Can," with its irresistible power-pop glam-rock drumbeat and Suzi's defiant voice. Thus began her reign of chart and radio success in the UK, Europe, and Australia.

Suzi's voice, bell-clear, has a slight rasp, sometimes tinged with a lyrics-appropriate snottiness. Tough, approachable, cute but dangerous, Quatro's bold authenticity and coolness were nearly unprecedented in the early seventies. Glam was full of dudes who looked like ladies; Suzi was the rare girl in touch with her masculine side.

lineup successfully toured and recorded for seven years. They were one of the first "girl groups" signed to Mercury Records, putting out the single "Light of Love" b/w "Good Kind of Hurt," before changing the band name and style to Cradle by 1969. (In 1974, Patti would join Fanny, another pioneering all-female rock band signed to a major label.)

It was at a Cradle gig in Detroit that Suzi

In 1974's seemingly self-referential "The Wild One," she sings of being a "hammer from hell" who will own the town. The phrase "I'm a red hot fox who can take the knocks" summarizes her killer combo of looks, skill, and bravado. (The song was used in the 2010 *The Runaways* movie, with actress Kristen Stewart as Joan Jett singing the song so influential to the band and Jett.) On "Devil Gate Drive" and "Your Mamma Won't Like Me," Quatro again flips the female-male script.

Quatro appeared on the January 1975 cover of *Rolling Stone* in a story by British author-socialite Anthony Haden-Guest. The cover photo was shot from behind to emphasize her, well, leather-clad behind; with her hands defiantly on her hips, Quatro looks back over her right shoulder, straight into the camera, at once coquettish and strong.

Two years later, cast in a recurring role (seven appearances from 1977 to 1979) on TV's retro hit *Happy Days*, Suzi's portrayal of the bass-playing singer Leather Tuscadero character inspired women, titillated men, and became part of the seventies culture conversation. In the midst of Quatro's small-screen success, she scored one of her biggest hits: in 1979, her duet on the soft-rock "Stumblin' In" with Smokie lead singer Chris Norman reached number four in the US and number one in Australia. In a 2012 interview with the *Detroit Metro Times*, Quatro acknowledged her place in music history: "I was the first to be taken seriously as a female rock 'n' roll musician and singer . . . I played the boys at their own game. For everybody that came afterward, it was a little bit easier, which is good. If I have a legacy, that's what it is."

If Quatro's 1980s and '90s musical efforts, many mellower than her glam-punk roots, didn't recapture her earlier buzz, 2006's *Back to the Drive*, made when she was fifty-six, did. The album is a stunner, a potent, timeless return to Quatro's harder rock roots. Ditto her fifteenth studio album, 2011's *In the Spotlight*, along with the video for the cut "Strict Machine," directed by Victory Tischler-Blue (aka Runaways bassist Vicki Blue).

All told, Quatro has sold more than 50 million albums. In addition to her decades of acting, writing, and touring, for years the mother of two has hosted popular radio shows on BBC Radio 2. 2017 saw the release of her first novel, *The Hurricane*, whose plot sounds suspiciously autobiographical: the heroine is a standout in an all-male rock band, where "she thinks like a man but has the emotions of a woman." Quatro still gigs regularly, whether she's paired with other seventies icons or up-and-coming bands; her leather-clad legacy and independent spirit still demands, and receives, respect. ■

CHAKA KHAN

MUKTA MOHAN

ILLUSTRATION BY JULIE WINEGARD

I n the Yoruba tradition, it is believed that people live out the meanings of their names. Names are taken so seriously that they're treated almost as spirits who are looking for a physical embodiment to live out their purpose. So in 1967, when an African Baba in all white renamed Yvette Marie Stevens to Chaka Adunne Aduffe Yemoja Hodarhi Karifi, he was breathing a new destiny into her being. Yvette was a teenage girl from an artistic yet broken home on the South Side of Chicago. But Chaka was a "Woman of Fire." A few years later, she went on to take her first husband's last name, completing the identity of the icon we know as Chaka Khan. We may associate Khan with her fire-like qualities of energy and passion, but what's harder to see are the ashes underneath the flame.

While soul music of the 1960s was the voice of the civil rights movement, the early 1970s gave birth to a fusion of jazz, R&B, soul, and Afro-Cuban rhythms that came together to create a danceable rhythmic style called funk. It was the sound of black power, celebration, and sensual indulgence. And at the center of it all with her bell bottoms and big hair was Chaka Khan, the Queen of Funk.

Khan's given name "Woman of Fire" comes with two sides: the glistening energy that pops and sparks and a darker underside that burns what lies underneath. As glamorous as her life may seem, Khan has struggled throughout. Khan's parents were both alcoholics and her father was addicted to heroin. They separated when she was twelve years old and Khan ran away from home at sixteen.

When Khan was eighteen, she was spotted by two members of the band Rufus while she was performing at a club in Chicago. They asked her to join as their lead singer, and within a matter of two years, the band shot to fame with the release of the 1974 album *Rags to Rufus*, featuring the Stevie Wonder-produced juggernauts "Tell Me Something Good" and "You Got the Love," which Khan co-wrote. It was just after the civil rights movement, and there was hope that the dust would settle to create an equal and integrated society. And then here was Rufus, a multiracial band with a larger-than-life frontwoman who not only belted messages of empowerment and pleasure with ferocity but also co-wrote and arranged songs with the band. Rufus's catchy, soulful music and Chaka Khan's star power catapulted the band to the top of the charts, earning them two platinum albums and four gold albums within a span of five

PLAYLIST

WITH RUFUS:

"Tell Me Something Good," 1974, *Rags to Rufus*

"You Got the Love," 1974, *Rags to Rufus*

WITH RUFUS FEATURING CHAKA KHAN:

"Hollywood," 1977, *Ask Rufus*

"Egyptian Song," 1977, *Ask Rufus*

SOLO:

"I'm Every Woman," 1978, *Chaka*

"Disrespectful," 2007, *Funk This*

years, from 1975 to 1979. They even renamed the band to Rufus featuring Chaka Khan in 1975, releasing an album of the same name.

Khan's powerful and complex vocal range coupled with her stunning looks and confidence caused her to be placed on the cover of magazines without the rest of the band. She wore skimpy outfits that showed off her toned body, and a megawatt smile complemented the furs, feathers, and fringe she'd wear on stage. She was deemed a sex symbol but was also graceful and chic. Her popularity placed pressure on the other band members, who were starting to be seen as her backing band rather than as collaborators. At first the band delighted in the commercial success they were achieving, but tension behind the scenes started to increase as Khan received more of the spotlight.

In 1977, the band released *Ask Rufus*, which gave each musician a chance to push their own artistic boundaries. It's quieter and more mature than their previous albums, and Khan's voice was given room to shine through the seductive jazz arrangements. On this album, she moves beyond the themes of pleasure and fun that typically marked her music, offering a critical analysis of the strive for fame in the song "Hollywood." She also traces her African ancestry and personal identity with "Egyptian Song." *Ask Rufus* went

platinum, but lineup changes and feuds started to break apart the synergy that the band once shared. They released three albums without Khan while she worked on solo material.

Although Khan mastered funk while working with Rufus, to pigeonhole her into one genre would be a discredit to the range of her voice and songwriting abilities. She had a successful career making disco, jazz, soul, and even rap albums and is the recipient of ten Grammys. In 1978, Khan released a solo album called *Chaka* featuring the hit song "I'm Every Woman." It crossed into disco and established Khan's career outside of Rufus. Shortly after, she worked on the Quincy Jones–produced Rufus featuring Chaka Khan album *Masterjam* while also recording more solo material. A few years later, Khan's sixth studio album, *I Feel for You* (1984), went platinum with multiple hit songs, including the title track, which was written by Prince and featured a harmonica solo by Stevie Wonder. In the introductory rap, Grandmaster Melle Mel repeats Chaka Khan's name over and over, a chant that made her name iconic. Since the 1980s, Khan has continued to release albums sporadically, including *The Woman I Am* (1992), which was dedicated to her friend and jazz legend Miles Davis, and *Funk This* (2007), featuring a collaboration with Mary J. Blige on the song "Disrespectful."

On the surface, Khan was a successful, self-assured, fun-loving party girl, but internally she struggled with the loneliness of being the only woman in Rufus and of constantly touring. She turned to drugs and alcohol, and struggled with alcohol, heroin, and cocaine addiction for years. She started a nonprofit organization called the Chaka Khan Foundation that assists women and girls at risk with an emphasis on education and autism. In 2004, her son, Damien Holland, was arrested for killing an aspiring young rapper who was living in Khan's family home. Khan dedicated a few years to court dates defending her son while simultaneously recording new music. A few years later, she gained custody of her granddaughter because of drug use in the family. After Prince passed away of an overdose in 2016, Khan checked herself into rehab for addiction to the opioid fentanyl, which is found in prescription painkillers.

Chaka Khan's vocal range and songwriting talent made her one of the most iconic women in the music industry. She's pushed through her pain to make music that we can all dance to and belt out with either heartache or joy. When the Yoruba priest renamed Yvette to Chaka, he probably saw a spark waiting to live out its full potential. With his hands rubbed together, he may have blown a little heat on the ember. But it has always been Khan's energy coming alive. ■

EMMYLOU HARRIS

KANDIA CRAZY HORSE

ILLUSTRATION BY JULIE WINEGARD

There is a Queen of Americana and her name is Emmylou Harris. Sometimes it seems the format was invented to enshrine Harris, so entwined is she in Americana's self-image. The roots-leaning music press loves to feature her in photographs gracefully aging beneath a mane of silver hair. She performs live with questers of American song from Neil Young to her frequent sonic partner Rodney Crowell. Her relationship with Gram Parsons is the tragic romance that birthed a nation of erudite singer-songwriters, even as she has firmly established her own musical career. Honoring her foremothers, she waved the flag for Dolly Parton and the women of the Carter Family, and then went on to inspire the likes of Alison Krauss, Tift Merritt, Rosie Flores, and Swedish sister act First Aid Kit.

Born in Birmingham, Alabama, in 1947 and raised as a wandering military brat, Emmylou Harris was not especially musical. By her own account, she was a bookish, dateless good girl who played saxophone in the high school marching band. She was close with her tight-knit family, eschewing anti–Vietnam War protest to honor her father; much later in life, she would share her home in Nashville with her mother Eugenia and older brother Walter (and a dog rescue organization named Bonaparte's Retreat). Harris began to demonstrate an adventurous inner world after she fell in love with the romance of Bob Dylan and Joan Baez. She joined the famed Greenwich Village folk scene after writing the genre's Johnny Appleseed of song, Pete Seeger, about whether she had the right in her relative privilege to sing about the downtrodden of the earth.

Harris found the New York City milieu in its waning days. She lived rough with young musician husband Tom Slocum and baby daughter Hallie in a Little Italy flat at the point when the city had yielded youth cultural pride of place to the innovative psychedelia emanating from San Francisco and the coming rise of Los Angeles country-rock. Still, she closed the decade with her recording debut, *Gliding Bird* (1969), for the small label Jubilee, sounding like a sweet woman who had absorbed the high soprano trills of early Joni Mitchell and the ringing clarity of her scene's female icon, Judy Collins. Harris would come to disown the album and spend the next three years bouncing between Manhattan, Nashville (which proved a professional washout), and her family's home area of DC/Maryland/Virginia, working with her Angel Band and the Capital's leading folk outfit, the Seldom Scene.

It was while plying her trade in DC that ex-Byrd and Flying Burrito Brother Chris Hillman discovered Harris—a fortuitous sighting that led to the most important creative partnership of her life.

She was enlisted to sing harmony and play rhythm guitar for two groundbreaking albums by Hillman's erstwhile bandmate Gram Parsons. The two Southerners relocated to Los Angeles. The audience for Parsons's vision of "Cosmic American Music" on his solo efforts *GP* and *Grievous Angel* (both 1973) was initially small, but their duets became as legendary in time as those of George Jones and Tammy Wynette, Dolly Parton and Porter Wagoner, and Johnny Cash and June Carter Cash. Parsons and Harris pointed a new way forward for the country genre.

Parsons died from an overdose in Joshua Tree, California, in 1973. Harris, who had served as his hungry acolyte, gaining a true appreciation for country music compared to the previous winking display she'd made on *Gliding Bird*'s Hank Williams cover "I Saw the Light," was left professionally and personally unmoored. She was rescued by a rare friendship with her fellow LA country-rock pioneer feminist Linda Ronstadt, who recommended her to Warner Bros., resulting in a deal that would show what the maturing artist Harris had learned from her Georgia-bred mentor. Starting with 1975's *Pieces of the Sky* (working with future husband Brian Ahern at the knobs), Harris released a slew of albums through the rest of the decade that would sound more traditionally country than much of Nashville's then current commercial product. Despite coming out of the often mistrusted California country-rock scene—*Pieces of the Sky* was cut in a house in Beverly Hills—Harris was embraced by country audiences. She covered hillbilly gems from the Louvin Brothers, Buck Owens, and Felice and Boudleaux Bryant, as well as standout track "Queen of the Silver Dollar" by Music City renegade Shel Silverstein, on the releases *Elite Hotel* (1976), *Luxury Liner* (1977),

Quarter Moon in a Ten-Cent Town (1978), and *Blue Kentucky Girl* (1979). She was celebrated for her ongoing collaborations with men of country music's Mount Rushmore, including Willie Nelson, Waylon Jennings, and Johnny Cash, and was adored by "Father of Bluegrass" Bill Monroe. Harris is pretty darn rare in that she has given equal shine to the oeuvres of female songwriters such as Parton (her co-songbird in the famed Trio projects with Ronstadt), Jean Ritchie, Anna and Kate McGarrigle, Kate Wolf, Sandy Denny, Julie Miller, Carole King, and Gillian Welch. In the 1990s she helped promote a feminist vision for popular music by performing on the Lilith Fair tour.

Emmylou entered the 1980s as a standard bearer for true twang amid the waning fad of disco country and the eventual rise of New Traditionalist Left Coast cowboys like Dwight Yoakam. Leading her nonpareil Hot Band featuring pickers like Crowell, her stature as Americana diva was assured by her inclusion in the Band's 1978 farewell concert film *The Last Waltz*, singing "Evangeline" (the title of her 1981 album, which highlighted the Robbie Robertson song). She relocated to Nashville and served as president of the Country Music Association, but her career and unknowable interior landscape remained haunted by Gram Parsons. By the new millennium, Harris would style herself as the "keeper of his flame," overseeing and performing on a Parsons tribute album produced by Ethan Johns with such followers as Ryan Adams, Raul Malo, and Beck, and lifting her longtime self-imposed

PLAYLIST

"If I Could Only Win Your Love," 1975, *Pieces of the Sky*

"Queen of the Silver Dollar," 1975, *Pieces of the Sky*

"Boulder to Birmingham," 1975, *Pieces of the Sky*

"Pancho and Lefty," 1976, *Luxury Liner*

"Even Cowgirls Get the Blues," 1979, *Blue Kentucky Girl*

ban on discussing her time with him. She never stopped airing out Gram's self-penned compositions nor covering country classics he had gifted to her consciousness.

Most critics count 1995's *Wrecking Ball*, with its atmospheric production from Daniel Lanois (U2, Peter Gabriel), as her masterpiece and credit it with causing Harris to transcend the roots briarpatch. But a far more arresting collection was accomplished between the poles of her 1975 ("Boulder to Birmingham") and 2011 ("The Road") Parsons homages: *The Ballad of Sally Rose* (1985). The concept album, produced by ex-husband Paul Kennerley, is notable not just because it's a thinly veiled song cycle delving into the heart of Harris's embryonic period as a country-rock star with Parsons—*Sally Rose* was her road alias—but because it took seven years for this artist prone to covers to write. *Sally Rose* was the first Harris album since 1969 to feature more than two of her own compositions. It is distinguished by its insight into one of the more mystical creative pairings of late modern times and, even more so, by the fact that it triggers conversation with one of the oldest traditions of American song. Harris's sonic alter ego is a Lakota woman born on the road and reborn through her encounter with the Singer (Gram's stand-in). Perhaps unsurprisingly Sally Rose—narrating a doomed romance between a Native American and a white man—was deemed a commercial failure yet shows the brave maverick Harris is. It is because of the creation of this riveting elegy of a "country opera" that Harris acts as a role model for this author-singer-songwriter of Cosmic Americana, for one.

The persistent impact of Harris's and Parsons's ethereal collaborations is perhaps best summed up by the finest song from the postmodern country aspirants First Aid Kit. Klara and Johanna Söderberg's "Emmylou" reifies that some voices were simply meant to sing together: "I'll be your Emmylou / I'll be your June / You'll be my Gram and my Johnny too . . . " ■

STEVIE NICKS

KANDIA CRAZY HORSE

ILLUSTRATION BY LINDSEY BAILEY

Stevie Nicks was a pioneering prophet of the New Age, informed by the hippie sub-culture's nineteenth-century neo-Romantic and German roots in Europe as much as by Janis Joplin's remix of the freak power of earlier Afri-cana mamas like Sophie Tucker and Eva Tanguay. Emerging from the wake of Joplin, the Jefferson Airplane's Grace Slick, and Fairport Convention's Sandy Denny, she eventually began to ply her rev-elations amidst a decade marked by Laurel Canyon ladies, rock heroes, druggies, alternative prophets, sexual revolutionaries, progressive politicos, liberated gays, and cult killers. With her steel-in-velvet lyrical perspective, signature hard bleat of a voice, and mys-tical visual sense, Nicks is the most enduring singer-spiritualist of rock and roll's season of the witch.

Stephanie Lynn Nicks was born in Phoenix, Arizona, on May 26, 1948. By four years old, she had learned to sing duets under the tutelage of her grandfather Aaron Jess "A.J." Nicks Sr., a country singer. Employing the Goya guitar that was a six-teenth-birthday gift, Nicks wrote her first song, "I've Loved and I've Lost, and I'm Sad but Not Blue." As an adolescent, she lived in a private world of sound centered around her stereo and early folk-rock group Changing Times. Nicks met her future romantic and sonic partner Lindsey Buckingham at a religious meeting when she joined him by adding harmonies

to the Mamas and the Papas' "California Dreamin'." They would continue to meld their voices together in blues-rock band Fritz, the duo Buckingham Nicks, and finally, in 1975, Fleetwood Mac.

Stevie Nicks became a revered California dream girl as soon as she came to wider prominence with Fleetwood Mac. With poetic lyrics rife with myths and symbols, her early work, like "Rhiannon," which she described as "a song about a Welsh witch," proved hypnotic and alluring to audiences. She came to stand for the earthy Isla de California, enspelling her global listeners with songs about an alternate reality. Women empowered by the sixties who quested in pursuit of "crystal visions" dominated Nicks's lyrical concerns perhaps even more than her romances. Her songs' arrangements tended to be resolved into a primal union of Afro-Celt sounds and loping Native American rhythms by her primary col-laborator Buckingham—when the gossamer traces of faerie were not present. The irrepressible twang in Nicks's hard voice caused her "Landslide" to become not just the standard that launched myriad millennial modern country groups and countless auditions for *The Voice* but also a favorite cover for urban alterna-tive artists looking to stretch their sonic wings. There is a late 1970s black-and-white photograph of Nicks in a black chiffon dress, grinning alongside San Fran-cisco Sound superstar and impresario Sly Stone—she composed her most enduring song, "Dreams," in his black velvet-upholstered room at Sausalito's Record Plant studio—that explains why many fans, such as this writer, identify as Fleetwood Black. Nicks's self-fashioning (realized with co-conspirator designer Margi Kent) as an amalgam of Joplin, Jimi Hendrix with his technicolor dreamcoats, and an anonymous Romani girl in ruffled skirts would decades later inspire an annual drag-and-sound event in Manhattan, the Night of 1,000 Stevies. Her flowy frock uniform transcends fads and makes her a fashion icon to many, including designer Anna Sui, and of course the fans who twirl at her concerts.

The more mundane sphere of the 1970s and '80s rock elite was pruriently preoccupied with the gold dust woman's rock-and-roll romances and friendships with Buckingham, Fleetwood Mac drummer Mick Fleetwood, the Eagles' Don Henley and Joe Walsh, and Tom Petty—with one notable exception. Prince, who inspired and contributed synth to Nicks's 1983 track "Stand Back," crucially remade himself in Los Angeles largely in thrall to Joni Mitchell and Nicks. He clearly copied her usage of lace, leg warmers, and ruched pantalettes. Although Prince flaunted his sexuality way more than Nicks ever did, he seemed to concur with what Stevie would tell *Rolling Stone* in 2002: "Personally, I think that sexy is keeping yourself mysterious." As an icon of gender benders, Nicks represents a curious imbalance: she willingly became a wage slave of feminine drudgery (i.e., a waitress) to support Buckingham's creativity so he didn't have to sully his bohemian poses. Yet at the same time, her vital appropriation of rock's most masculine volume via her voice—listen to Nicks and Led Zeppelin's

Robert Plant as a comparison in channeling Joplin—caused her to break out as Fleetwood Mac's frontwoman. And in pursuing her solo projects beginning with *Bella Donna* (1981) and *The Wild Heart* (1983), Stevie fostered an all-muses atmosphere, clannish in leather and lace and trading siren calls across such tracks as "Edge of Seventeen" and "If Anyone Falls."

Following the 2016 critically fêted reissue of her solo landmarks, Nicks launched a national tour. She has claimed she will record no more due to the state of the record business, but the "Sisters of the Moon" who follow her will not likely stand for the silencing of Nicks's voice. Long before the birth of Lady Gaga's Little Monsters, Nicks inspired a fierce following. Many of her fans would become musicians themselves. Her acolyte Sheryl Crow produced Nicks's *Trouble in Shangri-La* (2001). The case for Bella Donna Stevie Nicks enduring in a long season of Madonna clones has been made by her unacknowledged heiress Jenny Lewis, the Laurel Canyon Gold Dust Woman of the Aughts. Calexico wrote a 2003 song about the queen of desert rockers, "Not Even Stevie Nicks," and surely this description of witches from the 1968 manifesto from the Women's International Terrorist Conspiracy from Hell (WITCH) fits the siren of the Golden West like a velvet glove: "groovy, courageous, aggressive, intelligent, nonconformist, explorative, curious, independent, sexually liberated, revolutionary." ∎

PLAYLIST

WITH BUCKINGHAM NICKS:

"Long Distance Winner," 1973, *Buckingham Nicks*

WITH FLEETWOOD MAC:

"Rhiannon," 1975, *Fleetwood Mac*

"Silver Springs," 1997, *The Dance*

SOLO:

"Edge of Seventeen," 1981, *Bella Donna*

"Stand Back," 1983, *The Wild Heart*

DONNA SUMMER

ANN POWERS

ILLUSTRATION BY LINDSEY BAILEY

Donna Summer was a category basher seemingly put on earth to defeat listeners' preconceptions. She rose to prominence within disco, the musical milieu many feel was the most frivolous and tacky pop ever produced; yet her hits were consistently innovative, addressed serious themes, and rode on passionate, nuanced performances. Her longstanding collaboration with producers Giorgio Moroder and Pete Bellotte coincided with a time when women vocalists were often overshadowed by their studio Svengalis; yet once she achieved fame, Summer wrote or co-wrote most of her material, following her own muse in many different directions. Her legend was based around sex, or at least the sound of it, after the cosmically pornographic "Love to Love You Baby" sent her, Moroder and Bellotte, and the Casablanca record label into the stratosphere in 1975; yet far from embodying the hedonistic lifestyle of the free-love 1970s, she was a serial monogamist and mother who was born, and born again, in the Christian faith. Her gospelized singing style and African American identity have led to her being categorized as an R&B artist; yet she began her career in theater and rock, and remained a restless explorer of styles ranging from country to new wave to European synth-pop. Aretha Franklin influenced her, but so did David Bowie and Bruce Springsteen.

Summer's distinctive gift for blending soul sincerity with rock theatricalism (and pop glamour) is often attributed to her grounding in theater. Born in 1948 and raised in a large working-class Boston family, Summer became known on the local worship-service circuit as "the girl with the voice that can make you cry." She soon left the confines of the church, however, to try her luck in the theaters and clubs of New York City. A friendship with songwriter Paul Jabara led her to try out for a touring production of the countercultural smash *Hair*. The musical took her to Germany, where she enjoyed a sense of artistic and personal freedom she hadn't experienced at home. She married an Austrian artist and had her first child. She was working as a background singer in Munich when she met Moroder and Bellotte, whose first album with her, 1974's *Lady of the Night*, was eclectic in the spirit of the era that made stars of Bowie, Stevie Wonder, and Joni Mitchell. Its cuts ranged from the Cher-like story song "The Hostage" (a hit in the Netherlands) to the country-flavored "Born to Die" to the title track, whose girl group stylings celebrated a sex worker—a foreshadowing of Summer's biggest commercial success, the 1979 album *Bad Girls*.

The Italian Moroder and English Bellotte found a brilliant foil in Summer, whose American can-do spirit made her game for any role they devised together. In 1976 she told reporter Joe Esposito that the nonverbal pleasure cascade Summer devised for

"Love to Love You Baby" evolved out of some jovial studio banter: discussing the similarly expressive French hit "Je T'Aime/Moi Non Plus," Summer put on her best Mae West drawl and said she was ready to release her own blue record. Pete Bellotte said it wouldn't fit her image, a provocation that was enough to make Summer insist. In fact, "Love to Love You Baby" utterly refashioned Summer's image, making her "The Queen of Love," a title she fulfilled on five subsequent albums. "Well," she told *Ebony* magazine in 1977, by which time she'd become the official Aphrodite of the booming disco subculture, "you have to get people's attention some kind of way."

Disco depended on female voices to convey the emotions unleashed by the enmeshing beats and overwhelming melodies. Many great artists emerged or found second homes within its dance palaces. The girl group Patti LaBelle and the Blue Belles became the glorious sci-fi funk trio Labelle. Diana Ross, already a superstar, found new vitality in brawny hits like "I'm Coming Out" and "Upside Down." Journeywomen like Gloria Gaynor and Martha Wash (of the Weather Girls) claimed iconicity with enduring anthems "I Will Survive" and "It's Raining Men." For most of these women, disco was a rocket ship that sometimes felt like a segregated bus, with white male producers hailed as the geniuses steering up front, and African American singers providing the power of the ride in the back. Donna Summer became disco's enduring and transcendent star in part because her will, grit, and luck allowed her to stand side by side with her collaborators at the soundboard.

The luck part came from that journey to Europe she took as a young dreamer. Abroad, her eclectic taste and adventurousness were welcomed, instead of confounding the categories that often kept black and white artists in separate bins in American record stores. Moroder and Bellotte recognized that Summer's combination of style, voice, and brains was one in a million, and respected her enough to welcome her into their work as a peer. By the time *Bad Girls* became a number-one album on the *Billboard* charts, Summer was writing the bulk of her own material, including two of that album's major hits, the defiant title track and the wistfully romantic "Dim All the Lights."

Summer never got stuck within disco the way many of its superstars did. In 1979, she climbed another mountain by releasing "Enough Is Enough," a duet with Barbra Streisand that put her on equal footing with mainstream pop's most celebrated vocalist. And her last hits for Casablanca, like "Hot Stuff," had a rock edge that pointed the way toward a new era. She did, however, have to litigate her way out, suing Casablanca in 1980 after she and label honcho Neil Bogart butted heads over her music's direction. Disco was becoming a joke by then, and Summer refused to play the role of a punchline. "I felt like Marie Antoinette or Joan of Arc—great women of their time who had to deal with ridicule and misunderstanding," she told a reporter after winning the lawsuit.

Free from the dance floor's fantasy boudoir, Summer built a new sonic mythology. Albums like 1980's *The Wanderer* and 1984's *Cats without Claws* aren't generally acknowledged as masterpieces of rock's new wave—probably because Summer was African American, and African American artists not named Prince were still generally labeled R&B. In

PLAYLIST

"Love to Love You Baby," 1975, *Love to Love You Baby*

"Bad Girls," 1979, *Bad Girls*

"Cold Love," single, 1980, available on *The Wanderer*

"She Works Hard for the Money," 1983, *She Works Hard for the Money*

I'm a Fire," 2008, *Crayons*

fact, these discs belong next to Blondie's *Parallel Lines* and Pat Benatar's *Crimes of Passion* as classics that challenge rock's idea of itself. Ever restless, Summer explored reggae and African rhythms, pushed her upper range until she sounded like Kate Bush, and shouted out the chorus to "Cold Love"—a song that "sizzles like a block of dry ice," according to *Rolling Stone* scribe Dave Marsh. These daring moves have been lost to time partly because they didn't find a place on the radio, where Summer had dominated for so long; neither rock stations nor urban stations would play them. Summer found more commercial success, and eventually a comfortable home, with inspirational tracks like "Forgive Me," which expressed her renewed Christian faith and brought her back to her first musical love, gospel.

Summer continued to record throughout the 1980s, eventually slowing her pace as she devoted more time to raising her three daughters. (Her second husband, Bruce Sudano, was a frequent musical collaborator on her later albums.) Her many creative selves sometimes butted up against each other. Rumors surfaced in the mid-1980s that she had called the HIV/AIDS epidemic then ravaging the gay community a form of divine retribution. Summer always denied this, issuing a formal apology to the activist group ACT-UP in 1989 and suing *New York* magazine for libel when an article refueled the rumor in 1991. By 2008, when she released her last album, *Crayons*, Summer had fully embraced her role as doyenne of the gay disco: "Keep on screaming that you want your diva / I've always told you I'd never leave you," she wails on "The Queen Is Back."

Tragically, this hypermobile queen of so many scenes was back for only a few years. Summer died in 2012 of lung cancer. Her legacy lives on in the music of her daughter, Amanda Sudano, whose duo with her husband, Abner Ramirez, Johnnyswim, blends folk, rock, soul, and blues into an uncategorizable sound. And it survives within the spirit of every artist who finds, on the dance floor or in the studio, a place to wander and set herself free. ■

"PUNK IS MY GENDER"

By the mid-1970s, the Summer of Love had turned into the winter of our discontent. Watergate, the oil crisis, and the flaccid solos of cock rock had soured the American audience. Economic disparity, labor disputes, and the pomp of prog paralyzed England. The days of singing about kids in love were over; the black-leather-clad, all-teenage girl band the Runaways proclaimed themselves the "kids in hate" over pissed-off guitars and thundering drums.

A generation that had witnessed the failure of flower power turned to the raw power of a new sound and style. Evolving out of the raunchy put-on of glam, punk rock took its name from a middle-English term for catamites and strumpets, faggots and whores. Punk thrust a middle finger at the overemphasis on instrumental mastery that had sapped the crude energy out of pop and rock. It ripped to shreds conventional beauty standards and the sexist division of labor whereby female groupies serviced male rock gods. Abrasive and alienated, punk is the cry of emasculation, the roar of the outsider. It's Wendy O. Williams, taking a chainsaw to your television set. It's the all-dyke punk band Tribe 8, mock castrating a gang rapist on stage.

Wherever punk sprouted, women were front and center: in London, Siouxsie, the Slits, X-Ray Spex, and the Raincoats; in New York, Patti Smith and Blondie; in LA, the Runaways, X, Castration Squad, and the Bags; in San Francisco, the Avengers and Frightwig; in Athens, Georgia, Pylon and the B-52s; in Germany, Nina Hagen.

True to its etymology, punk offered a shelter and an outlet for queers. From the beginning, its pioneers have embraced androgyny and gender outlawry. Birthed in the sexual demimonde of Andy Warhol's Factory, the Velvet Underground featured the Teutonic singer Nico and Maureen "Moe" Tucker, who pounded standing toms with mallets, as well as the debauched and debased Lou Reed, who would go on to turn the phrase "he was a she" into a Top 40 hook. Iggy Pop sliced away at his flesh and just wanted to be your dog, whatever gender "you" were. Wayne County shouted "Fuck Off" as she became Jayne County. Patti Smith wore a tie in the Robert Mapplethorpe photo on the cover of her debut album *Horses* and sang about a beach where "women love other women."

For four decades and counting, punk has defied categories and labels. It's the Babel beyond binaries. In 2017, on the artists' panel of a conference about music and politics in Seattle, Meredith Graves, frontwoman for the band Perfect Pussy and MTV host, said it best: "Punk is my gender."

PATTI SMITH

SOLVEJ SCHOU

ILLUSTRATION BY ANNE MUNTGES

Sociologist Donna Gaines once proclaimed: "Music is the kids' religion." A musician, a song, an album, and a performance can inspire faith, devotion, and even catharsis like the most sacred of prayers and sermons. In the case of rock-and-roll high priestess, visual artist, and writer Patti Smith, fans have worshipped her for decades. Her New York City–steeped songs redefined modern rock and paved the way for punk. Her more than a dozen books of philosophical poetry and prose, including the lyrical *The Coral Sea* and award-winning memoirs *Just Kids* and *M Train*, have cemented her reputation as a literary heavyweight. Smith has thrummed with sorrow, rage, and joy on eleven studio albums, starting with her 1975 debut opus *Horses*. For more than forty years, she's also been a shamanistic performer, thrusting her raspy voice to the heavens and dancing barefoot, spitting and spinning on stage.

But back in 1966, at age nineteen, Patricia Lee Smith was just a glimmer of the legendary artist she would become. Raised a Jehovah's Witness while living in her lower-middle-class family's laundry room in rural New Jersey, she worked summers in a factory and attended a teachers' college. She was scrappy and wire-thin, with a lazy left eye and beatnik black long hair. She was fiercely dedicated to writers (Arthur Rimbaud, Charles Baudelaire, William Blake, Jean Genet), art (Diego Rivera, Frida Kahlo, Pablo Picasso), and music (James Brown, Little Richard, John Lennon, Bob Dylan). That year, Smith became pregnant, and then gave up her baby for adoption. She fled Jersey for the dark, sexual, and unfettered urban wilderness of NYC, where she met curly-haired photographer Robert Mapplethorpe—a misfit like her who became her longtime friend and she his muse. In New York, as protests over the Vietnam War dominated headlines, poetry and power chords sowed the seeds for *Horses*. Her ten studio albums that came after were all propelled by Smith's visceral, no-holds-barred lyrics about survival and liberation amid trauma, hardship, and loss.

In the early seventies, NYC's downtown was marinated in beer and piss; that grit fed into Smith's words and music. She gained a following with her freeform chapbooks, such as *Seventh Heaven* and *Witt*. She also painted, drew, and wrote for rock magazines including *Rolling Stone* and *Creem*. She started to perform her poems in the East Village with guitarist Lenny Kaye pounding out car crash electric feedback behind her. On the B-side of her first single, "Piss Factory," a 1974 jazz-rock spoken piece recorded at Jimi Hendrix's studio Electric Lady, Smith drawls about being a moral schoolgirl and hardworking "asshole" who escapes a factory filled with women she says—in her own vivid way—have no teeth or gums. In the song, she heads for NYC, and declares her aspirations of being a big star who's never coming back. Smith was ready to sing.

In 1975, after signing with Arista Records at almost thirty years old, Smith released *Horses*. Produced by the Velvet Underground's John Cale, the album features Jay Dee Daugherty on drums, Ivan Kral on bass, Kaye on guitar, and Richard Sohl on keyboards. "We imagined ourselves as the Sons of Liberty with a mission to preserve, protect, and project the revolutionary spirit of rock and roll," Smith writes in her 2010 National Book Award–winning *Just Kids*, a tender and passionate narrative about her early days in NYC and friendship with Mapplethorpe. Unrelenting and improvisational, with a nonconformist and spiritual raw authority, *Horses* sounded—and looked—like nothing that came before it. The album's famous black-and-white cover photo by Mapplethorpe features Smith standing alone and defiant, staring straight ahead in a white button-down shirt and black jeans, with a men's black blazer slung over her shoulder and her hair a shoulder-length shag. Smith said to a crowd of editors in 2015, of her look, "I just copied Bob Dylan and French symbolist poets," adding, with a smirk, "and Catholic schoolboys." She exuded an androgynous avant-garde swagger, the opposite of decidedly feminine rock stars, such as Linda Ronstadt, popular at the time.

"Jesus died for somebody's sins, but not mine," Smith sings bluntly, dryly, and blasphemously in her cracked East Coast twang on the slow piano and guitar intro of *Horses*' first song, "Gloria," a hybrid of her 1970 poem "Oath" and the garage stomp of Van Morrison's band Them. Speeding up with an urgent guitar strut, the song cracks open midway, and Smith's throaty vibrato fills the drawn-out call of "G-L-O-R-I-A!" "I was declaring my

existence, my right to make my own mistakes, my right to make my own choices," Smith told *Rolling Stone* in 2014. "Break It Up," about the death of Jim Morrison, soars as a howling anthem of grief. "Land" is a nine-minute punk poem that rips into the unconscious—guitars scratching and crawling—while Smith riffs on the homoerotic character "Johnny" from William Burroughs's book *The Wild Boys*. Not only did *Horses* propel the post-hippie early NYC punk scene, alongside the Ramones, Blondie, Television, and the Talking Heads; it influenced later artists, including PJ Harvey and R.E.M. Smith has continuously shown women and men—from seventies crowds at punk club CBGB to fans watching YouTube videos of her tribute to Dylan at his 2016 Nobel Prize ceremony—a path to freedom through the ceiling crack of creativity.

And while *Horses* is considered one of the most explosive debuts in rock history, deemed by *Rolling Stone* "a declaration of committed mutiny, a statement of faith in the transfigurative powers of rock and roll," Smith's later, less acclaimed, albums hold their own power. Experimental *Radio Ethiopia*, released a year after *Horses*, includes the driving and piano-led single "Pissing in a River," about the desperate and body-draining anguish of heartache. After Smith fell off the stage while touring, fracturing her back and neck, she returned in 1978 with the aptly named *Easter*, a rebirth. The album became Smith's main commercial breakthrough because of its punchy power ballad and

PLAYLIST

"Piss Factory," 1974, single, *Land* (1975–2002)

"Gloria," 1975, *Horses*

"Land," 1975, *Horses*

"Pissing in a River," 1976, *Radio Ethiopia*

"Because the Night," 1978, *Easter*

"Rock N Roll Nigger," 1978, *Easter*

"Dancing Barefoot," 1979, *Wave*

"People Have the Power," 1980, *Dream of Life*

"Beneath the Southern Cross," 1996, *Gone Again*

"Glitter in Their Eyes," 2000, *Gung Ho*

"This Is the Girl," 2012, *Banga*

worldwide radio hit "Because the Night," co-written by Bruce Springsteen, about unleashed desire.

Wave (1979), produced by Todd Rundgren, was more polished and less successful. Still, it includes one of her landmark compositions, "Dancing Barefoot," inspired by Smith's then soon-to-be husband Fred "Sonic" Smith, guitarist of Detroit garage band MC5. On the song, Smith lets her low, rumbling voice skim over an acoustic and electric twangy melody, with the word "heroine" sung like "heroin," a comparison of love to addiction. By the time Smith got married in 1980, she made the conscious decision to leave her band and New York to be a wife in Detroit, and then a mom, raising the pair's kids Jesse and Jackson in semi-retirement until her 1988 album *Dream of Life*, a collaboration with her husband. The album's rocking "People Have the Power" remains a heartfelt and relevant populist anthem, about people being able to wrestle the earth from fools. Smith again dove back into concentrating on family life but still wrote, releasing books such as 1992's *Woolgathering*, dreamlike in its recollection of childhood memories, and elegant 1996 prose tome *The Coral Sea*, about Mapplethorpe. In 1994, Fred died of heart failure; a few years later, Patti moved back to New York. In her stream-of-consciousness 2015 memoir *M Train*, which stretches from her world travels early on in her marriage to her present-day life in Manhattan and Coney Island, filled with books, coffee, and memories, she writes of her late husband, "My yearning for him permeated everything—my poems, my songs, my heart."

Horses hooked me for life when I first heard it as a Hollywood teenager in the mid-nineties, while grieving the childhood death of my mom by writing poems and exploding songs out of me. But it was *Gone Again*, Smith's triumphant, emotional return to music in 1996, that enveloped my soul. Within a five-year span, Smith's platonic soulmate Mapplethorpe died of AIDS, her pianist Sohl died of a heart attack, Fred passed, and her brother Todd suffered a fatal stroke. *Gone Again*, for Smith, was a heady and intimate immersion into profound grief, loss, and renewal, laid over a Native American tribal beat. On the deceptively simple acoustic song "Farewell Reel," for her late husband, Smith's voice cracks with vulnerability as she sings about the sky raining on her. "About a Boy," about then recently deceased Kurt Cobain, swells with raw poetry and atmospheric feedback. In 1997, when Smith played her first show at CBGB in more than fifteen years, to promote *Gone Again*, I was a college student in NYC and hustled my way to the back of the club beforehand to give Smith a poem I had written about her and a red rose. On stage, sweaty and exultant, gray and black hair flying, she feverishly ripped up the rose and made the club her pulpit for three frenetic hours. Death had brought her music raging back to life. She was fifty and on the precipice of releasing more books and albums—mortality and guitar-driven *Peace and Noise* (1997), rock manifesto *Gung Ho* (2000), antiwar *Trampin'* (2004), covers collection *Twelve* (2007), and spoken word-filled *Banga* (2012).

By the time Smith started performing *Horses* around the world for its fortieth anniversary, several years after the success of *Just Kids*, she had become a certified cultural icon, a Jersey factory girl turned punk poet hurricane. Her decades-long misfit ability to rebel, to use both written words and belted melodies to descend into the gut, and to espouse honest reveries on death, life, and love makes her singular. Her path continues to surge forward. "I'm going to remember everything," she declares in *M Train*, "and then I'm going to write it all down." ■

HEART

LUCRETIA TYE JASMINE

ILLUSTRATION BY LINDSEY BAILEY

Blood harmony is the heart of Heart. Led by songwriting sisters Ann and Nancy Wilson, Heart was one of the very few female-fronted bands who could be heard on album-rock radio in the 1970s. Ann's soprano voice and Nancy's mezzo-soprano and multifaceted guitar playing got listeners used to hearing women rock out on the radio, on TV, in music videos, and onstage. The sisters also play several instruments on their numerous albums, including acoustic guitar, autoharp, bass, drums, flute, lead and rhythm guitar, mandolin, mellotron, piano, and tambourine. Heart's seven Top 10 albums span the 1970s, the 1980s, the 1990s, and the 2010s, the longest span of Top 10 albums by a woman-fronted band.

Ann Dustin Wilson, born June 15, 1950, in San Diego, is the middle child of three sisters. Nancy Lamoureaux Wilson, the youngest of the three, was born March 16, 1954, in San Francisco. Since their father was a US Marine, the family traveled a lot. They eventually settled in Seattle, whose verdant landscape inspired Ann's writing. Key figures of that city, the sisters support Bad Animals, a music studio named after one of their albums, where an array of musicians, from newly emerging to legendary, have recorded.

Growing up, the sisters were not popular at school. But Motown and the Beatles offered an escape; one of the first 45s Ann bought was by the Supremes. Listening to records and playing guitar together, the sisters found musical solace in each other and in the music. Attending a Beatles concert galvanized the sisters not because they wanted to marry the band, but because they wanted to be the band. "It looked like a sublime way of survival," Ann said in the sisters' 2012 autobiography. Nancy explained: "To us, the Beatles were deadly serious stuff, something we studied like scholars, looking for meaning and wisdom." They formed the all-girl, four-part harmony band the Viewpoints in 1964. On Mother's Day 1967, the sisters played their first gig as a duo at First Congregational Church, in the center of Bellevue, Washington, the church their mom chose for the family.

Ann, a writer and artist, penned rock romances that she also illustrated and set to music with her own guitar playing and singing. Her childhood stutter disappeared when she sang. Nancy has said her first boyfriend was her guitar. Ann toured with the band Hocus Pocus, then as Heart, entreating college-going Nancy to join her in Canada, where Ann's boyfriend and bandmate was dodging the draft. With a plan to add more acoustic playing to the band, Nancy joined Heart.

Heart's 1976 debut album, *Dreamboat Annie*, yielded several hits that are FM radio staples. Every time I hear and see the 1978 concert footage of Heart performing the single "Crazy on You," I know I'm watching feminism in musical action. Ann wields

her voice and Nancy her guitar as powerfully—and as powerfully sexy—as any man, the entirety of their bodies unfettered by self-conscious constraints. Sisters in concert, Heart jangles go for the jugular. Ann kisses our ears and sings that the pleasure's all hers, and Nancy solos like a true guitar hero. "Magic Man," based on a real conversation Ann had with her mom, is suggestive and defiant; its protagonist tells her mother she's staying away from home to be with her man. "Dreamboat Annie" is a delicate road song, relentless and soothing as the sisters set forth in the diamond winds with their band: "Heading out this morning / Into the sun." Heart sisters set their course, playing it out in various musical styles, from acoustic and folk to metal and rock.

The album cover for their 1977 and second million-selling album, *Little Queen*, shows them confronting the camera, dressed in lace and capes, at the center of the frame; the men are mere backdrops along with the exciting vardo that awaits, the wild landscape their terrain. Indeed, somewhat controversially, the Wilson sisters have fired the men in their band several times, bringing in new talent.

Heart's managers and male bandmates told Ann her weight was interfering with record sales. The accusation was a devastating echo of her high school experience. Nancy was told to get Ann to lose weight. What Nancy did instead was true to Heart's form: when Ann had panic attacks and stage fright because of the body-shaming, Nancy would walk up to Ann, touch nose to nose, and say, "Hello, hello, come back come back, come here come here, I'm with you, look at me, keep looking at me," and Ann would.

The 1990s albums *Brigade*, *Desire Walks On*, and *The Road Home* continued Heart's popularity.

So did their new band, the Lovemongers. Nancy took a break from Heart and scored soundtracks for her filmmaker husband, Cameron Crowe (1996's *Jerry Maguire*, 2000's *Almost Famous*, 2001's *Vanilla Sky*, and 2005's *Elizabethtown*). Ann toured without Nancy. Heart re-formed in 2002, releasing more chart-topping songs and albums.

Heart and their music have been lauded in many ways. The band has sold 35 million records worldwide, with twenty Top 40 singles. The Grammys, the VH1 Rock Honors, ASCAP, and *Hit Parader* have honored Heart's influence and legacy, and in 2007, "Barracuda" was featured in *Shrek the Third*. "Barracuda" was also included in Guitar Hero III: Legends of Rock, the only all-female-fronted band in that iteration of the popular game. The Wilsons have raised funds for music education and performed at Royal Albert Hall with the Royal Philharmonic Orchestra. Heart played Led Zeppelin's power ballad "Stairway to Heaven" as the finale when Led Zeppelin was honored at the esteemed 2012 Kennedy Center Honors, with Led Zeppelin, the president, and the First Lady in the room.

The sisters have long endured sexist slurs and sizeist criticism but have never stopped writing and playing music. Ann has said they send out their hearts like javelins. As Nancy commanded at their 2013 induction into the Rock and Roll Hall of Fame: "Turn it up." ■

PLAYLIST

"Dreamboat Annie," 1976, *Dreamboat Annie*

"Crazy on You," 1976, *Dreamboat Annie*

"Magic Man," 1976, *Dreamboat Annie*

"Barracuda," 1977, *Little Queen*

"Heartless," 1978, *Magazine*

"Straight On," 1978, *Dog and Butterfly*

"Dog and Butterfly," 1979, *Dog and Butterfly*

"Bebe le Strange," 1980, *Bebe le Strange*

"These Dreams," 1986, *Heart*

"Alone," 1987, *Bad Animals*

"Stairway to Heaven (Live at the Kennedy Center Honors)," 2013, single

DEBBIE HARRY

THEO KOGAN

ILLUSTRATION BY WINNIE T. FRICK

Debbie Harry is the original punk goddess in kitten heels. A cover girl with a switchblade behind her back, a feminist "because how could you not be if you were a woman," she was one of the boys but undoubtedly female. Harry wrote most of the Blondie lyrics and was admittedly inspired by the songs and vocal stylings of 1960s girl groups such as the sultry Shangri-Las. Her voice—authentic, deep, angelic yet brawny—is part of what crowned her iconic stature in New York's music history. Blondie, the band Harry fronts, was the underdog of the punk scene in New York and would have been crowned "least likely to succeed" in the 1977 class of CBGB. They wound up topping the charts.

However, even in new wave, there were still rules. Debbie was thought by some to be excessively sexualized and perhaps exploited for her beauty. Being born a drop-dead stunner is not a crime, and what's wrong with using or even celebrating what you've been given by nature? Her personal style continues to be imitated today and has been a huge influence on me since I was nine years old and made a cassette tape consisting solely of the song "Heart of Glass" repeated over and over and over.

Named Angela Tremble by her birth mother, Deborah Ann Harry was born July 1, 1945, in Miami. She was adopted as a tiny infant by Richard and Catherine Harry and grew up in Hawthorne, New Jersey. After college Harry became a secretary at BBC Radio in NYC and then a waitress at Max's Kansas City. She was also a Playboy Bunny. She started her music career in the 1960s in a band called Wind in the Willows, which put out one album. She went on to sing for the Stilettos in 1974 and in Angel and the Snake with guitar player and partner Chris Stein, along with downtown punk icons Tish and Snooky Bellomo (of Sic Fucks and Manic Panic hair dye fame). Soon after, Harry and Stein formed Blondie. The name came from the catcalls that men would holler at Debbie on the street after she bleached her hair. To counteract the focus put on the high-cheeked front person, the group made T-shirts that said "Blondie Is a Group."

Blondie were a seminal part of seventies' New York punk and new wave. Along with Patti Smith, Television, Talking Heads, and the Ramones, they played the infamous CBGB and Max's Kansas City. Their self-titled first album (1976) was produced by Richard Gottehrer, who had produced the Shangri-Las' single "My Boyfriend's Back" and founded Sire Records. Blondie debuted with the song "X Offender," originally called "Sex Offender," about stalkers, showing that Debbie by way or by force openly did not give a fuck. "In the Flesh" expresses a sexy longing with lullaby grooves and girl

group–styled haunting "ooo's." "Rip Her to Shreds" has a slow vocal intro spoken in tough Shangri-Las fashion. Her looks may have given the band its name, but Harry's brains as evidenced in her lyric-writing skills, her dry delivery, and her sexy, low, and sometimes growling voice helped make Blondie the rare punk band that penetrated the Top 40 and the heartland.

Plastic Letters (1978), again produced by Gottehrer, included the international hits "Denis," partially sung in French with a classic upbeat feel, and "(I'm Always Touched by Your) Presence, Dear," a fast explosion of a love song. But it was on their third and seminal album *Parallel Lines* that Blondie achieved perfection. *Parallel Lines* had six singles, including "One Way or Another," written about a stalker of Debbie's and now a favorite of TV commercials (talk about making lemonade out of lemons). This is the work that toted "Heart of Glass," a song said to be inspired by Donna Summer's disco hit "I Feel Love." A punk band channeling a disco song was something that hadn't happened before. Perhaps the infamous nightclub Studio 54, where everyone who was anyone hung out, including Harry, was an influence on her musical tastes. Many of her brightly colored stage outfits were made by fashion designer Stephen Sprouse. The songs and these looks catapulted Harry to fashion divinity.

An album of videos for each song was released in conjunction with Blondie's platinum fourth album *Eat to the Beat*, a first for a rock band. The styles again ranged from punk to pop to reggae. "Atomic" is an epic dance song with a disco beat, electronic trance keyboards, and a surf guitar riff. "Dreaming" is a jump-around-and-shake-your-hair opener in which Debbie reminds us that dreaming is free, and "Union City Blue" is an ode to her beloved Union City, New Jersey.

Auto American (1980) debuted a deeper array of musical influences and a dive into more electronics. "Rapture" mixed funk, trance, and hip-hop and gave shoutouts to rap pioneers Fab Five Freddy and Grandmaster Flash; it was one of the first rap songs to hit the top of the charts, regardless of being sung and rapped by a blond white chick from New Jersey. "The Tide Is High," a groovy summery Caribbean hit, is a cover of the Jamaican ska band the Paragons. "Call Me," the theme song for the movie *American Gigolo*, was number one on the *Billboard* charts for six weeks straight. (Somehow "Call Me" hasn't been used for a cell phone commercial yet. Can you hear me now?)

After *Hunter* (1982) Blondie went on hiatus for many reasons. In the mid-1980s Stein became very sick with pemphigus, a rare autoimmune disease that affects the skin as well as the mucus membranes. Debbie took care of Chris during his illness, but they didn't stay together romantically. Her loyalty and partnership with Stein live on today.

Harry with Stein and producers Nile Rodgers and Bernard Edwards of Chic recorded her first solo album, *KooKoo* (1981). The cover features art by H. R. Giger, who was famous for creating the space creatures in the sci-fi film *Alien*. Harry's solo album

PLAYLIST

WITH BLONDIE:

"In the Flesh," 1977, *Blondie*

"Rip Her to Shreds," 1977, *Blondie*

"(I'm Always Touched by Your) Presence Dear," 1978, *Plastic Letters*

"Heart of Glass," 1978, *Parallel Lines*

"Fade Away and Radiate," 1978, *Parallel Lines*

"One Way or Another," 1978, *Parallel Lines*

"Atomic," 1979, *Eat to the Beat*

"Dreaming," 1979, *Eat to the Beat*

"Rapture," 1980, *Autoamerican*

"Call Me," 1980, on the original soundtrack for *American Gigolo*

"Maria," 1999, *No Exit*

Rockbird (1986), whose cover shows Debbie's face masterfully painted by makeup artist Linda Mason with black, smoky cat eyes and beige sex-kitten lips, became yet another iconic look. Over the next twenty-six years she released three more solo albums and scored international hits including "I Want That Man" and "French Kissin' in the USA." Harry, a visual as well as musical icon, has acted in over thirty films, notably *Downtown 81*, *Videodrome*, *Heavy*, *Six Ways to Sunday*, *Hairspray*, and *Spun*. She was a guest on *The Muppet Show* (1981), *Absolutely Fabulous* (2002), and *RuPaul's Drag Race* (2016)—a triad of small-screen fabulosity.

In 1999 Blondie was back with a bullet to make the album *No Exit*, which threw them back on the charts with the catchy song "Maria"—and they haven't quit since. More than two decades after I wore out my cassette of "Heart of Glass," Debbie and Chris saw me sing in an all-female Blondie cover band one night in NYC. Afterward they came into the dressing room and Debbie said to me, "You are brave . . . *very brave*." Then to top it off, she said, "We should do a duet sometime." I said, "*Anytime*. Call me." I immediately regretted the unintended pun. Singing backup on *No Exit* was a blast. Of course Chris was there, and longtime Blondie members Jimmy Destri and Clem Burke. In person, Debbie is warm and nurturing. She's also funny, smart, and snarky and knows she is the shit but at the same time is very relaxed about it. When I left the session I was floating on air. It was a superfan's dream come true.

Artists and bands like Madonna, the Sounds, Garbage, Paramore, No Doubt, Lady Gaga, and others have walked a parallel line to Harry's. Her groundbreaking singing and personal style continue to be mimicked with no signs of ceasing. Blondie dropped a new album in 2017 called *Pollinator*, just the latest splendiferous move by the Marilyn Monroe of punk, one of the most talented women ever to walk on planet Earth. ∎

JOAN JETT

CARYN ROSE

ILLUSTRATION BY WINNIE T. FRICK

There's a good reason Joan Jett's most well-known hit is her cover of "I Love Rock 'n' Roll." Jett is an unashamed acolyte, in love with the noise and the riffs and the stardust and the glory. As a teenager, she wanted to inhabit rock and roll, to write, play, and sing her own songs. She was determined to accomplish that by any means necessary, no matter how many obstacles she might face. A lesser person facing the bullshit Jett encountered would have given up, and her determination almost killed her.

Jett's musical idols give you the clues to what would become her unmistakable brand of rock and roll: Marc Bolan of T. Rex (whom she credits with teaching her how to scream), Paul Rodgers of Free (think of the rock solid riff of "All Right Now"), and Suzi Quatro, whose pioneering attitude as a leather-wearing frontwoman in pursuit of pop-driven hits gave Jett footsteps for her Chuck Taylors to follow.

It's ironic that Jett ended up as an icon of rebellion; as she told Katey Rich in 2010, "It wasn't about rebelling against family or school, it was more about rebelling against what people tell you you can't do." Joan Marie Larkin was born in Philadelphia, Pennsylvania, on September 22, 1958. She was told repeatedly by her mother that she could be anything she wanted to be. Joan eventually decided she wanted to be a rock musician, asking for (and getting) an electric guitar for Christmas. It'd be an unremarkable story if Joan was John, but in the seventies, despite Title IX and other advances of women's lib, girls would still be channeled toward pursuits judged more suitable for them (Jett's father wanted her to be a typist).

After moving to California in 1974, Jett assumed her *nom de guerre* as a habitué of clubs like the teen-friendly Sugar Shack and the English Disco, the latter the purview of influential radio DJ Rodney Bingenheimer. These were places where music-crazy kids could dress how they wanted to, be who they wanted to be, and find the rest of their tribe.

Jett met Kim Fowley—the rock impresario generally given credit for the creation of the Runaways—who introduced seventeen-year-old Jett to sixteen-year old drummer Sandy West. While Fowley had some master plan to infiltrate the music business via a band of young girls, the Runaways—including singer Cherie Currie, guitarist Lita Ford, and bassist Jackie Fox—just wanted to emulate their heroes David Bowie, Marc Bolan, and Jimmy Page.

But the music industry of the mid-seventies was not ready for a group of young women performing unadulterated rock and roll with power and agency. Arista's Clive Davis reportedly said, "I have Patti Smith, why do I need another [female artist]?"; the band's reception at radio also fell on deaf ears. Most of the critics likely never listened to the Runaways or saw them perform live; the 1977 footage from the band's tour of Japan offers tangible proof that people (mostly men) were deaf, blind, dumb, and stubborn.

The Runaways were reviled as strongly as they were ogled, with only a few champions on their side. Every step forward required a battle, and between the hostile climate and Fowley's legendary (mis) management and manipulation, the band lasted for four studio albums before disintegrating. Ford went solo, pursuing the heavy metal that was her first love; West failed to find another successful musical outlet and turned to drugs, before succumbing to cancer in 2006; Currie pursued music, acting, and memoir writing; and Jackie Fox moved to the business side of entertainment. Jett remained in LA and immersed herself in the burgeoning punk scene. She produced the debut (and only) album by the Germs—now considered a classic.

In 1979, Jett traveled to London, searching for new collaborators. She asked ex–Sex Pistols Steve Jones and Paul Cook if they'd like to help her record a song she loved and tried to cut with the Runaways: "I Love Rock 'n' Roll," originally recorded by the Arrows. Although Jones and Cook were game, it ended up as the B-side of a single only released in Europe, and went nowhere—the same place that Jett began to worry her career was destined for. She did not take care of her health. There were drugs. This is where these rock-and-roll fairy tales usually end, badly.

It was in this state that Jett—in her twenties, a grizzled rock-and-roll veteran—met Kenny Laguna, a producer, songwriter, and old-school "record guy." They went into the studio for a couple of days and were sufficiently sympatico for Laguna to emphatically agree to help Jett make a comeback. Laguna's sixties bubblegum pop sensibilities balanced Jett's punk heart and ear for a timeless riff. Together, they finished what would become *Joan Jett* (later retitled *Bad Reputation*) by the spring of 1980. She recruited Gary Ryan, Eric Ambel, and Lee Crystal for her backing band, the Blackhearts, thanks to an ad in the local paper reading, "Joan Jett is looking for three good men." (She would later say, "I love the Runaways too much to do another girl band.") The lineup changed over the years, but the Blackhearts power Jett's dynamite live act, keeping her on the road year after year.

Laguna shopped *Joan Jett* to twenty-three record companies, only to hear "No" twenty-three times. Time had not softened the industry's opinion of the Runaways, and the hostility toward a woman who wanted to define her own image was still firmly in place. Meryl Laguna, Kenny's wife, came to the rescue, emptying out their daughter's college fund to press the first run of *Bad Reputation*, which her husband sold out of the trunk of his car after shows.

Eventually, Casablanca Records gave Jett a home. They rereleased her first album and she began work on her second. Finally, "I Love Rock 'n' Roll" was going to be recorded the way Jett had always envisioned it. At first, reaction to the unabashedly rockist anthem was dismissive and indifferent. But all it took was a few radio stations

receiving positive listener response for the song to gain momentum. The track entered the *Billboard* Hot 100 and didn't stop until it reached number one. It would be only the first hit of many that landed in the Top 20, ranging from "I Hate Myself for Loving You" (co-written with hitmaker Desmond Child) to "Do You Wanna Touch Me," a Gary Glitter cover that Jett made her own.

Musically and sartorially, Joan Jett favors the classics; her style echoes the attitude of 1968-era Elvis and has inspired countless clones, none of whom wear a leather jacket and skinny jeans as well as she does. She has a bias toward a robust and crunchy riff fueling a sing-along chorus, powered by a sultry vocal possessing as much *oomph* as any of her heroes. She can yelp, shout, and then soulfully deliver a ballad like "Crimson and Clover." Lyrically, Jett embraces simple messages and universal themes—love, hate, friends, enemies. On "Bad Reputation" she flips the bird to the music industry, offering a message of empowerment for the women—musicians or otherwise—who followed in her footsteps.

Jett has tried her hand at acting on both stage and screen. In 1987, she starred as Michael J. Fox's screen sibling as the two of them fronted a band called the Barbusters in Paul Schrader's *Light of Day*; her rendition of the Springsteen-penned title track gave her another hit. In 2001, Jett played Columbia in *The Rocky Horror Picture Show* on Broadway.

In 1980, Jett and Laguna launched Blackheart Records. She was one of the first female recording artists to found her own label, allowing her to record and release twelve albums by 2013 and support other musicians, including female punk bands like Fea and the Dollyrots. In the nineties, she joined forces with the next generation, producing songs for Riot Grrrl progenitors Bikini Kill (and later, co-writing songs with Kathleen Hanna) and playing with Seattle's the Gits in tribute to their murdered lead singer Mia Zapata, in an outing called "Evil Stig" ("Live Gits" backward). For a rocker devoted to Elvis-retro style, Jett has maintained a savvy cultural relevance, working with cutting-edge artists from Fugazi to Laura Jane Grace (and, er, Miley Cyrus), and inspiring the punk-rock meme WWJJD? (What Would Joan Jett Do?).

In 2014, Jett appeared with Krist Novoselic and Dave Grohl as Nirvana was inducted into the Rock and Roll Hall of Fame. As she came onstage to play "Smells Like Teen Spirit," Novoselic said, "Here's an individual that I can't believe isn't in the Rock and Roll Hall of Fame!" This snub by the establishment would not last long. The following year, Jett was onstage in Cleveland, this time as part of the 2015 Rock and Roll Hall of Fame induction class: the ultimate mainstream validation of Jett's art and career. Her induction band included members of the Germs and the Blackhearts, Grohl, Kenny Laguna on keyboards, and Tommy James for "Crimson and Clover." In the background? Photographs of Jett flipping the bird. Revenge is sweet, and a dish best served cold. ■

GRACE JONES

ALI GITLOW

ILLUSTRATION BY JULIE WINEGARD

Picture iconic New York club Studio 54 in its 1970s heyday: giant mirror ball swirling, Champagne and cocaine flowing, disco tunes pulsating as hundreds of bodies writhe in total ecstasy. This was the domain of people deemed too fabulous to walk the earth in the light of day, including the inimitable Grace Jones. In environments like this the singer honed her party girl aura, fashion-forward personal style, and mutable approach to making music. After more than forty years in the limelight she remains known for espousing a full-throttle nonconformist agenda, causing her not only to remain relevant but to epitomize cool for multiple generations of music lovers.

Jones's life has been wholly shaped by rebelling against the circumstances under which she grew up. Born in Jamaica in 1948, she was raised under the strict regime of her father, a Pentecostal minister, and often beaten by her step-grandfather, who discouraged her from watching TV and wearing nail polish. It's no surprise, then, that after her family moved to upstate New York when she was thirteen, Jones hightailed it outta there as soon as she was legal, first to Philadelphia and then to New York City. Immediately, she was welcomed on the nascent disco scene for her glamazon looks, risqué clothes, and over-the-top personality. Many individuals who elect to live their lives on the fringes of

society find solace in the metaphor of the nightclub as church, and Jones is no exception. "I was a dancing disco queen," she told the *Stool Pigeon* in 2008, continuing, "My upbringing in the church had a lot to do with it. Disco was like the celebration of music through dance." For Jones, nightlife was the path to self-actualization.

It was in the experimental realm of nightclubs that Jones polished her singular look—on the dance floor, you really couldn't miss her. "I used to go [to Studio 54] before I started singing, when I was modeling, and just dance, dance, dance my ass off," she told the BBC in the 2007 documentary *Queens of Disco*. This early modeling stint took her to Paris in 1970, where her striking, androgynous visage was more readily appreciated. There, she became an inspiration to designers like Issey Miyake, Azzedine Alaïa, and Yves Saint Laurent, who hired her to walk their runway shows; she graced the covers of *Vogue* and *Elle* and appeared in fashion spreads shot by Guy Bourdin and Helmut Newton. She traded Studio 54 for Parisian clubs Le Sept and Le Palace, hanging out with the likes of Valentino and Karl Lagerfeld. The art world noticed her, too. Jones became close friends with Andy Warhol and Keith Haring, who rendered his famous cartoonish characters all over her naked torso. She looked great in the buff but could pull off wearing anything: draped

head coverings, skintight bodycon dresses, elaborate wigs, tuxedos, and military hats capped off by her flat-top hairdo.

However, it was her partnership with French artist Jean-Paul Goude that made her an icon of visual culture. Always playing with the form of Jones's body, Goude oiled her up and put her in an impossible raised leg pose for a 1978 issue of *New York* magazine. He created a Bauhaus-esque "maternity dress" comprising giant shapes when she became pregnant with his child in 1979. He consulted on her image and stage-managed her shows, too. History has it that Goude objectified Jones for her overt sexuality through the use of bondage motifs, and exoticized her blackness by photographing her in a cage for the cover of his 1982 book provocatively titled *Jungle Fever*. (Goude was most recently in the public eye for shooting Kim Kardashian's 2014 "internet-breaking" *Paper* magazine cover.) Yet Jones has always stood by her collaborations with Goude and the other powerful men in her orbit, telling the *New York Times* in 2015, "As much as I was a muse, they were also muses for me."

Over the course of her ten albums, Jones has proven herself to be a sonic chameleon, beginning as a disco starlet before shapeshifting into the high priestess of New Wave. Island Records boss Chris Blackwell discovered her in 1975 and put her in the studio with disco producer Tom Moulton; her debut album, 1977's *Portfolio*, earned her underground fame. Jones's unique vocal style was established via tracks like "I Need a Man," a slow-building stormer on which she switches between operatic quavering and low-range talk-singing. It became her first club hit, starting an enduring love affair with an army of gay fans. What she lacked in traditional musical talent she made up for in raw dynamism, allowing her to carry personalized disco renditions of Édith Piaf's "La Vie en Rose" and show tunes like "Send in the Clowns." After releasing another two disco LPs, Blackwell decided Jones should refresh her aesthetic and teamed her up with Sly and Robbie, who led Island's in-house band, Compass Point All Stars. The result was 1980's *Warm Leatherette*, which featured a mix of reggae rhythms and New Wave synths on covers of "Private Life" and "Love Is the Drug." This was quickly followed by 1981's *Nightclubbing*, which was awarded *NME*'s Album of the Year. It includes some of her most popular songs such as "Pull Up to the Bumper" (about which many of us have pondered: is it an anal sex reference?) and the title track, an Iggy Pop cover on which a thick dub bassline tangoes with Jones's paced incantations.

In the confines of the club, Jones could always express herself fully, living out the dream of simple existence as performance art. She describes early gigs in her 2016 autobiography *I'll Never Write My Memoirs* as "entertaining the creeps, freaks, strays, and lionized, living the un-American dream." From the get-go she has put on sensational live shows, seductively eyeing audience members, swaying her lithe limbs deliberately for slow numbers, and dishing out slip-sliding samba moves for fast ones. As a naturally outgoing entertainer, Jones tried her hand at acting for a short stretch, appearing in the 1984 flick *Conan the Destroyer*. She was even a Bond girl, playing May Day in *A View to a Kill* the following year.

PLAYLIST

"La Vie en Rose," 1977, *Portfolio*

"I Need a Man," 1977, *Portfolio*

"Do or Die," 1978, *Fame*

"Private Life," 1980, *Warm Leatherette*

"Love Is the Drug," 1980, *Warm Leatherette*

"Nightclubbing," 1981, *Nightclubbing*

"Pull Up to the Bumper," 1981, *Nightclubbing*

"My Jamaican Guy," 1982, *Living My Life*

"Slave to the Rhythm," 1985, *Slave to the Rhythm*

Jones has a reputation for extreme behavior, even by diva standards. In 1980 she repeatedly slapped British chat show host Russell Harty on live TV. She did ecstasy for the first time with Timothy Leary. Her baby shower was held at the famed New York club the Paradise Garage. When an airline once tried forcing her to check master tapes, she disembarked and laid down in the middle of the runway in protest. Throughout her career she has refused to be boxed in by categorization, embodying traits of femininity and masculinity in equal measure. Or, as she told *Interview* in 1984, "The future is no sex…You can be a boy, a girl, whatever you want." In 1996 she married her bodyguard Atila Altaunbay; they're neither together nor separated because, as she explains in her memoirs, she doesn't believe in divorce. She is renowned for being hours late (though she asserts this is because clubs asked her to delay performing so they could make money from the bar—otherwise, people would just leave after her set ended). This all said, watching interviews with Jones makes one thing abundantly clear: she's actually *really* nice. Just don't cross her.

Even now, Jones still occasionally haunts the world's nightclubs. In 2009 she told *Arise Magazine* that she can party harder than anyone else whenever she feels like it. Her speaking voice, now an untraceable mix of Jamaican, American, and multi-European accents, maps the story of her life, much in the same way that her body retains the sense memory to emote her heart out onstage, just like she did in her physical prime. In 2017, she was still stunning audiences, hula-hooping through the entire title track of her 1985 album *Slave to the Rhythm* wearing custom Philip Treacy headwear during live festival performances— oftentimes topless, slathered in body paint. ■

POLY STYRENE

STEPHANIE PHILLIPS

ILLUSTRATION BY LINDSEY BAILEY

The London punk scene in the late seventies was a chaotic, experimental, and sometimes violent place. It was the perfect setting for young people to rebel against the systems they saw as oppressive and old-fashioned. Some of the many middle-class art kids from the suburbs thought that being subversive meant daubing themselves in Nazi regalia and spiking their hair. Poly Styrene, a mixed-race working-class teenager from South London, took a different approach. As the singer and founder of anti-consumerist punk band X-Ray Spex, Poly decided to talk about the issues she cared about, such as environmentalism, identity, and consumerism, in her now infamous battle-cry yelp.

For a young black working-class girl, the restrictions of misogyny, racism, and the British class structure (a complex system that essentially boils down to the haves and have nots) must have been suffocating. X-Ray Spex gave Poly a way to escape. She was born Marianne Joan Elliott-Said on July 3, 1957, in Bromley, England. Her mother was a Scottish-Irish legal secretary, and her father was a dispossessed Somali aristocrat. When Poly was a child, her mother moved to Brixton with her so they could live in a more multicultural environment and escape the racism they experienced in Bromley.

Sensing her own dislike of mundanity, Poly ran away when she was fifteen and spent two years on the hippie circuit traveling from festival to festival. She eventually came back home at eighteen. After seeing the Sex Pistols play a ramshackle gig in Hastings on her nineteenth birthday, she decided anyone could do what they were doing. She put an ad in *NME* in 1976 looking for "young punx who want to stick it together." The ad caught the attention of fifteen-year-old Lora Logic, Jack Stafford (Jak Airport), Paul Dean, and Paul "BP" Hurding. X-Ray Spex was born.

The band played their first gig at punk staple the Roxy and were an instant success. Logic's saxophone, an unusual instrument for a punk band at the time, gave the band its distinct sound, accentuating each note and weaving in and out of Poly's vocals, the other unique quality to X-Ray Spex. Poly's discordant warble was a proto-feminist siren screaming "I'm nobody's little girl." Just listen to her spoken word opening to their classic first single "Oh Bondage Up Yours!," where she starts off sweet, citing the cliché that "little girls are meant to be seen and not heard," and ends up screaming the song's title. Poly knew she wanted to play around with the definitions of femininity. Many other women in the punk scene were also invested in this idea. Punk was all about rejecting social norms, and the submissive nature of gender was one of the first notions to go out the window. Though few women at the time

acknowledged their actions as feminist, whether it was ska icon Pauline Black of the Selecter dressing like a slick rude boy or the Slits messing up their hair and singing about societal expectations for women, it all laid the groundwork for better representation of women in music.

X-Ray Spex became the talk of the punk scene. Poly in particular caught everyone's eye with her unique sense of style and what was ever so slightly offensively referred to as her "unconventional look." Style was incredibly important to Poly. Her experience running a vintage stall in Beaufort Market on Kings Road when she was eighteen gave her a good eye for fashion. She knew early on that she had to wear braces and therefore couldn't just wear her "Carly Simon hairdos," as she calls them in the documentary series *The Punk Years*. So she decided to take a different approach to beauty. Mixing vintage dresses with army helmets, neon socks, and the tinsel on her teeth, Poly made her look work for her.

She appeared brash, but Poly was a vulnerable young woman. The industry tried desperately to sexualize her, but she resisted. Johnny Rotten tells stories of the "strange girl who often talked about hallucinating." In an interview with the *Guardian*, Poly stated that she shaved her head after a traumatic incident, adding that she read that girls in concentration camps did that after being raped. She refused to expand on what that statement meant.

Although there were a number of black punks around at the time, Pauline Black and Poly stood out as the only prominent black women in the scene. England in the seventies was awash with racist attitudes and a fear of the other; the punk scene was no different. Despite the noted influences of Britain's burgeoning multicultural society (Jamaican imports such as reggae and ska were a huge influence on early punk), the punk scene quickly became co-opted by fascist ideals and white nationalist groups, such as the National Front.

After Eric Clapton launched into a racist tirade at one of his gigs, Rock Against Racism was born. The campaign culminated in a gig in spring 1978 in East London to combat the rise of racism in music. Along with bands like Generation X and the Clash, X-Ray Spex played to the huge crowd in Victoria Park. Poly rarely spoke about her mixed-race heritage, perhaps because the English press were so crudely fascinated with it, but from her stance at Rock Against Racism, we can infer that Poly knew who she was and wasn't going to be pushed around.

X-Ray Spex signed to EMI and released their debut album *Germfree Adolescents* in late 1978. Although some punk albums of that era can sound dated today (for example, the Sex Pistols debut *Never Mind the Bollocks* [1977]), *Germfree Adolescents*'s original sound and forward-thinking lyrics ensured the album would always be relevant. Poly wrote about race, proto-feminism, materialism, environmentalism, youth culture, and liberation well before many people even considered thinking about those issues.

Poly was always a wild child. She quickly grew tired of punk, the media scrutiny, the mundanity of life on tour, and most importantly her greatest creation: Poly Styrene. In the 1979 BBC documentary *Who Is Poly Styrene?* Poly confesses that she was no

PLAYLIST

WITH X-RAY SPEX:

"Oh Bondage Up Yours!," 1977, on various artists, *The Roxy London WC2*

"Identity," 1978, *Germfree Adolescents*

"The Day the World Turned Dayglo," 1978, *Germfree Adolescents*

"Warrior in Woolworths," 1978, *Germfree Adolescents*

"Germfree Adolescents," 1978, *Germfree Adolescents*

longer interested in the character she created for the world and preferred to be herself. X-Ray Spex disbanded in mid-1979 after releasing a handful of singles and one album. The void they left wasn't truly filled until the Riot Grrrl era in the early nineties, which saw bands such as Bikini Kill and Heavens to Betsy take up Poly's gutsy attitude and propel it to its natural outcome: full frontal feminism.

After leaving the band, Poly gave birth to her only daughter, Celeste, and joined the Hare Krishnas. Unfortunately, Poly had numerous setbacks in her life. In 1978 she was watching a gig when she had a vision of pink light in the sky. Poly was misdiagnosed as schizophrenic, commited to a psychiatric hospital, and told she'd never work again. She wasn't correctly diagnosed as bipolar until 1991. Of course she did work again. She released several solo albums, re-formed X-Ray Spex in 1991 for a sold-out show at Brixton Academy, and the band released a second album, *Conscious Consumer*, in 1995. The band disbanded after Poly was hit by a fire engine in 1995 and suffered a fractured pelvis.

Poly was diagnosed with cancer after six months of agonizing back pain. Ever the optimist, she spent the last months of her life in a hospice promoting her last solo album, *Generation Indigo*. She died in April 2011. It's a testament to Poly's extraordinary talents that despite X-Ray Spex's rather slim back catalog her work is remembered as the pinnacle of the punk era. *Germfree Adolescents* has gone on to inspire musicians such as Neneh Cherry, M.I.A., and FKA Twigs, who said the album was one of her favorites of all time. Poly was an outlier in the pack, a revolutionary force who still inspires young people to pick up an instrument, write their own statement about the world they live in, and yell it in the faces of every person at sweaty dive gigs around the world. ■

SIOUXSIE SIOUX

CARYN ROSE

ILLUSTRATION BY WINNIE T. FRICK

Siouxsie Sioux of the House of Bromley, first of her name, the Uncowed, Breaker of Taboos, Mother of Goth. The woman born in London as Susan Janet Ballion in 1957 marched in the forefront of the phalanx of diverse, strong female role models in London punk bands, along with her compatriots in the Slits, the Raincoats, X-Ray Spex, the Pretenders, the Au Pairs, the Adverts, and so on. Sioux was inspired by the liberation theology of punk rock, first, as part of the Bromley Contingent, a group of Sex Pistols superfans inspired by the band's irreverence, and then, claiming the stage herself, creating Siouxsie and the Banshees and launching a career that spanned decades.

Ballion's first taste of the spotlight was inadvertent and unwanted. She was one of the fans brought along by the Sex Pistols on the UK punk shot heard 'round the world: the December 1976 television taping of the BBC *Today* show. Host Bill Grundy's ham-fisted, inappropriate attempt to flirt with Ballion on live television led to Pistols guitarist Steve Jones's now legendary outburst:

"You dirty sod. You dirty old man!" Uttered at the height of conservative Thatcherism, this chivalric if impertinent behavior was the equivalent of the Four Horsemen of the Apocalypse beaming into the heart of 1970s Britain at teatime.

Sioux found her way into what would become punk rock using a common roadmap: David Bowie, Roxy Music, *The Rocky Horror Picture Show*. She met her Contingent compatriots Steven Bailey (later Severin) and Simon Barker at a Roxy gig, where they were all dressed to the nines in repurposed stage costumes and other thrift shop finds that proper folks just didn't wear. Sioux's makeup mashed up kabuki, Frank N. Furter, and *Cabaret*'s Sally Bowles. Game recognized game. In the flat grayness of Britain in the post-glam mid-seventies, suburban kids longed for splashes of brightness, something to give them hope.

That something would be the Sex Pistols. Sioux and friends took to showing up wherever the band performed, wearing the most outrageous outfits they could fashion. They became the Bromley Contingent, christened by *NME* writer Caroline Coon after their North London neighborhood when they followed the Pistols to their first gig outside of the UK, in Paris. The Grundy TV appearance followed not long thereafter, putting Sioux's visage on the cover of the *Daily Mirror* tabloid in the aftermath: "SIOUXSIE A PUNK ROCKER."

PLAYLIST

WITH SIOUXSIE AND THE BANSHEES:

"Hong Kong Garden," 1978, single

"Switch," 1978, *The Scream*

"Happy House," 1980, *Kaleidoscope*

"Christine," 1980, *Kaleidoscope*

"Spellbound," 1981, *Juju*

"Israel," 1983, *Nocturne*

"Cities in Dust" 1986, single version

"The Passenger," 1987, *Through the Looking Glass*

"Peek-a-Boo," 1988, *Peepshow*

"Kiss Them for Me," 1991, *Superstition*

The media's attempt to capitalize on the ensuing moral panic brought the revolution to the hinterlands. Suddenly, kids were adopting the photos as a punk rock cookbook, and clones began to surface. The Bromley Contingent may have widely been dismissed as poseurs, but just like Bowie and Roxy had been to them, Sioux and her compatriots now offered the same path to freedom for other suburban kids. Sioux was personally upset about the clones simply because of their lack of originality.

Sioux's first performance was completely unrehearsed. She took the stage at the 100 Club's Punk Special along with Severin, friend Marco Pirroni (who would later join Adam and the Ants), and Sid Vicious on drums, where they played a fourteen-minute version of the Lord's Prayer. After that first gig, Siouxsie and Severin put together a proper band, recruiting drummer Kenny Morris and guitarist John McKay. They fashioned a sound that no one else was making, with the drama of a Brecht opera and the fury of proto-punk godfathers the Stooges and the MC5, filtered through the Velvet Underground's ennui. Sioux's vocal was fierce and full of defiance: unapologetically vibrant and compelling, which some critics (usually men, but not always) would somehow label as "icy" or "detached." Siouxsie and the Banshees provided a soundtrack for the disenfranchised, which connected those fans much in the same way Roxy Music and Bowie had done for Siouxsie. The Banshees—taking their name from the 1970 horror film *Cry of the Banshee*—sounded like the house band on the other side of Alice's looking glass, with songs that were catchy, hypnotic, and evocative, oftentimes utilizing nontraditional instruments and non-rock-and-roll rhythms and time signatures.

It was surprising how long it took the Banshees to get a record deal, not that that stopped them from being heard. They sold out gigs all over London, and what they lacked in recorded product they made up for in John Peel BBC sessions, until Polydor stepped up. To be fair, what kept many labels away was a

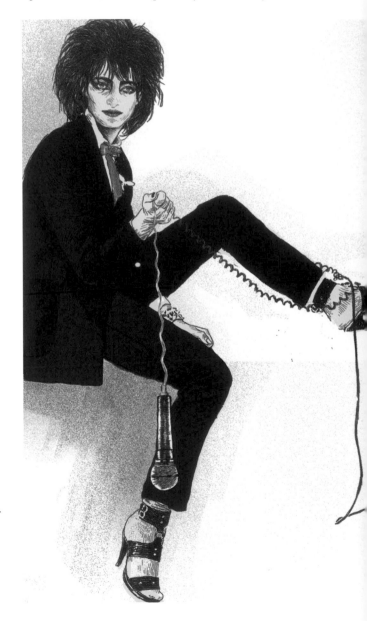

mixture of Sex Pistols backlash combined with the Bromley Contingent's early habit of donning swastikas, a practice that was stupid and thankfully short-lived. "Hong Kong Gardens," the band's first single, a story of the helplessness Sioux felt when skinheads would terrorize the owners of her local Chinese takeaway, showed that the group was smarter and more sensitive than their youthful fashion choices might have indicated.

The early Banshees albums are classics, with *The Scream* (1978), *Kaleidoscope* (1980), and *Juju* (1981) providing a blueprint for the eighties musical movement that would be known as goth. Goth poster boy Robert Smith of the Cure even filled in on guitar for the Banshees on a couple of tours, his performance captured on their cover of the Beatles' "Dear Prudence," their highest-charting record at number three on the UK singles chart in 1983. While not quite as commercially successful in the US, the Banshees' highly stylized videos became a fixture on the fledgling MTV, and their records were favorites at college radio—with the result being that the band topped the bill at the inaugural Lollapalooza tour in 1991.

The end result was a career made of both artistic and commercial success that spanned a quarter of a decade with the Banshees and later, the Creatures, a side project formed with bandmate (and briefly, husband) Budgie. Sioux wouldn't release a proper solo album until 2007. *Mantaray* sounds like the beginning of a career and not any kind of swan song, although she has not toured or recorded since then. Still, her influence remains pervasive. In 2011, Sioux received an award from *Q* magazine for her outstanding contribution to music, and Yoko Ono invited her to perform at 2013's Meltdown festival. Her songwriting, vocals, and visual style have been continually imitated but never equaled, inspiring musicians including U2, Johnny Marr, Depeche Mode, LCD Soundsystem, Garbage's Shirley Manson, PJ Harvey, and FKA Twigs. And in a bedroom somewhere, a lonely teenager is hearing that bold, resonant voice for the first time—maybe it's her cover of "The Passenger," perhaps it's the video for "Christine," maybe it's "Spellbound" showing up in *American Horror Story*—and a door opens. Behind it is a woman with bold, kohl-rimmed eyes and defiantly spiky hair, who looks and sounds like no one they've ever seen before. Suddenly, they feel less alone. ■

KATE BUSH

LIZ PELLY

ILLUSTRATION BY JULIE WINEGARD

From an early age, Kate Bush knew the importance of having complete control over her own creative vision. Even when she was misunderstood by the industry mechanisms that surrounded her, she strongly asserted her ideas: as an artist, an experimenter, a pop star, a performer, a thinker. Bush has embraced all the different sides of herself with abandon. Listening through her vast discography, one hears the beauty that shines through when artists win the fight to be their whole, complex selves.

Bush broke ground in the pop arena, bringing an adventurous synthesis of styles to a mass audience and making new spaces for women as the first female in the UK to have a chart-topping self-written song. Across ten studio albums, she has created a world drawing from pop, classical, glam rock, folk, and avant-garde sounds. Lyrically, her story songs are inspired by history, literature, film, comedy, and the darker corners of life on earth, turning tales that intrigue her into surrealist art-pop.

Born Catherine Bush on July 30, 1958, in Bexleyheath, England, the singer, songwriter, multi-instrumentalist, and producer was raised by an artistic family: her mother was a traditional Irish dancer, her father played piano, and her two older brothers dabbled in music, poetry, and photography. Bush played violin and organ, and taught herself piano at age eleven. She started writing her own songs at thirteen.

When Bush was sixteen, her brother's friend played demos of her songs for David Gilmour of Pink Floyd. Impressed, he paid for her to record a professional tape and helped her sign a deal with EMI. Bush spent two years writing and recording hundreds of songs, using her label advance to take mime lessons and interpretive dance classes from David Bowie's teacher Lindsay Kemp. During this time, she also played at pubs with the KT Bush Band.

In 1978, Bush released her debut album, *The Kick Inside*, a quick and huge critical success. EMI pressed her to make the first single the midtempo rocker "James and the Cold Gun," but Bush insisted that her debut be "Wuthering Heights" instead—an unusual slow burner inspired by the Emily Brontë novel. The song opens with dreamy piano and her theatrical soprano, before exploding into an enormous, operatic ballad, with soaring vocals from the perspective of character Catherine Earnshaw after she has died and become a ghost returning to her childhood love. Bush wrote the song all in one sitting at her piano late one night.

A testament to the strength of Bush's impulses, "Wuthering Heights" was a hit, reaching number

PLAYLIST

"Wuthering Heights," 1978, *The Kick Inside*

"Babooshka," 1980, *Never for Ever*

"Hounds of Love," 1985, *Hounds of Love*

"Running up That Hill (A Deal with God)," 1985, *Hounds of Love*

"This Woman's Work," 1989, *The Sensual World*

one in the UK and Australia (she also felt so strongly about the cover art that the release date was delayed). Based on the debut album's success, EMI pressured the artist to release a follow-up album quickly, a process she was unhappy with—she preferred to write, record, and release songs on her own terms.

She was also unhappy with the way her music was being marketed, when she realized how much emphasis the label was putting on her image, trying to sell her as much for her gender as for her music. "People generally weren't aware that I wrote my own songs or played the piano," Bush told *NME* in 1982. "The media just promoted me as a female body. It's like I've had to prove that I'm an artist in a female body." In order to have more autonomy over her work, early in her career Bush established her own publishing and management companies.

Naturally, it was not long before Bush gravitated to producing her own music. After her first tour (one of the only tours she's ever embarked on), Bush released her first self-produced record, the live *On Stage* EP. She co-produced her next and third full-length, *Never for Ever*, on which she used synthesizers and drum machines for the first time; eventually, she would become known for her frequent use of a Fairlight CMI digital synthesizer. With this record, Bush broke more chart records, becoming the first female British artist to reach number one on UK album charts.

Bush's music grew more experimental with the 1982 release of her first entirely self-produced album, *The Dreaming*, on which she fully embraced weirdness and theatrics. It felt as though all of her influences and ideas about creative work came to a head in the years that followed. After *The Dreaming*, which apparently her label did not care for, Bush created her own studio so she could take her time recording her next album, the legendary, visionary *Hounds of Love* (1985).

On *Hounds*, Bush created a masterful distillation of the different sounds found across her repertoire, making for an album ahead of its time. There are two different sides: the first is five pop songs, four of which became singles, including "Running up That Hill (A Deal with God)." The B-side is a seven-song soundscape presented as one track. The next year, Bush would be nominated for four BRIT Awards: Best Female Solo Artist, Best Album, Best Single, and Best Producer. In 1987, she won the Best Female Solo Artist Award.

After 1989's *The Sensual World*, her best-selling album in the US (which was inspired by the ending of James Joyce's *Ulysses* and includes the solemn single "This Woman's Work"), Bush took twelve years off from songwriting. During the hiatus, she gave birth to her child and got married. Bush has released three more albums since returning from the break in 2005, including 2011's intriguing *Director's Cut*—a project where she reimagined songs from her discography, offering an inquiry into what a new album can be and how perspective changes our relationship with music. It's the type of project that surely many artists wish they could realize, but don't. Bush has always pursued exactly what she imagined. For that, she remains one of pop's most influential voices. ∎

ALICE BAG

MICHELLE THREADGOULD

ILLUSTRATION BY ANNE MUNTGES

In 1977, the first Chicana punk frontwoman, Alice Bag of the Bags, took the stage at Hollywood's punk rock incubator and dive venue the Masque. She clasped her mic, wearing a literal bag over her head. The Germs' frontman, Darby Crash, ripped the paper covering off of her and Alice shoved him offstage, earning the nickname "violence girl"—it became the title of a Bags song and of Alice's memoir. She danced in a fearless femme style, not afraid to scream across the stage before slamming herself into speakers, walls, fans—or anything in her way. Her charisma struck her audience hard. At their first live show, the Bags performed two encores.

It was the moment that Alice had been rehearsing for all of her life, only this time, she was in control of the violent theatrics.

Born in 1958, Alicia Armendariz, the daughter of Mexican immigrants, grew up in East LA in what she later described in her memoir as a "cockroach-infested" slum. Her father ruled her home by terrorizing her mother, dragging her through the streets by her hair with her legs dripping blood, socking her face repeatedly with his fists, or ramming her into car doors or whatever was nearby. Alice would try to stop him, but often, standing in the way between her father and mother meant she might get a lashing of her own.

From this violent upbringing, Alice inherited a rage toward the patriarchy, machismo, and men who tried to keep her down.

Armendariz escaped the violence of her home through music, first, by listening to Mexican rancheras; next, to glam rock acts like Elton John and David Bowie; and later, through punk. She loved punk's flamboyant aesthetic, daringness, and total originality of sound. As a teenager, she took in the Ramones, Television, and Patti Smith, while reading zines and frequenting punk venues like the Roxy, the Masque, and Whisky a Go Go. But she was not content just as an audience member; she wanted to channel her rage onstage.

After practicing with her girlfriends in many incarnations of different bands, Armendariz reinvented herself as Alice Bag and became the frontwoman of the Bags, forming the band alongside her childhood best friend and bass guitarist Patricia Morrison. In 1976, the Los Angeles punk scene was hitting its stride, and Alice was close friends and often collaborated with members of the Zeros, X, the Go-Go's, the Weirdos, and the Germs.

The Bags became a nucleus of the Los Angeles punk rock scene. Early punks were as diverse in their sounds as they were in their backgrounds, and the Bags thrived in the experimental, hedonistic openness. The band toured throughout the West Coast, sharing bills with Iggy Pop, Dead Kennedys, and even the Sex Pistols.

Alice's fearlessness as a performer would live on in infamy after the Bags—dubbed Alice Bag Band due to the singer's break with Morrison—made an appearance in Penelope Spheeris's controversial punk rock documentary *The Decline of Western Civilization*. In her performance of "Gluttony," Bag prances onstage like a broken marionette, using her mic as a weapon, and shimmy-twerking in a Barbie-pink dress while screeching over heavy guitars.

"She held all this power in her performance, that I wanted, and that I could identify with," says Michelle Cruz Gonzales, the Chicana punk rock drummer of the nineties hardcore band Spitboy, and the author of *The Spitboy Rule: Tales of a Xicana in a Female Punk Band*. She described seeing Alice in the film for the first time and thinking, "It was very intense, and womanly, and [she had] this very indigenous, spiritual power when she sang."

The band disbanded shortly after *The Decline*, and although the Bags' influence on the Los Angeles punk scene was unquestionable, they only recorded one single while they were together.

Soon after her appearance in the documentary, Bag focused on college. She studied philosophy and education, and after being particularly moved by Paulo Freire's *Pedagogy of the Oppressed*, she briefly went to Nicaragua to help the Sandinistas with their literacy campaign. After spending time in such poverty, Alice chose to dedicate her life to highlighting inequity and bringing education to underserved members of her community.

While Alice was in school, her punk rock spirit

continued. She was a member of Castration Squad (along with LA punk pioneer Phranc) and Cholita—the female Menudo, featuring drag queen Vaginal Davis. Her career in education was balanced by her creative life and dozens of musical projects that she was involved in.

In 2011, Alice Bag released her memoir *Violence Girl*, the first autobiography written from the perspective of a first-wave punk and Chicana. In her book, Alice tells the tale of growing up working class and fiercely ambitious, and details what it was like to come of age in Los Angeles punk culture. For many Chicana and Latinx artists after her, the book served as proof of the diversity of the punk scene and that people of color, the queer community, and women actively shaped the culture.

"I feel that for women, we're told to create in our bedrooms when we're young, and we're told to put that behind us as sort of a girlhood experience.

But she [Alice] has created, and been a musician for her entire life," says Candace Hansen, a drummer who plays with Alice Bag and the queercore group YAAWN. "It has been really inspiring as a fan, to see how she has created work that has inspired and become a way for people to engage rage—and do it in a way that's fierce and femme and true to who she is, and enabled people to find a space to have that proxy with her in that space."

Alice Bag released her solo debut *Alice Bag* in 2016, her first album in four decades. It's an eclectic record with bits of punk, fifties pop, and danceable rock and roll; a followup, *Blueprint*, came out in 2018. Her subjects are political and feminist and deal with themes as varied as immigration and domestic violence. Since her album's release, Alice has been relentlessly touring, and even as she approaches 60, she remains Violence Girl: a force to be slamdanced with. ■

CHRISSIE HYNDE

WENDY CASE

ILLUSTRATION BY WENDY CASE

It's usually only in retrospect that you can accurately assesses good fortune, but when my high school sweetheart introduced me to the three-square-block radius of the State and Liberty area of Ann Arbor, Michigan, in the late seventies, I knew I'd hit the rock-and-roll jackpot.

Among the highlights was Marshall's Drugs—a dumpy, understocked convenience store located in the shadow of the State Theater. As teenagers, Ron and Scott Asheton of the Stooges used to buy their cigarettes at Marshall's, a fact that would have me eyeing the decaying floor tiles with reverence every time I stepped to the register. A few doors down was a T-shirt shop called Make Waves—most of us had our first encounters with the music, fashion, and fanzines of the booming English punk scene there. Up a few blocks at East William and Liberty was Music Mart, a hulking, preternaturally dusty instrument shop staffed by wisecracking, beat-up local musicians. These hungover reptiles were like gods to me—*real* musicians who played *real* gigs in *real* bars. That's what I wanted to be.

There were vintage clothing shops and used record stores on every corner, and plenty of options for the latest vinyl: State Discount was the cheapest; Schoolkids was there for the jazz and blues snobs. Discount Records, though pricier, was always a stop, simply because it was right across the street from Marshall's.

A young James Osterberg (aka Iggy Pop) worked at Discount Records in its early days. I used to think about that every time the rapey record store clerk invited teenage me down into its dank, moldy basement to smoke weed. It was on such a day, after the usual fending off of his pawing advances, that I staggered up from the depths to discover the first *Pretenders* album. It was on the wall display between Grace Slick's "Dreams" and a picture disk of Linda Ronstadt lacing up her roller skates. The cover was mesmerizing—in particular, the arresting gaze of the woman in the red leather jacket. Posed in a relaxed, pseudo-bondage posture—and staring directly into the lens—her affect suggested carnal knowledge and covert danger. I felt certain that hiding in that sleeve was the most rock-and-roll slab in creation.

From the first chugs of the floor tom and rhythm guitar, Pretenders was an explosive revelation. Up unto that point, my musical heroes had been predominantly male. But all that changed approximately two minutes and fifty-three seconds into my first listen when I heard Chrissie Hynde bark the immortal words: "but I'm too precious for *that*, baby—fuck off!" That f-bomb was titanic. It represented a seismic shift in my sixteen-year-old rock-and-roll education.

I began haunting Make Waves, snatching up every scrap of news I could get on the band. Through

UK rags like *NME* and *Flexipop*, I discovered that Hynde was from my birthplace of Akron, Ohio—a fact that geeked me to the gills. My aforementioned high school sweetheart, a talented guitarist with excellent taste, had acquainted me with the Yardbirds and, in particular, Jeff Beck—so when I saw Hynde dropping his name in the press and copping his roguish look, it further reinforced she was delivering quality I could trust. When it was announced the Pretenders would be playing up the road in Detroit, magical boyfriend and I went straight to work making a T-shirt for Chrissie. Forged in our high school print shop, it featured the robot kid from inside the jacket of the first album. I cut the sleeves off before folding it into a pink Bloomingdale's panty box rescued from my mum's garbage.

We were intoxicated with the promise of rock before the curtain even opened that night. Martha and the Vandellas' "Dancing in the Street" was tumbling out of the PA, flooding our brains with thunderous rhythm and soul as we waited for the main event. When the Pretenders hit, they were everything we'd hoped for. James Honeyman-Scott's guitar shimmered above the hammering rhythm section of Pete Farndon and Martin Chambers—and Hynde, hunched and raking on her telecaster, swiveled her hips like a floor show collision of Elvis Presley and Mae West. But what really got my attention was her fearless level of intimacy with the audience. Her unexpurgated stage banter crackled with provocative charm: "C'mon girls," she snapped, "shake your tits! Dry up the guy in front of you."

Much has been made of Hynde's voice, and justifiably so—it is a singular sound that gives few clues whence it came. Capable of both acid reportage and wrenching tenderness, it's only in her famously halting vibrato (splendorous on tracks such as "Kid" and the Kinks cover "Stop Your Sobbing") that one can hear echoes of Ronettes and Marvelettes. But it was her songwriting that seduced me, utterly. There was an integrity to it, an understanding that you were getting the truth, no matter what the subject at hand. Aggressive and audacious when it mattered, Hynde could gear down into gut-twisting proclamations of love, lust, and longing. "Brass in Pocket," the Pretenders' sparkling breakthrough track in the States, floated above Detroit's Zeppelin/Seger/Nugent FM din like Blake's ebullient newborn in *An Infant's Sorrow*—a veritable "fiend hid in a cloud."

It was clear from the start that Hynde had done her homework. The photo of her as a shadowy teen, clutching her Stones records, tells the tale—she was a fan, just like us. Previous to Hynde's public ardor for the Stooges and Mitch Ryder, Michigan kids of my generation had only a cursory understanding of their existence via arcane transmissions from *Creem* magazine. It's like she was waving her hands around saying, "Don't you know what you've got here?"

But Hynde was also the consummate rock star, herself. Whip-smart, volatile, and possessed of a caustic wit, she had a talent for messing with the equation. In her 2016 autobiography *Reckless*, Hynde detailed her experience at Kent State during the 1970 shootings, her arrival in London at the dawn of the UK punk explosion, and her relationship

PLAYLIST

WITH THE PRETENDERS:

"Kid," 1980, *Pretenders*

"Brass in Pocket," 1980, *Pretenders*

"Precious," 1980, *Pretenders*

"Tattooed Love Boys," 1980, *Pretenders*

"Message of Love," 1981, *Pretenders II*

"2000 Miles," 1984, *Learning to Crawl*

"My Baby," 1986, *Get Close*

"Gotta Wait," 2016, *Alone*

WITH UB40:

"Breakfast in Bed," 1988, on UB40's *UB40*

WITH JP, CHRISSIE, AND THE FAIRGROUND BOYS:

"If You Let Me," 2010, *Fidelity!*

with Kinks legend Ray Davies. Hynde's union with Davies produced a daughter, as did her marriage to Simple Minds' Jim Kerr. Infamously, the book also includes a passage about a violent sexual encounter with opportunistic bikers in Akron. Hynde's matter-of-fact observations about the experience and her "evolutionary psychology" take on navigating sexual threat created an international uproar during the book's release, forcing her into endless unwelcome conversations about sexual culpability.

Hynde makes feminists crazy. They love her—they can't help themselves. But she won't stay on the reservation; in fact, she's never set foot on it. *Real* rock and roll is a put-up-or-shut-up world—and it is not polite. She warned us back in 1980 that "if you mess with the goods, doll—you gotta pay." Maybe it's just Akron-bred pragmatism, but I agree with Hynde—and I appreciate her unflinching and unapologetic nature. She is interested in human relationships, not sexual politics; she's interested in rock and roll.

The drug-related deaths of Honeyman-Scott and Farndon in the early eighties brought a swift end to the chemistry that colored the band's meteoric rise. Hynde would go on to make many albums, both as the Prentenders and as a solo artist—often catching sparks in the fashion of *Pretenders* and *Pretenders II*. But the gravity of emotion and the intensity of purpose in the original lineup were undeniable. Hynde's loyalty to that shared experience is evidenced by the fact that her autobiography ends soon after the passing of her mates.

In true Midwestern style, Hynde's first communication to the audience at the Royal Oak Music Theatre that August night in 1981 was, "Do you guys know how lucky you are to be from Detroit?" I've thought about that question many times over the years. As a Detroiter by fortuitous default, it's unlikely I would have come into the totality of what that means without Hynde's blueprint. My faith in her decrees always paid off—still does.

Once the show was over, boyfriend and I positioned ourselves by the backstage door—hoping to catch a glimpse of the band as they exited. Pete Farndon was first, bounding out with a leggy brunette and a bottle of champagne. He and his date skipped past the waiting limo and headed straight for the tour bus. When Hynde emerged twenty minutes later, she had my pink Bloomies box tucked under her arm—beamed to her earlier in the evening by a generous roadie. We were thrilled.

Clad in a plain gray sweatshirt, she was all biz as she breezed past the clutch of admirers and hopped into the limo. I presumed she was off for a date with the hotel phone, poised to whisper into the waiting ear of Ray Davies—or perhaps to fight with him all night and cry her trademark black eyeliner onto a starchy hotel pillowcase.

Either way works—because that's life, and that's where the songs are. ■

EXENE CERVENKA

CARYN ROSE

ILLUSTRATION BY ANNE MUNTGES

Artist, poet, singer, songwriter, guitar player, author, teacher, mother. Exene (nee Christene) Cervenka arrived in Los Angeles in the pre-punk year of 1976 and headed straight for the literary community in Venice. She got a job at Beyond Baroque arts center, doing typesetting and layout. One night at a poetry workshop, a gentleman soon to be known as John Doe sat down next to her. They struck up a conversation when they liked each other's writing and developed a friendship. Doe took a liking to one of Cervenka's poems and asked if he could turn it into a song; he had a band with a friend who went by the name of Billy Zoom. Cervenka agreed, as long as she could sing it—despite no previous experience or ambition to be in a rock band. Her charisma and energy carried her through her first performance, fulfilling one of the essential tenets of punk rock. The band called themselves X, and the world shifted on its axis.

X didn't sound like anyone else in LA because they weren't like anyone else in LA. X's lyrics were written by poets, and while rock songs are not poems, the quality of Cervenka and Doe's lyrics elevated the band above their contemporaries. Zoom stood stage right and peeled nitro-flavored rockabilly riffs. DJ Bonebrake was the hardest hitting jazz drummer you've ever heard. But the key element that defined X's sound was the fusion of Cervenka and Doe's

voices. They sang the songs together in a poignant, passionate style that reached into your chest and ripped your heart open. Their vibe owed as much to Johnny Cash and June Carter Cash as it did to anything calling itself punk rock. Doe's warm, buttery, almost polished vocals provided a solid foundation for Cervenka to weave her haunting, silvery voice through. They created a harmony that was, and remains, unique to X. Watching the two interact vocally live was deeply meaningful: you believed every word they sang. The pair married in 1980, and despite divorcing just five years later, the creative partnership remained solidly intact, and the onstage dynamic remains authentic decades later.

From 1980 to 1993, X released seven albums, of which five—*Los Angeles*, *Wild Gift*, *Under the Big Black Sun*, *More Fun in the New World*, *See How We Are*—are insanely solid, undeniable classics of punk rock. They elevated West Coast punk to international attention, the only band among their peers to do so. The visual imagery of the records was also critically important, echoing their established aesthetic of thrift store, abandoned Americana, with the hand-inked liner notes painstakingly crafted by Cervenka.

The lyrics offered vignettes of suburban despondency and urban desperation, the scenes they witnessed on the tarnished underbelly of Tinsel Town, the places Exene (and John) left behind. Cervenka grew up in Florida, dropping out of high school at age sixteen to work odd jobs and take care of her sisters after her mother's death. She sold burial plots, waitressed, and worked in a toy department before taking off for the West Coast. So lyrics like "We're desperate / get used to it," "I could throw my lipstick / and bracelets like gravel," "The world's a mess / it's in my kiss" reflected Exene's reality. They were outsider observations delivered with a touch of dark humor between the lines; even the songs on *Under the Big Black Sun*, the band's third album, written in the aftermath of the terrible death of Cervenka's sister Mary (Mirielle) in a car wreck, have shades of gold. "Dancing with Tears in My Eyes" is sung against a boppy rockabilly beat; "Come Back to Me" is turned into a fifties teenage lament. Cervenka always points to the album as her favorite out of the band's catalog.

X went on hiatus in the early nineties. Cervenka started or joined multiple other bands and musical concerns: the country/rockabilly-flavored Knitters, which was three-fourths of X along with Dave Alvin; Auntie Christ—a faster, louder punk concern in which Exene was the only guitar player (an instrument she didn't even start playing until the mid-eighties)—formed in the late nineties with Bonebrake and Matt Freeman from Rancid; and in the early aughts, Cervenka fronted the Original Sinners, which leaned toward poppy surf punk. Throughout this entire continuum, Cervenka also wrote and recorded a handful of solo albums, most notably *Old Wives' Tales* (1989), the excellent *Somewhere Gone* (2009), and 2011's *The Excitement of Maybe*. Exene and John Doe went out as an acoustic duet in the mid-aughts, culminating in a live record,

Singing and Playing (2010). In 2016, the two supported the first leg of Blondie and Garbage's co-headlining tour, "The Rage and Rapture."

In 1987, Cervenka remarried, this time to a then up-and-coming actor named Viggo Mortensen, whom she met while beginning a brief acting career in the movie *Salvation!* The two had a son, then divorced in 1998; this matters to her creative history because it was during this time that Exene took a job as an assistant teacher and librarian in order to support her family. She was diagnosed with multiple sclerosis in 1996 and has alluded to some physical struggles as a result of the disease, but as her copious output illustrates, at no point did she ever stop working. (She would, however, offer, "Don't get married" when asked in 2011 what advice she would give to an aspiring female musician.)

In parallel to her musical projects, Cervenka pursued both her visual art and her writing. She published several books of poetry under Henry Rollins's 2.13.61 imprint, and collaborated with New York no wave pioneer Lydia Lunch on the poetry book *Adulterers Anonymous*, and with Wanda Coleman, who was known as "the unofficial poet laureate of Los Angeles," on the album *Twin Sisters* (1985). Cervenka's first comprehensive museum exhibition of her journals and mixed-media collages was held at the Santa Monica Museum of Art in 2005, and

PLAYLIST

WITH X:

"Johnny Hit and Run Paulene," 1980, *Los Angeles*

"The World's a Mess; It's in My Kiss," 1980, *Los Angeles*

"We're Desperate," 1981, *Wild Gift*

"Beyond and Back," 1981, *Wild Gift*

"Riding with Mary," 1982, *Under the Big Black Sun*

"Blue Spark," 1982, *Under the Big Black Sun*

"The New World," 1983, *More Fun in the New World*

"See How We Are," 1987, on *See How We Are*

WITH THE KNITTERS:

"The Call of the Wreckin' Ball," 1985, *Poor Little Critter on the Road*

SOLO:

"Brand New Memory," 2011, *The Excitement of Maybe*

she has been featured in over a dozen one-person, two-person, or group art exhibitions from 1998 to 2013. Cervenka's personal fashion aesthetic was well ahead of her time; her mix of Theda Bara meets *The Wild Ones* would be imitated by thousands of women but never equaled. (If you wear cowboy boots with your dresses, thank Exene.) Cervenka's eye is so legendarily discerning that when she decided to liquidate a healthy portion of her estate in 2014, there was insane demand for what she thought of as just a yard sale.

X revived itself as a live touring act in the mid-nineties to rapturous response and never stopped, only slowing down briefly when Billy Zoom was diagnosed with bladder cancer. (He, too, returned to the stage.) The young punks that never got to see X finally had their chance; the old punks brought their kids. The people who grew up listening to them had their own bands—Pearl Jam would take X on tour several times, culminating in 2011 when they played together in South America in front of fifty thousand rabid fans. In 2017, Cervenka threw out the first pitch at Dodger Stadium on a night dedicated to paying tribute to X, celebrating their fortieth year together. She is still writing songs; she is still making art. "Nothing affects my outlook," she said in 2011. "I have a straight line in front of me and I stick to it. It's all you can do." ■

POISON IVY

GILLIAN G. GAAR

ILLUSTRATION BY WINNIE T. FRICK

In a musical culture that elevated outsiders, the Cramps still seemed strange: characters from a creature feature playing blistering vintage-inspired punk rock. They were "the Addams Family of Rock," a band that created a new musical genre, "psychobilly," drawn from the detritus of American culture: comic books, horror films, and the primeval forces of rockabilly and rock and roll. Towering lead singer Lux Interior, who seemed even taller due to the pompadour piled on top of his head, threw himself around the stage, tearing off his clothes, appearing at times to be swallowing his microphone. Right by his side, from beginning to end, was lead guitarist Poison Ivy. She prowled the stage attired in something kitschy or glamorous, a sequined bikini or a leopard-print bodysuit, drawing sizzling surf-guitar licks from her beloved Gretsch hollow-body guitar. Ivy was the glue that held the Cramps together for over thirty years, gradually stepping up to take over more and more of the band's business, all while honing her skills as an exceptionally fierce guitarist.

Born Kristy Marlana Wallace on February 20, 1953, Ivy grew up in California. As a child, she favored novelty records like "Martian Hop" by the Ran-Dells and Sheb Wooley's "The Purple People Eater." She was later drawn to the slinky instrumentals of Link Wray and Duane Eddy, who would both greatly influence her own style. Her brother taught her to play the surf classic "Pipeline." Her attraction to instrumentals was a key factor in Ivy developing her own distinctive voice as a guitarist. In a piece without vocals, the emotion comes purely from the instrumentation, which pushes the players to become more expressive; they're the ones creating the drama.

In 1972, Ivy and Interior were both attending Sacramento State College. They met when Interior was riding in a car that stopped to pick up a hitchhiking Ivy; it was the day they both left "ordinary" behind. They moved in together and became consumed with music, drawn to flamboyant performers like T. Rex and the New York Dolls. But they also began investigating rock's past: fifties rock and roll, doo-wop, R&B, the blues, and garage rock, prowling thrift stores and junk shops for rare records and for clothing for their similarly vintage, glam look.

They'd already developed alter egos. "Poison Ivy" came from both the Coasters' song and the name of a *Batman* villain (her full name: Poison Ivy Rorschach); Interior used the names Vip Vop and Raven Beauty before settling on Lux Interior.

PLAYLIST

ALL SONGS WITH THE CRAMPS:

"Human Fly," 1978, *Bad Music for Bad People*

"Garbageman," 1980, *Songs the Lord Taught Us*

"You Got Good Taste," 1983, *Smell of Female*

"Can Your Pussy Do the Dog?," 1985, *A Date with Elvis*

"Get Off the Road," 1985, *A Date with Elvis* (reissue)

"Bop Pills," 1990, *Stay Sick!*

"Shortnin' Bread," 1990, *Stay Sick!*

"Wrong Way Ticket," 2003, *Fiends of Dope Island*

Deciding to start their own band, they moved to New York City in 1975, having investigated the new music scene emerging at nightspots like Max's Kansas City and CBGB. Ivy named the band the Cramps, inspired by another band, the Kinks, both names suggesting something twisted, sick, potentially dangerous.

The Cramps stood out even among that pioneering punk scene. They initially had two guitarists and no bass, and the lead guitarist was Ivy, a woman, a rarity (early Cramps lineups featured female drummers as well). Ivy immediately cut a distinctive sonic figure: on "The Way I Walk," the B-side of the band's first single, her guitar has the same menace as Link Wray's in "Rumble." Her precise descending line on "Human Fly" aurally brings the creepy crawly to vivid life.

Because the Cramps played rockabilly infused with the raw energy of punk, and their set lists included vintage songs like "Surfin' Bird" and "Fever," the band was sometimes described as a kitschy nostalgia act. But Ivy and Interior had no desire to be fifties-era revivalists along the lines of Stray Cats. They were inspired by the past but saw themselves as creating something new and entirely their own. As the two put it in the liner notes of the anthology *How to Make a Monster* (2004): "We wanted to be as shocking, sexy and original as the great culture-changing rock 'n' roll pioneers were during the '50s and '60s—not imitators, but the same kind of rebels that they were in their time."

Perhaps it wasn't easy to maintain the same level of devotion to the music that Ivy and Interior had. The Cramps' lineup changed continually over the years, which made it hard for the band to build momentum; continual problems with record companies had the same result. It was Ivy who emerged as the backbone of the Cramps, the driving force keeping the band together. She and Interior wrote most of the songs. From the second album on, she produced or co-produced every subsequent record. She ran the Cramps' own record label, Vengeance, and ultimately became the band's manager. It was easier, she said, to do it themselves than rely on other people.

Yet her skills were often overlooked in favor of her physical attributes. Granted, it was Ivy who was most often the sole band member seen on album covers, wearing something skin tight, revealing, or both. But she couldn't understand why, when she was the lead guitarist, interviewers would just ask about her clothes and not her gear. She'd started out on a solid body guitar, but in 1985 she picked up a 1958 Gretsch 6120 hollow body, "and there's no going back," she told *Vintage Guitar* magazine. It became her primary guitar for the rest of the band's career.

In the same article, Ivy's advice to aspiring guitarists was to not take lessons; you'd have a better chance of being more unique that way. It was certainly advice she lived by. As she became increasingly proficient, her guitar parts burned with a scorching intensity, providing an expert foil for Interior's over-the-top vocal performances. The best examples of her nimble finger work can be found on the Cramps' strongest album, 1990's *Stay Sick!* ("Bop Pills" and "Shortnin' Bread" in particular). Or consider "Wrong Way Ticket" on the band's last album, *Fiends of Dope Island* (2003), a track that brings the record to a searing conclusion, Ivy's guitar swooping and soaring, going flat out in a race to oblivion.

The Cramps came to an abrupt end, when Interior died on February 4, 2009, of an aortic dissection. Ivy has kept a low profile ever since. But if she's hung up her Gretsch for good, her legacy remains a body of work where her passion for the untamed spirit of rock and roll can be heard in every lick. ■

ESG

STEPHANIE PHILLIPS

ILLUSTRATION BY JULIE WINEGARD

If one were to write the ultimate story of a gang of struggling artists who changed the world but never got their due respect, it would most likely follow the journey of New York's first ladies of post-punk, new wave, funk, and hip-hop: ESG. Formed in 1978 in the South Bronx, the Scroggins sisters turned a hobby foisted on them by their mother into a genre-defying megalith. ESG is one of the most sampled bands of all time, yet the millions who hear their beats don't know of the women who are still chasing their royalties.

ESG's story starts back in the late seventies, when their mother, worried about the drug abuse and violence on the neighborhood streets that had already lured her older children, decided to preoccupy her young girls' minds by buying them instruments. Surrounded by the melee of Latin beats and funky jams that weaved in and out of the South Bronx, the girls—Renee (vocals), Valerie (drums), Deborah (bass), and Marie (congas and vocals)—quickly got to work. Soon they entered themselves in various talent competitions, to the delight of their mother.

ESG's take on funk was about whittling it down to its bare bones. Renee loved James Brown but specifically the part of his songs where he would "take it to the bridge," leaving just the bass and drums to build suspense. Renee wanted all of their songs to be one long suspense-filled bridge. ESG's music seems to be the result of a group of people being told to make pop having never heard a note before: a dark, otherworldly sound that fed into post-punk, No Wave, funk, dance, and the early hip-hop scene, their influence on which would be greater than the sisters could predict. They did know two things, though, and reflected as such in their name: the group would be a family band, and they wanted it to be successful. The E and S in ESG stand for Valerie and Renee's birthstones (emerald and sapphire) and the G refers to gold, how many records they wanted to sell.

The band met record store owner Ed Bahlman at a local talent contest and agreed to sign to his label 99 Records. The short-lived label captured an exciting moment in New York post-punk history, home to such seminal bands as Bush Tetras and Liquid Liquid. The music made during this brief period was known as No Wave. Bands such as Ut, Theoretical Girls, Bloods, and Teenage Jesus and the Jerks, all of which prominently featured women, embraced jazz, funk, noise, and dissonant sounds with a playful attitude. ESG became part of a scene that gave women the space to create experimental music that was both complex and amateur.

PLAYLIST

"UFO," 1981, *ESG*

"You're No Good," 1981, *ESG*

"My Love for You," 1983, *Come Away with ESG*

"Chistelle," 1983, *Come Away with ESG*

"Moody (Spaced Out)," 1983, *Come Away with ESG*

ESG also connected with another seminal post-punk scene, this one far from home. After meeting the English tastemaker Tony Wilson from the Manchester label Factory Records (Joy Division, Happy Mondays), the band agreed to make an EP with producer Martin Hannett in Manchester. According to legend, the sisters recorded "You're No Good" and "Moody" but still had three minutes left on the tape. Hannett asked them if they had anything else in their back pocket so the band recorded a song they had been practicing, "UFO."

Opening with a chorus of wailing sirens, "UFO" is a masterpiece in the proper use of a sliding guitar chord. The drums race back and forth trying to keep up, showing that perhaps Valerie didn't know the song that well, but it doesn't matter. The imperfections add to the beauty. The resulting EP, *ESG* (1981), feels like a rare moment in music when you know you're listening to the beginning of something, whether it's a movement or a new way of thinking. All you know is that no musician who listens to this will look at their instrument in the same way again.

ESG's music was danceable yet still undecipherable, leaving listeners craving more.

Thanks to their link to Factory Records, ESG played the opening night of the Haçienda in Manchester. Mainly funded by Factory Records and New Order sales, the club was the thriving hub of the "Madchester" scene and the birthplace of acid house and rave.

"UFO," in all of its cold, edgy brilliance, has become one of the most sampled songs of all time. Acts from Public Enemy to Nine Inch Nails have used the track to enhance their songs in one way or another. However, ESG was frustrated to discover their songs were being sampled without their permission, and they saw none of the profits. They were particularly disappointed that their music was used in songs that were derogatory toward women. Speaking to the Quietus in 2015, Renee explained: "I'm still saying to myself, don't these guys realise that women wrote this music? And yet you're calling every woman a bitch and a whore and treating them like garbage."

While other bands were living the high life on ESG's music, the band, though popular, hit a dead end in 1984 when 99 Records collapsed, and the Scroggins sisters had to take a break. They didn't forget about the bands that made money off them, though, and in 1992 they came back with an EP aptly titled *Sample Credits Don't Pay Our Bills*. The record still contained the essential elements of ESG, evolving slightly to include an early nineties club synth sound. The opener, "There Was a Time," is heavily influenced by James Brown's song of the same name, so much so that ESG affectionately include a note on the record's label that says "inspired by Mr. 'please please please' (don't sue us!) James Brown." Renee now pays a private investigator to track down any uncredited samples.

Disheartened and worn out from battling against constant unauthorized sampling, a defunct label, and lack of appreciation for their own uncategorizable music, the band kept a low profile for most of the nineties and early aughts. Then they got a new breath of life and started a successful run of gigs touring the US and Europe. Now a new generation of post-punk New Wave lovers have found the sisters. Bands such as London's Shopping and Glasgow's Sacred Paws have made their admiration of ESG known in the groove of their bass and the pace of their drum beat. They are creating their own experimental noise in the hope that they become successors to ESG's crown. ∎

GIRLS JUST WANT TO HAVE FUN

On August 1, 1981, shortly after the stroke of midnight, a cable channel changed the music world. It's no coincidence that the first two songs MTV played during those wee hours featured female vocalists: "Video Killed the Radio Star" by the Buggles, its chorus chanted by Debi Doss and Linda Jardim, and "You Better Run" by hard rocker Pat Benatar. At a time when FM radio had become increasingly locked into the album rock format that was a thin cloak for rockist male chauvinism, this "music television" offered an outlet for the new sounds and artists that were coming up from underground and over from Europe. It was the dawn of a new day, a new decade, and a new era in pop music, mostly for better but sometimes for worse.

The 1980s were a conservative decade in general, ruled by the paternalistic actor Ronald Reagan in the US and the Iron Lady, Margaret Thatcher, in the UK. But MTV offered a spot of bright, irreverent fun. By necessity as much as intention, its programmers looked beyond the usual chart acts to fill its twenty-four hours of music programming. At the same time, the housewives, college students, and schoolkids who tuned in were not necessarily interested in watching the aging men of album rock play another extended guitar solo. Instead, the burgeoning genres of New Wave, hair metal, and hip-hop starred young artists who honed a fresh visual as well as musical style. The effect of the videoization of music was perhaps most dramatic for female artists. Whereas the Runaways were locked out of radio and therefore the American market in the late 1970s, band members Joan Jett and Lita Ford both became MTV stars a few years later. The Go-Go's, Madonna, Blondie, the Eurythmics, Bow Wow Wow, the Human League, Sinéad O'Connor, the Bangles, 'Til Tuesday—all found success thanks to heavy video rotation. At first, MTV hesitated to break the color line that had long divided the music industry. But Michael Jackson changed all that, and soon his sister, Janet, and Whitney Houston, and Salt-N-Pepa, and Queen Latifah were bringing rap, pop, and R&B into the family room.

There was a downside to this emphasis on the visual, of course. More pressure to look good was put on artists than ever—and good often meant sexy. Some acts were happy to self-objectify. Others chose to playfully (or not) slap the male gaze in the face. Few managed the MTV platform better than Cyndi Lauper. She was thirty years old when her album *She's So Unusual* came out, and rather than writhe on the floor in her underwear, the Queens native adopted the punk beauty-disruption of partially shaved and technicolor hair. "Girls Just Want to Have Fun," she sang, and of course, fun wasn't really the only thing we wanted, but we did want it—on our own terms.

THE GO-GO'S

JEANNE FURY

ILLUSTRATION BY JULIE WINEGARD

I n a 1982 cover story, *Rolling Stone* dubbed the mega-popular, platinum-selling Go-Go's "America's rock & roll sweethearts" and described the five young women as "safe, wholesome, and proudly commercial." Fast-forward eighteen years to the LA band's episode of VH1's *Behind the Music*, which revealed a very different group. The Go-Go's, it turned out, were sexually voracious heathen drug fiends—a bracing revelation on par with photos of the moon landing or Kiss without makeup.

The band's candor simultaneously demolished their bubbly California cutie image and impaled the notion of "sugar and spice and everything nice" that girls are saddled with from birth. The Go-Go's prove that women can be just as gnarly as men.

Here are two other things that aren't affected by gender: musical ability and the potential for success. The Go-Go's had to teach the world about those, too.

On March 6, 1982, the Go-Go's debut, *Beauty and the Beat*, hit number one on the Billboard 200 album chart, where it would stay for six consecutive weeks, making the kitschy crew the first all-female band to top the chart with songs they not only wrote but also performed. This milestone in music history has an annoying flipside: It's never been replicated. The Go-Go's remain the only all-female band to have had an album for which they alone wrote and played all the songs themselves reach number one.

There should have been many successors. Although the talent was likely there, the same can't be said for labels willing to throw support (read: money and marketing prowess) behind bands of young women. For some reason, labels are perfectly comfortable unloading onto the public hundreds of spectacularly mediocre male bands, but they take a hard pass on patently talented female bands. Sorry, girls, you don't even get the chance to flop, let alone flourish.

Mercifully, the scene that bore the Go-Go's encouraged much flopping. The band had deep roots in LA punk, which, in the mid- to late seventies, was a hotbed of freaks on a creative streak. Bands like the Weirdos, the Bags, and the Germs had zero use for rock's bloated, archaic rulebook and instead believed opportunity could be self-generated—marketability be damned. This radical conviction made it possible for a bunch of musical novices to form a band.

The first incarnation of the Go-Go's began in 1978 and featured ex-Germs drummer Belinda Carlisle (vocals), Jane Wiedlin (guitar), Margot Olavarria (bass), and Elissa Bello (drums). Guitarist Charlotte Caffey was asked to join later in the year, reportedly because she knew how to plug a guitar into an amp. In 1979, the band got an enormous boost in musical ability when Bello was replaced by Gina Schock, who played with Edie and the Eggs, featuring Edith Massey, cult star of John Waters movies.

The Go-Go's caught the ears of UK label Stiff Records, which put out their single "We Got the Beat" in mid-1980. Featuring a rollicking melodic hook built around Schock's knockout drumming, the song became an underground hit that helped pack an increasing number of bodies into clubs whenever the Go-Go's were on a bill. By the end of the year, Olavarria was out, replaced by Kathy Valentine, whose badass pedigree included the UK metal band Girlschool, the Austin punk band the Violators, and LA punk band the Textones.

The Go-Go's signed to IRS Records and released *Beauty and the Beat* in the summer of 1981. Producers Richard Gottehrer and Rob Freeman deliberately tossed aside the band's punk upbringing in favor of a poppier, peppier sound. At first hesitant to embrace the new direction, the Go-Go's came around once they saw how much fans and critics dug it.

The finely crafted songs fit right into a niche previously carved out by punk bands that had an overt affinity for pop music's tunefulness: the tight jangle of guitars on "How Much More" recalls the hopped-up anxiety of the Ramones, and flickers of Blondie's lethal-cool attitude permeate the sullen darkness of "This Town." The first single, "Our Lips Are Sealed," reached number twenty on the *Billboard* Hot 100, and "We Got the Beat" made it all the way to number two, pushing *Beauty and the Beat* to the top of the album chart. It was certified double platinum by the RIAA, turning the Go-Go's into bona fide rock stars.

The next year, the band was nominated for a Grammy for Best New Artist and released their follow-up, *Vacation*. The title track reached number eight on the *Billboard* chart, and the album was certified gold by the RIAA. *Talk Show* followed in 1984, and although it generated two Top 40 hits, the Go-Go's were having internal issues, and the album was the last they would make for quite some time.

In the years since, there were reunion shows, retrospective albums, lawsuits, rehab, tours, a new album (2001's *God Bless the Go-Go's*), a star on the Hollywood Walk of Fame, more lawsuits, and a farewell tour—though they haven't officially disbanded.

Although the famed debauchery of the Go-Go's helped flip the script on what could be expected from a band of cherubic girls, their longevity is far more significant to their legacy. They have spent nearly forty years showing the world that women have the wherewithal to write original songs, play instruments, top the charts, sell tons of albums, and maintain a worldwide fanbase as capably as men. And yet, no other all-female band has been able to take their place alongside the Go-Go's as the sole songwriters and performers of a chart-topping album. After all these years, is the pursuit still a noble one?

Yes. Yes, it is. In addition to the financial security that songwriting royalties can provide, a sense of agency is at the heart of feminism. More so than "yes we can," the ethos is "yes we do," and sometimes, destiny's demands go far beyond sugar, spice, and everything nice. Through the Go-Go's, girls and women claimed a beat of one's own. *Yeah, we got it.* ■

PLAYLIST

"We Got the Beat," 1980, *Beauty and the Beat*

"Our Lips Are Sealed," 1981, *Beauty and the Beat*

"Vacation," 1982, *Vacation*

"Head over Heels," 1984, *Talk Show*

"The Whole World Lost Its Head," 1994, *Return to the Valley of the Go-Go's*

LAURIE ANDERSON

MICHELLE THREADGOULD

ILLUSTRATION BY WINNIE T. FRICK

"**I** do think that stories can cure you, but you have to find out what's wrong first," the experimental, electronic musician and multimedia artist Laurie Anderson told the Louisiana Channel in 2016. Anderson's ambitious, multifaceted body of work is not so much about finding the cure but finding the way to tell the story that is authentic to herself. The phrase "multimedia artist" best describes her because it houses all of the identities that she wants to be: singer, violinist, pianist, performance artist, poet, painter, sculptor, computer programmer, electronic musician, documentarian, installation artist—it gives her the freedom to walk a nonlinear path.

After all, Anderson likes to paraphrase the new wave French filmmaker Jean-Luc Godard: every good story needs a beginning, middle, and an end, just not in that order. Her work has been inspired by writers like Melville, Emerson, and Nabokov, who meander and reflect; Anderson's creations continue that tradition. She is interested in finding the story, the song, or the point as she goes, instead of trying to control her creativity.

As a child Anderson spent her time dreaming and reaching for the unimaginable. Born in 1947 in Glen Ellyn, a suburb near Chicago, she grew up in the woods, spinning stories, and telling adults and the neighborhood children that she was "from the sky." When she was thirteen, she ran for student body president and wrote a letter to John F. Kennedy, who was a senator at the time. She asked him for advice for her campaign, and he wrote her back, "Find out what the students want and promise it." The words of Kennedy helped her win the election, and she sent him a thank-you letter; he responded by sending her a dozen roses and a note of congratulations.

Life could, in moments, feel like a fairy tale.

When she wasn't dreaming, Anderson learned to play violin and performed in the Chicago Youth Symphony. She never fully committed to one art form, and studied painting and sculpture at the Art Institute of Chicago as a teenager, eventually designing her own instruments in her free time. Her curiosity revolved around how art worked, and how it was interrelated. After graduating high school, she set out to Mills College in California, before leaving to attend Barnard College and then Columbia University for her master's degree in the early seventies.

Living in New York on the Lower East Side, Anderson experimented with performance art. She made short films and accompanied them live, playing the violin or synthesizers. She also made friends with avant-garde composers like Philip Glass, David Van Tiegham, and the producer Roma Baran. It was with Baran that she recorded the song that would change her career, "O Superman."

"O Superman" was inspired by Jules Massenet's

aria on authority, "Oh Sovereign," from the opera *Le Cid*. Anderson saw a connection between the 1979 American hostage situation in Iran and the aria. She told the *Guardian* that in the aftermath of the failed rescue attempt, "We were left with dead bodies, a pile of burning debris and the hostages nowhere to be seen. So I thought I'd write a song about all that and the failure of technology."

Anderson wanted the song to echo the vibrations of a Greek chorus, so she found a way to loop the introduction, a breathy repetition of the phrase "ha ha ha ha," using a harmonizer and a vocoder. Her vocals had the effect of a stewardess giving terrifying instructions in a controlled voice, over a backdrop of electronics and synthesizers that oscillated between the sound of the twinkling of stars to a voicemail recording.

Anderson released one thousand copies of the single in 1981 on B. George's record label, One Ten Records. George was the founder of the ARChive of Contemporary Music, an organization dedicated to archiving pop music, and he had received a National Endowment for the Arts grant to produce music by visual artists. He was later invited as a guest on John Peel's popular radio show in London, where he premiered "O Superman." DJs across London began playing the song, until a British distribution company asked Anderson for eighty thousand copies of the record. Anderson approached Warner Bros. to help her with the printing, and they signed her for an eight-album record deal.

"O Superman" led to her debut album, *Big Science* (1982), an absurdist, futuristic, avant-garde release. Described as a "masterpiece" and featured on NPR's list of 150 most influential albums by women, the record would set the tone for Anderson's work to come. She collaborated with Peter Gabriel and released the poppy and minimalist *Mister Heartbreak* with him in 1984, which included a guest appearance by the beat poet William S. Burroughs. Then, in quick succession, Anderson released *Live* (1984), her concert film *Home of the Brave* (1986), and her first foray into singing instead of spoken word, *Strange Angels* (1989).

In 1992 Anderson met one of her most influential collaborators, Lou Reed, when she was performing at John Zorn's Festival for Radical Jewish Culture in Munich. Soon after, Reed and Anderson began a lifelong relationship in music and romance. Anderson focused on more multimedia works, including the interactive CD-ROM *Puppet Motel*, as well as an opera based on Melville's book, which became "Songs and Stories by Moby Dick." Reed and Anderson partnered on her sparse, ominous album *Bright Red* (1994), which was produced by Brian Eno. After releasing several experimental albums and focusing on art installations and multimedia projects—including working as the artist in residence at NASA and developing shows for the Whitney, Guggenheim, and Mass MoCA—in 2010, Anderson released another landmark album.

The record *Homeland* described living in New York shortly after 9/11, particularly Anderson's feelings of being disturbed by the willingness of citizens to surrender total control to the government. Anderson critiqued the way that people seemed to think that spying from the National Security Agency and the militarization of the police were worth the cost

PLAYLIST

"O Superman (for Massenent)," 1982, *Big Science*

"From the Air," 1982, *Big Science*

"Excellent Birds," 1984, *Mister Heartbreak*

"The Puppet Motel," 1994, *Bright Red*

"The Salesman," 1995, *The Ugly One with the Jewels and Other Stories*

"Only an Expert," 2010, *Homeland*

"A Different World," 2015, *Heart of a Dog*

of "safety," as if freedom of thought or expression had no value. The song "Only an Expert" served as a dystopian lullaby. Layers of synthesized vocals, guitar feedback, and instigatory piano lulled the listener into uncomfortable familiarity as she stated, "Just because the stock market's crashed, doesn't necessarily mean it's a bad thing." In this song, Anderson updated "Laurie Anderson's voice," as if it were software or code. Her spoken word once assumed an affect where she overly enunciated words, like she was drawing a picture with her mouth. But on *Homeland*, she abandoned this sound for a fast-paced tone that was almost automated, like the personal assistant Alexa, speaking on an airport intercom.

This is life sped-up. Do you like life at this speed?

Anderson wasn't interested in living life at the frenetic pace of mainstream America, and with Reed, she focused on slowing down. They practiced meditation together and believed in many of the metaphors in *The Tibetan Book of the Dead*, like the importance of hearing and being present, both in the moment and in the afterlife. When Reed passed away from cancer in 2013, after the two had spent twenty-one years together, Anderson thought of the connections between love, memory, and death, which provided the material for her film and soundtrack *Heart of a Dog*.

Released in 2015, *Heart of a Dog* explored the question, "What are the last things you say in life, before you turn to dirt?" Part memoir, part investigation of sound, part oral history of storytelling, Anderson wove tales of childhood and her beloved dog Lolabelle atop her art and music, and mythology from the *Book of the Dead*. Merging spoken word, music, paintings, and video, *Heart of a Dog* succeeds as a piece of multimedia that reflects all of Anderson's talent, and gives you a taste of what Anderson, at the age of seventy, is capable of. In her effort to explore her own pain and heartache, she also found and gave us her "cure"—her gift of storytelling. ∎

DIAMANDA GALÁS

MICHELLE THREADGOULD

ILLUSTRATION BY JULIE WINEGARD

Diamanda Galás is a *Macbeth* witch in human form, a wolf-woman who can howl to shrivel your heart, a dark spinner of revelatory truths about the despicable way that our country treats people, from women to AIDS patients. Though Galás is often described as "goth" because of her penchant for wearing black gowns and dramatic makeup, with death as her subject matter, her sound defies conventional music canons. She fuses opera-like wails with piano pummeling that sounds more like avant-garde, unrestrained, classical music experiments than pared-down jazz.

In some ways she is a performance artist. To watch her perform is to be possessed, to hear a voice with a three-and-a-half-octave range and the raspy whisper of sinners, the oppressed, and the forgotten. *I'm still here*, her hands seem to pound into the piano.

You will never be rid of me.

Performing "La Llorona" at the age of sixty-two, she seems to be trespassing on a forbidden culture. "La Llorona" is one of the most performed, revered ballads of Mexico, a song that the queer mariachi artist Chavela Vargas utterly owned. Vargas sang it like her vocal cords were ripping apart, with the strength and flair of a shot of mezcal served in the clay of madre tierra, her beloved Mexico. But to Galás, there are no boundaries. Instead, Galás personifies la Llorona, a ghost of a woman tired of being prayed to.

Dígame, dígame, dígame, dígame. ¿Que más quieres? ¿Quieres más? [Tell me, tell me, tell me, tell me. What else do you want? You want more?]

At the end of her performance, an audience member calls out: "Te amo!" (I love you). Galás reaches toward him with her arm and closes her talons in a fist toward her heart; "Yo, más!" (I love you more)," she responds.

Galás embodies fragments of multiple subversive cultures and identities. Born in 1955 to Greek Orthodox parents of Armenian, Turkish, and Syrian descent in San Diego, she was expected to be a good Christian girl. In fact, her father, who was the director of a gospel choir, associated secular music with prostitution and discouraged her from singing nonreligious music in her home. Instead, she became a classically trained pianist who had an affinity for avant-garde jazz and blues.

Escaping to San Francisco in the early seventies, Galás became spellbound by the free jazz of Albert Ayler and collaborated with Ornette Coleman. In a 2016 interview for Pitchfork, she said that when she heard their music, she realized, "The real star was

PLAYLIST

"Wild Women with Steak-Knives," 1982, *The Litanies of Satan*

"Let My People Go," 1988, *You Must Be Certain of the Devil*

"There Are No More Tickets to the Funeral," 1991, *Plague Mass*

"This Is the Law of the Plague," 1991, *Plague Mass*

"Insane Asylum," 1992, *The Singer*

"Skótoseme," 1994, *The Sporting Life*

"O Death," 2017, *At Saint Thomas the Apostle Harlem*

the saxophone. And it's not like me to want to play second fiddle to anyone. So I just said, 'Well, you guys are trying to emulate the voice—check this out. Let's take the voice to the highest place we can take it.'"

Galás does not have a linear music lineage; she has found solace in music ranging from spirituals, covering "Let My People Go," to collaborations with rock gods like John Paul Jones, the former bassist for

Led Zeppelin, with whom she created blues-tinged funeral music. She has been incorrectly compared to Yoko Ono because she is a woman, screams, and has a long history of performing with underground experimental artists. But to hear Galás scream is to hear a controlled, building, beautiful multi-octave release. Her music is rooted in her study of artists like Scriabin, Bach, and Thelonious Monk—artists like herself who deconstructed and then reimagined what chord changes could feel like.

Galás's training took her to the Bay Area, where she also developed a drug habit, and she became a prostitute, which gave her lifelong empathy for sex workers and the dangers they face, as well as a deep understanding of how women can be treated as bodies, disrespected, and dehumanized. The experience also sharpened her dark sense of humor. She told the *Independent* in 1994, "But I liked it . . . Not turning tricks—that was boring—but the whole thing of owning the street. I had these transvestite hooker friends, and if anyone messed with me, those 'broads' got out their knives and suddenly turned out to be built like football players—it was beautiful."

Her experience as a prostitute also informed her music. Her work took on complex subjects of what it means to be a woman in a repressive society, and what it would look like if women took power from the men oppressing them. She released two of her most avant-garde albums while in San Francisco: *If Looks Could Kill* (1979, recorded with Jim French and Henry Kaiser) and *The Litanies of Satan* (1982). Based on a poem by Charles Baudelaire, *The Litanies of Satan* included the song "Wild Women with Steak-Knives," which imagines living in a sexually perverse hell, narrated by Galás's supernatural and scary vocals. In the homicidal love song, Galás sounds like a wild creature in a cave tearing into her hunter, a man who mistakes himself as the ultimate predator. But instead, Galás shreds him with her words:

Wild women with veins slashed and wombs spread,
singing songs of the death instinct

Galás did not turn away from darkness but instead dove into it. She moved to New York in 1983, where she began experimenting more with different styles of music and her vocals. She deepened her collaborations and relationships with Bay Area and New York musicians and composers including Bobby Bradford, Mark Dresser, and Henry Kaiser. Galás also performed even more theatrically, sometimes embodying the characters that she wrote about in her avant-garde pieces.

During the height of the AIDS crisis, her brother and close friend Philip-Dimitri Galás was diagnosed with HIV, and Galás became involved with ACT UP, an AIDS activist group. In 1984, she began working on *Plague Mass*, a dark bel canto–style opera that denounced the church's inaction. Her brother died in 1986, before *Plague Mass* was completed, and Galás went on to perform the piece in his memory at the St. Patrick's Cathedral in New York in 1987.

Half-naked and covered in blood, Galás condemned priests at the altar of god. *Plague Mass* roused the ire of the church, and she along with sixty-three other people attending her concert were arrested after the show. Her performance defined her career, one of no compromises. The words "We Are All HIV+" are tattooed across her knuckles, a symbol of how easily she too could have died of AIDS and a permanent memory of the ones that she loved and lost.

Since that 1987 performance, Galás has released over a dozen albums and collaborations, exploring subjects such as genocide, inequity, and hell on earth. *In Masque of Red Death* (1988), Galás pays homage to Edgar Allan Poe with terrifyingly visceral poetry, and in *Vena Cava* (1993), her voice embodies the fear of those experiencing dementia brought on by AIDS. Because of her commitment to covering the tragedies of the most stigmatized people, she has toured Europe extensively and won Italy's career Demetrio Stratos International Award in 2005.

With a forty-year trajectory in music, Galás has yet to reveal herself at her darkest. In an interview she gave *Rolling Stone* in 2017, when describing her recent performance of a classic folk song that she reinterpreted as a jazz-possessed, soul-inspired ode to the afterlife, "O Death," she said, "When I finished that performance, there was blood all over the keyboard. I couldn't imagine why. What I had done is I had broken my nails, all of them, when I was playing. And I never enjoyed a performance so much in my life." ■

CYNDI LAUPER

JEANNE FURY

ILLUSTRATION BY LINDSEY BAILEY

In the eighties, an era known for flamboyant pop stars and audacious styles, Cyndi Lauper took the cake—then blew it up and wore it as a dress. The title of her 1983 debut *She's So Unusual* was an understatement. A gutsy New York City kid who became a pop sensation at the ancient age of thirty, Lauper presented a DayGlo riot of sight and sound in one of modern music's most defining decades. She, however, is not as easily definable.

Pop stars of the early to mid-eighties included benign, clean-cut acts like Huey Lewis and the News, Billy Joel, and Lionel Richie, as well as more risqué oddities like Prince, Madonna, and Duran Duran. Though Lauper had more in common with her contemporaries in the latter camp, neither her music nor her style leveraged sex appeal, which was unheard of, especially for a female. Lauper's peculiar ways prevented her from being considered conventionally sexy, and she never felt obliged to be.

For the past thirty-plus years, Lauper has been too busy busting her ass to worry about appealing to anyone's idea of femininity, class, or artistry. Her knockout voice—soaring, strong, soulful—songwriting smarts, and steadfast work ethic have earned her two Grammy Awards, an Emmy Award, and a Tony Award, not to mention global record sales that top 50 million.

Tiny in stature and with a half-shaved head of hair that was dyed fiery shades of red, orange, and yellow, Lauper appeared on the mainstream scene looking like a bonfire from the brow up. Her outrageous outfits were a vibrant mishmash of patterns and textures, outdone only by the primary-color makeup streaked across her face like warpaint. Add to that her Betty Boop speaking voice, awkward mannerisms, and professional ties to the gonzo characters in the World Wrestling Federation, and Lauper was among America's undisputed champions of pop culture weirdos.

But as artificial and cartoonish as Lauper appeared on the surface, this was not some elaborate game of dress-up. This was her natural state—her true colors—and it was rare to see anyone who was so seemingly content (titillated, even!) to inhabit their own skin. Not that it came easy.

Born in Queens, New York, in 1953, Cynthia Ann Stephanie Lauper grew up hearing tale after tale of dejected women who put aside their own happiness and potential because they were led to believe such sacrifices made them virtuous (if miserable).

The staunch conservative mentality of her Sicilian relatives was stifling—creatively, spiritually, and even geographically. The message was clear and routinely reinforced: good girls stay close to home. Good girls do not have—nor do they want to have—fun. Cyndi Lauper was decidedly not a good girl. At seventeen, she left home, determined not to fall in line and replicate others' choices.

Years later, a similar decision resulted in her first big hit. Written and recorded as a demo in 1979 by Robert Hazard, "Girls Just Want to Have Fun" was originally a gigolo's jumpy rock paean to carefree, horny girls. During the making of *She's So Unusual*, producer Rick Chertoff handed the demo to Lauper, who more or less gave him the middle finger. Girls want much more than disposable dick. But Chertoff persisted.

With the help of Brill Building songwriter Ellie Greenwich (who encouraged Lauper to sing the song in her naturally zany cadence), Lauper reworked the tune and lyrics, and inverted the message. On Lauper's version, "fun" was a thinly veiled code word for liberation, and it's kinda hard for girls to have fun when they're struggling in a socioeconomic system purposely designed to work against them. With bubbly exuberance, "Girls" kicked patriarchy square in the balls.

Lauper's ascent had begun. *Unusual* made her the first female artist to have four Top 10 singles on a debut album, two of which she co-wrote: the female-masturbation jam "She Bop" and the tender ballad about devotion "Time after Time." That's right, a woman who looks like a rainbow that threw up in a hurricane possesses the emotional capacity to write a

song about tipping the proverbial waitress and a song about everlasting love. Who'da thunk it?

On one hand, Lauper paid no mind to other people's hang-ups; on the other hand, she cared deeply about humanity, especially outcasts. The title track of her 1986 follow-up album *True Colors* was a torch song for anyone who ever felt shunned for simply being different. Amid a warm, pared-down arrangement, Lauper offered whispers of comfort and surges of solidarity: "I see your true colors, and that's why I love you. So don't be afraid to let them show."

"True Colors" topped the *Billboard* charts, and although Lauper didn't write it (kudos to Billy Steinberg and Tom Kelly), she can take full credit for its greatest triumph: becoming the anthem for the LGBTQ community. As with "Girls Just Want to Have Fun," "True Colors" was not only symbolic of a revolutionary movement but has also maintained its relevance decades after its release. An artist is beyond fortunate to have just one social anthem to their name. Lauper has two. Those songs weren't just lip service, either. A lifelong advocate for gender equality and LGBTQ issues, Lauper co-founded the True

Colors Fund in 2008 to work to end homelessness among lesbian, gay, bisexual, and transgender youth.

Though the onset of grunge and alternative rock in the early nineties nudged pop to the side, Lauper never stopped working. She's made nine albums since *True Colors*—really good albums, at that. Albums that produced hits, impressive reviews, and Grammy nominations. Her repertoire is as multifaceted as she is and includes an acoustic album, a dance album, a standards album, a blues album, and a country album. In 2013, she won the Tony Award for best score for her work on the Broadway musical *Kinky Boots*, making her the first solo female to achieve the honor.

It's hard as hell for a woman to maintain a career in a business renowned for its grotesque aversion to aging, but Cyndi Lauper was born to defy convention. "I had always struggled to live in a world whose language I couldn't speak and didn't want to know," she wrote in her 2012 book, *Cyndi Lauper: A Memoir*. Instead, she sang her truth in her own unusual way, blazing a technicolor trail for others to do the same. ∎

MADONNA

REBECCA HAITHCOAT

ILLUSTRATION BY ANNE MUNTGES

When a young singer who went only by her first name, Madonna, performed on *American Bandstand* in January 1984, she never stopped moving. From the moment the camera smiled on her, her hips popping in time with the drum kicks of early hit "Holiday," until a starry-eyed Dick Clark clutched her in mock frustration at the audience's relentless cheering, all that remained still on the soon-to-be cultural icon was her shelf of bleached, scrunched, and shellacked bangs. Over the course of her empowering, controversial thirty-plus years in entertainment, the only thing static about Madonna's career is the fact that she is in perpetual motion.

After all, before she sold more than 300 million records and was named the Best-Selling Female Recording Artist of All Time by the *Guinness World Records*, Madonna was a dancer. Born Madonna Louise Ciccone in Bay City, Michigan, she was six years old when her mother died from breast cancer. That loss, plus the fact that she was, in her words, a "weirdo," isolated her in suburbia. Raised strictly and Catholic by a single father, she bucked against patriarchies early. Throughout her life, she would alternately chafe under and embrace the religion. Ballet class provided her one sanctuary from home, church, and the 'burbs, and she studied dance at the University of Michigan—but college couldn't hold her for long. After one year, she sprinted to New York City in 1978 with only, as she tells it, thirty-five dollars in her purse.

Being a "weirdo" in New York was a good thing, and Madonna soon became a fixture in nightclubs. She took classes at Alvin Ailey American Dance Theater and fell in with a crew of dancers and musicians. Eventually, she decided to tout herself as a solo artist. Her style—floppy lace bows tying back her tangled, dishwater blond locks, jelly bracelets up to her elbows, fingerless gloves, mesh crop tops, and crucifix earrings—epitomized grimy, downtown DIY glam. Brimming with charisma and blessed with a heart-shaped face, flashing cat eyes, and a sexy gap between her teeth, Madonna was a magnet. Sire Records signed her, and by 1982 she'd released her debut single, "Everybody." Less than a year later, with help from her producer boyfriend John "Jellybean" Benitez, she dropped *Madonna*.

Madonna's early songs still best many current pop hits. Just listen to her first album. Instead of cynically aligning with whatever politically correct theme is in vogue, her songs indirectly carry their "girl power" message—she always discerned her first job was to entertain, confident that her own feminist bent would naturally imbue her music. Her voice might be thin, but she's a master manipulator, working its helium quality to her advantage and

writing sing-along hooks and singsong melodies while choosing catchy beats that pull you to the dance floor. "Borderline" is a hopeful, candy-sweet ballad; "Burning Up" and "Lucky Star" are taut jams that pulse with sexual tension. With the poppy bop of "Material Girl," the slinky, driving synths of "Into the Groove," and the glitzy skitter of "Dress You Up," she seemed to ask in those early years: Why dissect when you can dance?

Almost immediately, however, she realized she had a gift for pushing the envelope and could capitalize on her supremely confident attitude toward sex and her interesting sex appeal to do so. With *Like a Virgin*, the sophomore album that shot her to superstardom, she found herself in the news for the first—and certainly not the last—time. The title track, especially once her writhing-on-the-floor-in-a-wedding-dress performance at the MTV Video Music Awards had been attached to it, attracted the ire of conservatives across the country. They were positive she was determined to corrupt the youth.

But Madonna was not corrupting; she was encouraging. Women especially worshipped her unabashed pleasure in sex and utter self-assurance, and the way she urged them to stand up for themselves and grasp their power, too. One of the charming things about Madonna is the fact that she never closed the space between her two front teeth, recognizing that imperfections make a person memorable. There's a quirkiness to her beauty that gives it depth, a sassiness that draws you in deeper. She might've worn a belt buckle that read "Boy Toy," but she was nobody's plaything—unless she wanted to be. As she demonstrated by wearing a double-breasted suit and then being chained to a bed in the video for "Express Yourself," from 1989's *Like a*

Prayer, there could be pleasure in domination *and* in submission. You are your own boss, Madonna proclaimed: "A lot of people are afraid to say what they want. That's why they don't get what they want."

Once she was aware of how easily she could provoke the prudes, Madonna was fearless. Often, she'd juxtapose religious iconography from her Catholic upbringing with sex or explore kink in public. Pepsi dropped her from an endorsement deal when the church expressed outrage over her video for "Like a Prayer," in which crosses burned and she kissed a black saint. (The video also upset folks on the left, who critiqued her tenuous understanding of race and appropriation of black culture.) To Catholicism's chagrin, the controversy boosted her profile and income more than the check would have. She had the world's ear, and she eagerly accepted her role as an artist who forced people to confront difficult, sensitive subject matter—"Papa Don't Preach" was about teenage pregnancy, for example. That she was a mainstream pop star, not some underground performance artist, was the rub. Conservatives could not ignore her and they squirmed.

Perhaps her most eye-popping work, however, was a coffee table book simply titled *Sex*, which ushered in Madonna's most transgressive era and earned her the title the Queen of Obscene. Released in October 1992, the book, now out of print, was a collection of photographs of Madonna, then boyfriend Vanilla Ice, and other models both famous and unknown simulating various sex acts like analingus, bondage, and homosexuality. Overlaying the pictures were stories, essays, and poems that illuminated Madonna's positions on sex such as, "I think I have a dick in my brain." It sold over 150,000 copies on its first day.

Of course *Sex* drew ire from her detractors, but

it even went too far for some fans and anti-porn feminist groups who found her endorsement of the adult entertainment industry disturbing. She and the book were deemed desperate, uninteresting, soulless, self-righteous, tasteless, pretentious, derivative, and, in a first for the chameleon-like artist, even boring. Actress Isabella Rossellini, who posed for the book, later said she regretted her role in it. The LGBTQ community was torn between being excited over the exposure and feeling exploited.

Eventually selling 1.5 million copies, *Sex* is now heralded as an important postfeminist work. For her part, Madonna never buckled under the criticism and held strong to the themes underpinning her entire body of work: "I was interested in pushing buttons and being rebellious and being mischievous and trying to bend the rules," she told the *Sydney Morning Herald*. "There was a lot of irony in the *Sex* book and I am poking fun at a lot of things and I am being kind of silly and adolescent and I am being very f you, if a man can do it, I can do it." Digging in her heels, she dressed as a dominatrix in the video for her song "Human Nature," which includes the line "I'm not your bitch, don't hang your shit on me."

While withstanding critical blows, she continued to morph personally and artistically, never alighting on any one style or theme for very long. She'd start a trend with one album and then leave it behind for the next, whether it was the fifties soda pop girl of *True Blue*, the Old Hollywood glamour of her late eighties albums, the haute hippie vibe and Kabbalah practice of what might be her best album, the astonishing *Ray of Light*, or country kitsch and electro pop on *Music*. She became one of the first pop stars to warrant serious analysis, inspiring not just music journalists' essays but also academic examination. In "Madonna: Plantation Mistress or Soul Sister?" bell hooks censures the artist for her commodification of black culture, warning that Madonna's fascination with and envy of blackness—among her lovers were several black men, including Basquiat, Big Daddy Kane, and Dennis Rodman—ignores black pain in favor of fetishizing black pleasure. She drew criticism for being a "culture vulture" of the gay community when she brought vogueing, a manner of dance created in underground ball culture in which one hits poses that a model would in a *Vogue* editorial, to the masses. Yet Madonna also was one of the first mainstream pop stars to embrace and support gay men, hiring them to be her dancers, as well as toying with her gender identity herself.

Her personal life has been subject to similar scrutiny. In 1985, she married actor Sean Penn. Their tumultuous relationship was punctuated by Penn's violence toward photographers, including one instance that landed him in jail for thirty-three days. Madonna filed for divorce in 1987, then withdrew the papers only to file again two years later. Rumors that Penn assaulted Madonna were rampant until she dismissed them as false in 2015. After a string of romantic involvements, Madonna gave birth to daughter Lourdes Maria Ciccone Leon, her first child, in 1996, but within a year her relationship with Lourdes's father, trainer Carlos Leon, ended. In 1998, she met director Guy Ritchie and

PLAYLIST

"Borderline," 1983, *Madonna*

"Material Girl," 1984, *Like a Virgin*

"Like a Virgin," 1984, *Like a Virgin*

"Express Yourself," 1989, *Like a Prayer*

"Cherish," 1989, *Like a Prayer*

"Like a Prayer," 1989, *Like a Prayer*

"Vogue," 1990, *I'm Breathless (Music from and Inspired by the Film* Dick Tracy*)*

"Human Nature," 1994, *Bedtime Stories*

"Ray of Light," 1998, *Ray of Light*

"Don't Tell Me," 2000, *Music*

"What It Feels Like for a Girl," 2000, *Music*

settled into her longest relationship thus far. Two years later, they welcomed son Rocco John Ritchie, but eyebrows were raised in 2006 when Madonna adopted a boy from Malawi, David, amid reports that his biological father was unaware he had been put up for adoption. She and Ritchie divorced in 2009, and in 2017, she adopted two more children from Malawi, orphaned twin girls.

To no one's surprise, Madonna hasn't slowed with age. Her 2015 record *Rebel Heart* finds her dabbling in trap and dubstep and celebrating her proud, longstanding defiance of cultural norms and societal expectations. She can't be asked to quietly live within the boundaries society has determined befit women of a certain age. Constantly asserting her autonomy, she will always do whatever she wants, shrugging off criticism by reminding her detractors she's happily and forever an "Unapologetic Bitch." She's Madonna, and she still owns the throne—but don't expect her to sit on it. ∎

KIM GORDON

JANA MARTIN

ILLUSTRATION BY ANNE MUNTGES

If Patti Smith is punk rock's fairy godmother, Kim Gordon is its big sister/goddess. One of the three founding members of Sonic Youth, she showed women how to strap on a bass and hold their own with the guys. You can hear shades of Gordon—her voice, her guitar playing as well as her bass playing—in everyone from Karen O to Sleater-Kinney to Haim. Whip-smart and unafraid, entirely unmistakable for anyone else, she has always been way more than a "girl in a band"—also the title, irony intended, of her 2015 memoir. She's a visual artist, fashion designer, producer, director, curator, actor. And she's not done. Since the 2011 dissolution of Sonic Youth—arguably the most influential post–alt—noisecore/no wave/punk band in history—Gordon has been busy. When so many in rock seem to retire to a comfortable existence of past laurels and tame reappearances, she's singing on ratatat goth industrial track "Murdered Out" with drummer Stella Mozgawa and making noise/art in the duo Body/Head with guitarist Bill Nace—attracting cadres of new fans.

Born in 1953, in Rochester, New York, Kim Althea Gordon grew up in Los Angeles, a quiet and thoughtful girl who loved to paint. Dad was a sociology professor at UCLA; Mom made her daughter's clothes from Indian bedspreads. In *A Girl in a Band* she recalls being drawn to and also terrified by her big brother, Keller, a charismatic force of nature who became increasingly disturbed as he got older. She planned to be a visual artist, not a musician, but had an early attraction to freeform and expression: she cites free jazz (Archie Shepp, Art Ensemble of Chicago) and improv modern dance as early influences. In a recent conversation with Aimee Mann, Gordon talked about formative experiences making art in elementary school: "to me it was normal—that when you were learning something, you kind of embraced it—with your body, with your heart and soul and your mind."

That whole-hearted sensibility fit the no wave scene of 1970s NYC, thriving as Gordon arrived, fresh out of art school. This was the New York of old: cheap apartments, gritty streets, the city's creative life on a roll. Gordon performed the downtown bohemian's customary rites of passage: menial, low-paying, high-cred jobs (in a bookstore, and for uber-gallerist Larry Gagosian), crashing on couches (including in Cindy Sherman's loft), meeting everybody who was anybody. Witnessing the riotous fun of a one-off noise act, she thought, "I could do that." She took part in a short-lived girl band, CKM, and met a tall guitar player from Connecticut, Thurston Moore. Soon Gordon, Moore, and guitarist Lee Ranaldo started a band.

It was 1981, and the DIY, anyone-can-do-it

ethos of punk rock was still cresting. The prevailing belief was that anyone could play, and Gordon was one of the women fearless enough to dive in. In this era of smudged Xerox posters and shoestring indie record labels, Sonic Youth had that same heck-yeah spirit. But the band conveyed a novel, brainy self-assurance, conscious or not, that said they were going to last.

It wasn't that Moore postured like a punk-rock wannabe Jagger. It wasn't that Gordon was a girl. Sonic Youth's members were clearly all equals, and carried themselves with cynical pragmatism, record-geek enthusiasm, dare-to-suck ambition, and well-honed irony. Beginning with their early albums, including their eponymous five-song debut in 1982, *Bad Moon Rising* (1985), and *Evol* (1986), they also showed a penchant for gunning pop to its noisiest extreme. A tune could have a hummable hook—like the dreamscape verse and slithery chorus in "Expressway to Yr. Heart"—before crashing into a wall of deafening feedback or a maze of noise led by Gordon. Moore and Gordon shared most of the vocals, Gordon's voice fluid and expressive, shifting from throaty rebellion to girly sing-song to banshee scream. She didn't sing as much as chant, incant—her trademark a semi-tonal urging voice that managed to stay within the rough borders of melody and key but never really sounded out of tune.

With *Daydream Nation* (1988), Sonic Youth began their inevitable ascent into stardom. They signed with Geffen, releasing the astonishing *Goo* in 1990, with the hit single "Kool Thing" featuring Chuck D of Public Enemy, the catchy, grinding "Dirty Boots," and the heartbreaking "Tunic," Gordon's ode to Karen Carpenter, the singer and drummer who died of anorexia. The band took a then unknown Nirvana on tour with them in 1991, chronicled in the rockumentary *The Year Punk Broke*, and Gordon began a long friendship with Cobain. Sonic Youth headlined Lollapalooza in 1995. They made dozens of records, side projects, videos, and even voiceovers for *The Simpsons*. Gordon, by this point, was in her thirties and married to Moore, with a young daughter. As a couple she and Moore were considered indie rock's essential parents, dependable as a black T-shirt.

But Gordon also blazed her own grrrl-spirational trail. She started the street-fashion label X-Girl. She directed the Breeders' iconic nineties video "Cannonball," with Spike Jonze. She founded Free Kitten, whose shrill-femme sound was a refreshing change from the surging pop of Sonic Youth. She appeared on *Girls*. Whatever she does, it's intimidatingly cool.

Even as they shifted away from pop in the early 2000s, finally parting ways with Geffen in 2008 (Gordon describes her disgust for the company's sexist corporate mentality in her book), Sonic Youth rocked. It would be hard to put a fine point on just how powerful they were. And in the center of that rock hurricane was Gordon, a bobbing, wiry S-curve in a minidress and boots, throwing herself into the beat of a song. She kept the bass down low and braced on her right hip, and kept the groove going. She had a way of jumping into choruses like an awkward cheerleader, in a trance we all wanted to join. And that bass never wavered: she kept impeccable time. No matter the caterwaul or complex tunings swirling around her, she picked out those thick root notes, and the song never got lost. She also took her own turns up the neck, turning to face a bass cabinet the size of a truck, unafraid to shriek a buzzing mountain of feedback. That's what the girls in the audience got from her: don't be afraid to own that stage. In one of her last interviews as part of Sonic Youth, she sat alongside Moore and told the interviewer, "I get disturbed when I don't see enough girls in the audience. If I feel like it's shifting over to predominantly male, that makes me really nervous."

Much has been made of her post-divorce life, in that ridiculous double-standard kind of way—*Poor woman, her husband carrying on with that young thing while she was home with their child*. The shock of Moore's betrayal and resulting demise of Sonic Youth are discussed with whole-note clarity in her book: Gordon does not hold back. But the pain it caused seemed to galvanize a kind of rebirth. For the Rock and Roll Hall of Fame's induction of Nirvana, Gordon reemerged for her first post-divorce appearance and stole the show. She had been tapped to join three other women singing in place of the irreplaceable Cobain. She took to the stage to howl the B-side "Aneurysm," a favorite of Cobain's: "I love you so much it makes me sick." Storming around in foxcore silver boots and a striped short dress, windmilling her arms and throwing herself around the stage, she brought Cobain back to life. And she turned the staid, male-centric bastion of televised and sanctioned rock into a feminist primal scream. It was a balls-out punk rock expression of true grief: for the loss of her friend, and for the loss of her former life. At the end of the song she was down on the floor. But Kim Gordon is no victim. She got up. ∎

k.d. lang

LUCRETIA TYE JASMINE

ILLUSTRATION BY JULIE WINEGARD

The torch and twang of k.d. lang's voice, in country, folk, jazz, and pop, cross over. Gilded, fringed, or plain, her band, her vocal inflections, and her clothing choices allude to legends and icons, from Patsy Cline to Elvis Presley. She references music history even as she makes her own. A songwriting, guitar-playing, torch-singing rebel, lang, with her come-hither sneer and punk rock pompadour, displays the sexual command and self-assertion of a charismatic rock star icon—or "dykon," as lang says.

A cross between Virginie Amélie Avegno Gautreau, the subject in John Singer Sargent's controversial 1884 portrait *Madame X*, and film noir matinee idol Robert Mitchum, lang exudes undeniable and revolutionary sex appeal that crosses gendered identities and sexual mores. Her blend of alternative and country, androgynous fashion, onstage stance and croon, and the lower-casing of her name assure acquiescence to her rebellions. Kilts, suits, gowns—lang has worn them all.

And that voice: a smooth sheen that moves like a caress. lang perfectly controls vocal expression. The mezzo-soprano knows exactly when to unleash the power within. Even the breaks in her supple singing serve as careful emphasis. Photographer Catherine Opie's 2007 portrait of lang presents an unsmiling musician in the big outdoors, a guitar on her back and the road beyond. Experience appears limitless and like a long haul, and this musician is going the distance.

Singer, songwriter, guitarist, and actor Kathryn Dawn Lang was born November 2, 1961, in Alberta, Canada, the youngest of four children. She grew up on the Canadian prairie in a small town, with her mom, a teacher, and her father, who ran a drugstore. Her dad left them when she was twelve. Her mom drove long distances, too, to take her to weekly music instruction, encouraging lang's singing and piano playing.

In college, she loved the music of Patsy Cline, so in the early 1980s she formed the Reclines, a Patsy Cline tribute band that offered honky-tonk with butch cow-punk style. As she says with her trademark humor in her introduction to 1984's "Hanky Panky," "To dance is human. But to polka . . . divine." "Bopalena," also from 1984, celebrates women on the dance floor and at the microphone, centerstage—women who partner up with each other. The Reclines' albums, 1984's *A Truly Western Experience*, 1987's *Angel with a Lariat*, and 1989's *Absolute Torch and Twang*, show that they were as serious about making music as they were about having a good time (or singing about bad times).

lang's duet with Roy Orbison on his song "Crying" earned a 1989 Grammy for Best Country Collaboration with Vocals. Her solo album *Ingénue* (1992) yielded the chart-topping classic she co-wrote with Ben Mink, "Constant Craving." lang's sexy swoon of

a voice alternates restraint and release. The refrain inspired Keith Richards and Mick Jagger, who shared songwriting credit with lang and Mink on the Rolling Stones' 1997 song "Anybody Seen My Baby?"

k.d. lang delivers gender constructs with daring sexual implications and a sense of play. The August 1993 Herb Ritts cover of *Vanity Fair* showed supermodel Cindy Crawford shaving k.d.'s face: a rock star being tended by the most fashionably beautiful woman, as usual, but this time the rock star is a gay woman. lang's cover album, *Drag* (1997), also dares with its play on words and with clothes as it proffers cigarettes and cross-dressing. She gently resurrects Dory and André Previn's 1967 "(Theme from) the Valley of the Dolls," a hit for Dionne Warwick. On the passionate "I Confess" (2011), co-written by lang, Daniel Clarke, and Joshua Grange, she places herself in patriarchal dominance: "I confess / I'll be your daddy." In the music video, lang wields her guitar and voice with sexually sure and mature swagger amidst muscular and tattooed strippers who play with fire. Sex-role stereotypes have not changed, but women's place and power in them have.

The recipient of plentiful awards and nominations, including Junos and Grammys, lang was made Officer of the Order of Canada in 1996. In 2011, Q Hall of Fame Canada honored her for her LGBTQ activism. lang was inducted into the Canadian Music Hall of Fame in 2013. She has twice performed at the Winter Olympics (1988, in a fringed cowpunk dress for a fun-loving "Turn Me Round," and 2010, in a three-piece white suit for a powerhouse performance of "Hallelujah").

Appearing as an actor and/or as a musical performer in movies, sitcoms, TV shows, and theater, from *Christmas at Pee Wee's Playhouse* (1988) to *Portlandia* (2014), lang demonstrates her allegiance to the subversive. She contributes songs whose profits go toward multiple causes, including Tibetan human rights and HIV/AIDS research and care. When vegetarian lang announced her animal activism, many in her cattle-country hometown, Alberta, and the American Midwest denounced her and banned her music. lang kept on singing.

The happiness in her voice as she lets her vocals surge can also be seen in the subtle smile on her face as she sings. In a 2011 interview with *Xtra*, Canada's gay and lesbian news, lang discussed her career and her Buddhism, stating that neediness for an outcome eradicates its possibilities: "celebrate the fact that you get to be creative," lang postulates. Her creative collaborations include musicians as varied as Tony Bennett, Anne Murray, Dwight Yoakam, Madeleine Peyroux, and Ann Wilson. She formed a new band with singer-songwriters Neko Case and Laura Veirs, case/lang/veirs; like the lyric in their luscious song "Honey and Smoke" (2016), their sound is "exquisite to the detail."

k.d. lang is a heartbreaker, a rule maker, and a rule breaker. Just like any icon. Or dykon. She might be newly capitalizing the letters in her name to capitalize on a larger fan base, but even that shows her play with hierarchy. She makes rules. She can break them, too. ∎

PLAYLIST

"Hanky Panky," 1984, *A Truly Western Experience*

"Bopalena," 1984, *A Truly Western Experience*

"Crying," 1987, on Roy Orbison, *King of Hearts* (with Roy Orbison)

"Big Boned Gal," 1989, *Absolute Torch and Twang*

"Constant Craving," 1992, *Ingénue*

"My Old Addiction," 1997, *Drag*

"Theme from Valley of the Dolls," 1997, *Drag*

"Hallelujah," 2009, *Live in London* (with the BBC Concert Orchestra)

"I Confess," 2011, *Sing It Loud*

WITH CASE/LANG/ VEIRS:

"Honey and Smoke," 2016, *case/lang/veirs*

WHITNEY HOUSTON

REBECCA HAITHCOAT

ILLUSTRATION BY JULIE WINEGARD

When you quiet all the drama, the rumors and reality shows, the sleazy tabloid stories and gossipy headline teases that eventually turned Whitney Houston's life into a tempest, what remains is that voice. Pristine and bright as a cloudless day right after a rain, that voice flutters like a bird as she trills a snippet of the first song she ever sang in church, "Guide Me, O Thou Great Jehovah." For such a light and flirty pop song as "How Will I Know," that voice is surprisingly full-bodied. Tremulous and sweet, it skips lightly up and down her range as she unleashes a furious rendition of "I Have Nothing." That voice stretches out and renders anyone within its reach awestruck during her tour-de-force version of Dolly Parton's "I Will Always Love You."

Houston could shift from a belt to a purr in a finger snap, her voice billowing out in effortless, satiny waves. So exquisite was that voice, superlatives don't do it justice. So massive was that voice, the *New York Times* deemed her an "exceptional vocal talent" on her debut. And so powerful was that voice, it broke down the door to millions of white living rooms across the country so that one day Mariah Carey, Beyoncé, Rihanna, Zendaya, and so many more would also gain entrance.

Whitney Houston was born in Newark, New Jersey, on August 9, 1963, with music in her blood. Her mother, Emily "Cissy" Houston, was a gospel singer and cousin to Dionne and Dee Dee Warwick; Aretha Franklin was Whitney's honorary aunt. Growing up in a Baptist church, Houston learned to play the piano and was a soloist in the choir. Her mother taught her to sing and took her to nightclubs where she was performing. By the time Whitney was fifteen, she had sung background vocals for Chaka Khan.

Still, her mother shooed away record labels, insisting that her daughter finish high school before signing a deal. Houston found early fame anyway—her clean-scrubbed good looks landed her modeling gigs. Foreshadowing her later life, she quickly started breaking barriers in the fashion world, becoming one of the first black women to book the cover of *Seventeen* magazine. Eventually, the record executives couldn't be held off any longer, and Clive Davis signed Whitney. In 1985, Arista released her self-titled debut, which garnered four Grammy Award nominations, one win for Best Pop Vocal Performance, Female for "Saving All My Love for You," and high praise from publications like *Rolling Stone*, which deemed hers as "one of the most exciting new voices in years."

The rich layers of Houston's vocals ground the frothy pop confection "How Will I Know," the third single from her debut. The accompanying video spearheaded her breakthrough as a visual performer as well: it features Whitney wearing a Madonna-floppy bow and metallic minidress, bopping around a paint-splattered maze adorned with funhouse mirrors. There's some (very) loose plotline, a chorus of avant-garde dancers wearing black shifts, and a dude in shades "playing" a sax solo. In other words, "How Will I Know" meshed perfectly with the early aesthetic of MTV. Launched in the summer of 1981, the new music video channel was more popular than anyone had predicted. Yet with its high profile

came heavy criticism, especially of the fact that the channel played mostly white musicians. Houston helped break down that color barrier as well.

From "I Wanna Dance with Somebody (Who Loves Me)" to "Heartbreak Hotel," Whitney's videos were spun in heavy rotation, making her the first black female artist to be a regular, and beloved, presence on the channel and a visitor in white homes. Showcasing her voice, yes, but also her elegance, bubbly personality and girl-next-door appeal, the videos helped her became a universal sex symbol. Everyone—*everyone*—listened to Whitney Houston. No longer were black female singers constrained to urban radio. Whitney wasn't just on pop radio; she was pop radio. She dominated the airwaves for over a decade.

Houston continued to set records. With *Whitney* (1987), her sophomore album, she became the first woman to land four number-one singles from

PLAYLIST

"The Greatest Love of All,"
1985, *Whitney Houston*

"How Will I Know," 1985,
Whitney Houston

"You Give Good Love,"
1985, *Whitney Houston*

"Didn't We Almost Have It
All," 1987, on *Whitney*

"So Emotional," 1987,
Whitney

"I Wanna Dance with
Somebody (Who Loves
Me)," 1987, *Whitney*

"I Have Nothing," 1992,
*The Bodyguard (Original
Soundtrack Album)*

"I Will Always Love You,"
1992, *The Bodyguard
(Original Soundtrack
Album)*

"Exhale (Shoop, Shoop),"
1995, on various artists,
*Waiting to Exhale: Original
Soundtrack Album*

"My Love Is Your Love,"
1998, *My Love Is Your Love*

a single album. In the nineties, she accelerated her success even more via movies. Her first acting foray, *The Bodyguard*, was razzed, but its soundtrack, led by the best-selling single of all time by a female solo artist, "I Will Always Love You," won the Grammy for Album of the Year. *Waiting to Exhale* won more critical praise, and its sensuous, produced-by-Babyface soundtrack was another smash.

Her last great album, *My Love Is Your Love*, was released in 1998. Gone was the purely sweet tone, replaced with a new, welcome sharpness. After all, she was a grown woman who had experienced plenty of heartache and pain. Houston's image had shifted from the all-American girl to something edgier after she married R&B star Bobby Brown in the early nineties, but few knew the extent of the changes in her life. She suddenly was often hours late to interviews and performances, if she didn't cancel them outright. Airport security guards in Hawaii found marijuana in both her and her husband's bags. In 2002, she granted an interview to Diane Sawyer in which she announced, "Crack is cheap. I make too much money to ever smoke crack."

And then there was *Being Bobby Brown*, a reality show starring Houston as much as Brown that aired on Bravo in 2004: the *Hollywood Reporter* deemed it the "most disgusting . . . series ever to ooze its way onto television." Indeed, the two could be crude, with Houston elaborating on parasites as the family is eating. What struck viewers most, however, was the bizarre, if sometimes charming, world in which the couple alone existed, excluding even their children. Watching over a decade later, what's horrifying is not how doomed their union might be, but how desperately sad they seem. She's worn completely ragged by fans' constant hounding—forget eating dinner in peace, they can't even sit in the steam room without an autograph request. It came as no surprise when Brown later revealed these years to be the most tumultuous in terms of their both trying—and failing—to get and remain sober. The show ran only one season, but it tarnished Houston's golden reputation.

Still, when she was found unconscious and subsequently pronounced dead of a drug overdose in a bathtub at the Beverly Hilton hotel the weekend of the 2012 Grammy Awards, the world was shocked. She possessed that voice, that sweet, pellucid voice that propelled black female artists places they had never been. That voice that could whisper or belt. That voice that touched everyone who heard it. That voice that touches everyone who hears it still.

Houston even changed lives in death. She proved that no one, not a middle-aged mother nor the world's most famous singer nor simply someone gifted with a voice like that, is safe from addiction and mental unrest. And with all the number-one records, with all the new records set, with all the doors broken down, that might be the most powerful message that voice ever delivered. ■

JANET JACKSON

REBECCA HAITHCOAT

ILLUSTRATION BY WINNIE T. FRICK

T his is a story about control—straining against it, fighting for it, losing it, regaining it. It's a story that began with the first woman to ever walk the world, and the story of every woman since. It's a story during which many women have died. It's a story with no end.

I was too young to understand the war being waged for the wills of women when Janet Jackson's seminal album *Control* was released in 1986, but I was subconsciously cognizant of it. How else to explain the rebel thrill that careened through my eight-year-old body when I tore the cellophane off the cassette to see Janet looking like modern art—against a stark red background, she wears a sleek black suit outlined in gold squiggles. Slipping the tape into my jam box and pressing *play*, I felt my skin prick with chill bumps as her soft voice intoned that iconic introduction like a mantra:

> This is a story about control. My control.
> Control of what I say, control of what I
> do. And this time I'm gonna do it my way.
> I hope you enjoy this as much as I do.
> Are we ready? I am. 'Cause it's all about
> control—and I've got lots of it.

I latched on to the album with a ferocity that belied my age and experience. I didn't know that over the next two decades, I'd acquire a whole arsenal of ways to wrest back control—starving, binging, having sex, not having sex, working out, drinking and drinking and drinking, doing drugs, having more sex—but I intuited that the record was important. In Janet, I recognized myself: a woman trained to be sweet and agreeable instead of standing her ground, to smile and swallow her screams, to be seen but not heard unless the script was written by men.

With *Control*, however, Janet Jackson revealed that she'd been sorely underestimated. Watching the world reassess her buoyed me; maybe one day I'd also taste this sweet triumph.

There is something demeaning about being called cute. The word even sounds dismissive—it's a curt, one-syllable appraisal that's almost sniffed, unlike the musical "pretty," which is sung, or "beautiful," which is breathed, or "gorgeous," which is elongated and luxuriated in. The dress you bought half off is cute. The pile of puppies is cute. Kid sisters are cute.

On May 16, 1966, Janet Jackson was born in Gary, Indiana, the youngest of ten children—the cute kid sister. Her brothers were already singing and dancing as the Jackson 5, and Janet quickly began playing her part both in real life and on television. In photos from her days on the 1970s-era *Good Times*, she is almost always smiling, her eyes beaming, her

cherubic cheeks blushed as if a makeup artist had pinched them to mimic the bloom children get from racing around playing. Janet didn't have much time for such. Her big brother was Michael Jackson. Her father Joe instructed her to call him not "Dad," but by his first name. He managed her career, which included performing on the Las Vegas strip when she was only seven years old.

Hers was a showbiz family, and it already had its zenith, which was fine with Janet. By the time she was eighteen, her father had orchestrated a recording contract for her: two albums overseen by him. She'd eloped to try and escape her father's grip over her life, but the marriage had fizzled. Janet didn't need to be a big star; in fact, she was desperate to quit the role of kid sister. In those press pictures of her, there's an intensity to her gaze, too, one beyond her years.

She'd need every bit of that fire to blaze her way out from under her family's shadow. Harnessing it, plus the talents of Minneapolis producers Jimmy Jam and Terry Lewis, *Control* blasted to life in only six weeks. Full of taut jams and lyrics delivered in a sharp tone, it's exceptional, a 180-degree turn from her first two pop outings. "Nasty," "What Have You Done for Me Lately," and the silky sleeper hit "The Pleasure Principle" lash out at lazy, disrespectful men yet still manage to be the fun and sexy dance songs you'd expect from a nineteen-year-old. Rightfully, *Control* was hailed as her artistic breakthrough,

and its fusion of lean industrial music, danceable hip-hop, and beat-driven pop fixed a new template for contemporary R&B.

Yet most importantly, with *Control*, Janet proclaimed her independence and staked out her very identity. She would continue to refine her art and redefine herself over the years decisively and with guts. *Janet Jackson's Rhythm Nation 1814* (1989), which followed *Control*, had a socially conscious tone (in the iconic video for "Rhythm Nation," she wears a military ensemble and does army-like choreography). The bright and beaming, resplendent Herb Ritts-directed video for "Love Will Never Do (Without You)," which featured a glamorous yet fresh-scrubbed, crop top-clad Janet, established her as a sex symbol.

That status was further cemented in 1993 with *Janet*, her film debut in *Poetic Justice* opposite Tupac, and a jaw-dropping *Rolling Stone* cover that featured Janet in jeans—and not much else but a pair of hands covering her bare breasts. Simmering singles like "That's the Way Love Goes," "If," and the almost unbearable tease of "Any Time, Any Place" make *Janet* a must-have record for the boudoir.

Delving even deeper into sexual exploration, Janet released 1997's *The Velvet Rope*, the creation of which was spurred by bouts of severe depression and anxiety. The *New York Times* branded it her "most daring, elaborate and accomplished album." The five albums she's released since then might not have all been lavished so generously with praise, but throughout the years, Janet has never wavered in maintaining her creative control. Even when she was the subject of one of the biggest television controversies of all time, the "wardrobe malfunction" when Justin Timberlake exposed her breast during the 2004 Super

Bowl, she refused to cede any moral ground. She apologized gracefully, but refused to be shamed.

Despite loving *Control* as much as I did, it took me an embarrassingly long time to figure out that the best way to gain control is to do what Janet did: use my voice. My own voice was so rusty from disuse that it often simply did not work. Still doesn't at times. The thought of speaking my mind can be so paralyzing, I might face days, weeks, or occasionally even months of writer's block. I still tend to shove my feelings, desires, and needs down until my chest is so full of things unsaid that the slightest slight can topple the whole mess.

It's then that Janet most inspires me. Fed up with waiting for permission from other people, she struck off on her own and forged a path pop stars—and at least one regular ol' person—follow to this day: *This is a story about control. My control.* ■

SALT-N-PEPA

GILLIAN G. GAAR

ILLUSTRATION BY JULIE WINEGARD

It was 1987: the year that Easy-E boasted about his "Boyz-n-the-Hood," that LL Cool J asserted, "I'm Bad," N.W.A. begged the "Dope Man" for a hit, and Public Enemy declared themselves "Public Enemy No. 1."

But there was also a new crew on the block. Salt-N-Pepa crashed the party with their single "Tramp," reworking the Otis Redding/Carla Thomas song of the same name. In 1967, Thomas had teasingly taken Redding to task for not having a large bankroll and for wearing overalls. Twenty years later, Salt-N-Pepa took a more pointed stance, facing down the kind of man "who undressed me with his eyeballs," warning other women to not bother giving this guy the time of day.

"Tramp" gave rap's first female group their highest-charting R&B hit, but what happened next, when the single's B-side, "Push It," was remixed, changed everything. The song's a terrifically fun number about getting down on the dance floor, and the video has Salt-N-Pepa dancing all over the stage, wearing tight black outfits, letterman-style jackets embellished with a large "S" or "P," red knee-high boots, and heavy gold necklaces. It's a colorful, athletic look; these were young women who weren't afraid to move. "Push It" became their first crossover hit, cracking the pop Top 20. Without even intending to, Salt-N-Pepa had bum-rushed the mainstream. Over the next decade, they would become one of the most popular and important acts of this golden age of hip-hop, writing frank, er, salty raps about female desire and autonomy and laying down such classic jams as "Shoop" and "Whatta Man."

In the beginning, it didn't seem like Cheryl James and Sandy Denton would go together like salt and pepper at all. James, born March 28, 1966, in Brooklyn, was quiet and kept to herself; Denton's first memory of her bandmate was seeing her sitting apart from the other students at Queens College, reading a book. Denton, born in Kingston, Jamaica, on October 9, 1964, was the extrovert, who loved going out and having a good time. They became friends while working next to each other as telephone solicitors for the local Sears. Sometimes, Denton said, she could even drag James out for a night of fun.

Neither had given any thought to being a performer. It was James's boyfriend, Hurby "Luv Bug" Azor, who wanted to make it in music. Azor also worked at Sears and planned to start a rap group with a fellow co-worker, future comedian Martin Lawrence. When Lawrence's rapping skills proved not to be up to par, he thought of bringing James in. Then, as he later told *Rolling Stone*, he had a brainstorm: "Hey, it would be better if there were two girls."

The group, then called Super Nature, launched with "The Showstopper," an answer song to "The Show" by Doug E. Fresh and Slick Rick, in which the two men boasted of their skills on the mic. In "The Showstopper," James and Denton raised the stakes, poking fun at their rivals' clothing and accessories while touting their own rapping prowess. There was a tradition of answer songs in rap; fourteen-year-old Roxanne Shanté was one of the first females to score a hip-hop hit with "Roxanne's Revenge," her 1984 answer to a UTFO song. For women, who were so often denied access to the main stage, an answer song provided a way to get into the game.

Released in 1985, "The Showstopper" got immediate airplay before Super Nature even had a record deal; Denton recalled excitedly dancing on the hood of her car when she first heard it over the airwaves. The single was a moderate hit on the R&B charts, and the group expanded to include a DJ, Spinderella (Latoya Hanson). They also took on the name Salt-N-Pepa, after a line in "Showstopper" (James was Salt, Denton Pepa). Initially, the group was run by Azor, who wrote the songs and produced the records. Neither James nor Denton had wanted to record "Push It," finding it too pop; their opening, exaggerated "Oooh, bay-bee, bay-bee!" lines were their way of making fun of a song that they found, in Denton's words, "corny." But Azor insisted, and he had the final word. When the airplay for "Push It" began surpassing that of "Tramp," it was released as a single in its own right, selling over a million copies. The album the song appeared on, *Hot, Cool and Vicious*, sold over a million as well. It was a remarkable accomplishment; two years earlier, there wasn't a single all-female rap group in existence. Now the very first such act, Salt-N-Pepa, had gone platinum.

Hanson then left the group, and Deidra "Dee Dee" Roper (born August 3, 1970, in New York City), became the new Spinderella. Soon Salt-N-Pepa were the most popular female rappers in the country, regularly landing records on the pop and R&B charts. The group really claimed the game with their third album, *Blacks' Magic* (1990). The cover linked them to other African American musical trailblazers; they're depicted in a book-lined study, surrounded by the spirits of Billie Holiday, Jimi Hendrix, Louis Armstrong, and Minnie Riperton. It was the first album where Salt-N-Papa began to play more of a role in songwriting and production, with James's songs—"Expression" and "Independent"—celebrating the liberation of their creativity. James left no doubt as to who was now in charge, rapping with pride about being in command "in an all-girl band!" in "Expression" They were also more politically outspoken. In "Let's Talk about Sex," they urged their constituency to think about the consequences of having sex, in addition to its pleasures. They were pleased to find the song struck a nerve; Denton recalled in her 2008 memoir *Let's Talk about Pep*: "I started to see how much one song could change lives." The cut was later rewritten as a safe sex anthem, "Let's Talk about AIDS."

"Ain't Nuthin' but a She Thing" updated Donna Summer's song of female self-empowerment, "She Works Hard for the Money," for the nineties, with the group seen variously as mechanics, astronauts, and firefighters. "We all have little sisters and cousins who look up to us, and we see what they go through," James told former Supreme Mary Wilson

PLAYLIST

"Tramp," 1988, *Hot, Cool, and Vicious*

"Push It," 1988, *Hot, Cool, and Vicious*

"Negro wit' an Ego," 1990, *Blacks' Magic*

"Let's Talk about Sex," 1990, *Blacks' Magic*

"Whatta Man," 1993, *Very Necessary*

"Shoop," 1993, *Very Necessary*

"None of Your Business," 1993, *Very Necessary*

"Ain't Nuthin' but a She Thing," 1995, *Ain't Nuthin' but a She Thing*

in a Q&A in *Interview* magazine. "So we have to be an example." The song was later used as the title track of an album benefiting the Shirley Divers Foundation (which distributed funds to organizations dealing with women's issues) that also featured contributions from Annie Lennox, Queen Latifah, and Patti Smith.

They were an outgoing and friendly crew, playfully critiquing men's bodies in two of their biggest hits, "Shoop" and "Whatta Man" (the latter performed with the hit female vocal ensemble En Vogue), both on *Very Necessary* (1993). But they also cast a critical eye on what they felt were unfair demands on them, whether due to their gender or their fame. In the video for "None of Your Business," the group advises those with prying eyes to back off; they're joined by a racially and sexually integrated chorus of fellow travelers who gleefully shout the song's title. "None of Your Business" won the Grammy for Best Rap Performance in 1995, the first time a female rap act had won the honor.

Brand New (1997) was the first album the group worked on without Azor's help, but the record company went bankrupt when the album was released, and sales were flat. James had already stated in interviews she wanted to leave Salt-N-Pepa, and though there were still live dates, there was no more new music. The members eventually went their separate ways.

They reunited in 2007 for the reality TV program *The Salt-N-Pepa Show*, and the group eventually returned to live performance. Nearly twenty-five years after its release, *Very Necessary* (1993) is still the biggest-selling album by a female rap group. They turned up in an ad for Geico insurance, singing the song that started it all, "Push It." Denton had never dreamed they'd make the kind of impact of Run-DMC, Grandmaster Flash, or Public Enemy. "I couldn't see us in those same category as those guys back then," she wrote. "I do today, though." She was equally forthright when asked by *Billboard* in 2015 what she wanted people to remember about Salt-N-Pepa: "that we pioneered and did this damn thing for women and music. Period." ∎

SINÉAD O'CONNOR

PEACHES

ILLUSTRATION BY ANNE MUNTGES

I heard Sinéad O'Connor before I ever saw her face. It was 1988, and my friend had a copy of her debut album, *The Lion and the Cobra*. She busted it out in excitement, insisting I listen. The power, the anger, the vulnerability, the beauty; I was hooked immediately.

I'd never heard anything quite like Sinéad's songwriting before. There were traditional folk elements, to be sure, but there were also exciting new dance rhythms. While most pop music ebbs and flows through peaks and valleys, Sinéad's songs offered a slow, steady buildup of intensity and pain, adding layer upon layer of passion until it seemed like the music couldn't contain her emotion for even a moment longer. It flew in the face of tradition and the conventions of commercial radio. It wasn't particularly catchy, but damn, it was powerful.

Sinéad was a great singer. She wasn't always smooth in her delivery, but that was part of the point. The songs were about truth, not perfection. Her lyrics were direct, at times even scathing. There was no irony in what she sang, just pure emotion. Love, lust, anger, sadness, and joy all coexisted alongside one another, wrestling for power and attention. She mixed history, spirituality, and emotions, which came from a deeply personal place.

I was passionate about the songs, and that would have been enough for me, but then I *saw* her on TV. Big eyes and a bald head. Combat boots, black straight pants, and an oversized T-shirt. It was a revelation, a look that screamed feminism. She'd erased the conventional markers of beauty. If you were going to gaze upon Sinéad O'Connor, you were going to do it on her terms.

I still remember the way she took the stage with conviction and serious intent but how she couldn't manage to suppress the shy, innocent shadow of a smile that whispered across her face as the audience roared for her. Even through the TV, I could feel her shake and tremble as she sang of hurt and betrayal. One second, her voice was a delicate quiver, the next, a chilling snarl. Never had I seen someone convey such intimacy with their words and expressions.

In interviews, Sinéad was always straightforward and up-front. She talked about being a real human being, not a rock star. She spoke frankly about sexism in the music industry and what it meant to be a feminist. She addressed women's self-esteem and the need for society to move beyond its expectations of its female pop stars. I thought it was sweet the way, whenever she felt shy or insecure in an interview, she'd brush up on the back of her head. It must have helped her ground herself to touch the place where her hair had been.

From those interviews, I learned that Sinéad grew up poor in Dublin. She had a tough childhood

with an abusive mother, and she was in and out of strict Catholic boarding schools. She believed that the Catholic Church, as an institution, was the source of the destruction of Irish culture and the national violent frustration that came with this. Sinéad herself felt this through the domestic violence she endured from her own mother. Music was more than just self-expression for her; it was a way to stop the cycle of violence, a way to overcome her own trauma.

Though Sinéad was twenty-one when *The Lion and the Cobra* was released, she'd written most of the songs at seventeen, when she finally escaped conservative Dublin to live in London. Her mother, a devout Catholic, died shortly after Sinéad left home, and the two never had an opportunity to truly reconcile. The album earned a Grammy nomination for Best Female Vocal Performance alongside heavy hitters like Pat Benatar and Tina Turner, and O'Connor was invited to perform at the ceremony. Uninterested in flaunting fame, she took the stage by herself, wearing only a black sports bra and jeans, to sing her single "Mandinka," which was inspired by the West African coming-of-age ritual that includes male and female genital circumcision, as described in Alex Haley's *Roots*. It was a taboo-breaking performance and most Americans' introduction to her artistry.

Sinéad followed up *The Lion and the Cobra* with her second album, *I Don't Want What I Haven't Got*, in 1990. The emotion and anger remained, but this time, the production was slicker, and she was sitting on an enormous hit with "Nothing Compares 2 U."

Sinéad sang the song written by Prince with sadness and just the right amount of anger.

For the video, record executives apparently asked Sinéad to wear a miniskirt, so she of course shaved her head again. It didn't matter what she was wearing or how her hair looked, though. The resulting video, a simple close-up of Sinéad staring at the camera and pouring her heart out, is one of the most iconic in music history. She later revealed that she could conjure real tears and pain by thinking about her mother.

That year, O'Connor won three MTV VMAs, including Best Video of the Year, marking the first time a woman won the top award. She garnered four Grammy nominations, including Album of the Year, and would have taken home the inaugural trophy in the new Best Alternative Music Performance category had she shown up to the awards. Along with Public Enemy, she chose to boycott the ceremony in protest of its commercialization.

She threatened to cancel a concert in New Jersey when the venue wanted to impose their tradition of playing the national anthem beforehand. That was how Sinéad had always operated: things happened on her terms or not at all. She refused to perform on *Saturday Night Live* in 1990 because it would have meant sharing a stage with comedian Andrew Dice Clay, whose act reveled in misogyny and homophobia. When she did agree to appear on the show two years later, it would become one of the most memorable moments in modern television.

While O'Connor considered the Catholic Church to be a source of great damage to society, she still believed in direct contact with the divine and respect for all religions. She became fascinated with Rastafarianism, and during her fateful SNL performance, she boldly sang an a cappella version of Bob Marley's "War," which featured the words of the Rastafarian leader Haile Selassie. She tweaked some of the lyrics to denounce child abuse, and, just in case that wasn't revolutionary enough, held up a photograph of Pope John Paul II, determinedly shouting, "Fight the real enemy" as she ripped it up in front of millions.

No one clapped. No one cheered. There was dead silence in the studio. In later years, church abuse allegations would lead the front pages of newspapers around the world and come to be known as one of the great scandals of our time, but in that moment, in living rooms around the country, Americans were shocked, unwilling or simply not yet ready to hear the truth.

The move was no publicity stunt, though. Like everything Sinéad did, it came from a deep, dark place inside of her. Few knew at the time, but the photo O'Connor tore up was the same one that had been hanging in her mother's bedroom since 1978. Certainly, it was a provocative move, but one that was rooted in O'Connor's endless quest for healing and closure, not a desire for personal attention or controversy.

Weeks later, Sinéad was set to appear at a Bob Dylan tribute concert at Madison Square Garden, a thrilling prospect for an artist who considered Dylan one of her personal saviors. She was practically booed off the stage, though, only comforted by Kris Kristofferson as she walked off in tears. She had to retreat from America.

O'Connor has since made ten original albums, many critically acclaimed, but none ever reaching the mass appeal of her first two releases. In 1999, she was ordained as Priestess "Mother Bernadette" of the Latin Tridentine Church, a breakaway Catholic sect, and the following year, she was raised to archdeacon for her work on behalf of Dublin's homeless. In more recent years, her Facebook outbursts, suicide attempts, and pleas for help and understanding have landed her in the public eye. That Sinéad has struggled with PTSD and mental illness comes as little surprise to anyone who's followed her career. She's spoken openly and bravely about it in an industry where such revelations are discouraged from being shared publicly.

I remain, to this day, in awe of Sinéad O'Connor's talent, power, and courage. I have deep respect for her not only as an artist, but also as a woman, a fighter, a creator, a survivor, an advocate, a mother, and even a grandmother. With her music, she merged politics and emotion. Everything she touched was raw and real and forged a path for so many to follow, myself included. Nothing compares 2 that. ■

ANGÉLIQUE KIDJO

VIVIEN GOLDMAN

ILLUSTRATION BY LINDSEY BAILEY

The tiny teenage singer landed in Paris for the first time in 1983, a political refugee from Benin, West Africa. She possessed only what she was wearing—and a talent so formidable that it had forced her to flee. The success of "Pretty," her first album of lilting African pop recorded with her brother, had attracted the attention of President Mathieu Kérékou's Marxist military regime. To avoid being co-opted into the state-controlled cultural system, Angélique Kidjo had to slip away from a party, run to the airport in her hometown of Cotonou, and get right on a plane to France. Had she stayed, Kidjo, a performer since earliest childhood, would have been press-ganged into a paranoid noncareer of singing the despot's praises. Her bold breakout set her on a very different path; Kidjo is now internationally revered as both artist and humanitarian activist.

Smartly, Kidjo flips the "appropriation" script that presumes the usual flow of traffic of under- or unpaid influence, from the poor to the rich. In 2017 she offered an effervescent answer version of Talking Heads' African-inflected 1980 release *Remain in Light*, produced by David Byrne and Brian Eno. Her live performance triumphantly reclaimed the album for her continent.

Kidjo's roots were firmly planted in Cotonou. Since her actress mother first pushed her onstage as a little child, she learned how to use her multi-threat powers to sing, dance, and write in Fon, Yoruba, English, and French. When the family theater troupe folded, they channeled their energy into forming the children into an electric band, inspired by the Jackson 5. There was no doubt that in the parallel equation, Angélique was Michael. Her father smuggled the young girl into the hotel show through the kitchen to sing a few numbers onstage with her brothers, before hustling her home to bed to be ready for school in the morning. Her destiny was manifest.

The bouillon of early 1980s Afro-Paris was a multicultural magnet for artists from across the Francophone world. Working odd jobs to support her studies at the jazz school CIM, Kidjo joined the intriguing group Pili Pili, whose extended Afro-jazz-funk explorations set off her jazzy phrasing and unerring projection. Music was evolving with the advent of digitized sound and the compact disc, enabling genres that would likely have not crossed paths before to meet and meld. It was an exhilarating, exploratory moment for a generation born around the upbeat time of the colonial independence wave of the 1960s, whose ebullience would, in most cases, last less than a decade before outside forces soured the sweet promise. These were the years before the musical or cultural appropriation wars, right before the invention of the term "world music" by a cabal of enterprising British record retailers; for many immigrant Africans, the aesthetic challenge was how to embrace the increasingly digitized sounds of the West while retaining their African individuality. Kidjo's musical arc keeps testing the intracultural membrane with works like her cut with Carlos Santana, the dulcet, ethereal "Naima" from 1995's "Fifa"—named for her daughter with husband and creative partner Jean Hébrail.

The intelligence that illuminates all Kidjo's work makes her canon unusually directed and conceptual, even strategic. As an outernational artist, she takes the slave trade axis—Africa, North and South America, Brazil, Europe, the Caribbean—and spins it, her centrifuge shaking and compressing the dust of African ancestors' drums and bones into diamonds. From the supple, stinging guitars of "Pretty," Kidjo went on to explore facets of that multicontinental jewel, most clearly in her trilogy of albums divining the essence of the diaspora. On the first, *Oremi* (1998), she delves into the bond between Africa and the Americas (a theme she revisited on 2010's *Ôyo*) and audaciously covers Hendrix's "Voodoo Child" as the concept's rightful owner—after all Kidjo's native Benin, formerly known as Dahomey, was a major, not always unwilling, exporter of both human war captives and, with them, the ritual magic we now see in faiths like vodoun and Santeria. *Black Ivory Soul* (2000) is embedded in Brazil's sensuous, dreamy, and multirhythmic music, featuring such artists as Gilberto Gil, Carlinhos Brown, and Daniela Mercury. The trilogy's final album, 2004's *Oyaya*, bonds Cuba, the Anglo and Franco Caribbean, and Africa's Congo with sublime confidence and authority.

From her first internationally prominent album,

1991's *Logozo*, on Island's Mango label, Kidjo has made indelible anthems her trademark. Produced with Miami Cuban Joe Galdo, on signature tracks like "We We" and "Batonga," she grooves authoritatively over stabbing synthesizer, funk bass, and Cuban percussion. Her imaginative visual presentation, honed in sophisticated Afro-Paris, fused ancient ritual and symbolism with novel computer imagery and futuristic neon. Petite and agile, Kidjo wore a punky low flat-top hairdo and made her dazzling dance moves in tight, bright, graphic catsuits. Relocating to Prince's Paisley Park, Kidjo next recorded *Ayé* (1994) with Prince's producer, David Z. She soared again with "Agolo," a clarion call for the environment with an addictive background vocal hook over which she rises like a freed bird. Its sumptuous gold-drenched video, by French director Michel Meyer, won Kidjo her first Grammy nomination. She went on to win the award's World category three times: in 2016 for *Sings*, in which Kidjo melds African vocals and rhythms with the Orchestre Philharmonique du Luxembourg, with whom she had also worked with Philip Glass; the previous year's winner, *Eve*, was an album dedicated to African women, for which Kidjo made field recordings on a six-track in Benin and Kenya; and her first Grammy was for 2007's *Djin Djin*, whose poignant title track, sung by Kidjo with Alicia Keys, featured Branford Marsalis's saxophone.

Kidjo's participation was a moving force in the

PLAYLIST

"Wé-Wé," 1991, *Logozo*

"Batonga," 1991, *Logozo*

"Agolo," 1994, *Aye*

"Naïma," 1996, *Fifa*

"Voodoo Child (Slight Return)," 1998, *Oremi*

"Bahia," 2002, *Black Ivory Soul*

"Djin Djin," 2007, *Djin Djin* (with Alicia Keys)

"Senamou," 2007, *Djin Djin* (with Amadou and Mariam)

"Bana," 2014, *Eve*

"Malaika," 2015, *Sings* (with the Luxembourg Philharmonic Orchestra with Gast Waltzing)

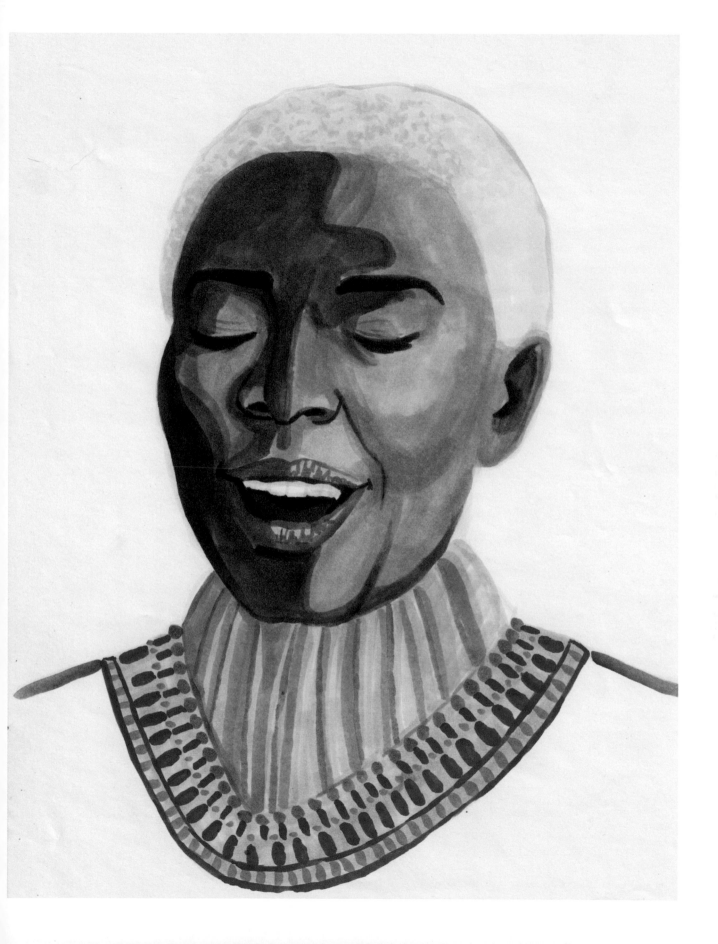

Amazones d'Afrique female supergroup of 2017, which united leading African female artists to raise funds for the Panzi Foundation, providing healthcare for the many thousands of women with brutal internal injuries from years of war in the Congo, described by the UN as "the rape capital of the world." It was the first time that a phalanx of such artists had united, and the collective was a reminder of Kidjo's powerful peer group; it includes Mariam Doumbia of the blind singers from Mali Amadou and Mariam; Nigerian pop star Nneka; and an Amazones co-founder who departed but remains a colossus, Mali's Oumou Sangaré, known for her throaty protest songs against regional ritual practices oppressive to females such as polygamy, child marriage, and genital mutilation.

Kidjo's memoir is aptly named *Spirit Rising*. From that vulnerable arrival in Paris, without powerful connections, Kidjo has indeed risen to be hailed by cultural arbiters like the *Guardian*, the *Daily Telegraph*, *Forbes*, *Jeune Afrique*, New African, and NPR. Amnesty International made her an Ambassador of Conscience in 2016. She has been a UNICEF Goodwill ambassador since 2002. She has been awarded honorary doctorates from Berklee College of Music, Yale University, and others. Few artists are bolder than Angélique Kidjo. Far from being a world music artist, the world's music is hers. ∎

LUCINDA WILLIAMS

KATHERINE TURMAN

ILLUSTRATION BY ANNE MUNTGES

Lucinda Williams's songs are the plain-spoken, gravelly voice of truth, rife with hard-won, whiskey-soaked wisdom and late-night longing. She's the girl you want by your side in a bar fight. A fight she herself might have instigated.

With one of her most beloved songs, 1988's "Changed the Locks," Williams sings of changing not only the locks, but her phone number, car, *and* the tracks under the train—because of a man whose pull is so powerful, he can bring her to her knees. It's a song that makes women want to cry out, "I've been there too!" and thank Williams—Lu, to her friends—for putting their feelings into words. Men aren't immune to the charms of her simply but perfectly wrought words and melodies either. Tom Petty, whom she opened for in 1998 and again in 2017, covered "Changed the Locks," and Ben Folds rendered a lush version of Williams's poignant 1988 song "Side of the Road."

Williams is an underdog: appealing but never fancy, cool but not intimidating, with a voice and mien that have the comforting patina of home. Like a Depression-era photo by Dorothea Lange, her voice has a sepia-toned timelessness, sad but resolute, a holder of eternal truths.

Even though *Time* magazine dubbed her "America's best songwriter" in 2002, Williams wasn't then—nor is she now—a household name. But that doesn't detract from the kudos, influence, or importance of a career that's been a slow burn. If she is too rock for country and too country for rock, the Americana scene—where she is a seminal figure—fits Williams well. The scope of her collaborators is a testament to talent rather than category, including Irish punk band Flogging Molly, Elvis Costello, Ramblin' Jack Elliott, David Byrne, Heart's Ann Wilson, and New York Doll David Johansen.

A title like America's Best Songwriter doesn't happen by accident. It's earned with a combination of hard work, innate talent, and, in Williams's case, genes. Her father, Miller Williams, an award-winning poet, editor, and professor, remained close to and an influence on his daughter until his 2015 death. She turned one of his poems, "Dust," into a song on *The Ghosts of Highway 20* (2016).

Williams was born in Lake Charles, Louisiana, on January 26, 1953; the town and the South exert a strong pull on her writing. Following her parents' divorce, the bookish Williams lived with her dad from her early teens. His progressive academic circle included the Southern Gothic author Flannery O'Connor. The antiwar movement of the late sixties, where she sang at demonstrations, was hugely influential on the young artist. At sixteen, she attended the 1969 March on Washington, and in

the following years she traveled and lived in Mexico and around the American South thanks to her dad's professorships.

Williams, whose grandfather was a conscientious objector, first heard sociopolitical songwriting while growing up in the sixties, worshipping Woody Guthrie and Bob Dylan. She'd later tell Greg Kot of the *Chicago Tribune*: "Dylan was my big hero as a songwriter—I wanted to write songs like 'Masters of War' and 'With God on our Side,' but I've always found it challenging to write topical lyrics. I try to push people's buttons, too, but I try to do it in a more subtle way."

Williams's first album, of covers, came and went in 1979. By the mid-eighties she had settled for a time in Los Angeles, finding traction as part of a roots-rock scene centered around the Palomino Club and groups including Lone Justice, the Long Ryders, and the Blasters. In 1988, her third, self-titled outing rightly found critical acclaim and a bigger audience, though still not entirely on her own terms. It was a song from that record, "Passionate Kisses," covered six years later by Mary Chapin Carpenter, who fought to record it, that earned Williams her first Grammy Award for Best Country Song in 1994, finally giving Williams's profile the nudge it needed.

At forty-five, when many artists' heydays are behind them, Williams's true commercial breakthrough came with the timeless *Car Wheels on a Gravel Road* (1998). The fully realized album featured such gems as "Drunken Angel," a plaintive song about a talented ne'er-do-well musician friend who was shot to death; the twangy "Concrete and Barbed Wire," and the midtempo sultry title track. *Car Wheels* won a Grammy for Best Contemporary Folk Album, and Williams found herself facing bigger venues and audiences with opening slots for Bob Dylan and the Allman Brothers.

Williams's songs are often melancholy but not hopeless and sometimes infused with hints of humor. While many of them mourn and mine relationship woes, Williams's personal life hit a high note in 2009 when she married manager Tom Overby onstage at Minneapolis's First Avenue club. Wearing black and saying her "I dos" to the cheer of her fans, within three minutes of marrying, the new bride had broken into song.

Her writing is by no means only focused on affairs of the heart and body or romanticizing and chronicling the smoky underbelly of a road-house lifestyle, though those topics are among her most forceful. *Sweet Old World* (1992) delved into death and suicide, while 2007's simple ode "Are You Alight" is a plea to her brother, who was no longer in her life. Williams consistently manages to ride the line between tough and touching, her immediate, plainspoken voice and songs folky but never folksy.

No matter the category Williams fits in—or doesn't—since 1998, she's been riding a fruitful, if out-of-the-spotlight, wave. In her seventh decade, her musical and personal power only continue to increase. And if she's particular about her writing and recording, taking her time to achieve what she hears in her head, well, the proof is in the grooves of every song she cuts. Journalist Holly George-Warren noted, "A lot of the things I've heard said

PLAYLIST

"Changed the Locks," 1988, *Lucinda Williams*

"Passionate Kisses," 1988, *Lucinda Williams*

"Sweet Old World," 1992, *Sweet Old World*

"Drunken Angel," 1998, *Car Wheels on a Gravel Road*

"Concrete and Barbed Wire," 1998, *Car Wheels on a Gravel Road*

"Get Right with God," 2001, *Essence*

"Sweet Side," 2003, *World without Tears*

"Unsuffer Me," 2007, *West*

"Compassion," 2014, *Down Where the Spirit Meets the Bone*

about Lucinda are sexist—that she's difficult, for example. You don't hear things like that about Bruce Springsteen and John Fogerty." With three Grammys and fifteen nominations, weeklong residencies at premier clubs, and fawning reviews, it's clear Williams's uncompromising approach is the right one. Author Flannery O'Connor said of writing: "A story is a way to say something that can't be said any other way, and it takes every word in the story to say what the meaning is." The same goes for Williams's songs: memorably perfect vignettes, precisely honed. ■

L7

KATHERINE TURMAN

ILLUSTRATION BY ANNE MUNTGES

Even a cursory glance at L7's song titles tells the tale: "Shove," "Shitlist," "Fuel My Fire," "The Masses Are Asses," "Fast and Frightening." Confrontational, unrelenting, aggro, powerful—the stuff that good rock and roll is made of. But created by women? There are no hints of gender identity in the titles nor the band name, either—fifties slang for square, or loser.

L7 is a dirty, punky hard-rock-verging-on-metal band who just happen to be women. In fact, they originally had a male drummer. They came together in Los Angeles in the mid-eighties, without an agenda, sans the big-hair image that both male and female bands were dubiously sporting at the time. As bassist Jennifer Finch remembers on her blog: "Punk Rock Was My Get-Out-Of-Van-Halen Free Card."

The members of L7—Finch, singer-guitarist Donita Sparks, guitarist Suzi Gardner, and drummer Demetra Plakas—*were* prescient, though, and while they adamantly did not want to be identified as a "girl band," they were keenly aware of sexism in the industry and society and were ferocious activists as well as musicians. As Sparks told Spin in 2012: "We chose fierceness and humor over vulnerability because we were, you know, navigating challenging waters—women in hard rock. You had to be tough."

To wit: the band's biggest hit, "Let's Pretend We're Dead"—a poppy, midtempo, fuzzy, buzzy (read: grungy) rocker that spent twenty weeks on the *Billboard* Alternative Song charts in 1992, climbing to number eight. The lyrics appear to offer snarky sociopolitical commentary. But, as Sparks admitted much later, the seeds of the tune arose from romantic heartbreak—a topic she felt she could not explicitly address in L7 lyrics.

What the band did address, through actions that galvanized the alt music scene of the early nineties, was everyday sexism. Onstage and off, they created a sociopolitical legacy equal to their memorable musical legacy of six studio albums and many hundreds of sweaty, incendiary performances. L7 railed against the "women in a band" pedestal they were put on, but they did inspire countless young women—and future peers—including Garbage's Shirley Manson. If female musicians were supposed to conform to societal standards for beauty and behavior, well fuck that. L7 kicked out the jams. Sparks wailed on her Flying V guitar, her changeable voice ranging from a passionate wail, to snarky punk snarl, to speedy, intimate grumble. Like the Northwestern bands they became associated with, from Nirvana to the Melvins, L7 were ordinary people making extraordinarily loud, important rock, taking no prisoners with their body-punishing stage diving, thrashing, and knee drops.

L7 partied hard, too. They enjoyed bonding and

debauchery on "girls' nights" that were as wild as any stereotypical "boys' night." In a 2011 *Vice* interview, Finch reminisced: "We rebelled against the decadence of the 1970s, making it filthier still. We were interested in all kinds of music and forms of art, and that's probably what inspired our behavior.'" Songs like "Off the Wagon" (and "on the town") proffer unabashed celebrations of sex, drugs, and rock and roll. Some people got it: the foursome received the blessing of MTV cartoon tastemakers Beavis and Butt-head, who grunted, "Is this the Bangles? No, the Go-Go's. Are these grunge chicks? Grunge chicks are cool."

L7 were more than cool, though cool translated into only semi-fame and moderate, fleeting fortune over the dozenish years of the band's duration, unlike many of their higher-flying contemporaries. In 1990, the group's second album, *Smell the Magic*, featured the anthem "Shove," a catchy salvo about pushing naysayers out of the way: boss, dad, neighbors, landlord, asshole dudes. The tune ended up on the *Tank Girl* movie soundtrack, and the band embarked on a tour in Europe, on the road with a pre-*Nevermind* Nirvana.

Back home, they spearheaded Rock 4 Choice, a buzzed-about pro-choice fundraiser produced in conjunction with the Feminist Majority Foundation. The 1991 debut show, at the Hollywood Palace, featuring L7, Nirvana, and Hole, was allegedly the show where Courtney Love, who had been in the San Francisco–based band Sugar Babydoll with Finch, met Kurt Cobain for the first time. The decade-long series of Rock 4 Choice concerts came to life concurrently with the Riot Grrrl movement brewing out of Washington state, though the factions weren't part of any unified movement. Thanks to Rock 4 Choice, many Gen X music fans who were burgeoning feminists joined their older sisters in instigating progressive personal and public conversations about women's issues. The organization brought together then up-and-comers next to A-list names, with Iggy Pop, Rage Against the Machine, Red Hot Chili Peppers, Soundgarden, and dozens of others supporting Rock 4 Choice.

Meanwhile, L7 were about to enjoy the commercial pinnacle of their success: their third album, *Bricks Are Heavy*, produced by Butch Vig (Nirvana, Sonic Youth), timed perfectly though unwittingly with the grunge explosion, proved their breakthrough. *Entertainment Weekly* described *Bricks* as "catchy tunes and mean vocals on top of ugly guitars and a quick-but-thick bottom of cast iron grunge." "Let's Pretend We're Dead" gave L7 new purchase in the music world, and they performed on *Late Night with David Letterman*. The band's give-no-shits stance made headlines. Several shenanigans threatened to overshadow the band's roaring musicality. At the 1992 Reading Festival in the UK, equipment malfunctions caused a delay in the start of L7's set and an impatient audience threw mud on the stage. Sparks's response? She removed her tampon and threw it into the crowd, shouting, "Eat my used tampon, fuckers!" The same year, she dropped her pants on live television, on the UK variety program *The Word*. The band was confrontational out of frustration and raw emotion, not by design. They didn't ask for forgiveness.

Hungry for Stink hit in 1994 and proved to be the last album to feature Finch, who quit to follow

PLAYLIST

"Shove," 1991, *Smell the Magic*

"Pretend We're Dead," 1992, *Bricks Are Heavy*

"This Ain't Pleasure," 1992, *Bricks Are Heavy*

"Andres," 1994, *Hungry for Stink*

"Off the Wagon," 1997, *The Beauty Process: Triple Platinum*

a solo dream. In 1997 came *The Beauty Process: Triple Platinum*. If L7 were still beloved by their peers—they opened for Marilyn Manson on a US tour, and Nirvana bassist Krist Novoselic directed a concert film *L7: The Beauty Process*—they nonetheless lost their record deal with Reprise and their internal momentum. Their sixth and final album, *Slap Happy*, came out in 1999 along with more non-music headlines: The band raffled a one-night stand with drummer Plakas at a London gig. The same year, L7 hired planes flying banners to communicate to festival crowds. At the Pasadena, California, stop of the mellow, female-centric Lilith Fair, the banner read, "Bored? Tired? Try L7." On the opposite coast, above the boisterous, male-centric Warped Tour date in Asbury Park, New Jersey, L7's banner opined: "Warped Needs More Beaver." Protesting—accurately—what the band perceived as the narrow scope of the festivals earned headlines rather than change or major kudos. They were too rock and outré for Lilith, and too estrogen-fueled and left-of-center badass for Warped.

L7's painful demise—Gardner quit via a phone call—is chronicled in the documentary *L7: Pretend We're Dead*, released worldwide in 2017. Finch described the era's declining music scene in her blog: "Radio stations had since gone back to the 'Same 20 Bands' played over and over again. It seems that once again bands are being fronted by aggressive, middle class white boys, playing middle of the road, watered down music and using women's body parts to escalate their sales." The dream of the nineties was dead, and so was the band.

Ironically, it was the 2015 Kickstarter campaign for the documentary that unintentionally rebooted L7. Director Sarah Price received $130,480 pledged on her $97,000 goal. The band saw the fan interest and began tentative steps toward reforming for live performances, which came to fruition at the end of 2015. If they'd spent a career resisting the unasked-for role as poster girls for women in rock, the reunion found L7 older, wiser but just as loud and unrepentant. Any inter-band conflicts were in the past, and the groundbreaking quartet were excited to bring back their "certain threatening element." If L7 spent a career too often lumped in by gender or genre, their return—and legacy—proved that ferocity and integrity know no limits. ■

SELENA

MICHELLE THREADGOULD

ILLUSTRATION BY WINNIE T. FRICK

Selena's death hangs over Corpus Christi like the thick, humid fog that envelops the coastal city of three hundred thousand residents. Everywhere you go, from the waterfront where her statue was erected, to the gay bars where the film *Selena* plays on repeat, to her old working-class neighborhood of El Molino, you will find roses, photos, and tributes to la gran muchacha del barrio. It's as if the city were a memorial that should be renamed Santa Selena.

Most of white America was introduced to the Tejana artist Selena Quintanilla-Pérez on March 31, 1995, the day that the twenty-three-year-old woman was murdered by her fan club president. But for the 25 million Latinos living in the US at the time, since 1991 they had watched her salsas and cumbias on Univision, they had seen her perform on *Sábado Gigante* or live in front of sixty thousand in Houston or Monterrey, Mexico. Her story gave women of color hope that during a time of welfare and immigration reform, and other legislation that seemed to otherize Latinos, one day someone like Selena could dominate the charts like Madonna. Selena held the promise of what could be, even when Latinos were disproportionately targeted by police and the eradication of bilingual education was championed. Even while a country was trying to get rid of you or force you to assimilate for a chance at the American

dream, Selena took her painted eyebrows, jet black hair, and proudly morena, Mexican American body, and—as she executed her Tejano dance moves and 360-degree turns—seemed to say: *I'm just as American as you, babe.*

Selena was a third-generation Mexican American born on April 16, 1971, in Lake Jackson, Texas, near Corpus Christi, where she would spend most of her adult life. Like many Mexican Americans trying to avoid the culture wars in America at the time, Selena did not grow up speaking Spanish but was surrounded by a hybrid culture where Tejano music reigned supreme. Raised in a strict Jehovah's Witness household, she was expected to fulfill the traditional role of being a loyal and obedient daughter, and eventually become a wife and have a family. But from a young age, it was clear that Selena wanted more for herself. Her father, Abraham Quintanilla, a former musician, noticed her perfect pitch when she would sing along to the radio. Envisioning a better life for his family, he began managing Selena, her brother, and sister in a band called Selena y los Dinos.

As a teenager, Selena began touring Texas with her family and band on an old refurbished bus nicknamed Big Bertha. While practicing her routines on Bertha, Selena would experiment with new fashions, designing her own costumes from studded bustiers to cropped fringed jackets. She also developed her

dancing style, incorporating Spanish folkloric elements via beautiful twists of her hand with Caribbean salsa and American hip-hop. Her performances were an expression of joy and Latinidad, with Selena nailing spins, smiling, salsaing, and belting out long notes at the same time.

Selena's life was not an assimilationist story but a fusion of the diverse cultures she was born into. Her brother, the musician and producer A. B. Quintanilla, loved the sounds that they grew up with in their barrio, and the two of them collaborated on making music that didn't fit neatly into any genre. Her songs borrowed and mixed many different styles; she was one of the first Latina artists to incorporate Afro-Caribbean beats, salsa, R&B, cumbia, ranchera, and Tejano music all alongside each other to create a sound uniquely her own.

In the nineties, Selena's popularity grew and she toured Mexico and the US. On the road, she met her future husband, the guitarist Chris Pérez, who became a member of her band. Over the course of her career, Selena released a total of five albums. Early on, she began trending on the Tejano music charts and received multiple accolades at the Tejano Music Awards. Her third album, *Entre a Mi Mundo*, released in May 1992, was certified six times platinum and sold nearly a million copies in the US and Mexico. A year later, she performed in Nuevo León, Mexico, for an audience of seventy thousand people, making her the most popular Tejano act in Mexico. *Entre a Mi Mundo* marked a turning point

PLAYLIST

"Baila Esta Cumbia," 1990, *Ven Conmigo*

"Como la Flor," 1992, *Entre a Mi Mundo*

"Amor Prohibido," 1994, *Amor Prohibido*

"Bidi Bidi Bom Bom," 1994, *Amor Prohibido*

"Si una Vez," 1994, *Amor Prohibido*

"I Could Fall in Love," 1995, *Dreaming of You*

"Dreaming of You," 1995, *Dreaming of You*

for Selena, featuring the song that would go on to epitomize her: "Como la Flor," a cumbia about love and the pain of heartbreak. On its call and response chorus, fans would reach out to Selena and scream, "Ayyyyyyyyayyyyyy, como me dueles."

In 1994, it seemed as if there was no barrier Selena could not cross. She received a Grammy for Best Mexican-American Album for *Selena Live!* and was recording what she hoped would become her "crossover," featuring her first-ever songs in English. But her life was ruthlessly cut short when her fan club president murdered her in a hotel room after it was discovered that the fan club president was stealing money from Selena and her family.

As a testament to Selena's staying power, her album *Dreaming of You* was released posthumously and went on to become a thirty-five-times platinum record, one of the biggest-selling records of all time by a Latino artist.

In her death, Selena made it possible for countercultures to find a home in her music, style, and image. The beloved, iconic 1996 film *Selena* gave Latinos a feel-good biopic about traditional Latino values like family, marriage, and the importance of being a good daughter and a hard worker. The film inspired Latinos to honor elements of their heritage in a way completely true to their culture. Today, we see many bands and artists remixing Selena's sound to pay homage to her, while setting out on their own path. From Latina DJ crews, like Chulita Vinyl Club, founded in San Antonio and featuring women who spin cumbia, salsa, and soul, to queer punk cover bands like Amor Prohibido, Selena can be found at the epicenter of counterculture movements. Cumbia punk, all-women Tejano groups, and Selena-inspired drag shows and tributes are all a vital part of her legacy—the different cultures seeking representation who found their voice in the voice of Selena.

When you visit Selena's old home in Corpus Christi, a deep sadness creeps in. You pass homes missing foundations, teetering on crates, and condemned. It is as if the people from her neighborhood never benefited from the promise of a better life for Latinos, as if you are walking onto the real-life set of "the other." After the devastation of Hurricane Harvey, whose floods swept six relatives of Selena to their death, many Latinos were left in even worse conditions.

It's poignant that Selena's story does not have a happy ending, because it reminds us of how far we still have to go as a society. As we stumble toward liberation, we will always have her music, and her inspiration to *baila esta cumbia* freely. ■

QUEEN LATIFAH

SHANA L. REDMOND

ILLUSTRATION BY LINDSEY BAILEY

In the pantheon of feminist provocations, the question "Who you callin' a bitch?" ranks high. Confrontational rather than diplomatic, it identifies a gross injury and refuses it, casting scorn back from whence it came. It's raucous and resonant, continuing to echo in everyday conversation as well as spectacular protest, highlighting its incendiary didacticism. This famed one-liner from the shape-shifting emcee Queen Latifah, from her 1993 anthem track "U.N.I.T.Y.," remains a benchmark for the entertainer who, at various moments in her career, used hip-hop to confront popular rap caricatures of black women as bitches and hos. This critical posturing beckoned me to her tribe like a teacher to a student; it was why I listened then and why I continue to do so almost thirty years later.

Born Dana Elaine Owens in 1970, Queen Latifah demonstrated a creative and inquisitive mind at an early age. Her adopted Arabic stage name, which means "gentle," "kind," or "pleasant," was chosen by her at the age of eight and, in adulthood, became a counterpoint to the stereotyped assumptions of aggression and masculinity too often associated with black female emcees. Originally a beatboxer with all-woman group Ladies Fresh, eighteen-year-old Latifah's rhymes grabbed the attention of Fab 5 Freddy of *Yo! MTV Raps*, who facilitated a deal at Tommy Boy Music. Though signed as a solo artist, the Newark,

New Jersey, native relied on and modeled an ethic of collectivity by announcing her crew and hinting at her Pan African sensibilities. During the 1990s she was one of two female emcees affiliated with the Native Tongues, a collective of hip-hop musicians who shared a distinctly and unapologetically Afrocentric style. Composed of Latifah, UK emcee Monie Love, the Jungle Brothers, a Tribe Called Quest, and De La Soul, Native Tongues bridged the urban stateside hustle of hip-hop with the sounds, dress, and dreams of a wider black world. Known in the early 1990s for wearing African-inspired hats and head wraps, Latifah used those symbols to reinforce her sophisticated lyrical content.

Marked on its cover with the colors of Marcus Garvey's black nationalist flag (red, black, and green) and a silhouette of Africa, her first solo album, *All Hail the Queen* (1990), is, in some ways, indicative of its time. Contemporary party jams ground the twelve original tracks. But *All Hail* mixes elements of house ("Come into My House"), Afrobeat ("Latifah's Law"), and reggae ("Princess of the Posse") into a diasporic sampler plate served at the end of a two-term Reagan administration that executed a deadly domestic War on Drugs and treated the apartheid government of South Africa as an ally. So yes, we wanted to dance, but we wanted our revolution, too, and Latifah delivered both. The biggest hit from the album was also the Queen's first popular anthem, "Ladies First." The video for the duet with Love shows Latifah playing a chess game for control of southern Africa. She knocks over the male figurines on the tabletop map only to replace them with black power fists. Lauding the power of women as emcees and mothers, "Ladies First" set the tone for a music career that first was organized around the concerns and experiences of black women. From domestic abuse to street harassment to empowerment, Latifah detailed the unique challenges and strengths of womanhood in a patriarchal industry, country, and world.

Two years later Latifah recorded her second and final album for Tommy Boy, *Nature of a Sista*. Toeing the line between bravado and positivity, she highlighted her lyrical skills while continuing to discuss Africa, love, and misogyny. Foreshadowing her later career, this album focuses more on vocals than her first, even if they still play second fiddle to a lyrical aggression. That confidence exploded on her third studio album, *Black Reign* (1993), for Motown. Dedicated to her brother, who died in a motorcycle accident, *Reign* introduces the Latifah from the Garden State. Gone are the African-inspired accessories; now wearing knit hats and baseball caps, jerseys and overalls, down coats and oversized leather jackets, she reflects the hybrid feminine-masculine aesthetic in contemporary R&B and hip-hop and represents for the curvy women who didn't bare their midriff like Aaliyah but nonetheless found and flaunted their sexuality in baggy jeans. She was our thick chick idol who proved that sexuality is to be enjoyed, not abused or taken advantage of, and multiple tracks on the album, including the stand-out "U.N.I.T.Y.," announce that women won't settle for anything less than respect.

With the key from her brother's motorcycle around her neck, Latifah used the success of *Black Reign* to begin a career transformation. She took a break from solo recording, joining the smash single "I Wanna Be Down (remix)" (1994) with singer Brandy and emcees Yo-Yo and MC Lyte, and moved into starring roles on television and film, including the comedy *Living Single* (1993–1998). In the 1996 bank heist film *Set It Off*, she portrayed the iconic butch lesbian character of Cleo, a woman who dies in a hail of gunfire rather than surrender to police. Her impressive performance heightened public interest in her sexuality, which she has consistently evaded in interviews even as her acting portfolio continues to include queer characters like the luminary bisexual blues artist Bessie Smith (*Bessie*, 2015).

Latifah's ascent to a regular television presence in the late 1990s signaled the end of an era in which she was known first as a hip-hop artist. In 1998 she released her final Motown album, *Order in the Court*, which was also her first to warrant a parental advisory. Her most recent three albums (2004, 2007, 2009) highlight her as a vocalist, and only on the last—*Persona*—does she reinvent her skills as an emcee and, even there, sparingly. In the wake of a highly decorated acting and producing career in television and film, as well as a limited record of longevity for female emcees, she may have abandoned her lyricism for more lucrative projects with crossover appeal. That would be understandable. But I hold out hope for a return to the source—a reintroduction of the badass, anti-pin-up Cover Girl who slays sixteen bars at the age of forty-eight, fifty-eight, and beyond. ∎

PLAYLIST

"Ladies First," 1989, *All Hail the Queen*

"Latifah's Had It Up 2 Here," 1991, *Nature of a Sista'*

"Coochie Bang…," 1993, *Black Reign*

"U.N.I.T.Y.," 1993, *Black Reign*

"Just Another Day…," 1993, *Black Reign*

"Paper," 1998, *Order in the Court*

ANI DIFRANCO

LUCRETIA TYE JASMINE

ILLUSTRATION BY ANNE MUNTGES

Ani DiFranco's do-it-yourself standards infuse everything she does. Singer, songwriter, multi-instrumentalist, and poet, DiFranco founded her own record label, Righteous Babe Records, by the time she was nineteen. She built her career through busking, touring, college gigs, word-of-mouth, and (early on) cassette tapes. By creating music through her own label and by performing at and contributing to benefits, rallies, fundraisers, and political events, Ani makes music of activism.

As of 2017's *Binary*, DiFranco has released more than twenty albums and worked with artists from Prince to Utah Phillips to Dar Williams to her own daughter, Petah Lucia (who sings backup on 2017's "Even More"). Throughout her career, Ani has written her own lyrics and music, producing and arranging her albums, too, sometimes recording in her own room. She contributes most of the instrumentation, including but not limited to guitar, ukulele, piano, congas, accordion, wurlitzer, optigan, space phone, and sound effects. She utilizes an open or alternate tuning, and plays with glued-on fake nails that she tapes down, rather than with a guitar pick, so she can more readily thump, pick, strum, and tear at the strings. The restrained rage of Ani's singing on 1995's "Not a Pretty Girl," from the album of the same name, emphasizes the song's meaning; like the kitty cat in the lyrics, she communicates entrapment and

the ability to work oneself free through one's own capabilities. So, too, does Ani find her way.

Born in Buffalo, New York, in 1970 to to a family she says was never very close-knit, Angela Maria DiFranco learned guitar when she very young. She played her first gig when she was nine years old, making the rounds of coffeehouses and bars as a teen, and releasing her debut album by age twenty. After her parents separated, Ani lived with her dad and brother, then moved to her mom's. But when Ani was fifteen and her breadwinner mom wanted to move away for a job, Ani decided to continue on in Buffalo, staying in her band, getting an apartment, and living as an emancipated minor.

Musically, artistically, and economically, Ani articulates her experimental essence. Her music of different genres (such as punk, funk, rap, and folk), her album cover art and book of poetry, and her indie record label all represent resistance to exploitation and hierarchy. Righteous Babe Records doesn't have to rely on formulas or past sales or traditional demarcations to guarantee future sales, and neither does Ani. In fact, DiFranco has stated her commitment to working within the system to change it. She turns down big-money offers from labels who might control her physical appearance and creative output or content, and then writes a song about it, and takes the song on tour.

That experimental versatility can be heard in her singing. The many moods of her multifaceted voice echo the many sides to each situation and person she examines in her lyrics. DiFranco's melodies can soothe or strike. When the music and lyrics are angry or hilarious her calm awareness comes across in her harmony and humor. On "Egos Like Hairdos," from 1993's *Puddle Dive*, she chants a childhood taunt in her soft and deep contralto voice and ends with a laugh as she works through competition among musicians: "There's more bad blood / In this bar than there is beer."

Ani's humor can be heartbroken, too. In the 1996 song "Dilate," her voice, close like a whisper on the phone or beside you in bed, and her looped longing of inarticulate singing that reinforces the words she does sing and say echo her passionate claims. She wipes up messes with her dress and doesn't apologize. "I like to take up space just because I can," she tells the lover who isn't there. A stuttering can be heard in her guitar-playing, too; judgments, betrayals, and disappointments stymie but don't halt her. DiFranco's voice smoothly ascends or lowers, lengthening into a bridge even as it distorts, as in the 1996 song, "Napoleon."

Thoughtful, Ani turns her emotional experiences into something she can work with. Her double live album *Living in Clip* (1997) attained gold record status. Her 2003 album, *Evolve*, which explores jazz and funk, won a Grammy for Best Recording Package, honoring the art she and Brian Grunert made for the cover: her signature, debossed and offset above an orange moth in blue space, with the die-cutting of the title like open windows, suggesting hands-on freedom. She has also won the National Organization for Women's Women of Courage Award, the Woody Guthrie Award, the Gay and Lesbian American Music Award, and the BMI Cable Award.

She speaks out and sings out about what she believes, working on behalf of others even as she finds a way to support herself. "I help myself to what I need / but I help other people too," she sings on "Egos Like Hairdos." Her record label distributes music by many artists, she contributes songs to benefit compilations whose profits go to the issues she supports, she provides soundtracks for films, and, tellingly, she gives voice to the feminist rocker on the popular sitcom *King of the Hill*. According to an article in the *New York Times*, DiFranco hired local businesses for her label's needs, from CD pressing to liner, poster, and T-shirt printing, despite the higher expense. She also champions causes that include death penalty rights and reproductive freedom. The Righteous Babe Store launched the Katrina Piano Fund, which replaces musicians' instruments lost in Hurricane Katrina. DiFranco serves on the board of Roots of Music, a group that offers academic support and tutoring as well as music education and mentorship for youth in New Orleans.

Ani personifies a zeitgeist, manifesting the revolutionary spirit of third-wave feminism in which she emerged. Her creative and grassroots independence dovetails with the Riot Grrrls' self-empowering ethos. An example of a woman who has forged her own path, DiFranco works outside of celebrity but inside the community, where it counts. ■

PLAYLIST

"Work Your Way Out," 1990, *Ani DiFranco*

"Anticipate," 1991, *Not So Soft*

"Egos Like Hairdos," 1993, *Puddle Dive*

"Not a Pretty Girl," 1995, *Not a Pretty Girl*

"32 Flavors," 1995, *Not a Pretty Girl*

"Dilate," 1996, *Dilate*

"Napoleon," 1996, *Dilate*

"Untouchable Face," 1996, *Dilate*

"Swan Dive," 1998, *Little Plastic Castle*

"Two Little Girls," 1998, *Little Plastic Castle*

GIRL POWER

The data was depressing: Girls were growing down. Instead of gaining strength and assurance as they began their transition into adulthood, females were slipping behind their male peers, according to several studies released in the early 1990s. Perhaps the most famous investigation was that conducted by Lyn Mikel Brown and Carol Gilligan, who interviewed one hundred subjects and found that "the crossroads between girls and women is marked by a series of disconnections or dissociations which leave girls psychologically at risk." The evidence dealt a blow to the legacy of second-wave feminism and especially Title IX, the government act that was supposed to level the developmental playing field.

But if you were a teenager, or a young woman who had just (barely) survived the conformist hotbox of high school, the findings came as more of a confirmation than news. No duh adolescence makes us want to die, even actually kills us (suicides . . . cutters . . . anorexics . . . addicts). How could we love life if we were being taught to hate our own bodies because they're too flat or too fat, too short or too long—never just right?

Around 1991—"the year punk broke," as one documentary put it—punk rock became the soundtrack of a new feminist revolt: "Revolution Girl Style," the band Bikini Kill called it. The word that had once been politically deemed patronizing and infantilizing was given the 1990s reclamation treatment: "Girly Sound," a songwriter bummed out by the "Guyville" of Chicago's indie scene proudly dubbed her music. Then the term got mashed up with the warning growl of a big cat: grrrl. The Riot Grrrls, a decentralized movement instigated by members of bands including Bikini Kill, Bratmobile, and Heavens to Betsy, spoke directly from and to the hearts of young women struggling with the Sisyphean loads of sexual abuse, incest, eating disorders, homophobia, gender dysphoria, the beauty myth, the feminist backlash, and so on. In the artist ephemera of fanzines, 45 sleeves, and meeting flyers, third-wave New Wavers whispered or screamed words of encouragement: "Support girl love." "Cry in public." The message was aimed at our mothers too; we were telling them we wanted not just "women's liberation" but "girl liberation" also.

Punks weren't the only artists getting into the sisterhood act in the early 1990s. Responding to Anita Hill's riveting Senate testimony recalling sexual harassment, writer Rebecca Walker called for a "third wave of feminism" in 1992. Rappers Queen Latifah and Monie Love declared "Ladies First." The funky divas of En Vogue channeled the ancient power of the girl group and urged their fans to "Free Your Mind." English blues singer Polly Jean Harvey declared herself a "50Ft Queenie."

Of course, the revolution got co-opted. The Riot Grrrl phrase "Girl Power" became the marketing slogan for a group of English models who peddled "Spice." The stapled-together manifestoes of Revolution Girl Style fell apart under the weight of media attention. But that idea—girl liberation—was like a virus unleashed upon the world. You could kill the host, but there was no containing—as one zine put it—Girl Germs. They might seem dormant, or to have burrowed underground, until suddenly, a rash of girl power would flare up. A suburban California ska singer named Gwen Stefani celebrated being "Just a Girl." A teenager in Chicago named Tavi Gevinson started a fanzine for rookies. And in Moscow, a group of feminist art students decided to start a riot of their own—a Pussy Riot.

KATHLEEN HANNA

GAYLE WALD

ILLUSTRATION BY ANNE MUNTGES

Kathleen Hanna didn't single-handedly invent Riot Grrrl, the early 1990s movement of women in independent rock, but she was an incontestable force behind the girl-style "revolution" that sent a welcome blast of feminist fresh air into the musty boys' club of punk and post-punk. Revered for her powerful vocals and fearlessness as a live performer, Hanna first garnered attention as the frontwoman of Bikini Kill, a band that appropriated the brazenness of punk to celebrate "girl culture" and rage against patriarchy, whether in the form of abusive fathers and boyfriends, oppressive beauty norms, or the quotidian sexism of the punk scene. Before it was co-opted in the mid-1990s by manufactured acts like the Spice Girls, Hanna and her cohort of feminist musicians advocated a notion of "girl power" centered on creativity, independence, emotional forthrightness, and frankness about female sexuality. Through her post–Bikini Kill bands, most notably Le Tigre and the Julie Ruin, and in various solo projects, Hanna has continued to explore popular music as a means of radical expression. And while she has expressed ambivalence about being elevated early on in her career as the "face" of Riot Grrrl, she remains one of third-wave feminism's most enduring icons.

Born in Portland in 1968, Hanna grew up in a working-class family, primarily in Oregon but also in the Washington, DC, suburbs. She credits her mother, a housewife drawn to the women's rights movement of the 1970s, for first exposing her to organized feminism. At the same time, she has spoken publicly about her parents', especially her father's, abusive behavior and insensitivity to her artistic ambitions. As an undergraduate at Evergreen State College in Olympia, Washington, Hanna explored photography, design, and spoken word before deciding to focus on music, after the writer Kathy Acker, an idol of Hanna's, suggested that she would have a bigger platform for broadcasting her ideas if she formed a band. Although the Pacific Northwest punk rock scene of the 1990s is most famous for having incubated alternative-rock trailblazers Nirvana and Pearl Jam, it also fostered an anti-corporate, do-it-yourself culture that emboldened young people like Hanna to pursue music regardless of their inexperience or lack of formal training.

In this fertile environment, it didn't take long for Bikini Kill—a quartet consisting of Hanna, Tobi Vail (drums), Kathi Wilcox (bass), and "token boy" member Billy Karren (guitar)—to begin producing compelling songs that combined punk attitude, feminist ideology, and the lo-fi aesthetic sensibility of earlier Evergreen State bands such as Beat Happening. But it was Hanna's vocals, which could range—sometimes in the course of a single song—from sweetly childlike to bone chilling, which set Bikini Kill apart from other bands in the Olympia scene. On tracks such as "Double Dare Ya" and "Feels Blind," first recorded for the group's 1991 self-released cassette tape "Revolution Girl Style Now," Hanna screamed and yowled her fury, amplifying the socially muffled feelings of other girls. While the band's raucous songs spoke of women's silencing, especially around sexual violence, Hanna's charismatic, no-holds-barred stage persona staged a furious rebuttal of good-girl norms. As one Bikini Kill song put it, "Suck My Left One."

Like punk shows generally, Bikini Kill's concerts could get rowdy and even violent, with audience members charging the stage or moshing aggressively at the front of the room. In response, Hanna and her bandmates made a point of calling "girls to the front," extending their critique of male-dominated culture to the spaces of their own live events. After the fashion of feminist artists like Cindy Sherman and Yoko Ono, Hanna used her body as a canvas for self-expression, scrawling the word "slut" across her exposed belly and appearing onstage in bikini briefs that revealed "unseemly" pubic hair.

Bikini Kill's eponymous EP *Bikini Kill* (1992) and LP *Pussy Whipped* (1993), both released on the Olympia-based Kill Rock Stars label, brought the band's music and message to a wider audience in the US and Britain, with *Pussy Whipped*, featuring the anthemic song "Rebel Girl," garnering critical approbation from outlets as seemingly un-punk as *Entertainment Weekly*. Yet even as Riot Grrrl gained traction as a decentralized movement, one that in many ways resurrected the collective activism of 1960s feminist consciousness-raising groups, Hanna and her bandmates found themselves increasingly alienated by the sensational media attention that followed Riot Grrrl and drained by the rigors of a punk circuit that remained particularly difficult for women. *Reject All American*, the band's final LP, appeared in 1996. Former Runaways member and girl-rock icon Joan Jett produced and contributed to *The Singles*, a compilation of Bikini Kill tracks released in 1998, after the group had officially disbanded.

In the wake of her hyper-visibility with Bikini Kill, Hanna turned inward, composing a solo album of electronic music and releasing it under the pseudonym Julie Ruin. Little noticed at the time, *Julie Ruin* (1998), an album that, in Hanna's words, sounded "like something a girl made in her bedroom," presages the sample-based synth pop of Le Tigre, a band Hanna formed with her friend Johanna Fateman and the filmmaker Sadie Benning, who was later replaced by JD Samson. Over the course of a career that spanned three albums, two of them on the San Francisco–based lesbian-centric label Mr. Lady, Le Tigre made witty, politically bold, and eminently danceable music. The feminist party band vibe is audible on such songs as "Hot Topic," a celebratory roll call of (mostly female) cultural icons from Gertrude Stein to Gloria Anzaldúa, from the band's *Le Tigre* (1999), and "Keep on Living," a spirited incantation of the will to survive sexual abuse, from *Feminist Sweepstakes* (2001). Released by corporate behemoth Universal in 2004, the band's third and last album, *The Island*, represented Hanna's first foray outside of small independent labels, although

PLAYLIST

WITH BIKINI KILL:

"Double Dare Ya," 1992, *Bikini Kill* EP

"Feels Blind," 1992, *Bikini Kill* EP

"Rebel Girl," 1993, *Pussy Whipped*

WITH LE TIGRE:

"Deceptacon," 1999, *Le Tigre*

"Hot Topic," 1999, *Le Tigre*

"Keep on Livin'," 2001, *Feminist Sweepstakes*

by that time the digital revolution in music had rendered largely obsolete the independent/corporate division that had animated and defined the Olympia punk scene.

The dissolution of Le Tigre roughly coincided with a years-long period, beginning in 2005, in which Hanna suffered from an unspecified but debilitating illness, later diagnosed as late-stage Lyme disease. In this period—which Hanna discusses openly in Sini Anderson's 2013 documentary *The Punk Singer*, although she was not public about it at the time—she worried that her symptoms, which included cognitive impairment, would permanently hamper her ability to make and perform music. Hanna's formation of a new band, the Julie Ruin, in 2010, which saw her reunited with Bikini Kill bandmate Kathi Wilcox, marked the end of this hiatus from the public eye and the beginning of a new phase of Hanna's advocacy, in which she has been outspoken about invisible disabilities, including chronic illnesses. *Hit Reset* (2016), the band's eclectic second album, features fuzzy guitar riffs and highly personal songwriting, much of it relating to her health struggle.

The twentieth anniversary of Bikini Kill's first vinyl release in 2012, combined with the 2013 debut of *The Punk Singer* at the annual South by Southwest conference in Austin, Texas, kicked off a period of renewed reflection about Hanna's influence. But she has been careful to refuse the garlands associated with being a venerated Riot Grrrl progenitor. In a 2015 interview with the *Portland Mercury*, Hanna cautioned millennials against romanticizing the Riot Grrrl era of the early 1990s, echoing critics who have pointed out Riot Grrrl's limitations as a movement that largely attracted white, college-educated women, remaining opaque in particular to women confronting racism as part of their everyday experience. In 2015, in response to a *New York Times* reporter's question about whether superstars like Beyoncé were commodifying or marketing feminism, she quipped, "Let's not put down people who have enough power to spread stuff beyond our little punk-rock world or our feminist academic world. Everyone is invited to this party." It's a party that lives on not only in Hanna's own music but in the many and varied heirs to the girl-style revolution she helped to foment. ∎

COURTNEY LOVE

LUCRETIA TYE JASMINE

ILLUSTRATION BY WINNIE T. FRICK

I wouldn't trust Courtney Love with my bank account, my closet, or my man, but Hole's first two albums are among those I would take with me to a desert island. She has been called a hot mess and a train wreck, and she calls herself a force of nature. Band mates have overdosed. She has been accused of killing her suicidal rock star husband, Kurt Cobain. Friends who know her tell me she can't be trusted, and documentaries about her question her musical skills and morality (did Cobain or Love's lover, Smashing Pumpkins' Billy Corgan, write the songs?). When I once met her I thought she could eat me for lunch. I'm scared of her. I'm in awe of her. She might be a natural disaster, but she's a natural wonder, too.

Love's peripateticism marked her as unclean when she was a youngster; children nicknamed her "Pee Girl." So, too, did her adult drug use and abusiveness mark her. But Courtney understands the transformative powers of persuasion and ambition. Her nonstop talk is like a form of bullying; her music is her true ally. Her thrift-store haute couture—tattered romance in satins of doom and glitter—recycles Hollywood movie-star enchantment; she's a farmer of the past. "While you were vanishing, this dirty girl got clean," she sings on Hole's "How Dirty Girls Get Clean" (2010).

Musician, songwriter, and actor Courtney Michelle Harrison, with the contralto voice, was born on July 9, 1964, in San Francisco to a psychotherapist mom and a dad who was the road manager for the Grateful Dead. She began therapy before she was three years old. Her mom worried that their divorce traumatized her angry child. A disruptive manner developed into defiance as Love got older. A repeat runaway who shoplifted and compiled probation violations, she landed in reform schools alongside teen killers. According to Melissa Rossi's most unauthorized biography, *Courtney Love: Queen of Noise* (1996), the all-girl band the Runaways were her role models; a life of crime meant subterranean cool. A trust fund allowed her to travel as far away as Alaska, stripping there and at Jumbo's in Hollywood to hone her street cred. Love taught herself how to play guitar, playing in bands Faith No More and Sugar Babydoll. She formed the Grammy-nominated band Hole, with lead guitarist Eric Erlandson, in Los Angeles in 1989.

Love made alliances that guaranteed her alignment with the stars. Canny Courtney's first marriage, to a cross-dresser, musician James Moreland, yielded his production of Hole's first single, 1990's "Retard Girl." Although it is hard listening, Hole's debut album, *Pretty on the Inside* (1991), becomes quickly addictive. Alt-rocker Kim Gordon produced it, and the weirdly beautiful cover art is by band bassist Jill Emery. Within its punk exterior,

the songs reference the 1970s Ladies of the Canyon. The track "Star Belly" begins with tantalizing bits of music by Fleetwood Mac, as a radio dial tunes in Stevie Nicks's voice. A powerhouse "Pretty on the Inside/Clouds" cover honors Joni Mitchell. Love also confesses and destroys girlhood's vulnerable concerns. Asking if she's pretty from the back in the title track, the enraged query counters critique. "Teenage Whore" shamelessly explains youthful prostitution to her mom, a grown woman screaming rights of ownership: "Get out of my house!" The music's relentlessness sounds on the surface like one long angry guitar wail. But beneath, the melodies and meanings make sense.

The infuriated "Asking for It," on Hole's amazing and second album, *Live through This* (1994), similarly subverts misogynist rhetoric. "Was she asking for it? Was she asking nice?" Courtney sings, her virago harmoniously tempered. Prettier sounding with its more radio-friendly music, though no less angry, perspicacious, or quick-witted, Hole's second album mocks revolutions even as it starts one, making fun of fascism and schoolyard punk rock as Love dons a tiara and declares herself the queen. Her battle cry, heard from the opening chords on the song "Violet," feels like a vintage gauntlet thrown down.

Hole's music deals with themes of rape, eating disorders, mental health, nonconformity, beauty pageants, suicides, and sex work. Her lyrics enact rock star lore of hotels and fancy locations as Love puts herself in the middle of the story. Friendships with women (many of her bandmates were females, including drummer Patty Schemel) and stories of selling a sister down the river by them intrigue; perhaps feminism is not so friendly after all. In her songs, Love tells listeners to learn how to say no, sets

boundaries, and says don't ever talk to her that way again. Unafraid to admit she doesn't like to share, she announces it: "I want to be the girl with the most cake," she sings lingeringly in "Doll Parts" (1994).

Both albums are perfect, each song a gem. She cuts and pastes her scrawled and scribbled lyrics, creating wholes out of parts. Love scattered her notebooks of lyrics and songs in different cities, at the homes of friends and former lovers, making a potential zine of an entire country, maybe the world. Literally, Love makes "Miss World" (1994) come true by leaving bits and pieces of her songwriting artistry wherever she hangs her tiara.

Love's talent for performance extends to the movie screen. Nominated and winning several awards for her acting in *The People vs. Larry Flynt* (1996), she shrewdly synchronized herself with roles that reference renegades, artistry, and punk rock: *Sid and Nancy* (1986, about the deadly romance of a Sex Pistol and groupie-cum-manager), *Basquiat* (1996, about the homeless artist), *Man on the Moon* (1999, about the comedian Andy Kaufman), and *Beat* (2000, playing Joan Vollmer, the writer killed by her common-law husband, writer William S. Burroughs).

Her real life seems like an incredible movie, too. Her husband died the week before the release of *Live through This*. Her bass player, Kristen Pfaff, died a couple of months after (she was replaced by Melissa Auf der Mar). The devastating fatalities detracted from and added to Love's

PLAYLIST

ALL SONGS WITH HOLE:

"Retard Girl," 1990, single

"Teenage Whore," 1991, *Pretty on the Inside*

"Good Sister/Bad Sister," 1991, *Pretty on the Inside*

"Starbelly," 1991, *Pretty on the Inside*

"Clouds," 1991, *Pretty on the Inside*

"Pretty on the Inside," 1991, *Pretty on the Inside*

"Asking for It," 1994, *Live through This*

"Miss World," 1994, *Live through This*

"Doll Parts," 1994, *Live through This*

"Violet," 1995, *Live through This*

personas. She toured the world like a pirate or a pillager during the 1990s, instilling fear and awe, giving music journalists a lot to write about and fans a lot to talk about. She and Cobain threatened a music journalist with death, and she allegedly assaulted another music scribe; she reportedly shot heroin while pregnant, resulting in the temporary loss of parental rights; she punched Riot Grrrl Kathleen Hanna backstage at Lollapalooza in 1995; she threw makeup at Madonna, interrupting a live red carpet interview at MTV's 1995 Music Video Awards. Love's loud, drug-addled, dangerous, sexual, insulting, and sometimes hilarious behavior harkens back to the legendary rock-and-roll debauchery of the 1970s. Men in rock have long warned listeners to lock up daughters. Love, as the title of Hole's 2010 album claims, is *Nobody's Daughter*.

Love's determined transformations can elevate her beyond personal crises. The "Pee Girl" pictured on the back of her second album became "the girl with the most cake." Courtney has attained everything she ever wanted: her own punk rock band, big-selling albums and world tours, solo albums, work with esteemed directors and famous actors in big-budget and low-budget films, a different face and body through plastic surgery. A rock star and a movie star, Love married a rock star, too. Plus, she's a mom and an artist. The babydoll look that she and Kat Bjelland of Babes in Toyland popularized has come to signify the 1990s. Love has developed her own clothing line, a glittering carnival couture that references the theatrical abundance of the GTO's. Her ambitions, struggles, and tremendous efforts have deepened her voice, much the way similar experiences intensified the singing voices of veterans Stevie Nicks and Marianne Faithfull. Her life, loves, movies, and music are ensconced in rock-and-roll legend.

Courtney Love is a bona fide rock star, rare for any girl or woman in any era. Wild, unpredictable, sexually voracious, and selfish, she is all appetite. Gloriously unstable and undeniably charismatic, astute and alluring, fast-talking chain-smoking Love with her movie star hair and punk rock glamour forces us to listen. And makes us like it, too. ∎

LIZ PHAIR

ALLISON WOLFE

ILLUSTRATION BY WINNIE T. FRICK

In early nineties post-Reagan-with-a-side-of-Bush America, times were a-changing. Identity politics flourished and the onslaught of grunge kicked off the mainstreamization of alternative culture. As Nirvana and punk broke, Riot Grrrls and gender queers in indie music were building their arsenal in response to musical sexism and heterosexism disguised in long hair and flannel.

A tiny, twenty-something girl from the Chicago suburbs pushed back in her own way, cranking out strangely arranged guitar ballads in the privacy of her own bedroom. Her name was Liz Phair, and she called her raw, rambling observations of gendered society "Girly Sound." Her deadpan delivery of frank meditations on loneliness, isolation, and relationships gone wrong shone a light on double standards in bed and beyond. Sometimes shocking in their honesty and self-incrimination, the thirty-plus four-track Girly Sound songs initially existed on cassettes that Phair only shared with a couple of friends in 1991.

Within two years, Phair signed to Matador Records and unleashed her 1993 debut album, *Exile in Guyville*, upon the male-dominated alternative music scene, challenging the reign of the debaucherous male rock god and inserting herself on his throne. Phair's girl-next-door image enabled her to slip in under the college radio radar and skewer mainstream stereotypes of womanhood with her sexually explicit yet feminist lyrics. The controversial indie rock darling seemed to ruffle feathers all over the place. Was she a good girl or a bad girl? She was neither marketable enough nor punk enough, and she didn't seem to care.

Born April 17, 1967, Elizabeth Clark Phair was raised by adoptive parents in Cincinnati, Ohio, and Winnetka, Illinois, an upper-middle class suburb of Chicago. Her mother was a docent at the Art Institute of Chicago, and her father was an infectious disease doctor specializing in HIV/AIDS research at Northwestern Memorial Hospital. Phair and her older brother, also adopted, were given the freedom to be what they wanted. "If you know that you come from somewhere mysterious, then everything is up for grabs," says Phair of her "identity turbulence," which kept her from fully identifying with any one group or ideology.

Phair had "already sort of pulled out of mainstream thinking" in high school, from which she did not graduate on time because she refused to take a state-required home economics class. Rejecting her conservative, North Shore environment, she took off to study visual art at the private, lefty Oberlin College. It was there, in an art history class, that Phair had an epiphany that became the driving force of her life's work. While thumbing through a massive, supposedly comprehensive art history book, Phair was outraged to find so few women represented. "I saw our invisibility. It wasn't that women didn't make art. They weren't allowed, encouraged, considered, or paid to. I wanted us to be seen and for our lives to count."

On school breaks, Phair wandered down to Chicago's underground music clubs. She began writing her Girly Sound songs in reaction to the male-dominated music community she was peripherally participating in. She recorded these confessionals by herself at different times in various homes over a four-year period but didn't intend to make them public.

It wasn't until after Phair graduated from Oberlin in 1989 and was living temporarily in San Francisco that she shared her taped songs. Fellow Oberlin alum Chris Brokaw, of the bands Come and Codeine, spent some time with Phair and got to know her music. "She's incredibly smart and articulate," says Brokaw. "Hanging out with her made you feel a couple of degrees more alive." He asked her to make him a tape of her songs, which she sent to him with the name "Rock Star" in the return address.

The only other person Phair sent tapes to was Tae Won Yu, frontperson for the indie duo Kicking Giant, whom she had hung out with in New York while interning for visual artist and activist Nancy Spero. Recognizing Phair's "freak genius," "bold swagger," and "secret trick of observation and reading people" in her four-track songs, Tae mailed copies of Girly Sound cassettes to any friend who would listen.

Word got out as Phair returned to Chicago and immersed herself in the Wicker Park music scene, where she became acutely aware of the psychic manspread of "Guyville." Phair asserts that men were always teaching her about what good music was. "They tried to *My Fair Lady* me. It's an interesting insult—the idea that men are the ones who know and women should listen and learn."

Phair doubled down on her brand of telling it like it is, signed to the influential Matador Records, and started working on her magnum opus, *Exile in Guyville*, at Chicago's Idful recording studio. Drawn to Phair's brave lyrics, producer-drummer Brad Wood says that she "was unabashedly literate in her writing and was a keen observer of the Wicker Park music world, circa 1991." Engineer-guitarist Casey Rice says that Phair chose to work with them because they listened to her and made the record she wanted to make. "She didn't really come from the punk world. She was being her real self and just wanted to make her music."

Full of bravado and brash, sexually candid tales, *Exile in Guyville* catapulted Phair into the alternative rock spotlight she'd asked for but didn't quite know how to navigate. "Male rock and roll singers have forever talked about sex graphically and gotten it on the radio. As a woman, I wanted to take that back," says Phair; the album was in part her response to the Rolling Stones' classic *Exile on Main St*. She was intentional with how she represented herself, but couldn't control the way it was received. "Oh my god, I was the 'blow job queen,'" reflects Phair on the media's obsession with only the sexual aspects of her work. Though she positioned herself as the subject, not the object, of her

PLAYLIST

"Open Season," 1991, *Girly Sound*

"Gigalo (Can't Get out of What I'm Into)," 1991, *Girly Sound*

"Divorce Song," 1993, *Exile in Guyville*

"Fuck and Run," 1993, *Exile in Guyville*

"Flower," 1993, *Exile in Guyville*

"Chopsticks," 1994, *Whip-Smart*

"Polyester Bride," 1998, *Whitechocolatespaceegg*

"Why Can't I?" 2003, *Liz Phair*

"Table for One," 2005, *Somebody's Miracle*

"You Should Know Me," 2010, *Funstyle*

music, Phair says "the complexity that [she] was displaying in a kind of novella turned into endless talk about two or three lines from one song." Surprised by the sexist backlash Phair incurred, drummer Brad Wood remembers a particularly inappropriate question asked of Phair's backing bandmates at a UK gig: "Even Liam Gallagher from Oasis showed his caveman nature by asking us if Liz paid us in blowjobs."

Phair's reputation exceeded her experience level, and she struggled with assumptions and expectations emanating from being thrust into the limelight. Having never played live before her first album came out, the singer-songwriter felt overwhelmed and suffered from acute stage fright. "What's the difference between bragging and knowing? I didn't know what it meant to perform or sell a record, what photo shoots projected or how interviews played out," recalls Phair. Instead of enjoying her new "It Girl" status, she spent the first two years following the release of *Guyville* feeling alienated, misunderstood, and out of control of her own image. Phair admits, "When you can't deal with what's going on, you sort of fly out of your own body."

Phair went on to put out five more albums with varying degrees of success, yet none of them have achieved the critical acclaim or cultural significance of *Exile in Guyville*. It was a hard act to follow, yet Phair's deep vocal articulations and songwriting chops shine brightly on several songs from each subsequent album. She continued to mine gems from her Girly Sound musical diaries with reworked songs

like "Chopsticks" on *Whip-Smart* (1994) and "Polyester Bride" from 1998's *Whitechocolatespaceegg*. New millennium offerings like "You Should Know Me" (*Funstyle*, 2010) and the heartbreakingly beautiful "Table for One" on *Somebody's Miracle* (2005) remind us that Phair's still got it.

After Phair signed to Capitol Records for her 2003 self-titled album, she was pushed into working with the Matrix, the hit song-writing factory known for elevating the likes of Avril Lavigne, Christina Aguilera, and Britney Spears. The indie music world came crashing down on Phair for "selling out" in a scene she never fully belonged to or identified with. But Phair lives more for the journey than the destination, and the decline in fame doesn't seem to have bothered her in the slightest. "I got so much shit for making a pop record," says Phair of the album which produced "Why Can't I?," her biggest hit to date. "As much as everyone hated it and hated on me, at least I got to fully inhabit that experience."

Phair's adventurous, take-no-prisoners spirit has propelled her through a ruthless music industry, marriage, parenthood, divorce, TV music composition, and book writing. She does what she wants, when she wants, and how she wants. The girl-turned-woman-next-door still revels in defying easy categorization. "Hearing my songs at the gym or somewhere like that and knowing that my somewhat provocative words slipped in under the guise of sanitized, adult contemporary pop—I take a great deal of pleasure in that." ∎

TLC

ALI GITLOW

ILLUSTRATION BY JULIE WINEGARD

I was eleven years old when TLC's second album, *CrazySexyCool*, took over the airwaves. It was 1995. At South Miami Middle School, the powers that be occasionally let us have parties in the cafeteria. These affairs were a mix of FUBU and Tommy Hilfiger, pungent food smells, and preteen sweat. Before the staff cottoned on and banned "booty dancing," everyone would grind on whatever was in sight: the floor, the speakers, each other. Windows got so fogged up that people could tag their names in the condensation, graffiti-style. However, when TLC's mega-hit "Waterfalls" would come on, the mood changed. Immediately, we'd clamber on top of the nearest chair, mimicking the song's sleek video, which featured the group's members standing on water through green-screen magic. We'd copy their dance moves, too, trying our gangly best at the bankhead bounce. The most fun part was when it came time for the rap; I was excited to know all the words and shouted them out with pride. TLC were huge, and we adored them.

Mornings before school were all Eggo waffles and MTV. There, we were able to put faces to the names Tionne "T-Boz" Watkins, Lisa "Left Eye" Lopes, and Rozonda "Chilli" Thomas, witnessing their superstardom as it grew. The trio initially came together in 1991 after Left Eye and T-Boz disbanded from a group called 2nd Nature. The day they met

Chilli, their lineup was complete. TLC's home city of Atlanta was, at the time, a hotbed for R&B and hip-hop. They quickly linked up with manager Perri "Pebbles" Reid, wife of producer L.A. Reid (who co-owned LaFace Records with Kenny "Babyface" Edmonds). With these rising industry talents behind them, TLC went on to record four multiplatinum studio albums, garnering scores of awards, including five Grammys, plus the title of best-selling American girl group of all time. Perhaps most importantly, they enchanted fans around the globe with their unwavering charisma. Writing in *Rolling Stone* in 1995, Carol Cooper noted, "As a unit, the girls exude the psychic allure of a secret club that you've always wanted to join."

Unlike other groups that had been, essentially, cooked up in a lab by producers, TLC had a vision. From the get-go Left Eye was the most involved, penning her own raps and sharing writing credits with the best in the biz, like Organized Noize, Jermaine Dupri, and Sean "Puffy" Combs. Their debut album, 1992's *Oooooooohhh . . . On the TLC Tip*, established LaFace as a force to be reckoned with. It defined TLC's unique blend of R&B, hip-hop, new jack swing, and straight-up pop. The formula remained unchanged throughout the course of their career, with T-Boz's sultry low register on the verses and Chilli covering harmonies and higher vocals on

choruses, all topped off by Left Eye's bouncy interludes, which oozed personality. The attitude was funky fresh, playful, and almost juvenile, with songs like "What about Your Friends" and "Ain't 2 Proud 2 Beg" peppered with samples from classic hip-hop, funk, and soul tracks.

TLC broke ground in the fashion arena, too. In 1992 they went on *The Arsenio Hall Show* to perform "Hat 2 Da Back," emerging onstage in a flurry of big-armed dance moves, wearing overalls embellished with tacked-on condoms and baggy shirts spray-painted in neon colors. Left Eye sported a large floppy bandana on her head and a pair of glasses with a plastic fried egg covering—you guessed it—her left eye. This became a wardrobe staple that eventually morphed into a more refined war paint–style black line on her cheek. When *CrazySexyCool* came out a couple years later, the vibe had changed. Gone was the loose-fitting clothing that questioned what is deemed masculine or feminine: TLC were now exploring their grown and sexy side through a more honed hip-hop/soul hybrid. In the video for "Creep" they donned colorful satin pajama sets, open at the middle to reveal toned bare midriffs. "Red Light Special" featured the suggestive chorus "Baby it's yours / All yours / If you want it tonight." They retained their early "girls from the block" realness, but their dancing became more overtly sensual. By the time their third record, *FanMail*, was released in 1999 they'd flipped the script again, appearing as futuristic cyborgs and hippie earth goddesses in the videos for "No Scrubs" and "Unpretty."

As their third album's title suggests, TLC had an overt and special bond with their followers. Their chemistry and camaraderie spoke to me, a young girl just starting to come to grips with the concept of womanhood. Though they also appealed simply by being pop stars, TLC never shied away from serious subject matter. "No Scrubs" recommends dropping deadbeat men and achieving financial freedom; "Waterfalls" is about the AIDS crisis; "Unpretty" tackles body positivity; "Ain't 2 Proud 2 Beg" affirms that women can desire sexual pleasure without inherently being hos.

My friends and I *loved* TLC but, man, was there drama. T-Boz was diagnosed with sickle cell anemia as a child, causing her to be in and out of the hospital and racking up costly medical bills. In 1994 Left Eye, who had grappled with alcoholism, set fire to her on-again-off-again football player boyfriend's mansion after the pair had gotten in a huge fight. She was ultimately sentenced to five years' probation and time at a rehab center, which is why she's featured less on *CrazySexyCool*. At the height of their success TLC filed for bankruptcy, mainly due to the fact they had worked out a bum deal with their management team in the first place. This struggle, coupled with an ongoing dispute with producer Dallas Austin, meant it took four long years to release *FanMail*. There was infighting, too, with Chilli and T-Boz calling Left Eye a loose cannon in 1999 after she'd begun to distance herself from the group, missing public appearances to visit a Honduran natural health guru with questionable methods. Her response? Publicly challenging her bandmates to each release a solo record and letting fans choose the best one.

PLAYLIST

"What about Your Friends," 1992, *Ooooooohhh…On the TLC Tip*

"Ain't 2 Proud 2 Beg," 1992, *Ooooooohhh…On the TLC Tip*

"Waterfalls," 1994, *CrazySexyCool*

"Creep," 1994, *CrazySexyCool*

"Red Light Special," 1994, *CrazySexyCool*

"This Is How It Works," 1995, on various artists, *Waiting to Exhale: Original Soundtrack Album*

"No Scrubs," 1999, *FanMail*

"Unpretty," 1999, *FanMail*

In April 2002, eight months to the day after the death of Aaliyah, Left Eye died in a car crash in Honduras, where she had taken a group of family and friends to shoot a documentary. I was eighteen, a senior in high school, and it felt like the world, or at least innocence, was crumbling to the ground. TLC's final album as a trio, *3D*, was released later that year, but their name was marked by tragedy. T-Boz and Chilli have soldiered on since, appearing on a reality show, performing, and even releasing a new album in 2017 using funds raised via Kickstarter.

Despite TLC's differences, their authenticity has always won out in the end, earning them the status of true legends. There were many other all-female groups on the scene during their initial ascent to fame, from En Vogue to Xscape, SWV to Total, Jade, 3LW, and more, but none of these outfits could match their level of crossover appeal. As Left Eye explains in *The Last Days of Left Eye*, which VH1 released after her death using footage from her trip: "We have three different individual styles, but we gel together as a group. TLC knows how to breathe life into songs." More than twenty years later, I can still recite the lyrics to her rap from "Waterfalls" by heart. *Believe in yourself / The rest is up to me and you.* ■

TORI AMOS

ADELE BERTEI

ILLUSTRATION BY LINDSEY BAILEY

Tori Amos is a rat charmer. The music video for her song "God" is a beauty of a tell; we watch her—as music as body as action—taming rodents and snakes, proving the power of music to calm the wild beast. If you haven't watched this Southern Goth video, check it and be stunned by the sheer number of rodents that wiggle, slither, and scurry, with affection, over Amos's anatomy. Hell, any human given the opportunity would do the same. Swarms of rats never take a nibble on her or any of the actors. I choose to believe it was the magic of Tori's music on the video set that turned scary vermin into playmates of her sacred duende.

Federico García Lorca talked of the duende, a phenomenon from southern Spain that describes a different type of call to inspiration than a muse. It's not outside of you as something whimsical, which may or may not appear when you wish for it. Tori often talks about muses in her interviews, and I don't doubt she has them, but I want to talk about her duende, an inspiration available to all artists, which I'll summon for you. It's a strange little fairy goblin that dances inside your deepest, darkest wounds, if and only if you are fearless enough to open those raw portals to beckon it in. Once having explored inside, it comes back out to play through your art with—in Amos's example—its bouquet of "Blood Roses." You cannot be afraid to look ugly when the duende is expressing itself, just

as you cannot be afraid to look ugly during the *Little Earthquakes* of orgasm. True art is always sexual at its root. Not all artists have duende, but you can instantly tell the ones who do. Jean Genet once said, "To escape from horror, bury yourself in it," and Tori does this; she crucifies, buries, and resurrects herself in her music, her duende on full view in each apex of song. Insecure men must be fucking terrified of her. This is a woman who has never made herself small—at least in her public persona and music—to prop up the ego of any man. And if she has in her personal life, that man has caught hell for it in a song.

You see her chromatic and emotional brilliance unfold not only in her compositions and lyrics but in the way she sings and moves, the way she straddles the piano bench, attacking and caressing the instrument as if it's a lover. She began playing the piano at two years old, entering the prestigious Peabody Institute at five on a full scholarship. She was given the boot at eleven for suggesting they open up their curriculum to contemporary music like rock and jazz. Nevertheless she persisted, on her own and playing by ear, until her technique became so ingrained it allowed her to completely let loose when playing live. Rebel girl fingers dance across the keyboard like the feet of a tiny ballerina, then pound the keys in primal rhythms, one hand flipping into a palm to slap the black shiny wood on the beat, ferocious notes embedded so deep in her memory and dancing out, so physical, the pianoforte becomes her and she, it. And her voice, a sexy mix of carnality and innocence. Using her breath as animal spirit she slips around her unique time signatures, silent rests and inhales punctuating emotions at just the right beats. She can work a microphone with the same feeling that accompanies the heat and danger of making out with an exciting new lover.

The importance of women artists like Tori Amos in our American musical canon cannot be diminished, because, let's face it, the greatest cultural gift our country has given the world is our music, and these are strange and challenging times for American women. When Tori entered our musical consciousness in the early 1990s, she was in good company with other brave, musically skillful female artists whose lyrical content was provocative and sometimes deservedly punishing, and playable on commercial radio. You could hear songs like Queen Latifah's "U.N.I.T.Y.," Sinéad O'Connor's "Emperor's New Clothes," Alanis Morissette's "You Oughta Know." Fiona Apple's "Criminal" was released just as President Bill Clinton was enacting one of his many deregulation bills responsible in part for the ruin of our democracy—the Telecommunications Act of 1996—which allowed Clear Channel to commence buying up every commercial radio station in the country, creating a monopoly that would in part dictate which female artists we would all hear on the radio, or not hear, as is the case today.

I listen to Tori still. I don't believe her recordings—fifteen studio albums, from 1992's *Little Earthquakes* to 2017's *Native Invader*—completely do her justice; she's somewhat restrained by the studio and feeds best on a live audience she in turn can bestow her banquet upon. I prefer to watch and listen to her via her live videos on YouTube or on the DVDs, imagining Freud experiencing the same visual and aural excitement of her in full throttle and applauding as his brain explodes into meat confetti. Not to get all psychoanalytical, but there is nothing binary about Tori's most sexual organ. She may dive into binary themes in her music, like in the song "Bliss," where she investigates herself in context of the church's hacking Mary in two; the Virgin Mary has her sexuality castrated and the Magdalene Mary becomes whore, devoid of spirituality. Woman, always in pieces, never the whole. Tori knows better. She is all prime numbers.

Being the daughter of a Southern minister may have set Tori on the path of her complex relationship with religion and its themes: sex and death, mythology and mysticism, nature and the church, relationships and why women betray one another. Songs such as "Spring Haze" and "Mother Revolution" explore mortality, feminism, sex, and the eternal "why," the sacrifices we make to receive certain gifts. She has been candid about having experienced three miscarriages and her own rape, the exploration of the latter having created her first stark, publicly arresting track, "Me and a Gun." Her music refuses the patriarchy's demands on women again and again. She understands, in her own words, "how to turn death into an expression of life" in her art. In America today, it's a theme we women should be all too familiar with. ■

PLAYLIST

"Me and a Gun," 1992, *Little Earthquakes*

"Crucify," 1992, *Little Earthquakes*

"God," 1994, *Under the Pink*

"Cornflake Girl," 1994, *Under the Pink*

"Bells for Her," 1994, *Under the Pink*

"Blood Roses," 1996, *Boys for Pele*

"Raspberry Swirl (Lip Gloss Version)," 1998, *Cruel/ Raspberry Swirl EP*

"Cruel," 1998, *From the Choirgirl Hotel*

"Spark," 1998, *From the Choirgirl Hotel*

"Father Lucifer," 2006, *A Piano: The Collection*

PJ HARVEY

SOLVEJ SCHOU

ILLUSTRATION BY ANNE MUNTGES

It was 1993, the year British singer-songwriter PJ Harvey's bluesy, punk, angry, thrashing, and raw second studio album, *Rid of Me*, established the arrival of a powerhouse new artist. The then twenty-four-year-old—her wiry body cinched into a gold dress, black hair slicked back, Telecaster guitar strapped to her chest—sang-slash-screamed the album's title track on *The Tonight Show with Jay Leno*. Alone, she played the revenge ode's distorted staccato riff and belted, "LICK MY LEGS AND I'M ON FIRE!" She had cracked open the male folk, rock, and blues canon of Bob Dylan, Robert Johnson, and Jimi Hendrix, and poured herself in. Later, Harvey discussed with Leno her upbringing on a farm in the English rural county of Dorset, where she grew up "ringing [sheep] testicles" with a rubber band so that they would fall off. The audience howled with laughter. Harvey smiled.

Through nine studio albums, three compilation albums, and two collaborative studio albums over the past twenty-five years, PJ Harvey has saturated her songs with desire, visceral literary and religious references, wry humor, allegorical storytelling, her own multi-instrumental prowess—guitar, bass, cello, violin, piano, autoharp, drums, percussion, saxophone—and, later, unapologetic sociopolitical commentary. Courtney Love and other musicians have worshiped her as a smart and experimental embodiment of art-infused nineties rock and beyond.

Rid of Me's "50Ft Queenie"—with lyrics such as "Tell you my name / F U and CK!!"—remains an empowerment anthem to many women.

Harvey has mastered genre bending and emotional versatility in her songs and performances, aided by a soaring contralto voice and lyrics that convey both vulnerability and strength, masculinity and femininity. Her music—from roaring *Dry* (1992), *Rid of Me* (1993), and breakout *To Bring You My Love* (1995) to *Is This Desire?* (1998), pop-rock *Stories from the City, Stories from the Sea* (2000), swaggering *Uh Huh Her* (2004), quiet *White Chalk* (2007), political *Let England Shake* (2011) and *The Hope Six Demolition Project* (2016)—speaks for itself.

Polly Jean Harvey has mostly kept her personal life private. She was born on October 9, 1969, to bohemian parents—quarryman Ray Harvey and stonemason and sculptor Eva—and was raised in a small secluded Dorset town on the likes of Captain Beefheart, the Rolling Stones, Neil Young, Jimi Hendrix, Robert Johnson, and Bob Dylan. The late Stones keyboardist Ian Stewart was a family friend, and live music permeated her decidedly non-city childhood, from shows her record collector parents hosted in the area to house guests such as Stones drummer Charlie Watts to nearby rollicking beach parties. Visiting musicians in turn gave Harvey saxophone and guitar lessons.

By the late eighties, Harvey had joined the band Automatic Dlamini, fronted by John Parish, who later became her frequent collaborator. She deferred getting a degree in sculpture at the prominent Central Saint Martins art and design college in London and signed a record deal with record label Too Pure, releasing 1992 debut *Dry* as an eponymous trio with Steve Vaughan on bass and Rob Ellis on drums.

Dry—packed with potent moans, power chord fuzz, and scorching, poetic, and biblical lyrics about female lust, revenge, and rejection, embodied by the single "Sheela-Na-Gig"—made a bombastic entrance. It pounded Top 10 lists and put PJ Harvey on the map as a singular musician whose very existence challenged commercial rock norms, from her exaggerated features to her swooning and growling voice and soul-shredding lyrics. That talent and passion, and a loyal fan following, have sustained Harvey through her twenties, thirties, and now forties.

Harvey wrote "Rid of Me" for the trio's second album in a damp, small apartment in a rough part of London. "When I was at art college, all I wanted to do was shock with my artwork," Harvey told *Spin* in 2013. "When I wrote 'Rid of Me,' I shocked myself." Exhausted by *Dry*'s quick success, touring, a breakup, and not eating and sleeping, she wrote the rest of critically acclaimed *Rid of Me* within the solitude of her native Dorset. It was released by her soon-to-become longtime label Island Records, and produced by Steve Albini (Nirvana, the Pixies). The trio disbanded later in 1993.

As a solo artist Polly cultivated a loyal cast of collaborators, including Parish, whom she later recorded two albums with as a duo, and producer Flood (U2, Nine Inch Nails, Nick Cave). Harvey shifted into new territory with 1995's melancholy global hit album *To Bring You My Love*. While *Dry* and *Rid of Me* aggressively rock, *To Bring You My Love* proceeds at a slower slinky strut. The change was evident in the cover image: Photographer Maria Mochnacz, who first met Harvey when Harvey was eighteen, has captured in unconventional photos, album covers, and music videos the musician's playful love of fashion and changing look album to album. In Mochnacz's 1993 video for the single "Man-Size," Harvey shimmies in loose underwear and a crop top. The photographer showcased the singer as nude, makeup-free, and flinging her hair on *Rid of Me*'s iconic black-and-white cover. At the time of *To Bring You My Love*, Harvey—a tomboy until her teens—had adopted a stage persona that offered an exaggerated image of femininity: red lips, fake eyelashes, scarlet gown. On the cover, Harvey floats on her back in the water, in her glistening and glamorous red dress.

With *To Bring You My Love*, Harvey set aside her bass-heavy snarling guitar, played the organ, and applied opera lessons. Awash in American blues influences but ominously inverted, the album includes the single "Down by the Water," a cool and elegant MTV favorite. Its synthesized organ, strings, and rhythmic percussion couch dark lyrics about infanticide. *Rolling Stone* called the album "astonishing" and named Harvey its 1995 artist of the year.

The more mainstream *Stories from the City, Stories from the Sea*—set mainly in New York

PLAYLIST

"Sheela-Na-Gig," 1992, *Dry*

"Rid of Me," 1993, *Rid of Me*

"50Ft Queenie," 1993, *Rid of Me*

"Down by the Water," 1995, *To Bring You My Love*

"A Perfect Day Elise," 1998, *Is This Desire?*

"This Mess We're In," 2000, *Stories from the City, Stories from the Sea*

"Who the Fuck?," 2004, *Uh Huh Her*

"When under Ether," 2007, *White Chalk*

"The Words That Maketh Murder," 2011, *Let England Shake*

"Dollar, Dollar," 2016, *The Hope Six Demolition Project*

City—ushered in standouts such as the stealthy, sexy, postmodern duet "This Mess We're In" with Radiohead's Thom Yorke. It also landed Harvey the United Kingdom's coveted Mercury Prize. Her 2007 album *White Chalk* added yet another layer of sonic complexity to Polly's palette, as a collection of mostly piano ballads. Harvey sings softly, conjuring up haunted visions of unease on songs such as the pared-down "When under Ether," seemingly about an abortion.

While earlier on in her career Harvey was unpolitical in her music, that changed when conflicts in Afghanistan and Iraq shook her soul. "I've always been extremely affected by what's going on in the world on a very deep level," Harvey told the *Guardian* in 2011. She just had wanted to avoid doing "dogmatic protest music." So in a reversal from previous albums, her ethereal 2011 album *Let England Shake* was about war and England's bloody roots and permeated with her newfound autoharp playing. It won Harvey her second Mercury Prize (she's the only artist to have won twice). On "The Words That Maketh Murder," behind a beautiful midtempo melody and handclaps, Harvey as tweeish narrator declares, "I've seen soldiers fall like lumps of meat."

The alt-blues singer had found her soapbox voice. Five years later, on 2016's *The Hope Six Demolition Project*, Harvey blew the sax fiercely. She took a journalistic approach to describing the lasting effect of war and poverty, based on trips she took to Kosovo, Afghanistan, and Washington, DC, with war photographer Seamus Murphy, whose photos illustrate her first book of poetry (2015's *The Hollow of the Hand*). The mournful song "Dollar Dollar" showcases the pure clarity of her voice, recalling the story of a boy begging next to her car.

In worldwide shows supporting the album and backed by a nine-piece band, Harvey dressed in leather and black feathers, stretching her arms out to the crowd like a modern dancer. Decades after she first belted "Rid of Me" alone and electric on *The Tonight Show*, she once again proved her lasting power as an artist, unleashing a sultry rebel yowl that—like her life and albums—defies categorization. ■

GWEN STEFANI

KATHERINE TURMAN

ILLUSTRATION BY JULIE WINEGARD

In No Doubt's breakthrough single, sassy, seeming-ingénue Gwen Stefani faux pouts about being "Just a Girl." But then she sings, "Don't you think I know exactly where I stand." That was a statement, not a question. The year was 1995, and the SoCal native was standing on the precipice of fame and fortune, a moment she had been prepping for since her brother convinced his younger, teenage sister to join his nascent ska band.

She's the glamour girl next door—whose adult braces make her relatable. Her perfect abs and signature red lips, to say nothing of her octave-spanning vocal talent, inspire envy, but Stefani possesses a guilelessness and gratefulness that belie an intensively driven and diversified career. She's topped the charts as both a solo artist and as a member of No Doubt and became a high-fashion icon with her L.A.M.B. line and, at forty-four, a TV celebrity as a mentor on The Voice. She does it all with a down-to-earth eagerness, simultaneously repping the suburbs—while leaving them behind.

Stefani, the second of four children, was born into a loving Roman Catholic family on October 3, 1969. She grew up in Anaheim, California, a suburb in the shadow of Disneyland—whose Magic Kingdom nickname inspired No Doubt's third, Grammy-nominated, 16-million-selling *Tragic Kingdom* album. Gwen was a typical teen in the commuter community of Orange County, mooning over boys, music, and clothing. She worked at Dairy Queen, hung out at the mall, and dreamed of becoming a mother. As she sang in 2006, she was an "Orange County Girl." Her fondness for that sprawling, traditionally Republican enclave was evident as she spun a traditional dis voiced by sophisticated Los Angelenos against their southern neighbors into a boast, proclaiming that a simple kind of life "behind the 'Orange Curtain'" is not "so bad."

In awe of her older brother, Eric, who turned her on to ska bands like England's the Specials, Stefani made her own stage debut with his group No Doubt in 1987 at Fender's Ballroom in Long Beach, California. Spewing Silly String into the audience, Gwen was all adorable, gawky manic energy. Her memorable vibrato captivated the crowd. The group's popularity spread quickly, as No Doubt opened for ska scene stalwarts the Untouchables and Fishbone. The buzz eventually found its way to the record companies a mere thirty-two miles north of the band's home—but a world away—in Hollywood. The SoCal third-wave ska scene, centered in Orange County in the late eighties and early nineties, was as young, racially diverse, and punky as its counterpart in the UK. Two-tone emerged from the landlocked center of England, but by dint of Orange County's western border—the Pacific Ocean—SoCal ska evinced a brighter, beachier mien, with homegirl Stefani its perfect icon.

Demos, sold-out gigs, and college all coincided for a few years while the band honed its chops, yet in a 1991 YouTube video, a pre-glam, brown-haired Stefani, twenty-two, is clearly possessed of the qualities that would send her into the fame stratosphere. Kneeling on the floor before a No Doubt gig, she's putting together a black-and-white-striped stage outfit—literally: with a glue gun. As she smiles up to the camera, she says proudly but humbly: "We've already been a band for over four years" and likens No Doubt's colorful energy to a "cartoon."

In 1994, her brother, the band's main lyricist, left No Doubt to work on *The Simpsons*. His departure allowed—demanded, even—that Gwen step up to the plate lyrically. At the time, grunge ruled. But instead of jumping on the Riot Grrrl wave, Stefani married the glamour and cool sexiness of Blondie's Debbie Harry with confessional pop lyrics. Her (love) life became her art: when Gwen was dumped by No Doubt bassist Tony Kanal, her boyfriend of seven years, a song cycle was born. The fraught, changeable emotions and relationship problems resonated with

women—and more than a few men—the world over.

Her emergence as No Doubt's focal point was inevitable: a November 1996 *Spin* magazine cover showed a grinning Gwen, abs on prominent display, sans her No Doubt band members, reportedly to the musicians' chagrin. Her initial goofy cuteness morphed into an early signature look of tank tops and low-slung cholo pants, setting off her cut midriff. She later became a platinum-haired, red-lipped siren in the Madonna/Harlow mold. When Stefani sported a bindi—a decorative Indian forehead jewel, inspired by Kanal's heritage—the South Asian symbol was appropriated by young women the world over.

If she explored her personal issues via song, her private life was never a public train wreck. Still, within No Doubt, fame and foibles caused a five-year break before *Return of Saturn* (2000), then *Rock Steady* (2001), both records fulfilling *Tragic Kingdom*'s wide-ranging alt-pop-ska promise, critically and commercially. The track "New" was about meeting her future husband,

British singer Gavin Rossdale, when his band Bush toured with No Doubt in 1995. "Home Now" laments her paramour's "vacant chair" in the "space we rarely share." Even more pointed was the melancholy hit "Simple Kind of Life," where Stefani muses about leaving music for the suburban housewife life she supposedly rejected: "Sometimes I wish for a mistake . . . You seem like you'd be a good dad."

While her biological clock may have been keeping its own time, Stefani's career ambitions and success surged rapidly ahead. In 2004 she released her first solo album and a clothing line as bright, adorable, and high-fashion as Gwen herself: L.A.M.B., an acronym for "Love. Angel. Music. Baby." More expensive than the average Stefani follower could afford, it nonetheless proved a huge success, solidifying her brand, with Gwen as its chic, cool, and together figurehead.

Stefani's solo success didn't diminish her self-doubt. In "What You Waiting For?" she chronicles her creative fears and societal pressures to be a "super-hot female" as she ages, and even nastily berates herself: "take a chance, you stupid ho." It was harsh self-criticism for such a successful superstar. Gwen's naked fear and honest output made her legions of similarly insecure fans fawn even more. The song also introduced her four back-up dancers, the Japanese, doll-like posse of costumed Harajuku Girls, who had an influence on not only Stefani's solo album but her clothing and perfume lines. While *Time* magazine accused the singer of "perpetuating extremely racial stereotypes," there was no public apology from Gwen and little or no backlash from fans.

For more than a decade, Gwen did seem to have it all: fame, fortune and family. Despite lyrical lamentations, outward success shone on all fronts, and Gwen found love, then in 2002, marriage. She had three beloved boys. Though her fourteen-year marriage imploded when Stefani discovered Rossdale's affair with their nanny, she weathered the tabloid scrutiny. Publicly, the general feeling seemed very much "his loss." And again, revenge is sweeter when sung: Rossdale was the target of "Used to Love You" where she keens, "I thought you loved me the most."

Three months after Stefani filed for divorce from Rossdale, her on-screen chemistry with *The Voice* co-coach Blake Shelton turned personal, and the country superstar and pop princess became a beloved pair both onscreen and off. Though in 2017 Stefani took a hiatus from her high-profile role on the hit program, she found her mentor role personally inspiring, explaining to *E! News*: "It's impossible to watch the talent be so great and not want to do that."

More than twenty years of mega-stardom—with even more opportunities looming—didn't change the down-to-earth California girl: in a 2017 magazine feature, Gwen admits to binge-watching *Beverly Hills 90210*, says she'd be a makeup artist if she wasn't a singer, and confesses that she loves to sleep late. Her appeal is not esoteric: less subversive and more sweet than Gaga, fifteen year her junior, less political and ambitious-seeming than Madonna, eleven years her senior, Stefani's unflagging appeal thrives in the sweet spot of vulnerability, talent, and relatability. ∎

PLAYLIST

WITH NO DOUBT:

"Just a Girl," 1995, *Tragic Kingdom*

"Spiderwebs," 1995, *Tragic Kingdom*

"Sunday Morning," 1995, *Tragic Kingdom*

"Simple Kind of Life," 2000, *Return of Saturn*

SOLO:

"Hollaback Girl," 2004, *Love. Angel. Music. Baby.*

WITH PRINCE:

"So Far, So Pleased," 1999, on Prince's *Rave Un2 the Joy Fantastic*

BJÖRK

DJ LYNNÉE DENISE

ILLUSTRATION BY WINNIE T. FRICK

Iceland is one of the most volatile places in the world, a hyper-monitored geological hotspot. On November 21, 1965, in one of the least populated countries on earth, Björk Guðmundsdóttir was born. Björk is a musicological hotspot—an uncategorizable triple Scorpio with an otherworldly understanding of the acoustics of ecology and the value of transdisciplinary art.

For most Americans, Björk surfaces in the collective national memory as the woman who wore the swan dress to the Academy Awards. Her appeal to the cohort of black women who follow her life may be influenced in part by our witnessing her objectification. She was read by the average consumer of popular culture as a freak of nature, and her place of origin was exoticized enough to be offensive—a phenomenon with which we are well familiar. And what do we make of the othering of her musicality as opposed to naming it as genius, a status historically reserved for men?

Björk is the product of parents who saw their voices as tools for social change. Her mother worked as an activist and a fortune teller, while her father organized as a union leader and wrote textbooks for fellow electricians. Her politicization and punk roots were informed by their social resistance and ferocious commitment to craft. Music and activism, as well as technology and mystical reflection, were very much

part of her development as a creative being. Perhaps this explains why Björk has been at the cutting age of technology, as indicated by the multimedia project *Biophilia* (2011), which was billed as the first interactive app album.

Although the point of entry to Björk's sorcery for most begins with the Sugarcubes, between 1977 and 1987, she established a rhythmic foundation and cultivated her identity as a singer. At the urging of her mother, Björk became a public figure and child celebrity at the age of twelve, releasing a self-titled record consisting mostly of covers. The experience left her with the desire to reclaim her privacy and produce music with her peers, leading to a series of collaborations with groups like the all-girl band Spit and Snot and the experimental post-punk bands Tappi Tíkarrass and Kukl. In 1988, she and other musicians frustrated by Iceland's obsession with British and American music and keen on pulling from traditional Icelandic sound modals gave birth to the Sugarcubes—a poet collective–turned–pop band. The Sugarcubes' rise to fame was ironic and met with suspicion about celebrity culture from its members. Björk and the Sugarcubes were pioneers of the Icelandic punk movement, and, impressively, this resistance to eminence remains a big part of Björk's personality, even as she's gone on to become the most successful solo artist in Iceland's history. The international

attention received with the Sugarcubes solidified her clarity around privacy as a nonnegotiable element in her career. And yes, while there have been a few outlandish moments (the physical assault of a journalist) and public breakups during her tenure as an artist, Björk buffs understand that most of what she's given us over the years—eleven superior studio albums, film appearances, magical live performances, music videos, and interviews about the artistic process—is nothing short of generous and intimate.

Björk never intended to use her voice as the leading instrument in her musical practice. Instead, she understood her voice as a necessary tool to further embody her compositions. But what comes out of her mouth cannot be detached from the spectrum of characters it offers. In one album she'll move from a guttural Viking sound to an ethereal viciousness. She screams, yells, whispers, and hollers, unearthing distant emotions few of us knew we had. Most impressive is the control she exerts over the wildness of her range. Björk's standout vocal performance on the Sugarcubes' first hit single, "Birthday," caught the attention of an audience who would follow her every move and secretly await her solo moment. The anticipation is comparable to the pre-solo careers of Michael Jackson or Lauryn Hill: you loved the Jacksons and the Fugees, but you also waited patiently for the "featured" artist to break out. It was Björk's quiet and, dare I say, visible boredom with the status of the Sugarcubes that signaled to fans that a volcanic energy was bubbling—we were sitting on the verge of an eruption. By 1992, the Sugarcubes disbanded, partly to save their friendship and partly to explore individual pursuits. During their run, Björk entered a one-year marriage and had her first child with the Sugarcubes' guitarist, Þór Eldon.

Fresh off the heels of success with resources generated from the Sugarcubes' reign, Björk went to the UK and made musical hajj to London. This holy land was in the prime of its production of acid jazz, UK soul, trip hop, drum and bass, dance music, and experimental electronica, reflective of the African and Caribbean immigrant contribution to the cultural fabric of England. The sound was dominated by Bristol DJ culture, which gave the world Soul II Soul, Massive Attack, Portishead, Sinéad O'Connor, and producer Nellee Hooper. Björk found her new tribe by going straight to the source of this developing movement: the clubs, the dance halls, and the studio with Hooper, where she recorded her first album less than a year after leaving the Sugarcubes. She speaks about carrying the first two albums, *Debut* (1993) and *Post* (1995), in her head for at least a decade and having unmistakable clarity about her musical direction from that point forward.

Homogenic (1997) is the first album she produced that hadn't been pulled from the archive in her mind. In an interview Björk described *Homogenic* as the album where she needed to "firmly establish her sound as an organically Icelandic one." The album integrates her trademark industrial influences with lyrical lovesickness and the musical unpredictability of Iceland's seismology. The strings on the album, she says, were intensely patriotic, most apparent in the song "Bachelorette." Her feeling was that this was the album that caught up with her voice and holistic artistry in real time.

Even then, she was surprised to be asked to produce a soundtrack for director Lars von Trier, but excited by the opportunity to expand her creative palette. Von Trier's *Dancer in the Dark* marked Björk's debut as an actress and as a film score composer. In many ways, this pivot to film was aligned with the cinematic component underlying her music videos. Pioneering directors like Michel Gondry and Spike Jonze were instrumental in helping to visualize Björk's music in a way that honored the integrity of her sonic force.

What can't get lost in understanding Björk's trajectory is her masterful ability to collaborate, something she describes as a "merging." Often, collaborations between men and women are mistaken for paternalistic relationships, with women being aided to reach their artistic goals. She dispels this myth. Her relationship with the late Mark Bell, longtime friend and producer, provides an example of Björk's belief that collaboration/merging is a "feminine quality" that is looked upon as a weakness but should be positioned as the next phase of feminism. For someone who appears so incredibly in control of her every musical move, her notion of surrendering, which is at the heart of collaboration, speaks to another angle of her brilliance.

The merging she describes also highlights a blurring of the line between the romantic and the professional. She partnered and produced work with visual and musical artists like Tricky and Goldie. This fruitful love life set the stage for her long-term marriage to artist Matthew Barney, with whom she had her second child, and with whom she merged to co-star in and arrange and produce music for Barney's film project *Drawing Restraint 9* (2005). Traces of her falling in love with Barney can be found on *Vespertine* (2001) and tragically, markings of their separation embedded in her ninth album, *Vulnicura* (2015). There is little separation between the state of her heart and her emotionally coded body of work. Each *known* relationship has a musical location, and through the practice of excavation can be identified in her orchestral bibliography.

Björk is a classically trained punk rock jazz head and a dance club kid who, like a DJ, understands a good blend. And perhaps Björk is no more experimental than a DJ making the connection between Frank Sinatra and Biggie Smalls. Her discography is in fact a repository for sounds and words she's collected along the way. She refused to stand in the shadows of men otherwise seen as the "minds" behind her projects. Instead she's increased their cultural capital through their association with her name. At the core of her genius is a rageful creativity and furious innovation. Amid her defining decades, we are left with only leads to her never-ending metamorphosis. The Museum of Modern Art's 2015 retrospective exhibition of Björk's entire career speaks to the volume of history she's left for us to climb. Björk best describes her biography thus far: "I feel like I'm trying to put an ocean through a straw." ∎

LAURYN HILL

SALAMISHAH TILLET

ILLUSTRATION BY LINDSEY BAILEY

In 1987, a thirteen-year-old Lauryn Hill dressed in her Sunday best—a green silk shirt and black pencil skirt—walked onto the Apollo Theater stage, and sang Smokey Robinson's "Who's Loving' You." At first, standing too far away from the mic, the bit off-key Hill was terrified by the mounting boos from Harlem's legendary tough crowd. Her face didn't betray her terror; instead she simply dug in, finding more confidence with each passing note, culminating her performance with a perfect "youuuuuu." By the song's end, Hill had the Apollo audience roaring with applause.

And yet Hill still thought her performance was a letdown. Trying to calm her daughter down, her mother said to a teary-eyed Lauryn, "Now, if every time they don't scream and holler you're gonna cry, then perhaps this isn't for you." Lauryn Hill had such an incredulous look on her face that her mother quickly realized, "To her, the mere suggestion that this wasn't for her was crazy." Ironically, after earning unprecedented accolades, Hill would soon discover fame could be a bitter pill.

Born in 1975 to Valerie Hill, an English teacher, and Mal Hill, a computer consultant, Lauryn Noel Hill and her older brother were raised in the middle-class suburb of South Orange, New Jersey. After discovering her mother's secret stash of 45s of Stevie Wonder, Aretha Franklin, and Donny Hathaway

tucked away in a corner of their basement, Hill fell in love with music. By age eight, she had an encyclopedic knowledge of soul, and at her high school, she founded a gospel choir. Having added acting to her repertoire, she got a recurring role on the daytime soap *As the World Turns*. By nineteen, she, was the rebellious teen gospel singer Rita Louise Johnson opposite Whoopi Goldberg in *Sister Act 2: Back in the Habit*.

At the same time, the straight-A student spent her days taking AP classes at her high school. Upon graduation she attended Columbia University, where she planned to major in history. Between classes, Lauryn would meet up with musicians Wyclef Jean and Pras Michél. In 1994, their band, the Fugees, released their debut, *Blunted on Reality*, a mashup of reggae-flecked, soul-inspired raucous romps that flopped, only selling twelve copies. Ever determined, they regrouped, honed their unique sound, and a mere two years later dropped *The Score*. It went to the top of the *Billboard* 200 and later was certified six-times platinum by the Recording Industry Association of America.

Leaving college after only a year, Hill became the face of the Fugees. In music videos, her natural hair, deep mahogany lipstick, Timberland boots, and newsboy caps offered a unique sartorial mix of hip-hop, bohemia, and vintage black glamour. But it was her voice that really stood out in the male-dominated hip-hop industry. She rapped alongside Jean and Michel, famously announcing, "I'll be Nina Simone / Defecating on your microphone" on "Ready or Not." On the Fugees' cover of Roberta Flack's classic "Killing Me Softly," Hill's raspy contralto voice not only updated soul music for a new generation but solidified her status as a star.

After *The Score* erupted, Jean started recording a solo album with the help of Pras and Hill. But when Lauryn began writing her own songs, Wyclef didn't support her, ultimately pushing Hill to record an album without any input from him. Jean and Hill, who had been secretly involved for years, split up, with Wyclef getting married and Lauryn falling in love with Rohan Marley, a former college football player and the son of Bob Marley. Two years later, Hill and Marley's first child, Zion, was born in August 1997, and the Fugees had officially broken up.

The next year, Hill released her career-defining solo album, *The Miseducation of Lauryn Hill*. The title was inspired by Carter G. Woodson's 1933 book *The Mis-Education of the Negro* and Sonny Carson's *The Education of Sonny Carson*, a film and autobiographical novel. Featuring the soulful D'Angelo, R&B singers Mary J. Blige and the then unknown John Legend, Latin-infused rocker Carlos Santana, and reggae inflections, *Miseducation* explored themes like romantic betrayal and motherhood alongside rap rivalries and racial pride. The album showcased Hill's unmatched genius as both a superb singer and dense, deft rapper, a dual talent captured best in the video for "Doo-Wop (That Thing)": through a split screen, she is at once Mary Wells and MC Lyte.

Miseducation topped the *Billboard* 200 for four weeks, selling 8 million copies in the US and 12 million copies worldwide. By 1999, Hill stardom had reached new heights. She not only graced the cover of *Time* magazine for its story "Hip-Hop Nation," but she became the first woman to be nominated for Grammys in ten categories in a single year, for *Miseducation*, for her remake of "Can't Take My Eyes off You" for a Hollywood movie, and for writing and producing "A Rose Is Still a Rose" with Aretha Franklin. Her album won five Grammys, a record for a female artist, and was the first hip-hop recording to be named album of the year. During her acceptance speech, a magnetic Hill, with flowing locks and in a fitted white cape and pants, said, "This is crazy because this is hip-hop music."

No longer needing to share the spotlight with Jean, Hill credited herself as the sole producer, writer, and arranger of all the music on *Miseducation* except one track. Four musicians, known collectively as New Ark, sued Hill, alleging that their contributions to the album were at least partly responsible for its sound and success. At first, Hill, fought the claims but eventually settled the suit out of court.

Feeling professionally betrayed and now a mother of two young children, Hill went into seclusion, only emerging on the stage while pregnant with her third child for a taping of an *MTV Unplugged* special in July 2001; the soundtrack was released as

PLAYLIST

WITH THE FUGEES:

"Fu-Gee-La," 1996, *The Score*

"Killing Me Softly," 1996, *The Score*

"Ready or Not," 1996, *The Score*

SOLO:

"Doo Wop (That Thing)," 1998, *The Miseducation of Lauryn Hill*

"To Zion," 1998, *The Miseducation of Lauryn Hill*

"Lost Ones," 1998, *The Miseducation of Lauryn Hill*

"Can't Take My Eyes off You," 1998, *The Miseducation of Lauryn Hill*

"I Gotta Find Peace of Mind," 2002, *MTV Unplugged No. 2.0*

"Mystery of Iniquity," 2002, *MTV Unplugged No. 2.0*

"Neurotic Society (Compulsory Mix)," 2013, single

"I've Got Life," 2015, on various artists, *Nina Revisited . . . A Tribute to Nina Simone*

"Feeling Good," 2015, on various artists, *Nina Revisited . . . A Tribute to Nina Simone*

MTV Unplugged 2.0. The album, featuring Hill on an acoustic guitar and singing about esoteric themes like spirituality, self-help, and crass materialism, divided fans and critics alike, ending up only selling five hundred thousand copies in the US. Nevertheless, her song "Mystery of Iniquity" was nominated for a Grammy for Best Female Rap Solo Performance and used as an interpolation by hip-hop producer-songwriter Kanye West for his single "All Falls Down" on his debut album, *College Dropout.* She later described this period of her life to *Essence*, saying, "People need to understand that the Lauryn Hill they were exposed to in the beginning was all that was allowed in that arena at that time . . . I had to step away when I realized that for the sake of the machine, I was being way too compromised."

Plagued by rumors and press reports that she had a nervous breakdown and joined a cult, Hill went into "self-exile" for an indefinite period, rarely granting interviews or doing any public performances. To the thrill of Fugees fans, she appeared for a brief moment on stage with the group in September 2004 at the filming of *Dave Chappelle's Block Party*, their first time performing together since 1997. The band went on to do a twelve-minute set at the BET Awards in June 2005 and launched a European tour later that year. Unable to resolve their differences, the Fugees split again.

In 2007, Hill launched her own solo tour, often amassing complaints for her chronic lateness, last-minute cancellations, and complex rearrangements of the songs from *Miseducation*. Still under contract to Sony, Hill released her first official single in over a decade, "Neurotic Society (Compulsory Mix)" on May 4, 2013, confessing on Tumblr that it was rushed

out due to an "impending legal deadline." Two days later, Hill's other legal woes caught up with her, and she was sentenced to a correctional facility for three months and house arrest for another three due to failing to pay taxes.

Upon release, Hill toured with Nas, with whom she collaborated on his 1996 breakout song "If I Ruled the World," and debuted "Black Rage," a rap about racial injustice. In August 2015, Hill rereleased it, dedicating the song to activists protesting the police murder of Michael Brown in Ferguson, Missouri.

Most recently, Hill appeared on the soundtrack for *What Happened, Miss Simone?*, a 2015 documentary about the life of Nina Simone, of whom Hill admits, "I grew up listening to Nina Simone so I believed everyone spoke as freely as she did. I thought everyone spoke their true feelings and that is what allowed me to speak mine." Hill recorded six songs, making it her most exciting song list since *Miseducation.*

While Hill is considered to be "the best female rapper of all time," the moniker denies how far-reaching her influence continues to be. Not only does Hill's hybrid style of rapping with gospel and R&B-inflected singing resonate in the music of Kanye West, Chance the Rapper, Drake, and Nicki Minaj, her lyrical meditations on black womanhood helped shape a whole generation of female artists who came of age listening to *Miseducation*, like Beyoncé and Solange Knowles. Reflecting on her unique style, Hill said, "I've always done things a little crazy a little earlier. I'm not embarrassed or afraid to be the person that I am, neither personally nor musically—whatever that means." ■

AALIYAH

STEPHANIE PHILLIPS

ILLUSTRATION BY WINNIE T. FRICK

Hidden behind a series of stylish, mysterious sunglasses was where you'd usually find Baby Girl, Missy Elliott's affectionate nickname for the princess of nineties R&B, Aaliyah. Known for her breathy soprano vocals and era-defining collaborations with Missy Elliott and Timbaland, Aaliyah began her promising career at a young age, leaving a definitive legacy even though she died when she was only twenty-two.

From the early days of her career at just fifteen, Aaliyah worked her signature look, sporting baggy jeans, crop tops, and sunglasses. Her image was sold as a streetwise ingénue, who appeared older than her years one minute and mysteriously aloof the next. For fans of Aaliyah, the feeling that you never truly knew the real her nagged at them throughout her short time in the public eye. Her death in 2001 at the height of her fame left fans reeling; she was poised to accomplish so much more.

Aaliyah Dana Haughton was born on January 16, 1979, in Brooklyn and moved with her family to Detroit, Michigan, at the age of five. She was introduced to performing at an early age, singing with her mother around the house, taking part in plays at school, and bagging the lead role as Annie in the first grade. Aaliyah and her family took her talent seriously. She took vocal lessons at the age of nine and appeared on the talent contest *Star Search* when she was ten.

At the age of twelve, Aaliyah inked a distribution deal with Jive Records and signed to a label owned by her uncle, Barry Hankerson, Blackground Records. It was here that the young singer was introduced to Chicago soul man R. Kelly, who was the lead songwriter and producer on her debut album, *Age Ain't Nothing but a Number* (1994). The album, recorded when she was only fourteen, was certified double platinum. The singles "Back and Forth" and "Age Ain't Nothing but a Number" showcased a depth and awareness greater than her years. Her breathy vocals contrasted effortlessly with Kelly's new jack swing instrumentals, capturing the style and sounds of early nineties R&B.

Despite the success, after the release of her debut it was clear something was amiss. Rumors spread about the extent of Kelly and Aaliyah's relationship. The seductive lyrics Kelly wrote for the teenager, who was twelve years younger than him; the album title, which seemed to be Kelly's way of dismissing her youth; and the disturbing album cover showing a shadowy figure of Kelly in the background looming behind Aaliyah led fans to assume the obvious. Vibe magazine revealed Kelly and Aaliyah's marriage

PLAYLIST

"Back and Forth," 1994, *Age Ain't Nothing but a Number*

"One in a Million," 1996, *One in a Million*

"Are You that Somebody," 1998, on various artists, *Dr. Dolittle: The Album*

"Try Again," 2000, on various artists, *Romeo Must Die: The Album*

"Rock the Boat," 2001, *Aaliyah*

certificate, which showed they wed in Illinois on August 31, 1994. Aaliyah was fifteen at the time, but on the certificate her age was listed as eighteen. The marriage was annulled by her parents in February 1995, and Aaliyah cut all ties with Kelly and Jive Records afterward. Years later Chicago journalist Jim DeRogatis revealed the extent of Kelly's dark obsessions with underage girls and the destructive effect he had on their lives. Aaliyah did her best to put Kelly behind her, refusing to discuss the matter in interviews and denying the marriage ever happened. She achieved a great deal in her life afterward, though it would be a misjudgment to believe that he didn't have an effect on her. In an interview with the *Village Voice*, DeRogatis stated: "I had Aaliyah's mother cry on my shoulder and say her daughter's life was ruined, Aaliyah's life was never the same after that."

Aaliyah certainly did seem to carry the reserved nature of someone who had been burned, but that is not to say the experience defined her. If anything Kelly was a short detour in her journey to finding her true mentors, friends, and collaborators in the legendary Virginia-based songwriting-and-producing team Missy Elliott and Timbaland. Then relative newcomers to the game, Elliott and Timbaland were at first nervous to work with the star who had recently signed to Atlantic Records and already had a double platinum album in her back pocket. Nevertheless, the pair were quickly won over by Aaliyah's charming nature.

The trio was one of R&B's greatest teams. Their work together spawned classics that still adorn DJ playlists today, such as "Hot Like Fire" and "If Your Girl Only Knew." Working with Timbaland and songwriter Static Major, Aaliyah recorded "Are You That Somebody," from the *Dr. Dolittle* (1998) soundtrack. Aaliyah's determined breathy vocals glide gently over Timbaland's stop/start production and harsh beats. Throw in a sample of a baby cooing, and it all made for the most astounding piece of experimental R&B, which is still being studied and replicated today by artists such as FKA Twigs, Tirzah, Solange, and Kelela.

After the success of her second album, *One in a Million* (1996), Aaliyah focused on graduating from high school and beginning her acting career. She landed her first film role in *Romeo Must Die* (2000) opposite Jet Li. The soundtrack featured her single "Try Again," which topped the *Billboard* Hot 100 and was nominated for a Grammy Award.

After some time away from the music industry, Aaliyah felt ready to make her next, and what would become her last, album. Recorded in 2000 during her time in Australia filming her role for *Queen of the Damned* (2002), *Aaliyah* (2001) showcased a new maturity and growth in the young artist. Working again with Timbaland along with a host of writers and producers, the album incorporated elements of rock, neo soul, and funk to continue Aaliyah's reputation as the number-one experimental R&B diva.

In August 2001, a month after the release of the album, Aaliyah and several of her crew were killed in a plane crash after filming a video for "Rock the Boat." Stunned by the loss, the R&B world mourned the star taken too soon. Her legacy continues despite the fact that ongoing legal disputes have prevented the majority of Aaliyah's music from adorning streaming sites, hindering the chances of millions from finding out about R&B's favorite Baby Girl. ■

SHIRLEY MANSON

ANNIE ZALESKI

ILLUSTRATION BY ANNE MUNTGES

One of the most original (and successful) bands to emerge from the alternative rock scene of the nineties, Garbage is a sort of supergroup of accomplished American musicians and producers. But the face of their brazen music is a Scottish firebrand, singer Shirley Manson. The Edinburgh native has a commanding presence, with her traffic-light-red hair, bold makeup and outfits, and thick brogue. (The latter is notable especially for how it amplifies her penchant for bawdy conversations.) Like two of her teenage idols—Chrissie Hynde of ragged rockers the Pretenders and punk icon Siouxsie Sioux—Manson exudes womanhood that upends expectations and projects bulletproof strength. An insightful conversationalist, she isn't afraid to speak up about weighty issues such as sexism and women's rights. "There was never a moment when I believed I was less-than," she told Yahoo! Music in 2016. "I will always meet a man toe to toe, and when I encounter sexism, I f—ing push right on through it." Manson is a proud loudmouth who doesn't suffer fools or injustices gladly—and she'll be the first one to admit this and announce it's a character asset, not a flaw.

Manson honed this outspoken nature growing up as the second of three sisters. Her father worked as a geneticist; her late mother was a big band singer. As a teen, Manson was bullied because of how she looked. The experience was devastating and formative: over the years, she has spoken candidly about how the bullying made her feel insecure and angry—among other things, she would purposefully cut her legs with razor blades—and adopt a rebellious stance.

Manson channeled some of her teenage rage into creative pursuits. She was a shop assistant at the department store Miss Selfridge, where she sharpened her colorful, striking sense of style while working at the makeup counter. Manson also studied at the Edinburgh Youth Theatre. In her late teens, she started playing keyboards in and singing backup for the artsy eighties and nineties alternative band Goodbye Mr. Mackenzie. Although the Scottish group only had middling commercial success with their four studio albums, the act received retroactive attention for providing the first showcase for Manson's unmistakable, piercing vocal style.

After Manson signed a solo deal, she fronted the rock band Angelfish in the early nineties. The gig lasted for only a few years, but it changed her life. The video for the Scottish group's grinding single "Suffocate Me" caught the eye and ear of American musician-producer Steve Marker after it aired on MTV's *120 Minutes*. Marker was especially impressed by Manson's voice—a formidable, dynamic instrument that captured the song's aura of menace and seduction—and thought she might fit with a new band he had formed with fellow producers and musicians Butch Vig and Duke Erikson.

That band was Garbage, which was then woodshedding a futuristic sound based on jagged, electroplated rock and roll. After a few shaky tryouts, Marker's instincts were proven right: Manson and the rest of the band found their footing with this analog-digital fusion. The band's 1995 self-titled debut sold more than two million copies and spawned a Top 40 hit ("Stupid Girl"), while 1998's *Version 2.0* produced four alternative radio chart hits, including the explosive "Push It."

Despite her outward brashness, Manson's transition into Garbage wasn't easy. She hadn't written lyrics before, for starters, and living in Wisconsin—where the band was working on its debut album—was a far cry from bustling Edinburgh. Manson channeled this stranger-in-a-strange-land experience to help craft and shape a cast of empowered characters: Garbage's early songs champion underdogs who exact revenge on people who underestimate them ("Vow"), clever women who turn the tables on oppressors ("Not My Idea"), and individuals who wield their uniqueness like emotional armor when faced with heartbreak ("Queer"). In a smart twist, Manson's vocal delivery is expressive but conversational, which makes her messages more potent.

Adopting this fake-it-until-you-make-it

confidence buoyed Manson. As Garbage released more music, and the band dabbled in space-age electronica, moody rock noir, barbed-wire punk, and lipgloss-shiny new wave, she demonstrated marked growth as a musician. The band's lyrics expanded to tackle androgyny, the allure and dangers of obsession, life-shattering heartbreak, and the importance of sex-positive perspectives. Manson amassed a versatile

arsenal of vocal tricks: a raucous rock-and-roll sneer ("Bad Boyfriend"), an intimidating snarl ("Hammering in My Head"), a desperate wail (the ecstatic trip-hop hit "#1 Crush"), and a majestic croon (the James Bond theme "The World Is Not Enough"). On the politically charged 2017 electro-goth single "No Horses," her voice even has the knowing tremble of a soothsayer who sees a dark, ominous future.

Manson is an equally audacious live performer. Energetic and charismatic, she stalks the stage, challenging the audience with intense gazes that amplify the music's confrontational themes. Her presence, when combined with the band's brazen live sound, puts Garbage on even footing with any of their tour partners, a list that's included Smashing Pumpkins, No Doubt, U2, and Alanis Morissette. Although Garbage took a break in the late aughts—which let Manson explore acting with a role on *Terminator: The Sarah Connor Chronicles* and work on a solo record (later scrapped)—the band's creative partnership endures. A pair of albums, 2012's *Not Your Kind of People* and 2016's *Strange Little Birds,* find Garbage settling into a midcareer hot streak driven by urgent, hungry songs.

Garbage has remained relevant because fans have been able to grow up with the band. That's largely thanks to Manson: a fearless and unapologetic feminist, she eschews traditional stereotypes of how women should act or dress after they reach a certain age. In fact, she is one of the loudest voices raging against rock-and-roll ageism and gender-based discrimination. "I have imaginary voices about what people might say about me having pink hair at 50," she told *Elle* in 2016. "But I'm at that point where I don't give a fuck if you think it's appropriate or not. Go fuck yourself and be boring!" As the years have passed, Manson has grown more comfortable speaking out about her own vulnerabilities, traumas, and past mistakes. She's talked about these tough truths with candor and wisdom, showing women that speaking out can have asteroid-crashing-into-Earth impact.

In music circles, women are often pitted against one another, as if there can only be one focal point at any given moment. "Stupid Girl" seems to criticize this kind of negativity: One reading of the lyrics holds that Manson scorns those who subsume their true selves as they lie and manipulate to get ahead. She has never had an interest in playing such games; in fact, she frequently amplifies the voices of other talented female musicians. Not for nothing did Deap Vally—a bluesy rock-and-roll duo comprising two women—open Garbage's summer 2017 tour with Blondie. Manson is comfortable enough in her own skin to be generous with her praise and encouragement. In this way, she's a hero to multiple generations of women, a unifying force of defiant femininity. ■

SLEATER-KINNEY

LIZ PELLY

ILLUSTRATION BY ANNE MUNTGES

Sleater-Kinney came from an underground community that didn't want to just create music; they wanted to create their own world, one that was socially conscious and feminist at a time when the rock-and-roll status quo reflected the opposite. Born of Olympia, Washington's intertwined mid-nineties local scenes, Sleater-Kinney took the influence of the radical Riot Grrrl movement to new heights. Drawing also from the decade's intricate indie rock guitarwork and the makeshift Northwest pop underground, the band's members stitched together an unprecedentedly visceral sound of their own, eventually breaking ground within national indie rock circuits and the higher-profile capital-R rock genre at large—never compromising their political beliefs as their platform grew.

Sleater-Kinney formed in 1994, growing out of a musical friendship between two singer-guitarists, Corin Tucker and Carrie Brownstein. The pair had met in the spring of 1993, when Tucker's band Heavens to Betsy played a gig in Bellingham, Washington. "She asked me to write her with more information about riot-grrrl," Tucker reflected in 2015, for the liner notes of *Start Together*, their reissue box set. "I didn't, but I had a feeling I would see her again. It was about a year later that we started writing music together, for fun." Tucker writes of the varied feelings that drove the project forward: joy, anxiety, anger, angst, "wanting to change things."

Born in Eugene, Oregon, Tucker spent her teenage years involved with antiwar and environmental activism, later channeling her rage into punk feminism as a student at Olympia's Evergreen State. During her first year in college, she interviewed the members of germinal Riot Grrrl bands Bikini Kill and Bratmobile for a documentary about women in music, an experience that was formative and mind bending. She wanted her voice to sound like that of Bikini Kill singer Kathleen Hanna. And yet, her booming, soaring instrument is like no one's else—a truly unique sound in punk through which she belts her sharp, critical lyricism, clearly articulating her words and demanding attention to every one of them.

Brownstein, born in Seattle, saved up to buy herself a guitar while growing up in Redmond, Washington. She started learning the instrument at fifteen, and a few years later would be playing in the band Excuse 17 when she met Tucker. Brownstein brought lead guitar lines so meticulous they create their own mesmerizing rhythms and thick countermelodies. Her iconic riffs, windmill kicks, and the deadpan punch of her backing vocals would give the songs and shows as much power as the percussion section.

Sleater-Kinney, named after a street near Olympia, was originally a side project for the two. On the last night of a trip to Australia in 1994, they stayed

up all night recording their self-titled full-length debut. Appropriately, urgency is laced throughout. Their early hard punk influences are on display, but so are their distinct senses of dynamic and melody, illustrated on the doubled vocals and dissonant post-punk guitar riffs of "The Day I Went Away." That first album, ten songs and twenty-two minutes long, was released on Chainsaw Records, the queercore label run by Donna Dresch of legendary Olympia punks Team Dresch. In line with all of the ways their songs rallied for autonomy, releasing music on local, independent labels was key for Sleater-Kinney: their fiercely independent music would be pressed by similarly independent labels like Chainsaw, Kill Rock Stars, Sub Pop, and Matador.

On Sleater-Kinney's second record, *Call the*

Doctor (1996), they honed their skill for countermelodies and dueling vocal parts—the beginnings of their signature sound and style, with Tucker and Brownstein's two voices intertwining and overlapping, pushing and pulling, as their electric guitars did the same. "Call the Doctor" proved to be a turning point, a song about resisting commodification and about the normalization and socialization that mainstream culture wants to push people through.

Their current and longest-running drummer, the California native Janet Weiss, joined the band in 1996, as they began writing their third album, *Dig Me Out*. (The band has never had a bassist.) Within the album's first two songs, the group pries open a whole spectrum of female emotional experience: from the desperation and anger of "Dig Me Out" (a soundtrack to someone clawing themselves out of an oppressive situation, where maybe the situation is society) to the heart-wrenching loss and longing of "One More Hour." Weiss's masterful drumming helped grow Sleater-Kinney into the more ambitious and expansive trio they were becoming: her muscular but expressive playing made their fury more palpable, their sadness more devastating, the highs higher, and the lows lower.

Sleater-Kinney released four more full-lengths during the next decade, often musing on feminism and social justice issues along the way. *The Hot Rock* (1999) was their darkest and moodiest, while 2000's *All Hands on the Bad One* offered their most direct feminist distillation. Before Sleater-Kinney found themselves opening for a 2003 Pearl Jam tour, they wrote *One Beat*, their most explicitly political statement, a reaction to life in post-9/11 America. The album contained songs like "Far Away," which directly criticized President George W. Bush and recalled seeing flames explode on

TV, making a city far away feel so close. The oppositional song "Combat Rock" called out the thoughtless patriotism of the time.

In 2006, the band played its last show before going on hiatus. They all started other projects; Brownstein and Weiss played in Wild Flag with Mary Timony, while Tucker started the Corin Tucker Band, writing songs influenced by having children. Brownstein also co-created comedy sketch show *Portlandia* and wrote a memoir, *Hunger Makes Me a Modern Girl*.

Sleater-Kinney hoped another band would carry the torch and channel their breed of intuitive, politicized rock. But as they explained in interviews, it never happened. And so they restlessly returned in 2015, with *No Cities to Love*, their eighth studio full-length album, just as explosive and urgent as ever. It kicks off with "Price Tag," a song about the anxieties of motherhood under a consumerist system and the struggles to make ends meet in post-recession America.

PLAYLIST

"I Wanna Be Your Joey Ramone," 1996, *Call the Doctor*

"Dig Me Out," 1997, *Dig Me Out*

"One More Hour," 1997, *Dig Me Out*

"Modern Girl," 2005, *The Woods*

"Jumpers," 2005, *The Woods*

Sleater-Kinney often use their band as a vehicle for commenting on the process of being in a band. In her memoir, Brownstein calls this dialogue with themselves "meta-songwriting." Early song "I Wanna Be Your Joey Ramone" flips gender stereotypes and makes fun of the gendered nature of rock and roll culture. "#1 Must Have," from *All Hands on the Band One*, critiques the marketing of music, and the need to resist being bought and sold. Toward the end of the song, Tucker sings defiantly, "Culture is what we make it, yes it is." Sleater-Kinney actively created the culture they wanted to see—on their own terms. ■

FIONA APPLE

REBECCA HAITHCOAT

ILLUSTRATION BY WINNIE T. FRICK

Since the release of Fiona Apple's stunning 1996 debut *Tidal*, journalists both male and female have tried to weaken her, infantilize her, reduce her. The *New Yorker* said she "looked like an underfed Calvin Klein model." A writer for the *New York Times* described her as tiny, a child, small, and shrinking, as well as referring to her as both "Lolita-ish" and an Ophelia, all in a single article. A critic at *LA Weekly* once opened a review with "There's something about Fiona Apple that makes you want to take care of her."

It's clear why so many writers feel an instinct to diminish her—she is a force, not only of talent but also of nature. Fearful instead of awestricken in that same gut-kick way we're terrified of a ferocious storm, or anything beyond our control, critics feel compelled to neutralize her power. In a 1998 *Rolling Stone* profile (its title, "Fiona: The Caged Bird Sings," renders her both fragile *and* captured), the writer describes a closet in Apple's bedroom at her mom's house. The wood is splintered where she has knifed it repeatedly. "Better than stabbing someone," she shrugs. Beneath those nicks, she had etched one word: *strong*.

To a generation of teenage girls spreading their wings just as *Tidal* dropped, Fiona Apple's strength was the encouragement and sustenance they needed to fly. Whether over the march of "Sleep to Dream,"

the slow shuffle of "Shadowboxer," or the flute that curled through the air on "Criminal," her raspy, scrubbed-raw voice told them it was okay to flirt, fuck up, and scream instead of smile. What they wanted was already inside of them. The cover of *Tidal* is cropped so that Apple's tangled locks, lean frame, and even her pillowy lips are cut away, leaving only her watery blue eyes staring calmly, intently. To girls wavering with the swell of new feelings, *Tidal* was steadying. It roiled with emotions but their owner never spiraled wildy, instead articulating her thoughts with a clean, crystallized fury. She made you feel as all-powerful as she. No small feat.

When she accepted her trophy for Best New Artist at the 1997 MTV VMAs, she snapped, "This world is bullshit. You shouldn't model your life on what we think is cool, and what we're wearing, and what we're saying and everything. Go with yourself." People made fun of her afterward in an attempt to temper her potency, but the speech wasn't some teenage tantrum. She simply was pushing her fans out of the nest, feeding them the tough-love message to rely on themselves and their own reserves, just as she'd had to do as a young girl who struggled with depression, anxiety, and an eating disorder. As the tattoo on her back reads, "FHW": Fiona has wings.

Born Fiona Apple McAfee-Maggart in New York City in 1977, Apple grew up living with her

mother and sister. She was trained as a pianist and was composing her own pieces before she was ten years old. In 1994, she passed along a demo tape to a friend who babysat for a music publicist. The tape reached a Sony Music executive, and her debut was released two years later. Containing songs like "Sullen Girl," which alluded to her rape by a stranger at age twelve, the album features Apple's signature banged-out chords and blues voice expressing the pain that ravages insides, from red-eyed rage to ripped-open desolation. Partnering with legendary producer Jon Brion, she released her sophomore album, *When the Pawn Hits the Conflicts He Thinks like a King What He Knows Throws the Blows When He Goes to the Fight and He'll Win the Whole Thing 'fore He Enters the Ring There's No Body to Batter When Your Mind Is Your Might so When You Go Solo, You Hold Your Own Hand and Remember That Depth Is the Greatest of Heights and If You Know Where You Stand, Then You Know Where to Land and If You Fall It Won't Matter, Cuz You'll Know That You're Right,* in 1999, but it would be another six years until her next, *Extraordinary Machine,* and another seven before 2012's *The Idler Wheel Is Wiser than the Driver of the Screw and Whipping Cords Will Serve You More than Ropes Will Ever Do.* All of her albums have been nominated for Grammy Awards.

In the years since she became a household name, she's increasingly withdrawn from the public's eye, emerging to tour or do press behind her albums and then retreating once more in a life she's largely

PLAYLIST

"Sleep to Dream," 1996, *Tidal*

"Shadowboxer," 1996, *Tidal*

"Carrion, 1996," *Tidal*

"Criminal," 1996, *Tidal*

"Paper Bag, 1999," *When the Pawn . . .*

"Fast as You Can," 1999, *When the Pawn . . .*

"Not about Love," 2005, *Extraordinary Machine*

"Hot Knife," 2012, *The Idler Wheel . . .*

"Anything We Want," 2012, *The Idler Wheel . . .*

managed to keep private. "I'd say that I've been reclusive for 34 years," a thirty-four-year-old Apple told Pitchfork in 2012. Scraps of information appear here and there, but they're tossed out by her, not unearthed by TMZ. In 2012, she made headlines when she posted a letter she'd written to her fans explaining that she was postponing a leg of her tour due to her dog's illness.

Apple has always rejected fame, taking care to keep something for herself and not be stripped dry by an industry machine. Early in her career, she said that she wrote her songs for her, but she was glad others found meaning in them. Even as she has protected her own heart and life, few artists are as adept at mining and examining the contents of the human soul. She does not care about being a star, and so that leaves her music, with its ferocious honesty and her husky voice, free to be consumed on its own terms.

"It occurred to me when I was making this album that I fucked myself by writing all those songs when I was angry and hurt," she once said. "Now, in order to live, I must rehash these memories all the time."

There is a video of Apple performing "Carrion," a song from *Tidal*, at the 2012 South by Southwest festival in Austin, TX. She has a faraway look in her eyes as she sings, her voice becoming an actual wail on the hook, the music slowing down and stretching like taffy. It is a brutal song that seems impossible to have been written by a sixteen-year-old girl, a song that imagines the love two people have been hanging on to as dead flesh rotting in the sun. The metaphor is the sort you don't understand until you've been battered by love a bit, when you sigh into middle age, but this teenage girl nailed it, and the music reflects the skitter of an animal before its slow decline to a stinking death. In the video, Apple throws back her head, arching into a backbend as emotion overtakes her. Her face scrunches up, as if she's experiencing the heartache that led her to write the song all over again. She looks wounded as she spits out the lyrics, and as the band continues to play, she slinks away to the shadows. It's the sort of performance that pricks desire in a certain type of person to mother, to pet, to take care of.

But look closer. The singer burns with a raw-boned power. A flame leaps in her eyes and her body is taut with steely resolve. No extra fat pads her frame, and her arms are sinewy with muscle. She is still the epitome of what a pop artist can be, at once sharing in the human experience, connecting us, and showing us truths we had yet to uncover. Frailty's name is not woman, she has always asserted with her art, and it certainly is not Fiona. ■

FLY GIRLS

In 1984 a fourteen-year-old Queens student decided to talk back. The rap group UTFO had just scored a hit with a B-side called "Roxanne Roxanne," about a "stuck-up" woman who refuses the men's supposed charms. Lolita Shanté Gooden decided it was time for females to stop being the object of raps and instead become the subject. "Roxanne Shanté" answered UTFO line for line with the hilarious "Roxanne's Revenge." Of course, no one was about to let a teenage girl have the last word: Shanté's retort was in turn answered by another hundred-plus records, in the so-called Roxanne wars. The bulk of the exchanges were silly roasts, but there was a disturbing underlying pathology, perhaps most clearly revealed when so-called "conscious" rapper KRS-One dismissed Shanté as only good for sex (only he didn't say sex).

Sadly, in hip-hop, as in musical genres from classical to jazz to rock, women have too often been dismissed as mere conduits for pleasure—or outright dissed as bitches and hos. In the 1980s, Salt-N-Pepa and MC Lyte showed that women were certainly capable of rhyme and flow. But it wasn't until Queen Latifah came along, demanding, "Who you calling a bitch?," that someone declared an end to the misogynist name calling. Dressed in regal Afrocentric attire and declaring "Ladies First," the Queen held the door open for Da Brat, Yo-Yo, Bahamadia, Sha-Key, and many more MCs projecting strong, positive self-images.

Lauryn Hill connected the history of soul singers with the future of hip-hop on her best-selling, award-gobbling solo debut *The Miseducation of Lauryn Hill*. Lil' Kim, Foxy Brown, and Trina proved you could be sexy and silver-tongued. And then a lady lyricist from Virginia took over MTV, demonstrating that you could floss in a garbage bag as well as a thong. Missy "Misdemeanor" Elliott was a true game changer, forging a sonic mixture of dance beats and dense raps and helping the career of other artists, most notably Aaliyah. She innovated in music, video, and fashion, donning bug-eyed goggles and declaring herself "Supa Dupa Fly." Fearless and uncategorical in her embrace of styles, Missy made it seem like anything was possible for women in hip-hop: breaking through in the clubs, on the streets, on the charts—having a career that lasts past your twenties.

Women were no longer the rule-proving exceptions in hip-hop; they just were. Bohemian rap-sodist Erykah Badu asserted hip-hop's blues roots and jazz pedigree. MIA milked its rage of dispossession and power of persuasion. And Nicki Minaj didn't just switch the code, she blew it up, writing her own *Pinkprint*. Like Elliott, Minaj humor-coats her provocations with cartoonish guises: Day-Glo pink hair, caterpillar-sized eyelashes, Tomb Raider breasts. But when she unleashes her rhymes, well, as she said on her debut mixtape: *Playtime Is Over*. Her verse on the Kanye West song "Monster" was declared by one magazine to be the greatest rap of the 2010s. As Nicki says, "You could be the king but watch the queen conquer."

MISSY ELLIOTT

REBECCA HAITHCOAT

ILLUSTRATION BY LINDSEY BAILEY

Rap has never been particularly kind to women. Generally, as Snoop Dogg explained in "Bitches Ain't Shit," females are assigned one of four unfleshed-out parts: bitch, ho, trick, or mom. Songs written in praise of any woman who did not birth the lyricist—even from "enlightened" rappers like A Tribe Called Quest—typically include a robust assessment of her physical assets. In the mid- to late 1980s, rappers including Shanté, MC Lyte, and Queen Latifah emerged to parry, not party, with their male counterparts and expanded the role of women in rap. Soon, however, sex appeal and a Coke-bottle-shaped body seemed to trump skill for women hoping to play with the boys—many of whom, it must be noted, sported figures shaped by smoking weed and eating McDonald's at the studio instead of situps at the gym.

So when Missy "Misdemeanor" Elliott, a BBW wearing bug-eyed sunglasses, a big, sweet smile, and what looked like a garbage bag, swerved into the rap world, the chances of her making it should have been slim.

Then "The Rain (Supa Dupa Fly)," the unearthly lead single off *Supa Dupa Fly*, Elliott's groundbreaking first album, beamed down.

Stretching out soul classic "I Can't Stand the Rain" as a canvas, Missy and longtime friend and producer Timbaland paint a simple picture with a hyper-vivid palette. Slicing away all but the cloudy, minor hook of Memphis singer Ann Peebles's hit, Timbaland gives Elliott a sparse, spacey track over which to rhyme. In a clipped, halting flow, she raps about blazing weed and heading to the beach, almost like a robot testing its voice ("Beep, beep, who got the keys to the Jeep? Vroooom").

Just as integral to Elliott's introduction to the world was Hype Williams's video, the director's signature rain-slicked, Technicolored, futuristic landscapes seemingly custom-made for Missy. Using a fisheye lens, he zooms in and out on the rapper and her friends (including R&B trio Total, for whom she'd written, and MCs Lil' Kim and Puffy), transforming their dancing and hamming with herky-jerky movements before landing on Elliott sitting atop a hill, dumping a guy, and announcing that anyone who gets to be with her is lucky. Flipping a middle finger to music executives who told her she was too fat to be a solo artist, she shuns bikinis, instead choosing to puff a balloon suit full of air to make her body appear even bigger. To a generation of girls like me, who wanted to be in the entertainment business but believed the execs' lie, Missy was a benevolent alien sent to prove size was irrelevant when it came to success. Whether doing the same slinky choreography as her dancers or shooting a lusty grin at the camera, Missy wasn't hearing any fat shaming, nor was she shy about broadcasting her libido.

Despite evidence to the contrary, Missy Elliott was born a mere mortal in Portsmouth, Virginia. Her father, a former Marine, physically abused her mother, and they were poverty-stricken. When Elliott was eight years old, an older boy in her family began molesting her. Music was her escape from bleak reality. She retreated to her room to write fan letters to the Jacksons, her favorite singers, and perform for her baby dolls. Finally, when Missy was in her early teens, she and her mother clawed their way out, escaping her father while he was at work.

High school was easier than home life, especially after her friend Magoo introduced her to Timbaland and Pharrell Williams. The threesome quickly began experimenting with sound, but Elliott also had a girl group called Fayze that scored a record deal when they auditioned for Jodeci in matching costumes—Missy's idea, of course.

Yet there were devastations, too. In 1993, Elliott wrote a song for Raven-Symoné, but when they shot the video, they cast a slim, light-skinned model to rap her verse. It gutted her so deeply that she gave up trying to be an artist herself and focused on songwriting. She won in the end: after she and Timbaland co-wrote and produced most of *One in a Million* for Aaliyah, record labels were more than willing to grant her creative control.

Also swaying the suits' decision was Missy's fantastical yet funky visual sense. Often, it seems like she is plugged into the wonderful and free (and demographically desirable) imagination of a child. In "Sock It 2 Me," she transforms into a video game character trying to dodge fireballs spit by outer space antagonists. She's a samurai bending her mind to

float across the room in "One Minute Man," and she's both a marionette and then on a hoverboard in "WTF." There's a plantation dance party with no gravity in "Lose Control" and girl-on-girl battles in "I'm Really Hot." Elliott builds a new world every time she makes a video, each one chock-full of choreography that makes you wish you were a dancer and boggling details that make your eyes spring out of your head, cartoon-style. Simply put, her mind is a marvel, and she's compelled to execute to the fullest whatever it dreams up.

"One thing I won't do is compromise," she said in a 2017 interview with *Elle* magazine. That's not lip service. With its boundary-stretching, digitally blipped soundscapes and the ease of Missy's transitions from sexpot to head-in-the-stratosphere imaginer, *Supa Dupa Fly* cemented Elliott as one of the most creative rappers of all time—and also one of the most forward-thinking. Long before electronic dance music became the monster EDM and married rap music, Elliott and Tim were incorporating elements of it into their sound. Instead of languid and syrupy like Southern rap, they shifted toward a manic pace and heady, industrial quality with Elliott's bot-like vocal delivery. From there, she simply leapt higher. On her 1999 sophomore album, *Da Real One*, she toyed with raunchier topics and a singsong delivery on tracks like "Hot Boyz" and "All n My Grill." *Miss E . . . So Addictive* was packed with

PLAYLIST

"The Rain (Supa Dupa Fly)," 1997, *Supa Dupa Fly*

"All n My Grill," 1999, *Da Real World*

"Get Ur Freak On," 2001, *Miss E . . . So Addictive*

"One Minute Man," 2001, *Miss E . . . So Addictive*

"Work It," 2002, *Under Construction*

"Gossip Folks," 2002, *Under Construction*

"Pass That Dutch," 2003, *This Is Not a Test!*

"I'm Really Hot," 2003, *This Is Not a Test!*

"Lose Control," 2005, *The Cookbook*

"We Run This," 2005, *The Cookbook*

"Teary Eyed," 2005, *The Cookbook*

"WTF," 2015, single

twangy club bangers like "Get Ur Freak On," while *Under Construction* and *The Cookbook* both cranked out frenetic dance numbers. In a world in which many artists could trade songs and no one would know the difference, Elliott marks her work. It is undeniably hers and only hers.

Beyond the genius-level creativity lies Missy's spirit. Throughout her career, Elliott has held the door open behind her for other female artists, from Aaliyah to Nicole Wray to Ciara, sprinkling some of her magic dust on each of them yet not overpowering their individual styles. Working with mostly female R&B singers, Elliott indulges her obvious soft spot for the genre, crafting softer, more smoothed-out songs like "Let It Go" for Keyshia Cole. All the while, she's seemed to be a woman's woman, never jealous of anyone else's success because she's so comfortable and confident in her own.

And instead of hiding in songwriting rooms forever after her appearance wasn't skinny enough or light enough or fit enough or whatever adjectives are used that inadvertently homogenize the music industry, Elliott shook off the mortal coil and animated herself, creating a whole new aspirational standard. Maybe the trash bag suit wasn't a "fuck you" to all the people who told her to shrink herself. Maybe it was just a metaphor, a reminder she is not regular. She's Missy. ∎

ERYKAH BADU

STEPHANIE PHILLIPS

ILLUSTRATION BY JULIE WINEGARD

Most recognizable when framed by a towering headwrap or gently waving an incense stick on stage, Erykah Badu is the multitalented singer, actress, and artist who, as one of the leaders of the neo-soul movement in the late nineties, helped bring soul back to its roots. The Dallas native took the spirit of artists like Chaka Khan, the street smarts of the hip-hop scene, and a burgeoning Afrocentrism found in arty black neighborhoods and created a raw, earthy sound that evoked a new age Billie Holiday on her debut album, *Baduizm* (1997).

It's fitting that Badu chose an album title that seemed to reference a zen attitude as listening to Baduizm feels like a spiritual experience. From her new age philosophies to her offbeat personality, Badu asked the world to adapt to understand her, rather than the other way around. Alongside her contemporaries the Roots, D'Angelo, and Lauryn Hill, in the short-lived but fruitful genre that was neo-soul, Badu created a template for artists who wanted to step outside the often restrictive R&B mold. Rather than opt for the polished, overly complicated vocal warbles loved by many R&B divas at the time, Badu cultivated a soulful, honest sound that could veer from a well-crafted rasp to honey-drenched purr in a second. When she debuted in 1997 her unconventional sound stunned listeners and set her up to become one of the most recognizable voices in R&B. Over the years she has continued to shake up her style and sound, reinterpreting what we think of as contemporary R&B as well as what we expect from Erykah Badu.

Badu was born Erica Abi Wright in Dallas, Texas, in 1971. Raised by her mother and grandmother, Badu was a precocious child who thought of herself as a bit weird. She loved listening to Chaka Khan records and music from the budding hip-hop scenes in other cities, like New York. Badu enrolled at Booker T. Washington High School for the Performing and Visual Arts and was a dancer and a rapper before she became a singer. While she was at college in Louisiana, Badu formed a duo with her cousin, Robert "Free" Bradford. At first Badu rapped over the beats her cousin sent via tapes in the mail, but one track, a sparse lounge piano melody with a repetitive whistle and tight snare beat, inspired her to sing. It later found its way onto her debut and became "Appletree." The duo released a demo under the name Erykah Free, which attracted the attention of record label executive Kedar Massenburg. Massenburg was managing D'Angelo and coined the term *neo-soul* to encapsulate the novel, stripped-down approach to R&B his artists were creating. He loved the demo the duo sent but only wanted to sign Erykah, who agreed, to the disappointment of her cousin.

Here began the next incarnation of Erykah. She settled on her now infamous stage surname, Badu, likening it to a jazz scat sound. She donned her most recognizable style—regal towering head wraps paired with incense and a plethora of ankh jewelry—and set to work on her eponymous debut album. With production from members of the Roots, her cousin Free, and others, *Baduizm* was released in 1997 to critical and commercial acclaim, debuting at number two on the *Billboard* 200. Her songwriting talents set her apart from the previous generation of R&B stars as she incorporated themes of spirituality, nature, and individuality into what could have been generic R&B love songs. "Next Lifetime" told the story of a woman in a relationship who falls in love with another man but doesn't want to cheat, deciding that fate will bring them back together in another life. Bursting out of the speakers like a lyrical mantra, "On & On" focused on reflection and self-love.

Though *Baduizm* defined her as an artist, many fans remember her for a stand-out moment on her live album, released eight months after *Baduizm*, where she debuted her scathing takedown of no-good men, "Tyrone." The call-and-response number connected with women everywhere who could rely on the memorable command to "call Tyrone." Witty and intelligent, the song showed Badu's comedic side. During this time Badu started a relationship with André 3000, from futuristic Atlanta rap duo OutKast, whom she met in a New York club in the mid-nineties. Badu gave birth to her first child, Seven, on the same day her live album was released in November 1997. Throughout her career she has balanced motherhood (she has two other children) with music, showing the world there is no divide between her life as a mother and as an artist.

After the release of *Baduizm*, Badu grew tired of being the queen of neo soul and began to try out new styles and reference points. For her second album, *Mama's Gun* (2000), she teamed up with the hip-hop collective Soulquarians, which featured musicians such as Questlove, Common, Talib Kweli, and Q-Tip; Badu was the only woman in the collective. *Mama's Gun* had a strong, throbbing hip-hop beat running through it and allowed Badu to step away from her love of cryptic lyrics to write directly about insecurities, relationships, and police brutality.

Before performing a song live, Badu will regularly halt to let the audience in on a secret: she's an artist, so she's sensitive about her shit. Basically she takes it seriously, so don't criticize. One can't help but wonder how Badu dealt with the public criticism toward the video for the single "Window Seat" from her fifth album, *New Amerykah Part Two: Return of the Ankh* (2010). Badu removed her clothes piece by piece in various locales around Dallas before lying down naked in Dealey Plaza, where John F. Kennedy was shot. Viewers missed Badu's original message about avoiding groupthink, and controversy ensued. She was charged with disorderly conduct and forced to pay a $500 fine.

Despite the criticism Badu continued to focus on her art and went in a new direction for her mixtape *But You Caint Use My Phone* (2015). Inspired by her reworking of Drake's viral classic "Hotline Bling" and her 1997 hit "Tyrone," the mixtape revolves around sampling, electronic beats, drum machines, and phone-based puns. No longer the "analog girl

PLAYLIST

"On and On," 1997, *Baduizm*

"Tyrone," 1997, *Live*

"Bag Lady," 2000, *Mama's Gun*

"Window Seat," 2010, *New Amerykah Part Two: Return of the Ankh*

"Cel U Lar Device," 2015, *But You Caint Use My Phone (Mixtape)*

in a digital world," as Badu often refers to herself, the former soul revivalist embraced new styles and sounds more willingly than many younger artists.

Over the years, along with her music style, her fashion sense has evolved. Badu has been seen rocking long, skinny braids with henna tattoos decorating her arms and towering black wide-brimmed hats with a piece of gold floss hanging out of her mouth. Many of her earlier fans would struggle to place the later Badu with the neo soul–era Badu. Of course this evolutionary ability is one of the many reasons the influential force has lasted so long in a difficult industry.

Today Badu is one of the most celebrated soul singers of the modern era. Her original approach changed what it meant to be a black female artist, freeing women from having to look like a variation of Toni Braxton or Destiny's Child and sound like a pitch-perfect copy of Mariah Carey. Badu proved you could have mainstream success creating music that was both challenging and nourishing. Her inability to stay still for too long will always result in something unexpected and engaging, though it won't necessarily be new music. Over the last few years Badu has hosted the Soul Train Awards, performed in her own one-woman show, and acted in the independent film *The Land* (2016). Even though various projects keep Badu distracted for now, make no mistake, when the time is right, Badu and her Baduizm will return to bring us back to center. ∎

NEKO CASE

ANNIE ZALESKI

ILLUSTRATION BY ANNE MUNTGES

In 2014, *Playboy* tweeted its review of Neko Case's 2013 album, *The Worse Things Get, The Harder I Fight, the Harder I Fight, the More I Love You*, with a teaser declaring that the fiery alt-country vocalist is "breaking the mold of what women in the music industry should be." Case—herself an avid, outspoken, and frequently hilarious Twitter user—was irate about the characterization. "IM NOT A FUCKING 'WOMAN IN MUSIC,' IM A FUCKING MUSICIAN IN MUSIC!" she retorted, also via Twitter. For good measure, she added a few more choice words, including a *Mad Men* reference: "DON'T PEGGY OLSEN ME, MOTHERFUCKERS."

A year later, Case had more to say about this topic in a lengthy, self-published essay on identity: "What the hell am I (and who the hell cares)?" The smart, honest piece touches on how she defines feminism in her own life, her complicated relationship with the term "women in rock," and how gender stereotypes play out in music, culture, and language. "Selfishly, I am doing this in part so I never again have to answer the question of, 'How is it to be a woman in rock?'" Case wrote. "Instead, I can direct people here for the full, thoughtful answer." Notably, in the intro she stresses that this essay is "not for publication, copying or paraphrasing"—simply Case wanting to share her own thoughts, unfiltered and without danger of them being twisted.

This willingness to detail her ever-evolving thought processes and perspectives, warts and all, speaks to the vulnerability Case brings to her music. Her openness starts with a big-hearted voice: She views country music's penchant for kicky twang and melancholic torchiness as a mere jumping-off point. More often, Case transcends genres and eras by singing in a bittersweet and haunted tone that's brushed with melancholy and empathy. On "Deep Red Bells," a song memorializing forgotten victims of the Green River Killer, her voice is a long, low wail—the sound of mourning and grieving. On the sparse "Maybe Sparrow," she exudes tender anguish over a vulnerable creature who becomes prey.

The almost a cappella "Nearly Midnight, Honolulu" is even more wrenching: she weaves a real-life encounter with a woman screaming at her child in between realizations of her own rough childhood. Case takes a detached, matter-of-fact approach as she details deeply personal, painful flashbulb memories. These recollections aren't hyperbolic. Case's parents, who are now both deceased, divorced when she was barely school-aged. The turbulence continued after they split. Her family was poor and moved around a lot, which meant she lived in Virginia, Massachusetts, Vermont, and Washington; Case has said both of her parents were drug addicts and alcoholics.

Left to her own devices, she dealt with the turmoil by hanging out with pet dogs (spawning a love of animals that endures to this day), drawing, and listening to music. She was captivated by the bold, brash sounds of classic rockers Heart and Queen, and absorbed country music via her cherished grandmother. And, like many disenfranchised teens, she was also drawn to aggressive punk rock: in fact, she left home at age fifteen and started drumming for noisy bands in the Pacific Northwest.

After matriculating to art school in Vancouver, Canada, Case continued with music, including stints drumming and singing for the punk-inflected rockabilly band Maow and indie rockers Cub. Still, her tastes remained eclectic. She listened to jazz and girl-group records, was a huge fan of the gothic-blues-twang act Flat Duo Jets, and had her DNA arranged after a friend gave her a record called "Swing Down, Sweet Chariot" by the Gospel Pearls, starring a passionate blues singer named Bessie Griffin. Case told *No Depression* in 2000 the latter was "the record that made me want to be a singer more than anything in the world."

These inspirations, combined with her growing desire to make a country-inflected record to please her grandmother, led to Case's 1997 solo debut, *The Virginian*. On this record, and the 2000 follow-up, *Furnace Room Lullaby* (both credited to Neko Case and Her Boyfriends), she sharpens her own take on the genre, exhibiting copper-colored twang ("Guided by Wire"), channeling a tough-talking rockabilly greaser ("Mood to Burn Bridges"), and unleashing a goofy, exaggerated drawl ("Honky Tonk Hiccups"). Case's love of aggressive music is never far from the surface, especially in concert. The 2004 live album *The Tigers Have Spoken* finds her playing a hotrodding cover of "Loretta," a song by Boston punk band Nervous Eaters.

The Tigers Have Spoken, on which Case is backed by Canadian alt-country shapeshifters the Sadies, illustrates how she thrives on collaboration. In fact, she is an integral member of fizzy power-pop band the New Pornographers, an exuberant sidecar that has let her indulge in hollering harmonies. Her solo concerts are just as engaging, thanks to frequent foils such as vocal powerhouse Kelly Hogan: Case howls like a wolf and trills like a songbird, soaring up to high notes with effortless grace, as Hogan adds keening harmonic shading. In contrast, Case's 2016 collaboration with Laura Veirs and k.d. lang (appropriately called case/lang/veirs) offers traditional country, folk, and fifties pop songs, with an emphasis on manicured, gorgeous harmonies.

Besides her original work, Case is also a first-class vocal interpreter who excels at putting her own imprint on other people's songs. In addition to a song called "Loretta," *The Tigers Have Spoken* includes Case doing justice to Loretta Lynn's gritty "Rated X" and the Shangri-Las' jangly girl-group classic "The Train from Kansas City." In 2011, she and My Morning Jacket teamed up for a live take on the frothy Kenny Rogers and Dolly Parton duet "Islands in the Stream," while a few years later, Case unleashed a brash, screeching lead vocal take on Iron Maiden's metal classic "The Number of the Beast." On *The*

PLAYLIST

"Deep Red Bells," 2002, *Blacklisted*

"Lady Pilot," 2002, *Blacklisted*

"The Train from Kansas City," 2004, *The Tigers Have Spoken*

"If You Knew," 2004, *The Tigers Have Spoken*

"Hold On, Hold On," 2006, *Fox Confessor Brings the Flood*

"This Tornado Loves You," 2009, *Middle Cyclone*

"People Got a Lotta Nerve," 2009, *Middle Cyclone*

"Man," 2013, *The Worse Things Get, the Harder I Fight, the Harder I Fight, the More I Love You*

Virginian, Case even puts a freewheeling, vintage country spin on her beloved Queen, via a version of "Misfire."

As these covers indicate, Case is adamant about not letting gender define her as an artist or a human being. The 2013 release of the song "Man," which speaks of embracing diverse gender identities, especially led to intriguing interview detours in which she spoke of reconciling her male and female sides. "I just want balance," she told the *Guardian*. "I want to be equal parts man and woman, no matter what I am at the gynecologist." Speaking to NPR about toying with gender perspective in songs, Case elaborated on her own self-perception: "I don't really think of myself specifically as a woman, you know? I'm kind of a critter. I'm an animal. Everyone's an animal." This refusal to be pigeonholed—and the fluid, human-first way she approaches her music—has helped redefine what alt-country looks and sounds like. Case is an iconoclast whose outspoken nature makes her a hero to anyone who marches to the beat of a different drummer. ■

DIXIE CHICKS

JEWLY HIGHT

ILLUSTRATION BY LINDSEY BAILEY

Often, the significance of an artist's body of work becomes clearer in hindsight, but it hasn't necessarily worked that way for the Dixie Chicks, a trio comprising Natalie Maines, Emily Robison, and Martie Maguire. Writing about them has fixated on their tempestuous departure from the mainstream country format, with the side effect of downplaying the bigger picture of their career. Their lasting influence—especially the way their musical choices, performing personas, and business decisions have emboldened a subsequent generation of country acts—gets overlooked. It's as though everything they did as country music's most vivacious ambassadors from the late 1990s to the early 2000s was invalidated when country radio blackballed them over right-wing reaction to an antiwar comment by Maines, and she and her band mates turned the controversy into grist for artistic re-invention. The self-determined way they ultimately handled the controversy grew directly out of the as-sertive, updated model of country femininity they'd been fleshing out all along.

The earliest incarnation of the Dixie Chicks was retro-minded. Sisters Robison and Maguire—who were then known by their maiden name of Erwin and had cut their teeth in fiddle and banjo contests—and co-founders Laura Lynch and Robin Lynn Macy performed a revivalist repertoire of Western swing,

bluegrass, and buckaroo ballads in kitschy cowgirl costumes. They became quite the draw on the Texas dance hall circuit, but their recognition was strictly regional. Macy was the first to leave, then Lynch departed, too. The sisters, who had more expansive aesthetic and professional ambitions, turned to a young singer whose father, the respected steel guitar-ist Lloyd Maines, had passed along her demo tape. In Natalie Maines, they found the potent voice and persona to transform the group. The dynamic new version of the Chicks signed a deal with a division of Sony Nashville.

Right away, they found themselves in a defiant posture. The commercial country template of the nineties relied on arena rock bluster and had little room for string band standbys like banjo. Besides, it was far from a given in the Nashville studio scene that the members of a band would actually play on their own albums. But the Chicks insisted on it, reveling in their virtuosity and solidarity, despite the fact that the media, unaccustomed to country groups showcasing female instrumentalists, had supplied the dismissive nickname "Country's Spice Girls." They and produc-ers Blake Chancey and Paul Worley joined mod-ern country-pop drive to the string-band chassis of Maguire's fiddle and mandolin and Robison's banjo, dobro, and acoustic guitar on *Wide Open Spaces* (1998). Maines was a lusty livewire. All of twenty-three years old when the trio entered the spotlight, the sassing twang, fiery flourishes, and uncurbed youthful passion of her performances contributed to her magnetic appeal. Maguire and Robison, also in their twenties, intensified their vocal attack to blend with her in brassy-sweet, three-part harmony.

The Chicks' projection of forwardness and fun spoke to lots of women their age. Their first single, "I Can Love You Better," was a lighthearted boast about possessing prowess as a lover, while their second, "There's Your Trouble," directed wry, bubble-bursting real talk at an object of affection. Their third, "Wide Open Spaces," became an anthem for young women determined to enlarge their experiences of the world. Those songs sounded like little else on country radio, but they became smashes regardless, generating millions-strong record sales that enabled the Chicks to really flaunt their freedom on their next album, 1999's *Fly*. They put the acoustic picking further out front, dove into co-writing their material, and recorded headstrong songs like the effervescent "Ready to Run," whose willful protagonist behaves as though standard scripts of feminine domestication don't apply to her.

Maines's vinegary, taunting delivery of "Goodbye Earl," the colorful tale of a battered wife whose best friend helps her dispose of her abuser by poisoning his black-eyed peas, showcased her wicked wit, and all three Chicks brought lightheartedness to songs like "Sin Wagon," a rollicking declaration of the intention to act out. To them, it was daring fun to simultaneously acknowledge and kick against constricting codes of feminine, middle-class propriety. The Chicks didn't view themselves as being seriously subversive so much as true to their impulses. Their down-home angle on audaciousness was an expression of personality that connected with country audiences—who needed to believe and identify with performers' personas before buying in to them—and young women who were used to pop stars' demonstrations of empowerment and alt-rockers' displays of autonomy. In 1999 alone, the Chicks landed on tour with paragons of conventional country masculinity George Strait and Tim McGraw and on the main stage at the implicitly feminist, genre-bridging Lilith Fair.

The trio developed a reputation in the country music industry for a more threatening form of rebelliousness by going head to head with Sony, seeking a better contract and unpaid royalties. Sony responded with a lawsuit, and the Chicks countersued, eventually reaching an agreement, the terms of which they couldn't disclose. Still, the legal battle itself was public knowledge, and the group was conscious of the fact that their intrepid actions were being watched. "I think that it's good for girls to see that we stuck our necks out and did what we believed was right," Maines observed to *Country Music Today* in 2002.

While the lawyers were working toward a resolution, the Chicks retreated to Texas and took a low-key, acoustic approach to recording what would become the unlikely hit album *Home*, for which they shared production credit with Lloyd Maines. Its pop-savvy polish was subtle; what people primarily picked up on was that it amounted to drum-free, contemporary bluegrass treatments of singer-songwriter material. The trio's mischievous humor surfaced here and there, in "White Trash Wedding" and the radio-panning puns of "Long Time Gone," a single that got airplay despite its bite. But mostly there were melancholy moments: a lilting cover of Stevie Nicks's "Landslide" and the modern mountain-style story-song "Travelin' Soldier" among them.

The latter song was yanked from country radio

after Maines criticized President Bush's hawkishness on stage in 2003. It was a startling chain of events. Maines wasn't known for explicitly political speech, but she'd taken the stage with the Chicks in London, troubled by the impending American invasion of Iraq, and informed the crowd, "Just so you know, we're on the good side with y'all. We do not want this war, this violence, and we're ashamed that the president of the United States is from Texas." Conservative American talk shows and blogs seized on what she'd said, urging people to bombard country radio stations with complaints. Acutely averse to anything polarizing, country stations quickly scrubbed the trio from their playlists. And that was just one aspect of the unambiguously gendered backlash the Chicks faced.

Typically, country superstars would endure a long, slow fade from radio dominance as they moved into middle age, so it was entirely understandable that the Chicks, darlings of country radio up until then, felt a profound and disorienting sense of betrayal when they found themselves shut out of their format. They became the targets of hate mail, death threats, and vitriolic protests delivering the silencing message that they should keep their opinions to themselves. Robison and Maguire supported Maines unequivocally. Together they regarded the new public scrutiny of their words as a provocation to embrace the role of statement making. It was their idea to pose nude for the cover of *Entertainment Weekly*, their bodies branded Riot Grrrl–style with examples of sexist insults they'd received: "Saddam's Angels," "Dixie Sluts," "Big Mouth." In a move both symbolic and artistic, they enlisted LA rock guru Rick Rubin to produce *Taking the Long Way*, a collection of West Coast country-rock and adult pop that made tangible their determination to chart a future for themselves outside of the country format. The serious-minded songs, all of which they had a hand in writing, were introspective but wholly unrepentant, and political in the sense that they were pointedly personal, cathartic narrations of the rejection they'd experienced.

Though the Chicks have kept their distance from Nashville, recording side projects—Robison and Maguire's tasteful Court Yard Hounds albums and Maines's broody, solo rock set *Mother* (2013)— and touring only sporadically, their influence has remained present in the invigorating brashness of Miranda Lambert, the exuberant sisterhood of Lambert's Pistol Annies trio, and the sly, feminine wit of Kacey Musgraves and Maddie and Tae. Lambert, Little Big Town, and other country hit makers have signaled that they admire, identify with, and miss the Chicks' music by covering "Goodbye Earl" live. When the long-absent trio appeared on the 2016 Country Music Association Awards telecast, stealing the show alongside Beyoncé, Maines, Robison, and Maguire carried themselves with the fierce pride and rascally defiance you'd hope to see from a group whose attitude has galvanized country music in so many different ways, take it or leave it. ■

PLAYLIST

"There's Your Trouble," 1998, *Wide Open Spaces*

"Goodbye Earl," 1999, *Fly*

"Ready to Run," 1999, *Fly*

"Sin Wagon," 1999, *Fly*

"Long Time Gone," 2002, *Home*

"Travelin' Soldier," 2002, *Home*

"Truth No. 2," 2002, *Home*

"Not Ready to Make Nice," 2006, *Taking the Long Way*

"Lubbock or Leave It," 2006, *Taking the Long Way*

BEYONCÉ

NEKESA MUMBI MOODY

ILLUSTRATION BY JULIE WINEGARD

O f all the debates that raged after Beyoncé's *Lemonade*, the most talked-about recording of 2016, lost the album of the year Grammy to Adele's commercial juggernaut *25*, perhaps the haughtiest argument came from a writer who suggested Beyoncé didn't win because she was *too* ambitious.

Apparently, King Bey, as her fans have crowned her, made folks a bit weary by doing too much. She overwhelmed us with her star power, syncopated choreography, arresting videos (she prefers to call them films), top-notch singing, and songs that interweave political commentary with almost every modern music genre, from country to reggae to R&B to dance to rock to adult contemporary.

It's an all-too-familiar knock for women who journey outside of the lines society draws for them. From Madonna to Hillary Clinton, there's something about a woman who has achieved but still yearns for more that provokes a nasty backlash.

Beyoncé Gisele Knowles has never been one to stay inside her lane; instead, she creates new highways to traverse. After all, this is a woman who took two years off after having daughter Blue Ivy in 2012 and then dropped an album with (1) no advance warning (2) as an iTunes exclusive (3) on a Friday (when traditional music releases came out on a Tuesday) and still went platinum. (The release helped change the industry release date and encouraged a flurry of other artists to release surprise albums, with varying success.)

She reached her artistic apex thus far with *Lemonade*, listed in 2017 as number six in NPR's list of the 150 greatest albums made by women. More than an album, it was a cultural milestone, both deeply personal and political, as she exposed the pain of infidelity and the strain of repairing a broken marriage through the prism of the particular burden of the black woman. The visual accompaniment—complete with poetic soliloquies—commanded its own HBO special when it debuted and led to an avalanche of analyses, from college campuses to newsrooms to barber shops and nail salons.

Certainly, to create a masterpiece such as *Lemonade* requires plenty of ambition—the kind that has made Beyoncé a superstar without peer. But Beyoncé is more than a superstar, even more than a cultural phenomenon. She has become the voice of her generation.

Knowles is not a provocateur, joyously pushing buttons and challenging societal norms for a reaction. Instead, she makes the personal universal and political. Take, for example, "Sorry," from *Lemonade*. At first, the song appears to tread familiar broken heart territory as she sings of revenge after confronting an ungrateful lover. Then Beyoncé sings the final line,

"He better call Becky with the good hair." She takes a song that was for every wronged woman and centers it around the pain of black women, long made by society's beauty standards to feel inferior to white women—Beckys—because of the texture of their hair, the color of their skin, the width of their noses. With that one utterance, Beyoncé gave voice to the anger and frustration of a particular people while laying bare her own insecurities.

On "Flawless" from the *Beyoncé* album, she serves up one brag after the next, as the queen demands respect from the pop princesses flitting around her, reminding them that "since you were a little girl, you dreamt of being in my world." One verse later, the woman once declared *People* magazine's "Most Beautiful" turns the song into not only a rallying cry for every woman but an explicitly feminist anthem, with her deft use of a speech by award-winning writer Chimamanda Ngozi Adichie that questions sexual and social standards for women. Then there's the song's rallying cry: "I woke up like this." While it could come across as cocky, Beyoncé

brings her sisters with her in the next line, saying, "WE FLAW-LESS; ladies, tell 'em." It's not a celebration of vanity, but of women managing the burdens of society and still managing to come through it all and look good too. "Say I look so good tonight, God damn, God damn; Say I look so good tonight; God damn, God damn GOD DAMN!" she exclaims: Beyoncé is our hype woman, our counselor, our healer; Beyoncé lifts us up with her.

It seems as if Beyoncé has always been famous. Born in Houston, Texas, in 1981, she first appeared on the music scene in late 1997 as the poised, polished, and gorgeous frontwoman of Destiny's Child, the R&B foursome that started off with Kelly Rowland, LeToya Luckett, and LaTavia Roberson (the band would famously fracture and go through personnel changes before finally becoming a trio with Beyoncé, Rowland, and Michelle Williams). In a crowded girl-group field that included multi-platinum R&B

funksters TLC, silky Xscape, and hitmakers SWV, it looked as if the band was to be forgettable also-rans when their first single, the pleasant ballad "No, No, No," was released. But a Wyclef Jean–helmed dance remix gave them new life—and their first Top 5 hit.

From there, the Beyoncé hit train barely slowed down. First as part of Destiny's Child, then when she went solo in 2003, she racked up hit after hit with funky girl-power anthems ("Independent Women," "Single Ladies," "Upgrade U"), sexy club bangers ("Crazy in Love," "Baby Boy"), and torch ballads ("If I Were a Boy," "Halo"). Vocally, she developed into a powerhouse singer (some classify her as a mezzo-soprano), and her range was as varied as her musical styles: though her music was rooted in hip-hop-inflected R&B, her albums smartly wove in a mix of styles that appealed to a mass audience.

She became more than just a pop star. She forayed into acting with mixed results (the critically acclaimed and Oscar-winning *Dreamgirls*, the flop *The Fighting Temptations*), became part of a super duo with her union to Jay-Z, landed top endorsements, graced the covers of elite magazines like *Vogue*, and sang at both of President Obama's inaugurations.

She was undeniably a superstar, and yes, also an artist (Beyoncé has been listed as a co-writer on most of her hits since she was a teen). But while her songs became part of the international conversation and her lyrics became catchphrases (surely many men got tired of the phrase "Put a Ring on It"), her projects didn't reverberate in the culture as social commentary until the *Beyoncé* album.

While it's not hard to pinpoint when the pivot in her music happened, it's less clear as to why. Some point to her dismissal of her father, Mathew Knowles, as her manager; Knowles had called the shots in her career since she was a child (with her mother, Tina, styling Destiny's Child from the hair to the outfits) and had an almost singular focus to make his daughter a sensation but steered her away from controversial political or social movements that could make her unpopular.

Some credit husband Jay-Z; his gritty background and refusal to play on anyone's terms but his own may have rubbed off on his wife. There's also the influence of sister Solange, who after attempting to go the pop route as a teen singer eschewed the mainstream for alternative, edgy fare, stretching her artistic wings without concern for where her songs landed on the charts (Solange co-wrote one of Beyoncé's edgier songs, "Why Don't You Love Me"). And of course there was the life-changing event of 2012, the birth of daughter Blue Ivy, who Beyoncé said changed her artistic mission. "[Having a daughter] just gives you purpose, and all of the things that my self-esteem was associated with, it's all completely different," she said in an interview that same year.

Or maybe, after all those years being the perfect pop star with the perfect lock-in-step dance moves, the perfect outfits, the perfect style, the perfect body, Beyoncé craved something that, while potentially imperfect, perhaps had more meaning.

"I'm climbing up the walls cuz all the shit I hear is boring / All the shit I do is boring," she declares in a husky monotone on "Haunted," on *Beyoncé*.

PLAYLIST

WITH DESTINY'S CHILD:

"Say My Name," 1999, *The Writing's on the Wall*

"Independent Women (Part I)," 2001, *Survivor*

"Survivor," 2001, *Survivor*

"Bootylicious," 2001, *Survivor*

SOLO:

"Crazy in Love," 2003, *Dangerously in Love*

"Single Ladies (Put a Ring on It)," 2008, *I Am . . . Sasha Fierce*

"Drunk in Love," 2013, *Beyoncé*

"Flawless," 2013, *Beyoncé*

"Sorry," 2016, *Lemonade*

"Formation," 2016, *Lemonade*

A harsh and, safe to say, unfair assessment. But after years of studio time spent trying (and typically succeeding) to create a hit record, the process had surely become rote. Perhaps that's why, as ambitious as Beyoncé is, she decided to be downright ambivalent about pleasing radio and instead mined what was in her heart and mind and started making the most important work of her career.

Beyoncé still has hits, but not with the regularity that she had earlier in her career. But at the 2017 Grammys, after Adele captured the Album of the Year trophy, it was the British singer who deemed herself not worthy, almost literally bowing down to her queen—who gave inspiration to an eleven-year-old Adele when thoughts of a music career were just childhood dreams.

"The way that I felt when I first heard 'No, No, No' was exactly the same way I felt when I heard *Lemonade*," Adele would tell reporters backstage that night. "For her to be making such relevant music for that long a period and still affect all of us . . . what the fuck does she have to do to win Album of the Year?"

It's a question many were asking, except likely Beyoncé. Pregnant with twins, she had performed at the show with a spectacular visual display that framed her as a golden Madonna but also as a luminescent black queen radiating the beauty of her fellow sisters, standing on stage with her, all hues represented.

After winning for best R&B album, Beyoncé—who likely knew she wouldn't take home the top trophy—didn't do the usual stream of thank-yous to loved ones, collaborators, and fans. Instead, she used her platform to once again make a statement. "My intention for the film and album was to create a body of work that would give a voice to our pain, our struggles, our darkness and our history. To confront issues that make us uncomfortable," she said in part. An ambitious goal, for sure. And the vision of a true artist.

At the end of the night, Beyoncé was the epitome of unbothered. She was photographed partying with husband Jay-Z, mother Tina Knowles, and sister Solange. One of the most circulated photos of the night featured Beyoncé wearing a large fedora, a white gown that accentuated her cleavage, and her protruding bump—with her middle fingers squarely up. While it was widely seen as a message to the Recording Academy, it could have also represented the attitude toward that commercial, radio-friendly career she once held on to dearly.

Clearly, she didn't need it to be the queen that she remains today. ■

TEGAN AND SARA

JENN PELLY

ILLUSTRATION BY ANNE MUNTGES

On the first song off the debut record from Tegan and Sara Quin—the identical twin sister duo from Canada who have been making sincere pop-rock under their given names since 1995—they offer a nearly impossible directive. "Go ahead / Try to figure out what my future looks like," goes that somber acoustic tune "Divided." It's a bracingly inquisitive genesis song from a band whose path you could not have readily predicted.

Tegan and Sara are the rare group who, over the course of eight sharp studio albums to date, have grown steadily and assuredly, from living-room recordings to the *Billboard* Top 20. Their vulnerable lyrics always cut to the bone, splitting the difference between emo and something more classic, often speaking directly to depression and ways of coping. Their hooks, crucially, are muscled. From the beginning, their singing was bold, slightly soured, and forthright: like your only friend, a fellow misfit, talking straight to you. A naturally towering ascent like Tegan and Sara's is typically cordoned off to dreams—as rare as a comet streaking slowly across the night sky, glittering only at moments for all to see.

The Quin sisters—both singers, songwriters, and multi-instrumentalists—began writing together as fifteen-year-old punks in Northeast Calgary. They made their own cassettes and used a school photocopier to print the artwork. In 1999, the eighteen-year-old twins tracked their debut album, *Under Feet Like Ours*, at their mother's house; a year later, they were signed to Vapor Records, the label founded by a fellow Canadian, Neil Young, and his manager, Elliot Roberts. It was Vapor that afforded the duo the time to evolve on their own terms. One day, Tegan and Sara will have an unstoppable *Greatest Hits* compilation: the songs will vary in style, from strummy ballads with airtight, Alanis-like inflection, to dizzied indie rock, to fully bloomed pop bangers—all tied by the rawness of emotion that powers great popular music. Tegan and Sara are consummate artists because they change.

The first two Tegan and Sara albums contained several high-water marks, songs that subtly spoke of outsiderdom—like the devastating "Clever Meals," which seemed to capture the stark loneliness of eating disorders, or the stormy "My Number," in which Tegan wisely, wearily intoned, "It's a silly time to learn to swim when you start to drown." But it wasn't until 2002's astonishingly catchy *If It Was You* that they

PLAYLIST

"Clever Meals," 1999, *Under Feet Like Ours*

"My Number," 2000, *This Business of Art*

"City Girl," 2002, *If It Was You*

"Not Tonight," 2002, *If It Was You*

"Where Does the Good Go," 2004, *So Jealous*

"Walking with a Ghost," 2004, *So Jealous*

"The Con," 2007, *The Con*

"Nineteen," 2007, *The Con*

"Now I'm All Messed Up," 2013, *Heartthrob*

"Boyfriend," 2016, *Love You to Death*

made a great album, really arriving as a songwriting voice for the open-hearted LiveJournal generation. *If It Was You* offered signature Tegan and Sara songs like the complexly sad "Not Tonight" or the coolly swaying "City Girl": "I got so / City girl on you" is a lyric that captured an entire self-possessed way of being—a picture of a woman in motion—while remaining efficient like Tegan and Sara's best songs.

By 2004, Tegan and Sara had embraced a relatively synthier sound with another remarkably varied LP, *So Jealous*. That album's swaggering single "Walking with the Ghost" was for some time the best-known Tegan and Sara song thanks to the White Stripes, who covered it on an EP. Its central image—the ghost, or the memory, of a lover that hovers and haunts and echoes inside you—is vividly rendered in Sara's strikingly minimal lyrics. For most bands, one Jack White cosign would be enough for a lifetime of rock-and-roll authenticity, but Tegan and Sara have always survived on legitimate connections with their fans rather than sweeping critical acclaim. And those connections would multiply with their 2007 Warner Bros. debut, *The Con*, which charted at number thirty-four on the *Billboard* 200 in the US. The Quins' dynamic sound rocketed further on *The Con*, with the explosive angles of its title track and the soaring queer yearning of "Nineteen."

When Tegan and Sara made a more deliberate appeal for mainstream radio play, crafting songs redolent of 1980s synth-pop beginning with 2013's *Heartthrob*, it was not entirely surprising. Their music always contained all the hallmarks of stadium-filling pop (and they'd performed in arenas, opening for the likes of Cyndi Lauper); their songs just hadn't been presented as such. As a fan of Tegan and Sara since my early teenage years, I was thrilled by their pivot toward a wider audience: This was a band you wanted the whole world to hear, who could make the simplest romantic line feel purposeful.

Tegan, for one, felt like there might be something blocking their attempt at world domination. Reflecting on that moment in a 2016 BuzzFeed profile, she recounted her thought process—"I can't think of a gay woman that's on the pop charts"—to which her then label-head replied, "Well, why can't that be you?" With that, the anthemic come-on "Closer" was Tegan and Sara's first Top 20 single. *Heartthrob*'s stunning penultimate track "Now I'm All Messed Up" offered genius new wave melancholia. On 2016's sleek, sparkling *Love You to Death*, the single "Boyfriend" felt like a legitimate triumph, a bubblegum plea from one woman to another to not keep their love a secret.

Their unusual journey is even more miraculous given that, along the way, Tegan and Sara have persevered through a music culture that could be hostile and mocking toward queer women making earnest songs. They've also struggled to navigate their own at-times fraught relationship, but they've survived well enough to warrant the beautifully self-reflective title *Love You to Death*—a moving statement of the girl love their careers so wholly embody.

Tegan and Sara's success story sets an important precedent in modern music. An unorthodox perspective need not diminish an artist's visibility—indeed, it should be reason to amplify it. Formally, the barebones songs the twins were producing as teens in their mother's living room are a world away from the glossy radio pop they've envisioned two decades on. But Tegan and Sara always dealt in supreme catchiness, in heartache, in telling the truth. They are masters of intimate emotion—if their latest albums are perfect pop, then they spent a lifetime preparing for it, pinpointing the magic at its beating heart. Through it all, Tegan and Sara have offered proof that there is no more powerful or daring spark for music than being yourself and giving voice to that self than pure honesty. ■

PEACHES

JANA MARTIN

ILLUSTRATION BY JULIE WINEGARD

Peaches's blunt-force beats, her refusal to be a corporate slave, and her ferocious stage presence have garnered her an intensely loyal following. She's a vag-tastic provacateur, stomping onstage like a she-satyr, hair done fork-in-a-socket style and eyes a kabuki rainbow. Gorgeous in her own skin and with a sneer like Elvis, she spouts pornalicious joy to banging beats. "Whistle blow my clit"—she sang/urged/recited in 2015 on *Rub*'s title track, which had a video so NSFW it kept tripping the YouTube censors. The premise was vintage Peaches: unshackled by any male gaze, she and a throbbing posse of female adult-movie stars romp in the desert in Joshua Tree. Body positive, sweaty, juicy, filthy, unforgettable—it was a perfect collective feminist orgasm as a form of protest. And the song has a one-word hook that sticks like Velcro.

What makes Peaches stand apart from the herd of today's voices-over-rhythm-track makers is her uncompromising wildness, her gender-fluid hotness, and her refusal to kowtow. In the face of music that's increasingly sanitized, she rips off the plastic wrap and makes it real. Her voice can slide from a throaty yowl to a declaratory grunt, a supple and punchy

instrument for such sex-positive, pussy-power songs. And thank the ejaculating goddess that having reached fifty, she's not going anywhere, because we need her fearlessness more than ever.

Peaches began performing in the nineties. She was a nice Jewish girl named Merrill Beth Nisker who got bullied by her schoolmates and had the good sense to aim for better things. As part of the Toronto music scene that included her sometime roommate Feist, she made her punk rock debut, *Fancypants Hoodlum*, in 1995. In order to not have to rely on other musicians, she shifted from indie rock to electro—and found plenty of room inside its hammer-thump sparseness to spout, shout, incant, and sing. *The Teaches of Peaches* (2000) included the hypnotic anthem of sexual healing for the millennium, "Fuck the Pain Away." *Fatherfucker* (2003) featured "Kick It," a raucous collaboration with Iggy Pop that proved that Peaches has the rare balls to meet the godfather of punk's raw power halfway, then kick it up a notch. In the video, the two toughs cajole each other flirtatiously while killing zombies. The combination of the pair's aggressive sexiness and the retro sleazoid story line was a perfect mix of *fuck off* and *fuck us*.

With her cleverly titled *Impeach My Bush* (2006), Peaches took her place as supreme ruler of electroclash—a synth-pop-meets-new-wave variety

PLAYLIST

"Fuck the Pain Away," 2000, *The Teaches of Peaches*

"Kick It (Peaches feat. Iggy Pop)," 2003, *Fatherfucker*

"Boys Wanna Be Her," 2006, *Impeach My Bush*

"Talk to Me," 2009, *I Feel Cream*

"Vaginoplasty," 2015, *Rub*

"Dick in the Air," 2015, *Rub*

of electronica that fit her punk intensity. With her backing band the Herms (a play on the seventies act Peaches and Herb and another gender-politic label), she performed at Coachella and opened for Bauhaus and Nine Inch Nails. The album also gave the world the genius anthem for gender fluidity "Boys Wanna Be Her"—its lyrics miles ahead of their time: "the boys wanna be her / the girls wanna be her." A former teacher, Peaches slyly trolled both the religious right and the ridiculous way we treat certain stars as being bigger than Jesus: "You lick so hot / Are you conceived / Kids receive / Crawling up the sleeve."

But Peaches is also more than a stomping diva dressed in giant vagina collars that make her look like the sex queen of space. Yes, she's hilarious—she puns worse than Dad. Yes, she's so much fun to work with that Kim Gordon, Joan Jett, Margaret Cho, Kathleen Hanna, Christina Aguilera, Pink, and a host of others have joined forces with her. But she's also a deeply thoughtful musician and performer. One of the first artists to organize efforts to support the imprisoned Pussy Riot, she embodies and enacts girl power. Under the smeared makeup and seventeen breasts she sometimes wears, she's a pop mastermind. The "Boys" song has been used in car commercials, video games, and television shows, including as the theme song for *Full Frontal with Samantha Bee*—its hook so infectious that corporate America wants it bad. And when a Peaches track lands on the *Billboard* charts or she wins an award—she was voted Electronic Artist of the Year by the Independent Music Awards in 2010, the year after her fourth album, *I Feel Cream*, came out—we all get to feel like we've won.

Like her zombie-killing teammate Iggy, like Nina Simone (whose song "Four Women" gave Peaches her stage name), like Sid Vicious, like any iconoclast, Peaches in concert is mesmerizing, magnetic, frightening, and inspiring, her hot-button content and boy-girl beauty groundbreaking. In 2010 she performed the entire score for *Jesus Christ Superstar*, accompanied only by her longtime collaborator Chilly Gonzales on piano: *Peaches Christ Superstar* was Jesus and Judas and Mary Magdalene and, of course, King Herod—an ambitious, hilarious, and powerful undertaking. Her larger-than-life persona is made even bigger by the aplomb with which she costumes herself in vulvas and breasts, by her spot-on phrasing and the way she can deliver a line with a combination of allure and out there. She's got a warm and goofy unpredictability, as if she's well aware of how freaking important what she's doing for us all is—and also wants to protect our souls from fear and shame. Her purest form of fighting back is to throw a gigantic delicious vagina in the face of the Man: a deliberate, outsized, crotch-grabbing fuck-you. But it's anything but a cheap shot. Behind her gleaming appearance—with all its ferocity, its lunacy, its hypersexy spirit—is compassionate brilliance and a great big heart. ■

SHARON JONES

SOLVEJ SCHOU

ILLUSTRATION BY LINDSEY BAILEY

When retro funk-soul singer Sharon Jones performed—jumping, shimmying, twisting, and strutting on stage—the full-throttle emotion of her quick moves and raspy, bluesy voice shot into the audience like lightning bolts, whipping people into a dancing frenzy. She wasn't just a singer and performer. She was an *entertainer* whose concerts were sweat-drenched events that surpassed even those of her childhood icon James Brown. From the early 2000s until her death from pancreatic cancer in 2016, Jones toured relentlessly with her taut multi-piece band the Dap-Kings, singing and speaking her truth as a woman in her forties and then fifties. A record executive once dismissed her as "too fat, too black, too short, and too old," she said in the 2016 documentary *Miss Sharon Jones!* She stomped on those ageist, sexist, and racist comments, ushering in a new age of robust sixties-style soul years before younger white singers Amy Winehouse and Adele reaped Grammys and financial success for a similar sound. "God gave me a gift, and that gift is to sing. I'm at my happiest when I'm on this stage, and this mic is in my hand," Jones—wearing a blue spangled dress, her head bald from chemotherapy—told the crowd at the Montreal Jazz Festival in July 2016. Months later, following a stroke on election night that she attributed to Donald Trump's becoming president, she died at age sixty, a fighter and artist until the very end.

On Jones and the Dap-Kings' two compilation albums and seven studio albums, she sings about love, heartbreak, female strength, and societal injustice with all the blunt fierceness of someone who fought against multiple odds. Like many in the revival Mod scene, whose throwback heroes were sixties Motown and Stax singers, I fell in love with Jones as a singer and survivor who fully embodied the spirit of that culturally explosive era. I would place myself in front of the stage to be one of the men and women she pulled from the crowd—which she did during every concert—to dance, prance, and sweat alongside her. In that sense, in her own egalitarian way, Jones gave fans a taste of what it was like to feel the heat of stage lights, of a roaring audience, of the exuberant joy of singing. A nightly twenty-minute Dap-Kings intro of rollicking horns, bass, guitar, organ, drums, and backup singers would lead to her bursting forth from behind the curtain like a locomotive dressed in fringe. She—in the words of her and the Dap-Kings' only Grammy-nominated album, *Give the People What They Want* (2014)—gave the people what they wanted: raw power.

But Jones's journey to being recognized as "an unstoppable frontwoman" by the *New York Times* took decades. Born the youngest of six kids in Augusta, Georgia (where the Godfather of Soul Brown grew up), then living with her family in South

Carolina, Jones soaked up Brown's fiery funk and soul, along with the music of Aretha Franklin and other big-voiced belters. Her mother moved Jones and her siblings to the projects of Brooklyn, New York, when Jones was a young girl, to escape an abusive husband. Sharon began singing in church with her sister Willa, and was the first in her family to go to college. She went on to play in funk groups in the seventies, while also singing in church and performing in wedding bands, but musical stardom didn't materialize. Years spent working as a prison guard on New York's Rikers Island and as an armed security guard for Wells Fargo instilled in Jones the resilience that would later pervade her albums.

By the time Dap-Kings bandleader and bassist Gabriel "Bosco Mann" Roth heard Jones singing backup during a 1996 recording session for Southern soul singer Lee Fields, he was hooked. Roth released Jones's first solo single, "Damn It's Hot," a rhythmically skittering funk ditty, in 1996, when she was forty. In 2002, Roth and Dap-Kings saxophonist Neal Sugarman put out Jones and the Dap-Kings' debut album, *Dap-Dippin'*, on their newly formed Brooklyn independent label Daptone Records. The album surges with old-school seventies electricity, and songs such as "Ain't It Hard"—with Jones crooning narratives about poverty and violence—have an activist edge. The group started out "playing in lofts and garages, little greasy places," Roth told the *Los Angeles Times* of those early days.

On equally rambunctious *Naturally* (2005), Jones took the Woody Guthrie classic "This Land Is Your Land" and transformed it into a grooving political funk anthem that became a live staple. Then the

British wave of sixties-inspired chanteuses took hold. Beehive-haired tabloid darling Winehouse started gaining massive attention for her 2006 hit album *Back to Black*, which featured members of the Dap-Kings. The bump in accolades for the Dap-Kings directed attention Jones's way, but she never incorporated pop-centric hip-hop or contemporary beats, like Winehouse did, or experienced the same kind of fortune and fame. She stayed faithful to her vintage gospel, soul, and funk roots. On *100 Days, 100 Nights* (2007), Jones slows things down to a slinky simmer, with most songs—including the lovelorn title track—harnessing a smoother sixties R&B vibe. "Better Things," off 2010's *I Learned the Hard Way*, incorporates handclaps, trumpet, and piano trills and a loose, jazzy, Muscle Shoals–style rhythmic arrangement, with Jones wailing passionately—a gritty warmth in her voice—about holding her head high after a breakup.

Jones's 2013 cancer diagnosis and its life-altering impact, captured in heartbreaking detail in Oscar-winning director Barbara Kopple's *Miss Sharon Jones!*, suddenly thrust Jones into a different kind of spotlight. Through chemo treatments, remission, and then a recurrence, still gracious, honest, and funny on stage and off, Jones never wavered discussing her cancer. Shivering, in pain, she wrapped herself in blankets before giving 120 percent of herself during live shows. "I say to the cancer, get up and get out. GET. UP. AND. GET. OUT," she shouted to the audience while opening for Hall and Oates in 2016, at that point playing twenty-thousand-seat venues. Her party tunes and ballads on *Give the People What They Want*—nominated for a Best R&B Album Grammy, recorded prediagnosis, and released postdiagnosis—reflect her chutzpah amid illness. "We get along / Through sorrows and strife," she sings with gospel verve as backup singers call back to her on the midtempo "We Get Along." On "People Don't Get What They Deserve," Jones chants, "Money don't follow sweat / Money don't follow brains."

In the last moments of her life, in November 2016, Sharon Jones left the world as she lived and loved it: surrounded by music. Band members packed into her New York hospital room. She couldn't speak, but could hum in tune, and they accompanied her on guitar, playing gospel hymns such as "Amazing Grace" and "His Eye Is on the Sparrow." Exactly a year after her death, in 2017, her posthumously released album *Soul of a Woman*, produced by Roth, included her belting an emotional farewell on the spiritual slow burner "Call on God," which Jones wrote decades earlier, and singing confidently about civil rights on the funky and hopeful "Matter of Time." "She was the strongest person any of us had ever known," Roth told the *LA Times*. "That part of her that made music and that loved music and that was musical just didn't want to go. It was just so strong." ■

LAURA JANE GRACE

KATHERINE TURMAN

ILLUSTRATION BY WINNIE T. FRICK

The moniker Against Me! is at once confrontational and invitational. The preposition "Against" conveys hostility—or is it intimacy?—and, when emphasized by the exclamation point, fervency. The "Me!" can reasonably be presumed to reference the singer, or person who named the band.

That person was indeed Against Me! frontperson Tom Gabel. But the true "me" was unclear. It took nearly thirty years for a clear answer to definitively emerge: Me = Laura Jane Grace.

Gabel, born in 1980, grew up in a transient military family, the eldest son of an Army general. As a boy who felt he should have been a girl, Gabel understood he was operating against society's norms, but more importantly, he was fighting against himself, grappling confusedly with "her," as he called his female interior identity. He moved through life as a boy, a teen, then a man. But inside, he was a girl, then a woman. Before knowing the term, Gabel struggled with gender dysphoria.

The fraught, decades-long journey to become the woman she knew she was culminated in 2012, when Grace came out in a *Rolling Stone* article titled "The Secret Life of Transgender Rocker Tom Gabel." The decision to go public made her into an unasked-for but eloquent spokesperson for transgender awareness, on top of her already considerable punk rock

bona fides. Grace found adoration from kids who previously hadn't seen anyone like "them"—young, tattooed, punk, and trans.

Against Me!'s bold 2014 *Transgender Dysphoria Blues* album marked Grace's own musical outing, followed by 2016's *Shape Shift Me*. Her ongoing emotional and physical growth—and the world's reaction—is emotionally wrought in song: "Walking on broken glass while holding my breath / I wouldn't dare step on a single crack . . . Just because I can intellectualize it doesn't mean I feel it in my chest," she sings in "Norse Truth." Grace's frank 2016 memoir, *Tranny: Confessions of Punk Rock's Most Infamous Anarchist Sellout*, furthered her role as thoughtful truth teller.

Grace's early childhood as Thomas James Gabel provided clues to who she really was. Was it natural curiosity or the first inkling of gender misalignment that led Gabel to play with Barbies and try on his mother's nylons in secret? By the age of five, he wanted to be Madonna; in *Tranny*, the writer recalls the shock of realizing he wasn't a girl, and could never be.

Never say never.

Gabel's parents divorced, leaving a puberty-perched twelve-year-old with yet another reason to be confused. His naturally rebellious nature led him first to metal, notably an obsession with Guns

N' Roses, whose androgyny and acting out surely mirrored his own. Ultimately, GNR represented a lifestyle that Against Me! Would rail against not only in theory but on an actual album: *Against Me! Is Reinventing Axl Rose*. (Pitchfork called the album "a bit like the Clash or Billy Bragg on the first take— hardly polished, ragged, and throaty.")

As American music shifted toward the stripped-down anti-fashion of grunge, Gabel shifted with it. In his early teens, he was already playing guitar. He sought relief from his personal demons by, variously, playing live music at church talent shows, watching MTV, and cross-dressing. The dive into drugs and alcohol started around the same time.

The musical journey for the self-proclaimed "Teenage Anarchist" began with a self-titled 1997 demo, recorded in his mom's Florida bedroom. Dropping out of high school, Gabel was an autodidact, politically and socially conscious. The Trotsky-quoting teen who interviewed Black Panther Bobby Seale for his zinc was bold and defiant. At fourteen, an insolent Gabel got beat up by cops, a defining moment, spurring songs and solidarity with other misfits in the beach community of Naples, Florida. It was the start of a hardscrabble life that included dumpster diving and punk rock squats. But a prolific creativity as a songwriter coupled with an honest, passionate likability as a frontperson would lead Gabel and Against Me! to both commercial and critical success.

PLAYLIST

ALL WITH AGAINST ME!:

"Reinventing Axl Rose," 2002, *Against Me! Is Reinventing Axl Rose*

"Don't Lose Touch," 2005, *Searching for a Former Clarity*

"Thrash Unreal," 2007, *New Wave*

"Stop!," 2007, *New Wave*

"I Was a Teenage Anarchist," 2010, *White Crosses*

"True Trans Soul Rebel," 2014, *Transgender Dysphoria Blues*

"Black Me Out," 2014, *Transgender Dysphoria Blues*

"Norse Truth," 2016, *Shape Shift with Me*

Success, however, did nothing to quell Gabel's gender dysphoria. Whip-smart, if not book-steady, Gabel followed a path not unfamiliar to suburban teens and twenty-somethings, involving bad decisions and self-abuse, tempered with dreams and musical strivings. Listening to English punk, notably the anarchist collective Crass, Gabel embraced its DIY ethics and insurgent attitude. A youthful but informed idealism guided many of Against Me!'s songs.

Gabel emerged as a singer-songwriter able to articulate injustice and inequity in infectious, melodic, but urgent punk songs. The band vibe, angry but not alienating, set the stage for a slow, steady-ish climb for the foursome. When commercial success came calling in 2005, in the person of Sire Records, punk purist fans cried sellout. At twenty-five, Gabel was at once thrilled, fearful of a credibility hit, and terrified that cross-dressing would interfere with the band's career. So, he stopped. But the torturous angst continued.

The albums *New Wave* (2007) and *White Crosses* (2010) and endless touring solidified Against Me! as a consistently powerful presence in the punk scene. But beneath the rise to success and numerous relationships with women, the omnipresent, pained ghost of a girl lurked. Clues were blatant in lyrics such as "Confessing childhood secrets / of dressing up in women's clothes / Compulsions you never knew the reasons to" in "Searching for a Former Clarity."

In 2007, Gabel married for the second time (his first he dismissed as a youthful foible), and he and his wife had baby daughter Evelyn two years later. But it was becoming increasingly clear he couldn't keep "her" down. In a 2009 journal entry, Gabel wrote: "I need to kill Tom Gabel, destroy his ego."

It still took three years to begin that process. In

2012, he began hormone replacement therapy and became "Laura," the name his mother would have chosen if he'd been born female. Outing herself en masse via the *Rolling Stone* article, Grace garnered support from the music industry and most fans. Her father, however, hasn't spoken to her since the magazine came out.

If Grace knew who she was, the rest of the world was not always certain. But Grace has been glad to chronicle—in song—and explain, in gracious interviews. As she notes in the title track on *Transgender Dysphoria Blues*, "you want them to see you / Like they see every other girl / They just see a faggot / They'll hold their breath not to catch the sick."

Grace continues her own transition and education, along with her fans. When she asks them to shape-shift with her—"What have you got to lose"—the answer is "everything," despite the bold punk posturing of the lyric that follows: "fuck it."

Yet shape-shifting she is. Six foot two, blue eyes rimmed in black pencil, long brown hair, short painted nails, and solid but wiry physique, Grace is a powerhouse. She still dresses mostly in black, the occasional sundress subbing for black jeans. It's about comfort and onstage functionality, she says. But as she sings songs written when she was an angry, aggravated twenty-year-old boy, the same spirit, talent, and soul shine through. The only thing that's changed are the pronouns. "I'm still me," she says in *Tranny*.

Thomas Gabel was a teenage anarchist for sure. But Laura Jane Grace is a punk princess and transgender heroine, and, as she told me in an interview, "it's made me a better person. I'm much nicer to be around. I think that just by coming out, just by accepting who I was and moving on, I was able to clear a huge weight off my shoulders and really genuinely change as a person." ■

AMY WINEHOUSE

STEPHANIE PHILLIPS

ILLUSTRATION BY WINNIE T. FRICK

"Amy, Amy, Amy." So goes the refrain and title of a lesser known song from the late North London soul singer Amy Winehouse. The last track from her debut album *Frank* (2003) contains the essential ingredients for which Winehouse was known: expressive contralto vocals and tongue-in-cheek lyrics. The prophetic song and its admonishing refrain focus on Amy's craving for the opposite sex, but knowing the troubled singer's life, it's probable this wasn't the only context in which her name was strung together thrice—like a tsk, tsk, tsk. Much like the jazz singers she idolized, Winehouse didn't listen to advice, instead continuing fatally down the well-trodden self-destructive artist's path strewn with creative highs, debilitating addictions, and dramatic outbursts.

From the moment she burst onto the music scene, Winehouse's modern take on jazz coupled with her gregarious personality made her an unforgettable presence. Her world-weary voice harked back to the greats, such as Ella Fitzgerald and Billie Holiday. Her lyrics were often warm, witty, and honest observations on life, making her even more relatable. Along with Adele, Amy seemed to be one of the inheritors of the crown for queen of blue-eyed soul, a vacancy that had not been filled since the death of British soul singer Dusty Springfield in 1999. Despite her short-lived, tumultuous career, she achieved critical and commercial success, winning a cavalcade of awards, including several Grammys and three of England's prestigious Ivor Novello Awards. She will forever be remembered for her bad-girl look and classic songs such as "Rehab" and "Back to Black." In death, and for the last few years of her life, her demons and the crushing nature of celebrity obscured her original talent as one of the great British soul singers.

Winehouse was born on September 4, 1983, in North London. She had a relatively normal Jewish upbringing, living with her older brother, Alex; her mother, Janis, a pharmacist; and her father, Mitch, a cab driver who factored heavily in her life. In the posthumous documentary *Amy* (2015), directed by Asif Kapadia, we learn that her parents' separation when she was nine was a life-changing moment for the young Amy. She later went through the normal terrible teen behavior expected after her parents' divorce: drinking, talking back, getting expelled from school. She also displayed problems that pointed to her later struggles with depression and bulimia.

Beginning at a young age, Winehouse sang with her father, who influenced her music tastes. She grew up listening to such classic jazz artists as Frank Sinatra, Dinah Washington, Sarah Vaughan, Thelonious Monk, and Tony Bennett, the latter of whom she later worked with on his album *Duets II* (2011). Her grandmother saw potential in the young Amy and told her family to enroll her in theater school. After becoming a featured vocalist in the National Youth Jazz Orchestra, her big break came when her friend singer Tyler James gave her demo to Nick Shymansky, a young A&R rep at a management company owned by Simon Fuller, who famously managed the Spice Girls. Shymanksy instantly warmed to the young Winehouse and gave her studio time to record a demo, which she used to bag a record deal with Island Records and a management deal with Fuller's company in 2002.

Winehouse was only nineteen at the time but was already tipped for success. At a time when the public was growing tired of the unwieldy mass of lookalike pop stars churned out by reality TV shows, Amy represented real talent. She was a headstrong young woman who was determined to be an authentic artist. Most important, she was honest and didn't lie to her audience. If she was bored, you'd know about it; if she thought you were fake, you'd know about that, too.

Her debut album, appropriately titled *Frank* (2003), stayed true to Winehouse's nature. She worked with producer Salaam Remi to craft a portrait of her world, documenting her tales of wild nights out ("Fuck Me Pumps"), lost loves ("Take the Box"), and pathetic boyfriends ("Stronger than Me"). Amy clearly challenged herself, singing at the top of her range on songs like her cover of "Moodys Mood for Love," showcasing her unique skills as a vocalist. The album was a critical success and earned her an Ivor Novello for her songwriting, though she later stated that there were parts of the album that she disliked. Behind the honesty and witty jokes in *Frank* is a sadness that Winehouse tried to mask. On "What Is It About Men" Amy sings about her destructive side, seemingly at peace with her inevitable collision with fate. She believed in the tortured jazz singer trope, seeing her drinking and chaotic love life as fodder for her songs, a belief she would continue to push to its extreme.

After her first album, Winehouse spent years, in her own words, playing pool and drinking in her local Camden pub until she finished her second album. *Back to Black* (2006), produced by Salaam Remi and Mark Ronson, was inspired by her breakup and eventual reconciliation with her boyfriend, Blake Fielder-Civil. The album almost didn't happen when the label threatened to drop her as her drinking steadily got out of control. At a loss, they recommended she go to rehab, a move her dad infamously decided was not for her. It was a pivotal point in her life, when Amy could have possibly received the help she needed. But she was at heart a daddy's girl, so she didn't go. Instead she made a hit record, "Rehab," out of the incident and proceeded to collide headfirst with a new level of fame and notoriety. With influences from the Ronettes to Motown, *Back to Black* signified Winehouse's arrival as the tortured woman of the blues. Winehouse used veteran New York singer Sharon Jones's backing band, the Dap-Kings, to achieve the sound of the sixties in the studio and on tour. She abandoned some of the perfection of her earlier jazz stylings to explore the lower register in her vocals and revel in melancholy. Horns and delicate piano keys float around her every tale of woe, almost playing down the severity of her songs.

PLAYLIST

"You Sent Me Flying," 2003, *Frank*

"In My Bed," 2003, *Frank*

"Love Is a Losing Game," 2006, *Back to Black*

"Rehab," 2006, *Back to Black*

"Back to Black," 2006, *Back to Black*

During this time Winehouse worked on her defining look, pairing Ronettes-inspired beehives and thick eyeliner with tank tops and tiny jeans. The look was brought together by the multitude of 1950s pinup tattoos covering her now petite and fragile frame. So precise was her look that lead singer of the Ronettes, Ronnie Spector, credited Winehouse with making her know that her work mattered and began incorporating a cover of "Back to Black" into her live shows.

As her success grew and the accolades rolled in, Winehouse descended into self-destruction. She married Fielder-Civil, who introduced her to hard drugs, which further accelerated her downfall. The media circus that surrounded Winehouse turned her into a laughingstock. Propelled into a world that wasn't her own, she found herself in a place she didn't want to be. Her fame was at odds with who she saw herself as at heart, which was just a musician. In early interviews she laughed at the idea that she could become famous, insisting she wouldn't be able to handle it if she did.

After a stretch of disastrous gigs, Winehouse tried to get herself together. She had already separated from Fielder-Civil, had stopped drinking and taking drugs, and was dating someone new. She seemed on the road to recovery until July 23, 2011, she was found dead in her Camden home, a result of alcohol poisoning. She was mourned and celebrated as fans tried to recover from the shock of losing someone they thought was working through her demons.

As Winehouse was such a huge fan of jazz, it's poetic that her last recording was a cover of "Body and Soul" with one of her idols, Tony Bennett. Nervous at first, Winehouse perked up when Bennett compared her style to Dinah Washington. The pair seemed to connect, harmonizing as if they had been singing together for thirty years. After one recording session, Bennett captured a sense of who Winehouse really was. Speaking to *Entertainment Weekly* about the late singer, Bennett said: "Some people think that anyone could sing jazz, but they can't. It's a gift of learning how to syncopate but it's also a spirit that you're either born with or you're not. And Amy was born with that spirit." ■

A SEAT AT THE TABLE

She's striding down the street in a yellow ruffled dress and braids, wielding a bat. Her husky voice is at its thickest and deepest, all funky Southern drawl over a languid reggae beat, as she reminds her lover of her considerable assets, number one: the other women "don't love you like I love you." "Miss Thing" is on fire. Flames shoot out as if from gas explosions behind her, as she mounts a one-woman riot. With pure intentional devilish joy, she swings the bat into car windows, a fire hydrant, a piñata, store windows, more cars, a security camera, and finally, staring straight into the lens with delicious malice aforethought, the camera that has been shooting this whole scene. The artist who for two decades has dominated pop with her vocal prowess, progressive anthems, irresistible beats, and looks so perfect that one prominent feminist dubbed her a "terrorist" knocks the male gaze out cold, then climbs into a monster truck and rides over a line of cars.

Don't mess with Beyoncé Knowles.

The 2016 film and album *Lemonade* was a masterpiece of beats, words, and visuals, the emotionally raw but aesthetically baroque statement of a lifelong pop star who was finally claiming the R-E-S-P-E-C-T long overdue her, personally, professionally, and artistically. And politically: Beyoncé had already declared herself a feminist with the 2013 song "Flawless" (and an independent woman years before that), but with *Lemonade*, she connected directly to a growing movement of black activists tired of systemic racism and proud of their own culture. The film quotes Malcolm X: "The most disrespected person in America is the black woman." Sadly, the Grammys proved the continuing truth of that statement when they passed *Lemonade* over for album of the year. Even the winner was outraged; Adele was in tears as she tried to share the trophy with the artist who had inspired her own career, a noble gesture demonstrating the ongoing wattage of girl power.

In the twenty-first century female musicians smashed windows, boxes, ceilings. Kesha sued the producer who had guided her pop hits, accusing him of sexual abuse. Taylor Swift and Adele set sales records. Lady Gaga wore a meat dress to an awards show. Pussy Riot stormed the citadels of Russian patriarchy. And Beyoncé won the Super Bowl with her all-girl band.

But it was another Knowles who made clear women's minimum demand moving forward: *A Seat at the Table*. With that 2016 album, Solange stepped firmly out of her big sister's shadow. The Knowles girls were clearly drinking the same lemonade, crafting compelling protest statements about black identity and female empowerment. But where Beyoncé channeled rage with the powerhouse techniques of Tina Turner and Patti LaBelle, Solange offered a seemingly mellow, jazz-tinged reflection in the soprano stylings of Minnie Riperton and Diana Ross. Don't be fooled by her sotto voce: the younger Knowles was not requesting a seat; she was declaring it. For at least one hundred years, since Bessie Smith was anointed the Empress of the Blues, through Aretha Franklin being declared the Queen of Soul, to Solange's sister the King Bey, music has given otherwise disempowered women regal authority. "Don't touch my crown," Solange warns on "Don't Touch My Hair," an homage to black beauty standards and pride. Then she takes her seat not just at the table, but at its head.

M.I.A.

ALI GITLOW

ILLUSTRATION BY WINNIE T. FRICK

In the 2004 music video for M.I.A.'s first single "Galang," the rapper dances energetically, invoking classic hip-hop swagger and busting moves that appear like attempts at taking flight. The song offers a thoroughly modern mishmash of UK grime drum machine thuds, Caribbean dancehall vibes, and video game bleeps topped off by singsong, cocksure vocals that culminate in a joyous battle cry. M.I.A. wears a variety of hyper-colored outfits, from a pink and black ski jacket paired with massive, intricate gold earrings to a hoodie with a cartoonish-yet-menacing face on it. The animated background features her own vibrant stencil art. Looking closely, the viewer realizes that palm trees, tigers, and Nokia cell phones are mingling with much more sinister imagery, including bombs, tanks, fighter jets, and bundles of dynamite.

Though her videos have become flashier over the years, M.I.A.'s primary project has always remained the same: to trick us into nodding our heads along to slick pop tunes with banging beats, all the while shining a light on the plight of underrepresented Third World populations, most specifically those affected by the Sri Lankan civil war. As she revealed to *Nirali Magazine* the same year the "Galang" video was released, "I wanted to see if I could write songs about something important and make it sound like nothing."

Born Mathangi Arulpragasam in 1975 in west London, the woman who goes by Maya moved with her family back to Sri Lanka when she was six months old. Her father—an engineer, activist, and co-founder of the separatist group Eelam Revolutionary Organisation of Students—wanted to be involved firsthand in the fight for the country's Tamil minority to establish a sovereign state apart from the Sinhalese majority. There, M.I.A. experienced a fraught childhood, dodging war-torn neighborhoods with her mother, a seamstress, and rarely seeing her father. Just before her eleventh birthday the family returned to London minus Dad, settling as refugees on a council estate in the city's southwestern outskirts. There, she learned English and developed the persona of a true British rude girl: streetwise and cheeky, a chancer with "good chat." While traveling through the multicultural metropolis she came into contact with many types of music blaring out of flats and cars, from American hip-hop to Indian bhangra, punk, and Britpop, to African tunes, chart pop, and R&B, to electronic dance tracks of all stripes. This exposure ultimately informed her entire aesthetic and worldview, inspiring her to create intricate mosaics of urban sounds.

Eventually, M.I.A. attended university at the prestigious Central Saint Martins, where she studied film and visual art. Although she had no formal musical training, in 2001 friends convinced her to start writing her own songs using a Roland MC-505 groovebox. She uploaded the resulting six-track demo to her MySpace page, making her one of the world's first recording artists to garner widespread attention via the internet. This demo caught the ear of XL Recordings, who signed her in 2004 and released her first album, *Arular*, named after her then basically estranged father, the following year. Featuring career-defining singles including "Pull Up the People" and "Sunshowers" (which was censored by MTV for its reference to the PLO) and album art once again using her confrontational graffiti imagery, she became an underground sensation. The hipster set loved her immediately—members of the iPod generation used to having thousands of songs at their fingertips identified with her multi-genre approach. Her sound was cemented through an early alliance with Diplo, a then unknown fellow tastemaker who introduced club kids to styles as disparate as Brazilian baile funk, Miami bass, and Angolan kuduro via sweaty, raucous DJ sets. The pair started dating in 2004 and collaborated on a mixtape, *Piracy Funds Terrorism*. On tour together, M.I.A. gained notice for her Day-Glo garments designed by young brands like Cassette Playa, associated with London's then burgeoning New Rave scene.

M.I.A. has released five studio albums addressing a large swath of issues, including guerilla warfare, the global refugee crisis, daily life in London, the internet, and government surveillance. However, it wasn't until the Clash-sampling tune "Paper Planes" that she gained mainstream attention. Co-written with Diplo (after a rough breakup) and his frequent collaborator Switch, it features a syrupy slow tempo—yet, by the time the chorus is reached, a cacophony of cash register cha-chings and gunshots ring out in a way that is, somehow, really catchy. First released on her second studio album, *Kala*, put out by XL and Interscope in 2007, "Paper Planes" gained major traction once it was included on the *Slumdog Millionaire* soundtrack in 2008. It was also sampled by Jay-Z, T.I., Kanye West, and Lil' Wayne in their monumental hit "Swagga Like Us," which they performed onstage with a heavily pregnant M.I.A. at the 2009 Grammy Awards, where both versions of the song were nominated. In true provocateur form the female rapper wore a sheer black dress with pop-art-style polka-dot patches covering her breasts and stomach. Three days later her son Ikhyd (pronounced, fittingly, i-Kid) was born. (His father is Ben Bronfman, a musician, environmentalist, and Seagram's heir to whom M.I.A. was engaged.)

What's perhaps most striking about M.I.A.'s career is her choice not to water down her music or her message, despite pressures to do so. As the only Tamil widely known in the West, she has said she feels a responsibility to act as a spokesperson for those who don't have the luxury of expressing their views. She maintains that she has never taken sides in the Sri Lankan conflict despite her father's involvement. Because the media has often incorrectly linked him to the militant Tamil Tigers, she's even been accused of supporting terrorism and denied US travel visas at various times. As she has achieved a certain level of renown, this burden of representation has gotten her into trouble, whether for depicting an imagined genocide of red-haired boys in her video for the 2010

PLAYLIST

"Galang," 2005, *Arular*

"Sunshowers," 2005, *Arular*

"Bucky Done Gun," 2005, *Arular*

"Paper Planes," 2007, *Kala*

"Bird Flu," 2007, *Kala*

"Born Free," 2010, *Maya*

"Bad Girls," 2013, *Matangi*

"Borders," 2016, *AIM*

single "Born Free," flipping the bird while performing with Madonna at the 2012 Super Bowl, or asking WikiLeaks founder Julian Assange to open a stage show via Skype. M.I.A.'s fame has also caused some to question her authenticity. The fact that she went to art school, performs for large crowds of white kids, and moved to a fancy neighborhood in Los Angeles has caused journalists to accuse her of perpetuating "revolutionary chic."

Many critics have gotten bogged down with the nitty-gritty of M.I.A.'s political beliefs. In doing so, they've missed the bigger picture: by refusing to be silenced, she's almost singlehandedly made the Western world aware of Sri Lanka's violent past and proved that pop music and serious subject matter don't need to be mutually exclusive. As she explained in a 2016 *New York Times* interview, "I had the choice to shut my mouth . . . in order to catapult my fame and popularity and my bank balance. But that's not the choice I made." ∎

RIHANNA

REBECCA HAITHCOAT

ILLUSTRATION BY LINDSEY BAILEY

In every young female pop star's life, there comes a moment when, having sung scales with the vocal coach, run trails with the personal trainer, boosted her follower count with the social media expert, been plucked and bleached and contoured and primped by the glam squad, her music label executives present her with an opportunity to shed the sweet, bubblegum image that endeared her to parents everywhere and rise to her potential . . . as a sexpot. Whether that entails playing up the pigtailed schoolgirl gimmick or trading in jeans and a T-shirt for a pushup bra and lip-plumping injections, these transitions are typically orchestrated by marketing and publicity departments, suits who haven't read *Lolita* but pant over the Stanley Kubrick movie poster.

Rihanna played along with the standard "good girl gone bad" narrative. In fact, she named her third album exactly that—*Good Girl Gone Bad* (2007). But the cheeky self-consciousness of that title revealed that the Barbadian Bardot knew she was playing a role.

And then, Rihanna stopped playing.

The night before her cover shoot for the album, she sliced off her beauty pageant-long hair without permission, much to her label's dismay. They'd wanted edgy, but this was too edgy.

Too bad. From the beginning, Rihanna planned on steering her own career. In 2005, as her star was just beginning to streak through the sky with "Pon de Replay," the lead single from her debut album *Music of the Sun*, she did an interview with MTV News. She was only seventeen years old, but she already burned with determination and intention: "[I want to be] remembered as Rihanna . . . Just remembered as me."

Born Robyn Rihanna Fenty in Bridgetown, Barbados, the future Caribbean pop queen's childhood was tumultuous due to her father's drug and alcohol addiction. She was a loner and suffered from crippling headaches but found respite in music, listening to everything from reggae trailblazers like Barrington Levy to pop divas like Whitney Houston. In 2004, she entered a local audition and ended up singing for two American record producers who happened to be in the audience, Evan Rogers and Carl Sturken. She moved in with Rogers's family in Connecticut while they worked on securing her a deal. She'd always been shy, but when she auditioned for a group of executives at Def Jam that included Jay-Z, L.A. Reid, Jay Brown, and Tyran "Ty Ty" Smith, Brown said the sixteen-year-old had fire in her eyes. Rihanna signed with Def Jam.

That fire fueled her swift ascent to pop royalty, as did her appearance. With perfectly symmetrical marble-green cat eyes, a caramel complexion that

looks good with hair colors from tawny blonde to Ronald McDonald red, and Coke-bottle curves, Rihanna emanates sultriness. She never quite cultivated an innocent image to dismantle—see "There's a Thug in My Life" on *Music of the Sun*—and if there has been a constant in the pop icon's career, it's her open embrace of her sexuality. Even when she was seventeen, she seemed determined to do what she pleased, and not simply out of teenage rebellion. A glint in her eye hinted that she already understood what was expected of her, what wasn't, and, most importantly, how she'd toy with both of those unspoken directives when given the chance. "I just have a way of breaking the rules even when I don't intend to," she told *NME* in 2015.

"Pon de Replay," a grinding, sweaty dancehall track whose name and riddim played on her Caribbean roots, first sent her soaring. Several excellent pop songs followed, including "Umbrella," which established her signature nonsense vocalizations, cribbed from co-writer the Dream: *"eh-eh," "na-na," "ay-ay-ay."* By the time she was out of her teens, Rihanna had already won a Grammy Award for Best Rap/Sung Collaboration for "Umbrella" and handily moved away from her early "island girl" image, experimenting with rock, pop, and electronic music.

Upon leaving a pre-Grammy party in the wee hours of February 8, 2009, Rihanna suddenly found the media spotlight trained on her for an entirely different reason. While driving in L.A. with then boyfriend R&B singer Chris Brown, the couple began to fight. According to a detective's affidavit, Brown tried to push Rihanna out of his car, punched her repeatedly, bit her on the ear, choked her to the point of her almost losing consciousness, and allegedly threatened to kill her. Brown eventually was charged with two felonies, to which he pled guilty. Later, Rihanna said being asked to discuss the night with journalists was like being "punished over and over."

Clearly, the assault colored the music she was making. *Good Girl Gone Bad* had matured her sound, but it was *Rated R* (2009), her risky fourth album she was writing during that turbulent time, that revealed a personal maturation and set her on her current creative course. L.A. Reid reportedly told Rihanna he was "scared about" it. Something seemed to have been loosened internally, and "Rude Boy" sounded as if it came from an altogether different artist, one who delighted in the earthy joys of being a woman and in her sexuality. Like most pop artists, she'd toyed with sex talk by using double entendre before (2006's "Shut Up and Drive" imagines her as a sleek, high-speed vehicle just desperate for someone to drive it). But by dropping the smokescreens, she was going boldly where few bona fide pop stars ever dare— openly championing a healthy sex drive. With her languid delivery of bold lyrics ("Kiss It Better," she urges before diving into "Sex with Me": "And it's always wet . . . I'ma need you deeper than six"), she made it clear she enjoyed sex, but not in the performative, "for men" way burgeoning female pop stars often do. This was the work of a woman unafraid of her appetites.

Since breaking down that barrier, Rihanna has continued to stake out space for modern women, dipping into ever-racier fare with surprisingly little blowback, considering her mainstream audience.

PLAYLIST

"Umbrella," 2007, *Good Girl Gone Bad*

"Rude Boy," 2009, *Rated R*

"What's My Name," 2010, *Loud*

"Cockiness (Love It)," 2011, *Talk That Talk*

"Birthday Cake," 2011, *Talk that Talk*

"We Found Love," 2011, *Talk That Talk*

"Stay," 2012, *Unapologetic*

"Work," 2016, *Anti*

"Sex with Me," 2016, *Anti (deluxe edition)*

"Love on the Brain," 2016, *Anti*

"Cockiness (Love It)" finds her pumping out sly, almost-explicit phrases like, "Suck my cockiness, lick my persuasion"—a working girl's anthem. On "What's My Name," she assumes the typically male, dominant role, demanding Drake say *her* name, not the other way around. *Anti* (2016), which was certified platinum two days after its release, is the work of an artist at her creative peak and a woman at her most confident. "You was just another nigga on the hit list . . . Didn't they tell you that I was a savage?" she purrs on "Needed Me," a delightful appropriation of the wham-bam-thank-you-ma'am jam. If the record label thought chopping off her hair was edgy, imagine the conversations they had around the XXX "Sex with Me."

From the knowingness in her smile to her ballsy delivery of songs that even a male artist would've been discouraged from recording two decades ago, Rihanna has become a symbol for freedom of expression, for doing what the fuck you want when the fuck you want, simply by being herself. She's a sex symbol, yes, but that's reductive. She is what we collectively desire—what we desire *to be*, free from society's expectations of female politeness and propriety. If the dream is for women to be as comfortable within their skin as men, then Rihanna is the woman we put on the poster. She can brag about being the best in bed, throw middle fingers at the world, wear her pajamas in public, and walk out of a restaurant still holding her wineglass. Remembered as Rihanna? Easy. ∎

ANA TIJOUX

MICHELLE THREADGOULD

ILLUSTRATION BY ANNE MUNTGES

On September 13, 1973, Victor Jara, the Chilean folk hero and founder of the Nueva Canción (New Song) movement, was tortured with his hands nearly severed from his wrists, shot forty times, and murdered by the Chilean government alongside hundreds of others in front of a stadium of thousands. Two days earlier, military general Augusto Pinochet had overthrown the democratically elected socialist president of Chile, Salvador Allende, launching a forty-year reign of terror during which thirty thousand Chileans disappeared, two hundred thousand were imprisoned, twenty-two thousand were widowed, and sixty-six thousand were orphaned.

It was the moment song was silenced. Or, the moment Nueva Canción began its resurrection as a global protest movement.

Four years later, in France, two prominent leftist sociologist exiles from Chile gave birth to a girl who would bring Nueva Canción into the twenty-first century: Ana Tijoux.

Tijoux's parents did not choose the label *exiles*, they were exiled, a difference that Tijoux noted in an interview for *Emeequis*. And so Tijoux was born with the anger of being violently dispossessed. In her hit song "1977," the rapper and singer explains that during the year of her birth, the phrase "no me digan no" or "don't tell me no" became her guiding

light. She describes her body as an instrument, beating out of step with her surroundings, and fighting feelings of impotence as she watched her home country become increasingly militarized.

For sixteen years, the only Chile she knew was from afar. Her relatives back home sent her tapes of Victor Jara and Violeta Parra, and their voices informed Ana's own resistance. Parra, part indigenous herself, was the first woman to travel to remote parts of Chile and find traditional songs of the native people, transforming them into feminist critiques of the wealthy elite, songs that would inspire Jara to join her alongside the socialist and communist movement and support Allende and his bid for presidency. Her songs fought the classist ideas of who could make art and what art could be about, and even in her love songs, she flipped the patriarchy script. When Parra killed herself in 1967, her beautifully difficult work lived on in the covers of her song "Gracias a la Vida" by Mercedes Sosa and Joan Baez. These artists translated the suffering of Chileans without a pop veneer; instead a raw, luminescent anger emboldened their work, as it would for Tijoux.

As Tijoux developed her voice, she saw solidarity between her struggles and those of the poor, working-class, indigenous, and oppressed populations of the world. Instead of numbing herself to a type of cultural amnesia prevalent in the pop culture of Chile today, Tijoux chose to confront subjects like feminicide, police brutality, sexual assault, environmental destruction, patriarchy, and political corruption. And she chose to tell the stories of those who don't have a voice, from Palestinian refugees to the imprisoned in the US.

You could say that for Tijoux, even her choice of form, rapping, is confrontational—it challenges the prevalence of anti-Blackness within Latin America. The way that she interprets the genre offers a modern mestizo of different facets of her culture. Tijoux's flow has Zack de la Rocha elements, with lyrics that serve as a poetry of resistance. Yet, unlike most rappers, her singing hooks you. Her voice is emotional, glorious, possessing the clarity and pitch of a classically trained cabaret singer. Her compositions offer the unexpected, juxtaposing record scratches against Colombian flute playing and tribal Chilean drumming—all of which creates a sound that has deeply indigenous roots with themes that speak to now.

Soon after her homecoming to Santiago, Chile, in 1996, Tijoux began rapping with her newly found crew, Makiza. The group had an old-school, nineties sound, influenced by underground hiphop from New York, but with lyrics about protest and global unity. Makiza split ways after almost ten years together, and soon after, Tijoux collaborated with Mexican pop star Julieta Venegas, on the hit song "Eres Para Mi"; they set out on a world tour together. After the success of "Eres Para Mi," Tijoux worked on several side projects before finally striking out on her own.

Throughout her solo career, Ana's commitment to social progress has never waned, and she has continued to highlight issues of class, injustice, and sexism to critical acclaim. Three out of four of her full-length solo albums (*1977*, *La Bala*, and *Vengo*) have been nominated for Best Latin Rock Album at the Grammys. Her songs have caught the praise of Thom Yorke of Radiohead and were featured in *Breaking Bad*. Success has only strengthened her mission, and her latest work discusses Black Lives Matter, the Palestinian and Israeli conflict, and the violent government response to Chilean student protests. Tijoux's music reveals what intersectional rap, politics, and feminism can look like.

For Tijoux, feminism is not a commercialized product for pop stars to coronate themselves with; rather, it's an ideology that she feels needs to be adopted by all in order to combat the machismo, high rate of sexual assault, limited opportunities for women, and feminicide plaguing not only Latin America but the world. In her song "Antipatriarca," the lyrics are both her declaration of freedom and a manifesto against patriarchy. The song discusses all of the roles women can take on: ally, partner, teacher, daughter, mother, friend—anything that women want to be.

Tijoux's music and ideology are about transcending the roles assigned to women and deconstructing the imposed idea of women as sex objects. In her critical essay for *Walker Magazine*, "La Cultura de la Basura" (The Culture of Garbage), Tijoux portrays the ways that women performers are made to denigrate themselves, by performing for the male gaze.

PLAYLIST

"1977," 2010, *1977*

"Shock," 2011, *La Bala*

"Somos Sur," 2014, *Vengo* (featuring Shadia Mansour)

"Antipatriarca," 2014, *Vengo*

"Oro Negro," 2014, *Vengo*

"Luchín," 2016, single

"Calaveritas," 2017, single (featuring Celso Piña)

Every female singer must compete in an infinite game of provocation. Now nothing is enough, and nothing is too much, the goal is to put everything on display, always setting a new challenge with a higher bar: who can show more and more, who can achieve the most extreme contortions in the most acrobatic way, who is the most desirable, and who has the highest ability to annul the most beautiful femininity, to transform it into something and not someone.

To the former exiled, patriarchy is like oil seeping into our water and our environment, contaminating everything it touches. The only way to stop it is to fight back. Tijoux's music gives voice to women who can see the role that society wants to give to them and instead of passively accepting it, seek to remake their roles into the visions of themselves that they want to be. Like the founders of the Nueva Canción movement, Tijoux can see that the global struggle for liberation is a matter of life and death, and, as for those before her, the only life worth living is one that honors this struggle. ■

TAYLOR SWIFT

NEKESA MUMBI MOODY

ILLUSTRATION BY ANNE MUNTGES

Taylor Swift didn't exactly brim with confidence as a young teen.

Gangly and awkward, Swift would pour out her insecurities in her diary and then mine those pages to write the kind of country tunes that she hoped would make her famous. Her own mother described her as a bit of an "oddball" who suffered from classmate taunts for pursuing dreams of being a country singer—particularly because she grew up in Pennsylvania, which seemed a lifetime away from Nashville.

But while Swift may have been struggling with the same kind of self doubt most teens have, when it came to her songwriting talent, she was supremely assured—so much so that when a major label offered her a development deal, she turned it down because they wouldn't let her record her own songs.

She was fifteen years old.

"You don't just walk away from a big record label like that when you're an unsigned artist," Swift told me. "But I had a gut feeling about it, and some of the best decisions I've made in my career have been based on solely gut feelings and my instinct."

Certainly that label has rued their decision many times over. Not only did Taylor Swift come to dominate country music, she has also emerged as one of the premier songwriters of her time. Music critic Robert Christgau compared her favorably to Leonard Cohen; Ryan Adams was so taken with her craft that he rerecorded her songs for *1989* for his own album, also named *1989*. James Taylor—for whom she was named—called her remarkable.

Over time, she would shift from a country-centric sound to an overall pop groove that would include shades of dance, hip-hop, even EDM. (She famously revealed that she was the co-writer, under the pseudonym Nils Sjoberg, of ex-love Calvin Harris's hit for Rihanna, "This Is What You Came For.") No matter what genre she straddles, Swift has emerged as arguably pop's most influential figure. The music industry watches what she says like Wall Street monitors what the Federal Reserve does: both can cause seismic shifts with their actions.

Case in point: when Apple Music's then fledgling streaming service was trying to grow its subscription base, it offered fans three months free. But Apple had decided not to pay royalties to artists during that time. Some grumbled over the tech titan's policy, but it wasn't until Swift published an open letter to the company explaining that she would be withholding her music from the streaming service because of the equity issue that Apple changed its tune. Even Grammy-winning star Ed Sheeran owes his breakout in part to Swift, who took the fledgling singer-songwriter on tour and touted his music before he was well known in the States.

Of course, Swift's magic includes her own stunning sales numbers: her last four albums (*Reputation*, *1989*, *Red*, and *Speak Now*) all debuted to more than 1 milllion in sales in their first week, numbers that even superstars like Drake or Beyoncé can't match.

Just a few years ago, Swift was the fledgling artist. She first made her self-titled debut in 2006 as a wide-eyed country ingénue who longed for a career like her idol Tim McGraw, whose name she used to title her very first hit, a longing romantic ode that held out hope of "when you think 'Tim McGraw,' I hope you think my favorite song, the one we danced to all night long." "Tim McGraw," co-written with her then songwriting partner Liz Rose, was a tender hit that belied Swift's age; she was just fifteen years old when the song was released. The song had all the hallmarks of a veteran Nashville songwriter, but Swift was hardly a veteran. She wasn't even from Nashville.

Swift, the daughter of a stockbroker father and a stay-at-home mom, was born in Reading, Pennsylvania, but grew up with country dreams. She started playing guitar at eleven and was performing her favorite tunes by her favorite artists at local events until she convinced her parents that her talent was worth heading to Nashville for.

Taylor Swift was a triple-platinum success and garnered crossover buzz, but it wasn't until her second album, 2008's *Fearless*, that her career skyrocketed. Her gift for songwriting grew even stronger on her sophomore effort with songs like "White Horse" and "You Belong with Me." Though she was just eighteen when the album was released, the imagery and wistfulness of her lyrics showed a depth that songwriters ache to achieve. One could wonder where she got the life experience to write such tales, but Swift insisted they were all true emotions, perhaps more amplified in song than what she penned in her diaries at night. She was no vocal powerhouse like Carrie Underwood—her voice was lithe, and some would criticize it as downright thin. But it was expressive and had the emotional heft needed to bring her words to life.

Swift was already soaring when a career-defining moment—for the worse, not the better—occurred the next year. As is now part of pop folklore, Swift beat Beyoncé's "Single Ladies (Put a Ring on It)" and others for an MTV Video Music Award for best female video. She was accepting her VMA when Kanye West came on stage, grabbed her trophy, and infamously said, "Yo, Taylor, I'm really happy for you, Imma let you finish, but Beyoncé had one of the best videos of all time!"

While perhaps true, West's intervention left Swift onstage looking like a clubbed seal. The backlash was immediate; he was trashed by everyone from Pink to President Obama, and the public, already growing weary of his boorish antics, turned on him to such a degree he was forced to cancel a joint tour with Lady Gaga later that year. (It would also mark the beginning of a tortured relationship between West and Swift that would include songs about each other, a reconciliation, and yet another bitter fissure.)

West defenders (and West himself) would go on to claim that that moment, which cast him as the villain and Swift as the wounded girl next door, would

---

PLAYLIST

"Tim McGraw," 2006, *Taylor Swift*

"Our Song," 2006, *Taylor Swift*

"You Belong with Me," 2008, *Fearless*

"Fifteen," 2008, *Fearless*

"Mine," 2010, *Speak Now*

"Dear John," 2010, *Speak Now*

"I Knew You Were Trouble," 2012, *Red*

"We Are Never Ever Getting Back Together," 2012, *Red*

"Bad Blood," 2014, *1989*

"Blank Space," 2014, *1989*

make her famous, but Swift was already a star. The sales of *Fearless* were outpacing her first (it would eventually sell more than seven million copies in the US alone and win Swift her first Album of the Year Grammy) and she was already emerging as the It Girl of the moment. She even had a taste of tabloid attention with a failed romance with Joe Jonas.

As her fame grew, that taste became a steady diet. High-profile romances with very public images drew scrutiny and sometimes scorn, as did the pop-star feuds she would become entangled in. All were fodder for her music. While Swift prided herself on never revealing names in interviews, she also made it clear that despite her fame, her songs were still based on her diaries, and fans need only listen closely to decipher the clues.

One of her most brilliant—and brutal—take-downs in song would come on her third album, *Speak Now* (on which she wrote every song except one, which she cowrote). "Dear John" offers a blistering dressing down of a romancing cad who took advantage of her innocence. The song came a few months after tabloids reported a failed romance with John Mayer, and the lyrics seemed to hint at his woman-izing ways, but what may have been the tell-tale clue was the music: a wailing guitar centered the song, reminiscent of Mayer's own tracks.

While her honest lyrics were appreciated by fans and gossip editors, others used them as a point of con-tention, accusing Swift of trading her celebrity and personal life for hits—an odd criticism, given that most singer-songwriters rely on their own malaise or triumphs for inspiration. Swift couldn't help but vent about whether some of the criticism she endured was due to sexism. Certainly male pop stars weren't derided for the length of their relationships or the number of their partners, or questioned when they sang about their failed romances.

"No one says that about Ed Sheeran. No one says that about Bruno Mars. They're all writing songs about their exes, their current girlfriends, their love life and no one raises a red flag there," she bristled to one interviewer.

Swift would learn to take criticism and use it to her advantage. She eviscerated reviewers who took aim at her vocal abilities in "Mean" on *Speak Now*, and on *1989*, named for the year she was born, she pushed them to the side on the bouncy pop groove "Shake It Off": "Haters gonna hate hate hate, hate," she sang with a cheery dismissiveness.

She also managed to poke fun at her own image on "Blank Space," parodying her reputation as an obsessive lover: "Got a long list of ex-lovers / they'll tell you I'm insane / 'cause you know I love the play-ers / and you love the game."

Even the most ardent critic couldn't deny the wittiness of a table turned. Oddball no more, an adult Taylor Swift deftly used the taunts that used to draw tears to make hits, her confidence clearly soaring. ∎

ADELE

ANNIE ZALESKI

ILLUSTRATION BY JULIE WINEGARD

When Adele performed "Rolling in the Deep" at the 2012 Grammy Awards, it was the most anticipated—and anxiety-inducing—appearance of her career to date. The previous fall, she had vocal cord microsurgery to fix a hemorrhaging benign polyp, a condition that had caused the cancellation of multiple tour dates. The high-profile Grammys performance would mark the first time she had sung in public since the procedure, and questions swirled about how her voice might sound post-surgery.

With a defiant look on her face, Adele immediately demolished any such concerns. She sang the first few lines of "Rolling in the Deep" a cappella, in a clear and strong voice frilled with trills, and kept that steely resolve going as the song progressed. Adele effortlessly arced up to the chorus high notes and emphasized the tune's biting tone—courtesy of lyrics replete with kiss-offs toward an unworthy romantic partner—with stinging glee. By the song's end, she was teary-eyed as the star-studded audience rose and gave her a loud standing ovation. None other than Sir Paul McCartney raised an arm in triumphant solidarity.

No matter where she goes, Adele attracts this kind of universal affection. She's an artist for whom people root, a musician whose success and confidence draw plaudits, not jealous sniping.

That's largely because of her incomparable voice—a multi-octave holler with a dusky, lived-in tone that exudes longing—and a tender-but-tough underdog veneer she honed growing up as the only daughter of a hardworking single mom. Her ferocity is also an asset. As a songwriter, she favors brutally honest, raw-nerve lyrics about how to protect the heart after shattering breakups. Adele verbalizes the things everyone wants to say to an ex—whether vengeful and bitter, or wistful and pleading; she's a champion of the heartbroken.

Adele's music smartly places her voice and these sentiments front and center, favoring relatively simple instrumentation: soulful piano and guitar, majestic strings that unfurl like peacock feathers, and the rare burst of lively horns. These traditional sounds receive a modern polish thanks to producers such as Paul Epworth, Mark Ronson, and Greg Kurstin, whose input ensures her songs fit seamlessly on contemporary radio stations. Reconciling timeless and modern influences has made Adele enormously likeable. Her 2011 breakthrough, *21*, has sold more than 14 million copies in the US alone, and its follow-up, 2015's *25*, sold 3.38 million during its first week of release, shattering sales records. Adele has taken home fifteen Grammy Awards overall, including the prestigious Album of the Year Grammy for both *21* and *25*, and also landed an Oscar and a Golden Globe for her James Bond theme, "Skyfall."

With such impressive statistics, Adele has earned the right to boast about her achievements. Instead, she possesses an affable and unpretentious personality that makes her feel like a best girlfriend to her fans, the type of down-to-earth confidant you could call when you're looking to drown your sorrows over a dud dude or want to gush about Beyoncé. Adele herself showed off this humble nature—and her Queen Bey fandom—by using most of her 2017 Album of the Year acceptance speech to praise the superstar, whose *Lemonade* had been heavily favored to win this top award. She called *Lemonade* "monumental" and "beautiful and soul-baring," and addressed Beyoncé directly from the stage. "All us artists here, we fucking adore you," Adele said tearfully. "You are our light. And the way that you make me and my friends feel, the way you make my black friends feel, is empowering. And you make them stand up for themselves. And I love you. I always have and I always will." Adele's "black friends" remark attracted controversy: although many understood its heartfelt intent and saw it as a nod of respect to Beyoncé's status as a powerful role model for black women, others decried Adele for being racially insensitive or patronizing.

However, such off-the-cuff, honest banter is very in character for Adele. In concert, she makes arenas feel like intimate cabarets due to her casual demeanor (sample topics: cheerfully admitting to having a "potty mouth," taking selfies with fans, and joking about her lack of "happy songs"), while her press interviews are refreshingly candid and reveal her humility. She's also never hesitated to give back: in the wake of the devastating fire at Grenfell Tower,

a twenty-four-story apartment building in West London, Adele has been a constant and supportive presence, creating a fund for survivors and even renting out a movie theater screen so affected families could see *Despicable Me 3*.

This lack of pretense stems in part from her working-class roots. Born Adele Laurie Blue Adkins, the voracious music fan grew up in the London districts of Tottenham, Brixton, and West Norwood without her dad, who left when she was a toddler. Adele has occasionally been accused of appropriating R&B culture, but, as a budding vocalist, she reverently soaked up inspiration from the greats: jazz icon Ella Fitzgerald and soul legend Etta James; R&B powerhouses Lauryn Hill, Destiny's Child, and Alicia Keys; and pop mavens Céline Dion and the Spice Girls. Her mom, Penny, even added moodier sounds to the mix by sneaking her into a concert by the Cure. Adele, who also learned how to play guitar as she honed her voice, was empowered by such eclecticism. As a teen, she attended the BRIT School for Performing Arts and Technology, where classmates included sister

PLAYLIST

"Chasing Pavements," 2008, *19*

"Rolling in the Deep," 2011, *21*

"Someone Like You," 2011, *21*

"Set Fire to the Rain," 2011, *21*

"Rumor Has It," 2011, *21*

"Lovesong," 2011, *21*

"Skyfall," 2012, single

"Hello," 2015, *25*

"When We Were Young," 2015, *25*

"Send My Love (To Your New Lover)," 2015, *25*

pop stars Jessie J and Leona Lewis. After graduation, her career took off like a rocket: XL Recordings heard her demos posted on the then popular social network MySpace, and Adele signed a record deal.

The title of her 2008 debut, *19*, refers to how old Adele was when she was piecing together the album, not that the record makes it easy to guess her age: Adele is a precocious and perceptive writer who can zero in on exactly how she's feeling in the aftermath of a breakup, and describe it using poetic and elegant language. These descriptions of relationship fissures are so believable because Adele has lived through them all: both *19* and *21* are inspired by messy splits she's experienced in her own life. In fact, in interviews, Adele has made it clear that her litmus test for a successful song is whether she herself becomes emotional when recording it.

But although her depictions of angst, understandably, can be dramatic—"Set Fire to the Rain" uses fire-and-brimstone imagery to invoke an imploding relationship, and "Hello" possesses the grandeur of an old-school Hollywood epic—Adele also calibrates songs for maximum impact in subtle ways. That's most evident on *25*, a record that finds her grappling with more mature relationships,

such as the one with her now-husband, Simon, or the bond she has with her son, Angelo. In a nod to Adele's growth as a songwriter, *25* takes a more complex view of breakups—"When We Were Young" explores past slights and turmoil with a nostalgic tint—and incorporates a more modern sound based around slick keyboards and pop-leaning rhythms.

This album especially demonstrates that Adele's supernova success is no fluke. Better yet, it signals that she refuses to be stuck in heartbroken mode for her entire career, and isn't beholden to classic traditions. Although Adele's stylish music boasts soulful rigor, it isn't stuffy. Instead, she's crafted a singular approach to pop music, one that's a sophisticated throwback without being slavishly retro or too old-fashioned. Adele has singlehandedly redefined the sound of global superstardom. ∎

JANELLE MONÁE

DAPHNE A. BROOKS

ILLUSTRATION BY WINNIE T. FRICK

We are the ones we've been waiting for.
—June Jordan, "Poem for South African Women"

During that first year of Janelle Monáe's Afrosonic underground ascent back in 2008 to 2009, it was the mantra that I couldn't get out of my head whenever I caught her frenetic, rebelliously euphoric live show: "We are the ones we've been waiting for." True, it was also high-flying Obama time, and this was a line that the junior "hope and change" senator from Illinois was invoking on the presidential campaign trail quite a bit. But it was the late great black feminist activist, scholar, and poet June Jordan who first authored those words that so aptly capture what it felt like to watch Monáe back then, if you were a black girl rock nerd of a certain age who'd grown up wishing for her very own superhero. She was the manifestation of all of our Prince–Bowie–Parliament–Funkadelic–Grace Jones–Sun Ra–Octavia Butler dreams, an impish, androgynous beauty decked out in a tuxedo and a fancy coif that recalled the golden age of rock and soul. And she was armed with an arsenal of hypnotic moves and seductively mad skills: punk velocity, black new wave body music, James Brown squeals mixed with Poly Styrene screams, and silky R&B crooning that, taken together, felt both retro and otherworldly.

In that moment of her arrival on the pop scene in the wake of her breakthrough EP *Metropolis: The Chase Suite* (2008), she was inviting us to run with her right into the heart of an epic, Ziggy Stardust–style backstory. Here was the mythology: her alt-ego, Cindi Mayweather, a cyborg from the year 2719 and a fugitive from the state, might save us from straitjacketed notions of blackness, womanhood, and sexual desire and, likewise, turnstile-jump the pop music lanes in which black women artists are expected to stay put. *Transgress genres, break all the rules, and stage dive while you're at it.* This is what her sound and look whispered to me. And this is what Janelle Monáe's act was telling those of us who watched her burn through electrifying sets at venues like the Highline Ballroom in Manhattan in the summer of 2008 and the Afropunk Fest in Fort Greene Park, Brooklyn, soon after, as well as her much-hyped South by Southwest set in Austin, Texas, that following spring. Witnessing Monáe at each of these shows fearlessly bodysurfing the crowd with a sea of hands keeping her afloat, it felt as though rock and roll, black feminism, and science fiction had colluded in birthing the manifestation of what historian Robin Kelley calls our "freedom dreams." Afro-Gen X and Millennial avant-garde passions writ large had found a mythically rendered

(post)human host in which to spread the good news of black girl magic.

She came out of the Midwest—born Janelle Monáe Robinson in Kansas City, Kansas, on December 1, 1985—with a penchant for musical theater. The daughter of a mother who did janitorial work and a father who drove trucks, Robinson first studied drama at New York City's American Musical and Dramatic Academy before making her way to Atlanta, where she befriended OutKast's Big Boi, who served as an early champion of her cause. But the masterful and most inspired connection she would make once she arrived in black America's Southern capital were with a cluster of daring and bookish black bohemian artists: former Morehouse College students Chuck Lightning and Nate "Rocket" Wonder (known as the duo Deep Cotton) who, along with Wonder's fellow musician-composer brother Roman GianArthur, shared Monáe's Afrofuturist vision and love of boldly hybrid pop sounds. They ultimately co-founded the Wondaland Arts Society, a collective of black sonic experimentalists and activists whose manifesto pronounces, in part, that they "believe songs are spaceships," that "music is the weapon of the future," that "books are stars . . . " Together, Monáe and her Deep Cotton brothers declare in this retro, radical grassroots art statement that "[w]e believe in our own state, our own republic."

With Wondaland as a place, a state of mind, a cultural collective, and more recently a record label that she and her co-conspirators have launched in partnership with Epic (a division of Sony Entertainment), Janelle Monáe has pressed forward for nearly a decade now, forging a musical movement that shrewdly and whimsically absorbs, navigates, collects, and repurposes fragments of modern culture, history, and politics. With each successive album (*The ArchAndroid* from 2010 and *The Electric Lady* from 2013) and with each accompanying tour, she continues to spin the epic Mayweather escape narrative with metaphorically rich liner notes and orchestral soundscapes infused with dazzling cinematic (Fritz Lang's *Metropolis*, Ridley Scott's *Blade Runner*, Sun Ra's *Space Is the Place*) and literary (Butler's *Kindred*, Nalo Hopkinson's *Brown Girl in the Ring*) allusions. Monáe assembles a dense array of pixelated pop music culture citations as she beckons us to time-travel with her at a fast and furious pace. She gives us back our sonic cultural past in the form of that Little Richard pompadour, Godfather of Soul cape routine (a gesture that evokes the pinnacle of entertainment exertion and exhaustion as well as unbridled, unstoppable performance fervor), Stevie Wonder–inspired, empathic urban anthems, Bad Brains body-slamming jams, Jackson 5–era upper-register angst-ridden serenades, Mothership funk grooves, Hendrix psychedelia, and Minnesota Purple revolution rock all folded together as new millennium maelstrom.

From the Afro indie-alternative roots whence she came (and which she still claims as her home base), Monáe has, nonetheless, made bionic leaps into the bright lights mainstream, adding soaring vocals to Fun's 2012 global prom smash "We Are Young" and hitting the Hollywood jackpot with notable roles in two of 2016's most high-profile films. As "Theresa" in *Moonlight*, the best picture Oscar winner for that year, Monáe delivers a quietly stirring performance as a mentor figure to the adolescent outsider protagonist in Barry Jenkins's heartbreaker bildungsroman.

And as NASA mathematician Mary Jackson, she holds her own opposite seasoned vets like Taraji P. Henson and Octavia Spencer in *Hidden Figures*, the surprise box-office smash that celebrated the unheralded achievements of African American women who played pivotal roles in the space race.

Both films are clear extensions of the boundary-pushing vision that courses through Janelle Monáe's music. Repeatedly she takes us to the edge of our imagination and then pushes us far beyond. On, for instance, the slinky duet with her beloved mentor Prince, *The Electric Lady* track "Givin 'Em What They Love," the burn-this-mother-down ambition of the song's lyrics takes on a quietly ferocious tenacity with its menacing rhythm section, its sinuous rhythm guitar, and the reciprocating androgyny of Monáe and the Purple One's tense, powder-keg vocals. It is a song that reminds us of her sly virtuosity and the playful danger and risk that shape and drive Monáe's thrillingly eclectic and eccentric iconicity. Her existence is an affirmation of all that we have been and all that we may still be. With her we wage the "Cold War" of which she sings, continuously reminded by way of her sui generis pop artistry of exactly what it is that we're fighting for. ∎

PLAYLIST

"Violet Stars Happy Hunting!!!," 2007, *Metropolis: Suite I (The Chase)*

"Many Moons," 2007, *Metropolis: Suite I (The Chase)*

"Cold War," 2010, *The ArchAndroid*

"Tightrope," 2010, *The ArchAndroid*

"Come Alive (The War of the Roses)," 2010, *The ArchAndroid*

"Q.U.E.E.N.," 2013, *The Electric Lady* (with Erykah Badu)

"Electric Lady," 2013, *The Electric Lady* (with Solange)

"Givin 'Em What They Love," 2013, *The Electric Lady* (with Prince)

"We Were Rock and Roll," 2013, *The Electric Lady*

"Victory," 2013, *The Electric Lady*

LADY GAGA

ANNIE ZALESKI

ILLUSTRATION BY WINNIE T. FRICK

When Lady Gaga kicked off her 2017 Super Bowl halftime show with a simulated jump from the roof of Houston's NRG Stadium, the move was shocking, but totally in character. The flamboyant go-getter from a supportive Italian family has built her glitter-encrusted empire on daring leaps of faith.

Her boldness starts with a boundary-free musical vision, which borrows liberally from modern electronic and dance culture, futuristic hip-hop, classic rock and roll, and punk and new wave's anything-goes mentality. Beginning with the 2008 release of her debut *The Fame*, Gaga has bent musical trends to her will, subverting the charts with her bawdy vernacular and performative quirks such as stuttering choreography and a gesture whereby fans curl their hands into claws. Weirdness has always been an asset, not a liability, in Lady Gaga's universe.

The woman born Stefani Germanotta pairs this askew perspective with both intuitive and trained musical talent. An emotive and versatile performer, she hopscotches between horn-bolstered Broadway struts ("Teeth"), electro-flamenco sizzles ("Americano"), glam-punk swerves ("MANiCURE"), and guitar-seared power ballads ("Yoü And I"). Her voice can be smoky and torch song ready, seasoned by whiskey-fueled nights and too much heartbreak. At other times, she channels soaring soft rock legends such as Barbra Streisand or nods to the bluesy boogie of piano balladeer Elton John. Gaga knows when to make a performance pristine and when a ragged, grittier touch will work. No wonder she thrives on working with diverse collaborators, including Marilyn Manson, Queens of the Stone Age's Josh Homme, T.I., and Beyoncé.

Chalk this malleability up to her upbringing in culturally diverse New York City, shaped by clubs, church, and classic rock. Born in 1986, Gaga spent her childhood soaking up the works of musical greats. She gravitated toward eighties iconoclasts Michael Jackson, Cyndi Lauper, and Boy George, and absorbed the songwriting and swagger of the Rolling Stones, Led Zeppelin, and Billy Joel. The "Gaga" in her name refers to Queen's 1984 hit "Radio Ga Ga." *Aladdin Sane* by the chameleonic David Bowie altered her life, she has said. She learned how to play Bruce Springsteen's "Thunder Road" on piano in exchange for her dad getting a loan so they could buy a baby grand.

Gaga was raised on the Upper West Side and attended Convent of the Sacred Heart, a Catholic school known for its rigorous academic and religious curricula. This foundation occasionally tints her music and outlook. For example, in "Judas," a song brimming with biblical allusions, Gaga characterizes the titular character's betrayal as irresistible, akin to

a bad influence coming between a good girl and her devout faith.

Her spiritual solace, however, came from New York and its vibrant club scene. By age fourteen, she had already started performing at the Bitter End, a venue she returned to years later while singing and playing piano with a band. Later, Gaga frequented other Lower East Side haunts with more outré acts, especially after she dropped out of New York University's Tisch School of the Arts at age nineteen. Among her endeavors was the cheeky Lady Gaga and the Starlight Revue: the hodgepodge showcase found her playing songs on a keyboard amid antics such as her and pal Lady Starlight lighting hairspray on fire and dancing awkwardly onstage while wearing bras and underwear.

This fearless performance style fueled her transformation into a larger-than-life pop star. Gaga manifested a fabulous persona, like Dr. Frankenstein constructing his monster. Her stance was that of an outsider infiltrating pop music's inner circle. On *The Fame* (and its 2009 expanded reissue as *The Fame Monster*), she was hyper self-aware of celebrity culture and its pitfalls yet obsessed with accumulating and assimilating glamour. On *Born This Way* (2011) and *Artpop* (2013), she continued developing a manifesto based around reconciling striking individuality with fame's glitz. Throughout, Gaga exuded contradictions—she was bulletproof and vulnerable, messy and self-assured, emotionally damaged but strong.

Such unabashed quirkiness also helped Gaga amass legions of devoted fans. Fittingly, these loyalists became known as Little Monsters, with the star herself colloquially becoming Mother Monster. Both nicknames reclaim the negative connotation of the word as a badge of honor—a sign of how she's the grand marshal of a parade of freaks, outcasts, and rebels.

With the help of Haus of Gaga, a crew of artistic visionaries who make her surrealist fantasies come true, our Lady cultivates an outrageous visual veneer. She once accepted an MTV Video Music Award while wearing a dress made from flank steak and showed up at the 2011 Grammy Awards in an egg-like contraption from which she then "hatched" onstage to perform the misfit-empowering anthem "Born This Way." Gaga crafted sci-fi punk couture: impossibly tall high-heeled shoes, bras constructed from disco ball facets or seashells, and impractical clothing made out of space-age material. Even arriving at an airport, she is fully committed to the attention-getting Gaga lifestyle: in 2013, she was spotted at LAX wearing a sheer black skirt and a complicated black shirt with giant shoulder pads, looking rather like a stingray.

Lady Gaga intuitively understands that she can use pop music and fashion as a springboard for loftier pursuits. She has given millions of dollars to charity and, along with her mom, created the nonprofit, youth-oriented Born This Way Foundation. From speaking out against discriminatory legislation to being a vocal ally in the aftermath of the Pulse nightclub shooting, Gaga is an outspoken, tireless advocate for the LGBTQ community. She has toyed with gender conventions, assuming a male persona named Jo Calderone in 2010 for performances and photo shoots and releasing songs such as "G.U.Y.," a playful treatise on inverting relationship and sexual stereotypes. And she has never shied away from addressing weighty topics. In 2015, she leveraged her voice and platform and collaborated with Diane Warren on a sweeping orchestral ballad, "Til It Happens to You." The Oscar-nominated song appeared in a documentary called *The Hunting Ground* and addressed the deep impact of sexual assault.

Gaga's voracious creative appetite has led her far beyond the pop world. In 2014, she dueted with jazz legend Tony Bennett on *Cheek to Cheek*, an album of standards that won the artists a Grammy Award. Concurrently, Gaga pivoted to an acting career encompassing variety shows (2013's *Lady Gaga and the Muppets Holiday Spectacular*) and movies (a forthcoming role in a remake of *A Star Is Born*). She won a Golden Globe for her work on the TV show *American Horror Story: Hotel*.

With 2016's deeply personal *Joanne*, Gaga unveiled yet another chapter in her musical evolution. What hasn't changed is her underlying thirst for reinvention. A thoroughly modern pop star who revels in risk taking, she still operates like an aspiring performer scrapping in New York City clubs with nothing to lose, throwing caution to the wind in the name of artistic adventure. ∎

SANTIGOLD

DJ LYNNÉE DENISE

ILLUSTRATION BY LINDSEY BAILEY

The Philly-born, punk-schooled singer, songwriter, and producer Santigold comes from a lineage of fierce, independent, business-savvy, cutting-edge, socially conscious women who find a way to produce and not be (publicly) swallowed up by the by-products of success. Her fifteen-year presence in the music industry is no small thing, and when you check her ghostwriting credentials you'll see she's written for many of your favorite artists (Lily Allen, Ashlee Simpson, and Blaqstarr, to name a few). As a DJ, I'm a witness to her maturation, her growing global presence, and her interdisciplinary approach to the arts. Santigold embodies voices of the unsung.

Santi White was born and raised in Philadelphia, where her ear caught wind of the regional rhythm for which Philly is known. Not only was she within listening range of the Philadelphia soul sound and the masterful ministers of dance-floor activism (Gamble and Huff); she grew up alongside the burgeoning Soulquarian movement, a Questlove-led crew heralded as the founders of the annoyingly misnamed neo-soul music.

Santigold is a formally trained musician. She took her Philly soul education to one of the nation's most prestigious music schools, Wesleyan University, and double majored in African American studies and music. Significantly, sonic cultural knowledge and intellectual curiosity show up in her vocal arrangements, drum patterns, and lyrics. Equally curious is the fact that she dropped out of college to become an A&R rep for Epic Records—a partial nod to her do-it-yourself punk roots, choosing the alternative route to her future.

Between 2003 and 2005 White worked with Bad Brains bassist Darryl Jenifer, placing herself in direct conversation with black punk (pre-Afropunk) royalty. Santigold was the founding member and lead singer for the Philly-based punk band Stiffed, and she and Jenifer co-produced the band's two albums. This moment is significant due to the fact that black women have existed on the margins of punk music and culture for years. With her work with Stiffed we can trace Santi's footprints to NYC's and Philly's early 2000s underground punk and post-punk scene. Both Stiffed albums, *Sex Sells* (2003) and *Burned Again* (2005), are now part of a black punk archives that should be excavated.

It was on the East Coast punk scene where she was courted by London-based independent label Lizard King Records. This wouldn't be the first time that the UK, while poking their heads into American underground culture, would find some of our brightest; see N'dea Davenport, Jhelisa, Carleen Anderson, and early Detroit techno pioneers for proof. The UK soul scene (Soul II Soul, Massive

Attack, D'Influence, etc.) drew influences from diasporic Caribbean riddims, continental African polyrhythms, and black American funk. Santigold fits well within this tradition—this transnational artists community. By 2006, she was offered a solo contract by Lizard King.

When she finally dropped *Santogold* in 2008, she had staying power and exciting force behind her creative process. The album introduced us to the experimental nu-dub sounds of producer Diplo and pulled off that hard-to-achieve mature blend of electronic music and the "one drop," a style of reggae described by Louis Chude-Sokei as dropping out the beat on the dominant 1 and 3 beats in 4/4 time, so that you begin your rhythm with absence. These musical devices were then accentuated by an unexpected black woman's new wave voice floating between and on top.

Santigold didn't rush into her next album, showing her to be a student of the school of Sade, who averaged a new album every two to four years. And I say yes! Let it marinate, experience life, take your time, do it right. By the time Santigold's *Master of My Make Believe* dropped on March 1, 2012, the second album was indeed a demonstration of artistic investment. She made bold musical decisions, pushing in the direction of a fusion that seems to draw on everything from the Talking Heads to the vocal antics of Poly Styrene. What came through most was Santigold's signature ability to deliver cross-pollinated music with measurable confidence.

When Santigold released her third studio album, *99¢*, in 2016, it sent me to Joan Armatrading and from there to Grace Jones. In the retrospective glance, I found a thread—a shared dance on the lines that connect UK new wave to roots reggae and Caribbean punk—musical elements of the Black Atlantic coupled with rhythmic traces of migration. I understand Santigold and her place in music to be somewhat of an anomaly, but only when juxtaposed against pop artists who shine bright under the light of America's marketable musical mediocrity. Santigold has been functioning at capacity in an underworld—a world that must be sought out and unearthed, an underworld without super video budgets and automatic radio play, where ticket prices do not exceed that of a car note.

I'd like to challenge readers to think of Santigold as a variation of Beyoncé, or better yet, think of them as variations of each other. While the two are read as opposite, it's only because we're not given much of an opportunity to interface with the large number of multifaceted black women who make music. I would argue that both women stand in their craft with high levels of artistic integrity and did so for at least a decade before being "discovered." Both women have a clear commitment to the mastery of technical skills. And while the distinctions between the two are worth investigation, I'm moved by their collective drive and the evolutionary aspect of their respective practices. The fine tuning of every part of their projects is largely ignored because they are black women. People get real stingy when assigning the title genius to these particular bodies, and too generous in framing their work as naturally good versus ruthlessly perfected.

PLAYLIST

WITH STIFFED:

"Hold Tight," 2005, *Burned Again*

WITH RES:

"Golden Boys," 2001, on *Res's How I Do*

SOLO:

"You'll Find a Way," 2008, *Santogold*

"Creator," 2008, *Santogold*

"Disparate Youth," 2012, *Master of My Make-Believe*

"This Isn't Our Parade," 2012, *Master of My Make-Believe*

"Walking in a Circle," 2016, *99¢*

"Run the Races," 2016, *99¢*

Collectively, Bey and Santigold's work share impact—different scales of impact, but recognizable impact. That said, Beyoncé doesn't have to be the standard against which all black women are measured. I am very aware of her hyperexposure, but the comparison between the two felt like an outlandish and therefore exciting way to think about how even the most visible black women are unseen.

Santigold is one of those artists who is vulnerable to the belief that hers is not black music, but from my gatekeeping position, my work here is to place her where she belongs, squarely between the tradition and the future of black music. ■

NICKI MINAJ

ALI GITLOW

ILLUSTRATION BY LINDSEY BAILEY

Nicki Minaj embodies dichotomies. Feminist and sexpot. Barbie and anaconda. Or, as she explained to gossip blogger Perez Hilton in 2012, she's "a crazy psychopath with great intentions." The rapper uses multiple personalities as a way to express diverse points of view—and avoid the usual gendered pigeonholes. With an approach that appeals to streetwise urban dwellers and down-home suburbanites alike, Minaj is the first woman to make it big in the pop *and* rap genres. A bona fide star with unapologetic ambition and laser determination, she insists on having her cake and eating it, too—even (or maybe, especially) when her outsized appetite raises eyebrows.

Born Onika Tanya Maraj in Trinidad and Tobago in 1982, her family moved to Queens, New York, when she was five years old. She had a rough relationship with her father due mainly to his alcohol and drug abuse (he set fire to their family home once). With dreams of making a better life for herself, Minaj attended LaGuardia High School of Music and Art, aka the *Fame* school, where she studied acting. After graduation she held down a string of random jobs while trying to forge a music career, joining a group called the Hoodstars for a short stint. In 2007 she signed to Dirty Money Entertainment after CEO Fendi discovered her on MySpace; it was his idea to supersize her name in an effort to attract more press

attention. When Lil' Wayne heard her buzzworthy mixtapes *Playtime Is Over* and *Sucka Free*, he recognized a need in the market for a smart, sexy female rapper in the wake of Lil' Kim, Foxy Brown, and Trina and signed her to his own label, Young Money, in 2009. Weezy mentored Minaj as she created a third mixtape, *Beam Me Up Scotty*, which helped her secure a place on the wider rap universe's radar and put her in position to achieve mainstream chart success.

Her three studio albums have established her as a fierce rhymesmith, on tracks like "Did It on'em" from 2010's *Pink Friday*, "Stupid Hoe" from 2012's *Pink Friday: Roman Reloaded*, and "Feeling Myself" from 2014's *The Pinkprint* (which also features Beyoncé). Yet no other song has bolstered her reputation as a serious rap contender more than her contribution to Kanye West's "Monster," released in 2010. On it, she puts Jay-Z's, Rick Ross's, and even West's verses to shame, taunting, "Okay first things first / I'll eat your brains."

To the untrained ear Minaj may seem like a textbook rapper, asserting her bad bitch supremacy through fast, hard wordplay. Anyone more familiar with her oeuvre will know, though, that she has multiple bizarre alter egos. The most prominent one, Roman Zolanski, is an angry British gay man. When she personifies him she sounds possessed, dipping into the lower reaches of her vocal range

and trembling like an earthquake poised to erupt. Sometimes she also appears as his do-gooder mother Martha, adopting a whiny Cockney accent. At the 2012 Grammys she put on an elaborate performance—the ceremony's first ever by a solo female rapper—of the song "Roman Holiday," focusing on the wayward character's exorcism. It included religious iconography and krumping clergy members, angering the Catholic League. Minaj even teamed up, as Roman, with Eminem's own furious alter ego Slim Shady on 2010's Swizz Beatz–produced "Roman's Revenge." Other recurring characters include the sweetie pie Harajuku Barbie, slutty Nicki Lewinsky, and spiritual healer Nicki Teresa, each with her own distinctive twang. "I feel it's like one big theater piece," she told the *Guardian* in 2012. "It's a show."

No matter how much fire Minaj may spit, it doesn't stop "real" hip-hop heads from accusing her of being too bubblegum. That's because Minaj is also known for ginormous hits like the can't-get-it-out-of-your-head "Super Bass" and EDM-tinged "Starships," which have highly palatable singsong choruses. Her collaborations with artists like Britney Spears and Justin Bieber also have the power to lure in even the most vanilla of listeners. At times, her two personas conflict.

Minaj easily earns a place in the pantheon of hypersexual female rappers with suggestive tunes like "Whip It" and "I Endorse These Strippers." Crucially, she retains complete control of her own objectification. "There are sexual things that I do that aren't for a man," she once told *Vogue*. In the video for 2014's Sir Mix-a-Lot–sampling paean to booty "Anaconda," she dons a tiny pink G-string, twerking with a squad of similarly blessed backup dancers as she intones, "Pussy put his butt to sleep / Now he calling me NyQuil." When a wax sculpture of her curvaceous form bent down on all fours was installed at Madame Tussauds in Las Vegas in 2015, visitors lined up to take photos with it in explicit poses—and she didn't seem to mind.

However, all this raunchiness became complicated when, due to her poppier numbers, her penchant for fluorescent wigs and Japanese street style–inspired outfits, and her overall cartoonish appearance, Minaj started to gain an unexpected fan base: kids. She has struggled to toe the line between the adult world and that of children, joining eight-year-old British YouTuber Sophia Grace Brownlee on *The Ellen DeGeneres Show* for an adorable duet of "Super Bass" and voicing a character in the animated film *Ice Age: Continental Drift* in 2012. She even refers to her fans as "Barbz" and "Ken Barbz" in a nod to her playful Barbie-esque image of unrealistic body proportions and technicolor hairdos.

Minaj sees world economic domination as part of her feminist agenda. In 2014, she revealed her plan to amass $500 million to *Dazed*: "Then no other woman in rap will ever feel like they can't do what these men have done," she noted. She's well on her way to reaching this goal, making *Forbes*'s annual Hip-Hop Cash Kings list of the highest-grossing rap stars year after year (she is the only female artist to have ever been included on it). In March 2017 she became the woman with the most *Billboard* Hot 100 entries of all time, surpassing Aretha

Franklin's hold on the title after almost forty years. She's won numerous awards and been nominated for a slew more, including ten Grammy nods. Her high-profile endorsement deals range from MAC Cosmetics and OPI nail polish to Adidas and Pepsi. Plus, she touts her own products in her videos, including the fragrance Pink Friday, the pink Beats Pill speaker, and Myx Fusions wine.

While Minaj works tirelessly to spread messages about women's empowerment—especially in the business realm—she is not above getting embroiled in beefs with other celebs, ranging from Miley Cyrus, Taylor Swift, and Mariah Carey (whom she sat with on the judging panel of *American Idol* in 2013) to Remy Ma and one of her inspirations, Lil' Kim. Her widely publicized breakup with rapper Meek Mill in 2017 even spurred her old pal Rick Ross to dis her in his track "Apple of My Eye." You can't please everyone.

For all of these contradictions, one fact rings true: Minaj adores her fans, and it seems they're willing to stick with her through anything. On the E! network's 2012 documentary about her life, *My Truth*, she confessed, "I think that if I were to stop having that kind of relationship with my fans, I would quit the business. Because that is sometimes the only thing that gets me out of bed." She's America's sweetheart, reloaded. ∎

PUSSY RIOT

KATHERINE TURMAN

ILLUSTRATION BY ANNE MUNTGES

Music is but one platform for Pussy Riot's dispatches, espoused via guerilla live performances, videos—and deed. A 2012 protest performance against the authoritarian, anti-free-speech regime of Vladimir Putin's Russia instantly demonstrated that while the members of the Moscow-based feminist group—a collective of about eleven women in their twenties and thirties—were incendiary, they had history on their side. The name Pussy Riot is not so much a band moniker as much as a movement.

Pussy Riot's rise from obscurity to international fame was swift, kick-started with a provocative February 21, 2012, appearance on the altar inside Moscow's Cathedral of Christ the Savior. It was the group's fifth-ever live outing; a previous "rehearsal" was in the famed Red Square. Five Pussy Riot members, including Nadezhda (Nadia) Tolokonnikova, Maria (Masha) Alyokhina, and Yekaterina (Katya) Samutsevich, began what would be a thirty-second "performance" before it was halted by church security. Internet-spread footage of the shambolic act shot Pussy Riot into the headlines. The potent, pointed, and shouted lyrics to "Punk Prayer," the song they performed, rage against the melding of church and state, beseeching the Virgin Mary to take the protesters' side in the fight against patriarchy: "Fight for rights, forget the rite / Join our protest, Holy Virgin"

(translated from Russian). As Malcolm Forbes wrote in the *Columbia Journalism Review*, "Their agitpop is intentional noise, a cacophony tantamount to a clarion call to sit up, take heed, and join the cause."

Within days, the three women were arrested and charged with "hooliganism." The prisoners of conscience became an international cause célèbre. The trio's goals of "transforming consciousness," being the "voice of the voiceless," and "revolution" resonated both positively and negatively in their home country and, almost instantly, abroad. The pro-LGBTQ, free-speech agenda Pussy Riot espoused had huge international impact, language barriers be damned. From Madonna—live in concert—to Amnesty International to Yoko Ono to Peaches to Björk, support for Pussy Riot was manifold, and as bold and colorful as the balaclavas Pussy Riot wore to remain anonymous and keep the focus on issues rather than individuals. Like the band name itself, the head coverings were subversive signifiers, indicating Pussy Riot's goals of positivity and power versus danger and destruction, while also referring back to the masks of feminist activist artists like the Guerrilla Girls.

The road from inception to action to deftly calculated viral video fame was a short trip for Pussy Riot. It was the 2012 election of Putin as president of the Russian Federation that incited Tolokonnikova, a mid-twenties mother, art student, and activist, to action. The intent, she said, was peaceful, using "metaphor and art" to expose and explode Russia's totalitarian oppression and anti–human rights actions. Never has so little—Pussy Riot released seven songs and five videos—achieved so much, sociopolitically speaking. The abbreviated, intent punk of their early protest songs reflects the influences of Riot Grrrl and classic oi! punk of the early 1980s: Angelic Upstarts, Cockney Rejects, Sham 69.

The execution and planning of their cathedral appearance may have been ramshackle—in court, Alyokhina even called the church escapade "small and somewhat absurd "—but the trial helped expose, she also said, "the grotesque mask the government wears." The closely observed court proceeding and voluminous press coverage illuminated the three accused, the loose idea of Pussy Riot as a whole, and the oppressive nature of Putin's government. If the unmasking and governmental persecution and personal probing were antithetical to the idea of Pussy Riot as an anonymous group focused on action and issues, the women's solid grounding in musical, political, and religious history shone through the court system drama, particularly in the articulate scholarship of their closing statements (published by Feminist Press in the US in the book *Pussy Riot! A Punk Prayer for Freedom*).

After a month-long trial in August 2012, they were sentenced to two years in prison. In October Samutsevich appealed and was released on a technicality, but her comrades continued their two-year sentence in prison camps. In July 2013, support for the jailed freedom fighters was still growing: more than one hundred musicians, including Adele, Kesha, Patti Smith, Yoko Ono, and Bruce Springsteen, and members of U2 and Radiohead, signed Amnesty International's open letter calling for Pussy Riot's release.

Yet the unincarcerated members of the collective didn't jump on any of the offered bandwagons. An anonymous Pussy Riot spokeswoman said of invitations to join luminaries onstage: "We're flattered, of course . . . But the only performances we'll participate in are illegal ones. We refuse to perform as part of the capitalist system, at concerts where they sell tickets."

Two days before Christmas 2013, after twenty-one months in prison, a grant of amnesty freed Tolokonnikova and Alyokhina. Upon release, the two added prison reform to their agenda. Appearances on *The Colbert Report*, Amnesty International's Bringing Human Rights Home concert, *Today*, and *Charlie Rose* saw the pair continuing to excoriate Putin's regime, bringing death threats on themselves and families, while concurrently earning nominations for human rights prizes including the European Parliament's Sakharov Prize for Freedom of Thought and the Martin Luther "Fearless Word" prize. They have been the subjects of two documentaries, *Pussy Riot: A Punk Prayer* and *Pussy versus Putin*, as well as a book by noted Russian expert Masha Gessen.

"Official" Pussy Riot output continued sporadically, their fervor and fight for justice no longer confined to Russia. The group's first song and video in English came with February 2015's "I Can't Breathe," which features Tolokonnikova and Alyokhina and was made "for Eric [Garner] and for all those from

PLAYLIST

ALL SONGS AVAILABLE ONLY AS ONLINE VIDEOS:

"A Punk Prayer: Virgin Mary, Chase Putin Away," 2012

"I Can't Breathe," 2015

"Straight Outta Vagina," 2016 (featuring Desi Mo and Leikeli47)

"Make America Great Again," 2016

"Organs," 2016

"Chaika," 2016

Russia to America and around the globe who suffer from state terror—killed, choked, perished because of war and state sponsored violence of all kinds." The haunting, stripped-down ode features punk poet Richard Hell reciting Garner's last words, the song's title. Their post-prison recorded output is more studied and layered than their early songs, and often sung in English. "Make America Great Again" (2016) is a musically bright, bare, folky ditty, in stark contrast to the acerbic political lyrics. "Straight Outta Vagina," featuring American rappers Desi Mo and Leikeli47, is irresistible, an electronic hip-pop anthem, a reminder to a politician who "grabs pussy" that "Vagina's where you're really from." "Organs," sung in Russian, casts a darker shadow, still with hip-hop underpinnings, insinuated with cinematic, classical flourishes, the video portraying Tolokonnikova in a bathtub of blood.

In addition to Pussy Riot's musical and video creations, the two most visible members of the once anonymous group have engaged in various civic and artistic pursuits, sometimes together but increasingly on their own. They founded a news company focused on exposing the Russian government's malfeasance and appeared on *House of Cards*. They both authored books and became interested in theater. From their advocacy of prisoners' rights, to their continuing acts of civil disobedience, to their solo releases, their crimes and punishment as Pussy Riot continue to define their work. Tolokonnikova announced a Kickstarter campaign to support an immersive theatrical production that will allow the audience to "become a participant, experiencing exactly what Pussy Riot went through during our imprisonment."

If the future—and history—of Pussy Riot "the collective" is amorphous, it's no matter. The flashpoint created by their bold 2012 actions allows like-minded rebels to forge forth under the auspices that, as they said, "anyone can be Pussy Riot." As Tolokonnikova urged in her closing court statement: "Come, taste freedom with us." ■

BRITTANY HOWARD

SHANA L. REDMOND

ILLUSTRATION BY WINNIE T. FRICK

Shakes. The word describes as well as conjures an action, a motion, a sensibility. Singers know the rapid, radical expansion of vibrato well, perfecting its delivery. Even in those moments when it appears to be loose and free—two exceptional states of being—the shaking is controlled and focused by skilled singers. With her jaw just shy of unhinged, Brittany Howard is the shakes and shook of Alabama Shakes, leading the band's vocals as well as its guitars through a virtuosic tremor that reminds us bodily that we're in this moment with her. Her performances demand that we be exceptionally present. Let's begin the story of being here.

Approximately halfway between Nashville and Birmingham sits Athens, Alabama, a town with a population of just under fifteen thousand at the time of Howard's birth. Along with her older sister, Jamie, Brittany grew up among auto debris and dust in the junkyard where her father fixed cars. There, she was always into something that might get her hurt. This adventurousness, in tandem with profound loss, sparked her musical acumen. She became an autodidact on guitar, an instrument that she began in earnest after her sister died of retinal cancer and her parents split. By high school she was writing her own songs and playing with a friend, bassist Zac Cockrell, who was joined shortly thereafter by Steve Johnson (drums) and Heath Fogg (guitar). Now a unit, they began to rehearse and perform short sets in local venues under the name the Shakes, soon catching the attention of indie bloggers and labels with a demo including "Hold On," the song that announced the force of Brittany Howard.

Starting with a low Rhodes piano drone and joined by a straightforward drum snare, the song is driven by a rootsy guitar sound that supports the story's arc of perseverance. Howard's sustained note on "hold" exposed to a popular audience the now characteristic form of her mouth, ajar and full with vibration. This autobiographical song served as a natural lead single for the band and an accessible point of interiority for their star, Brittany. Eventually named the song of 2012 by *Rolling Stone*, "Hold On" was the catapult to *Boys and Girls* (2012), the band's Grammy-nominated debut, which created, in the midst of an industry year marked by female vocalists Rihanna, Taylor Swift, and Adele, a new lane for a singer who had no intention of slowing down.

The band's sophomore effort *Sound and Color* (2015) debuted at number one on the US *Billboard* 200 charts. Composed exclusively in the recording studio after a grueling tour, the album shows Howard flexing her songwriting skills, incorporating more lush and intricate harmonies and instrumentals than were heard on the debut. Quiet and intimate or fiery with passion, *Sound and Color* exhibits the

spectrum of knowledges and influences that guide Howard's writing and performance. The standout track is "Don't Wanna Fight." Thirty-eight seconds in, the vocal equivalent of a string scratch tone interrupts. That scene-setting sound of frustration leads into an examination of a contentious relationship, in which Howard asks, "Why can't we both be right?" The album similarly raises this question in relation to musical forms; in spite of being labeled "alternative" by iTunes and indie, folk rock, blues rock, roots rock, Southern rock, and Americana by various other outlets, *Sound and Color* also cozies up to classic soul, for example, in the head-nodding vamp at 2:14 on "Gimme All Your Love."

The album's eclecticism—as well as its title—may have been a result of Howard's reported synesthesia, through which she sees sounds as colors. Its bid to a soul tradition, while heard multiply, is first apparent with Howard herself. Her voice—an open, unassuming tonal mix of cigarettes and passion, which leaves its listeners humbled and envious—was shaped by appreciation for icons such as Nina Simone, Bon Scott, and David Bowie. These same showpeople undoubtedly influenced her unique aesthetic and performance choices, from playing barefoot to wearing clothing that fluctuates between the retro styles of her grandparents' generation and the wide metallic collars and capes of Sun Ra futurism. She travels these spaces of time and genre fluidly, just as she once traveled

PLAYLIST

WITH ALABAMA SHAKES:

"Hold On," 2012, *Boys and Girls*

"Driva Man," 2013, on various artists *12 Years a Slave (Music From and Inspired by the Motion Picture)*

"Don't Wanna Fight," 2015, *Sound and Color*

"Gimme All Your Love," 2015, *Sound and Color*

WITH THUNDERBITCH:

"My Baby Is My Guitar," 2015, *Thunderbitch*

"Heavenly Feeling," 2015, *Thunderbitch*

WITH RUBY AMANFU:

"When My Man Comes Home," 2013, single

ground distance as an employee of the US Postal Service.

Like the genre-bending talents of Screamin' Jay Hawkins, you never quite know what will be next on deck for Howard, and it's because of that, not in spite of it, that I seek her out even at the risk of being lost in the Bermuda Triangle. With a bio that simply reads, "Rock'n'Roll. The end.," Howard's second major band, Thunderbitch, is a composite group of other established Nashville musicians. She's the frontwoman and guide between sixties surfer pop ("Eastside Party") and blues rock inspiration ("My Baby Is My Guitar"), between the US South (rock and roll) and Britain (proto-punk). Sporting a punk aesthetic of white face paint and leather, the music is less aggressive than the band's name suggests, but her performances provide all of the animation and intensity needed. With roots in the South and skills from the future, her voice is a coupling between where popular music has been and where it's going. In the summer of 2017, Howard announced participation in yet another new group, a new trio named Bermuda Triangle—her third in under ten years.

Beyond her continued work as leader of Alabama Shakes and the two bands that followed, Howard's short but stunning career is marked by a number of collaborations and guest appearances. From a Grammy ensemble performance with Elton John, Mavis Staples, and others (2013), to performing at the 2016 Ray Charles Tribute at Obama's White House, to the single "Darkness and Light" (2016) with John Legend, to sharing the stage with Paul McCartney for "Get Back" at Lollapalooza (2015), she is called again and again, darting across genres and audiences. This rare dexterity is evident in her choice and execution of cover songs, which lead her into elderly genres that welcome her unique vocal textures. Alabama Shakes's "Driva Man" for the *12 Years a Slave* soundtrack (2013) follows the slow build of jazz icons Max Roach and Abbey Lincoln's field holler but adds the bulbous southern drawl of Howard's cries. One year later, "dream" collaborator Jack White (formerly of the White Stripes) brought Brittany together with singer Ruby Amanfu to cover the 1940s blues song "When My Man Comes Home" for his Third Man Records label. In it, the women trace each other's voices, with Howard's providing the gravity to Amanfu's airy atmosphere, producing a unique collaboration in which neither attempts to outshine the other. It's a true blues moment due not simply to their clear expressions of pleasure, desire, and longing for a man taken by Uncle Sam but also for their vocal intimacy, which reveals itself in their slow drag during the chorus. This is not the Brittany who wails but the one who whispers, too, revealing both her power and her subtlety. With this range and talent, I have no problem believing Howard when she says, "I feel like I'm capable of anything." ■

ACKNOWLEDGMENTS

There are two people who are as important to *Women Who Rock*'s genesis as I am. Black Dog & Leventhal Publishing Director **BECKY KOH** had the initial vision for a book that would match iconic female artists, writers, and artwork. She let me take it from there, always providing her trust and support, while keeping walls up so I didn't veer off track. I'm delighted to find an editor who was so simpatico and impassioned about music's disruptive and transformative power.

    SARAH LAZIN brought this book to me, and vice versa. She has been my agent since the start of my career, the person who has made my childhood dream of writing books a reality for more than two decades now. Her assistants, **MARGARET SCHULTZ** and **JULIA CONRAD**, were also essential to making *Women Who Rock* happen.

    The initial editorial board for this book, including **DAPHNE A. BROOKS, KANDIA CRAZY HORSE, GILLIAN G. GAAR, ALI GITLOW, REBECCA HAITHCOAT, DREAM HAMPTON, LUCRETIA TYE JAS-MINE, JANA MARTIN, NEKESA MUMBI MOODY, STEPHANIE PHILLIPS, SHANA L. REDMOND,** **SOLVEJ SCHOU, MICHELLE THREADGOULD, KATHERINE TURMAN,** and **GAYLE WALD,** helped me decide which musicians were imperative to include. All of the writers who rock treated their subjects with care and R-E-S-P-E-C-T. It was an honor to work with you, **ALICE BAG, ADELE BERTEI, WENDY CASE, DJ LYNNÉE DENISE, JEANNE FURY, HOLLY GEORGE-WARREN, VIVIEN GOLDMAN, JEWLY HIGHT, THEO KOGAN, MUKTA MOHAN, JESSICA CARE MOORE, PEACHES, JENN PELLY, LIZ PELLY, ANN POWERS, CARYN ROSE, SALAMISHAH TILLET, ALLISON WOLFE,** and **ANNIE ZALESKI.** I'd particularly like to thank **JANA** and **VIVIEN**—my longtime sisters in the Fictionaries—for always being there to sound out ideas and directions. I am grateful to the illustrators—**WINNIE T. FRICK, ANNE MUNTGES, LINDSEY BAILEY, JULIE WINEGARD**—for matching visions with sound. Their art is integral to this book.

    I was fortunate to have two Loyola Marymount University students who assisted me in researching and organizing this immense project. Watch out, world, for **JANIE MCMANA-** **MON** and **ALEXANDER SIMON**! Thank you to the university for giving me a sabbatical to make this happen, and to my colleagues and Dean **ROBBIN CRABTREE** for their support. In **TIMOTHY SNYDER**, I have a president I can always talk Björk with.

    Copy editor **LORI PAXIMADIS** saved our butts over and over again, and made sense of those complicated playlists. **ELIZABETH VAN ITALLIE** made it all look good, and **AMANDA KAIN** created the bitchin' cover.

    I was lucky in life to help teach two beautiful girls, **KARLIE** and **KENDA**, to be women who rock. I grew up in a household where the radio and stereo were almost always on: Thanks to **DAD** and **BRETT** for helping me discover great artists. **JUDY CHRISTENSEN**, you are a saint for taking care of Dad.

    My husband, **BUD SHANKLE**, and son, **COLE SHANKLE**, put up with many late nights of me stressing over missing subjects and playlist formats. They rock, too.

    Most of all, I am grateful to the many musicians who have inspired me over and over again with their songs and their lives. I am so sorry I could not include you all. Next time.

ABOUT THE CONTRIBUTORS

ALICE BAG. Alice Bag is a singer-songwriter, musician, author, artist, educator, and feminist. Alice was the lead singer and co-founder of the Bags, one of the first bands to form during the initial wave of punk rock in Los Angeles. The Alice Bag Band was featured in the seminal documentary on punk rock, *The Decline of Western Civilization*. Alice went on to perform in other groundbreaking bands, including Castration Squad, Cholita, and Las Tres. She has published two books, including the critically acclaimed memoir *Violence Girl* in 2011 (Feral House) and the 2015 self-published *Pipe Bomb for the Soul*, based on her teaching experiences in post-revolutionary Nicaragua. Alice's work is included in the Smithsonian exhibition American Sabor. Alice's self-titled 2016 debut album received critical acclaim and was named one of the best albums of the year by All-Music. Her second album, *Blueprint*, will be released in March 2018 on Don Giovanni Records.

ADELE BERTEI. Adele Bertei is a multidisciplinary artist and writer working in music, poetry, performance, and film/video. Bertei was an original member of the Contortions in 1977–1978 and appeared on the incendiary no wave LP No New York. She played a lead role in Lizzie Bor-den's Born in Flames and has acted in several no wave films. Her writing has appeared in several compilations. Adele has recorded as a solo artist and has written songs, toured, and recorded with various artists such as John Lurie, Whitney Houston, Tears for Fears, Asia Argento, Culture Club, Lydia Lunch, Arthur Baker, Thomas Dolby, Jellybean, and Scritti Politti.

DAPHNE A. BROOKS. Daphne A. Brooks is a professor of African American studies, theater studies, American studies, and women's, gender, and sexuality studies at Yale University. She is the author of two books: *Bodies in Dissent: Spectacular Performances of Race and Freedom, 1850–1910* (Durham, NC: Duke University Press) and *Jeff Buckley's Grace* (New York: Continuum, 2005). She is currently working on a three-volume study of black women and popular music culture titled *Subterranean Blues: Black Women Sound Modernity*. The first volume in the trilogy, *Liner Notes for the Revolution: The Archive, the Critic, and Black Feminist Musicking*, is forthcoming from Harvard University Press. Brooks is also the author of the liner notes for *The Complete Tammi Terrell* (Universal A&R, 2010) and *Take a Look: Aretha Franklin Complete on Columbia* (Sony, 2011).

WENDY CASE. Wendy Case is an Akron-born musician, journalist, and fine artist who criss-crossed the US and various parts of the world as frontwoman for Detroit-based rock outfit the Paybacks. A singer-songwriter and guitarist, Case's songs have been featured in film and television, as well as in the 2004 broadcast of the Academy Awards. Case came off the road in 2008 and embarked on a new career as a licensed psychotherapist and art therapist specializing in trauma and addiction. Case lives and works in the northern suburbs of Detroit with her musician husband and their critters. Her new band, Royal Sweets, is currently active in the Detroit music scene.

KANDIA CRAZY HORSE. A standout in the crowded Americana field and the burgeoning rise of black country, Kandia Crazy Horse expresses an authentic and rich sonic vision of Appalachian (Affrilachian) lore and Native American twang. Born in the nation's capital, Kandia has resided in Bamako, Mali; Maseru, Lesotho; Alexandria, Egypt; Accra, Ghana; Atlanta; Philadelphia; Charlotte, North Carolina; and near Branson, Missouri, and is now based in Harlem. Her Blue Ridge mountain music and Laurel Canyon–influenced songwriting skills, voice infused with a honeyed rasp, and deft arrangements have yielded performances at the Grand Ole Echo party at South by Southwest and at Lincoln Center and garnered critical acclaim from outlets such as *Mojo*, the *Village Voice*, *Acoustic Guitar*, *Relix*, *ß*, and celebrated indie radio station WFMU. Praised for her all-encompassing fluency and facility with varied country and folk music traditions, Kandia unifies the ancient with indigenous futures.

DJ LYNNÉE DENISE. DJ Lynnée Denise is an artist and scholar who was developed as a DJ by her parents' record collection. Her work is inspired by underground cultural movements, the 1980s, migration studies, theories of escape, and electronic music of the African diaspora. She's the product of the historically black Fisk University with an MA from the historically radical San Francisco State University Ethnic Studies Department. DJ Lynnée Denise is a visiting artist at the California State University Los Angeles Pan African Studies Department.

JEANNE FURY. Jeanne Fury has been writing about music for nearly two decades and has been published in the *Village Voice*, *Billboard*, *Decibel*, and more. She volunteers at Willie Mae Rock Camp for Girls in Brooklyn, New York (williemaerockcamp.org), where she has the honor of working with the next generations of strong, brave, badass kids and teens. Her heart belongs to the Lunachicks.

GILLIAN G. GAAR. Gillian G. Gaar has written for numerous publications, including *Mojo*, *Rolling Stone*, and *Goldmine*. Her previous books include *She's a Rebel: The History of Women in Rock and Roll*, *Entertain Us: The Rise of Nirvana*, *Return of the King: Elvis Presley's Great Comeback*, and *Green Day: Rebels with a Cause*, among others. She served as a project consultant for Nirvana's *With the Lights Out* box set. She lives in Seattle.

HOLLY GEORGE-WARREN. Holly George-Warren is a two-time Grammy nominee and an award-winning writer and editor named one of the top women music critics "you need to read" by Flavorwire.com. She is the author of sixteen books, including: *A Man Called Destruction: The Life and Music of Alex Chilton*, *Public Cowboy No. 1: The Life and Times of Gene Autry*, *The Cowgirl Way*, and a forthcoming biography of Janis Joplin. She served as co-producer of the box set *RESPECT: A Century of Women in Music* and the Wanda Jackson tribute album *Hard-Headed Woman*, among other

recordings, and as producer or consulting producer of such documentary films as *Nashville 2.0*, *Hitmakers*, and *Muscle Shoals*. She also teaches at the State University of New York–New Paltz.

ALI GITLOW. Ali Gitlow commissions and edits books about popular culture, art, design, photography, and fashion for Prestel Publishing. Her projects have covered topics including Japanese cute culture, emojis, Juggalos, British subcultural style, toy cameras, cosplay, and images banned from Instagram. She's also a freelance writer mainly covering electronic music and has contributed to outlets like the Red Bull Music Academy Daily, Thump, *Crack Magazine*, and Resident Advisor. She hails from Miami and now lives and works in London after a ten-year stint in New York. Her favorite thing on earth is Notting Hill Carnival. Find her online at aligitlow.com.

VIVIEN GOLDMAN. Vivien Goldman is a London-born, New York–residing writer, broadcaster, educator, and post-punk musician. Her sixth book, *Revenge of the She-Punks*, will be published by the University of Texas Press, following *The Book of Exodus: The Making and Meaning of Marley and the Wailers' Album of the Century* (Three Rivers Press/Random House). She's an adjunct professor at

NYU's Clive Davis Institute of Recorded Music. New York University's Fales Library acquired her archive as the Vivien Goldman Punk and Reggae Collection. *Cherchez la Femme*, the musical she co-wrote with August Darnell, aka Kid Creole, premiered at the La MaMa Theatre in 2016. "Resolutionary," a compilation of Goldman's music (Staubgold), was selected as a top reissue of 2016 by the *Wire* magazine and others.

REBECCA HAITHCOAT. Rebecca Haithcoat is a writer living in Los Angeles. She was the assistant music editor and a theater critic at *LA Weekly*, as well as a staff writer for the new MySpace. Her writing has been published in the *New York Times*, *GQ*, the *Guardian*, *Playboy*, *Billboard*, Pitchfork, *Spin*, and *Vice*, among others. She earned her MA at the USC Annenberg School for Journalism and is the recipient of two NEA fellowships. She once did tequila shots with Lil Jon in Las Vegas.

JEWLY HIGHT. Jewly Hight is a Nashville-based music critic and journalist who's contributed to the *New York Times*, NPR, Vulture/NYMag.com, *Billboard*, the *Oxford American*, Pitchfork, MTV.com, and a number of other outlets. Her work frequently focuses on country, roots, pop, R&B, and gender. She's the author of *Right by Her Roots: Americana Women and Their Songs* and was the inaugural recipient of the Chet Flippo Award for Excellence in Country Music Journalism.

LUCRETIA TYE JASMINE. With wild interests and an inclination to rage against the machine with a self-destructive flair that could equal the groupies and rock stars who fascinate her, writer and artist Lucretia Tye Jasmine earned a BFA from Tisch (University Honors Scholar, 1988) and an MFA from CalArts (2006). Alien She, the Fales Special Collections Library, the Getty Center, Joanie 4 Jackie, MoPOP, and the Punk Museum Los Angeles have featured her work. Recent publications include *Let It Bleed: How to Write a Rockin' Memoir*, edited by Pamela Des Barres (2017). Current projects are the oral history mixtape zines *riot grrrl Los Angeles* and the *Groupie Gospels*.

THEO KOGAN. As the lead singer of NYC's Lunachicks, Theo was widely known for her signature avant-garde style, high-energy performances, and powerful lead vocals. During her ten years on the road with the Lunachicks, her day jobs ranged from babysitting, to go go dancing, to modeling, which led to acting. Her writing credits include *Paper Magazine*, *Time Out NY*, *Nylon Magazine*, and *Gen Art Pulse*. She was MOLI.com's fashion and design contributing editor and advice columnist. In 2009 Theo launched her lip gloss brand, Armour Beauty, and started her journey as a professional makeup artist. In 2010 she had her daughter, Lucy. Today she continues to rock her pro makeup artistry and is working on writing, film, and music projects—so stay tuned!

JANA MARTIN. Jana Martin has written about electronica, bluegrass, postwar design patents, pigeon racing, wedding veils, and cigarette packaging. She's a contributing editor for TheWeeklings and the author of nonfiction and fiction books, including a forthcoming novel. Her work appears in the *New York Times*, the *Village Voice*, *Marie Claire*, *Elle*, *Glimmer Train*, and Tinker Street.

MUKTA MOHAN. Mukta Mohan is a radio host, DJ, and podcast producer based in Los Angeles. She has produced pieces for *MTV News*, Crooked Media, *Marketplace*, and NPR affiliate stations. Mohan is the co-founder of the feminist music and arts collective Honey Power. She also creates audio art installations using voicemails left anonymously. She was named best radio DJ in Los Angeles by *LA Weekly* in 2014 and has appeared in *LA Record* and on BBC Radio 6. Mohan is a graduate of Loyola Marymount University.

NEKESA MUMBI MOODY. Nekesa Mumbi Moody is an award-winning veteran journalist who has broken and covered some of the biggest entertainment stories in recent memory and interviewed its biggest stars. As the global entertainment and lifestyles editor for the Associated Press, she directs a multiformat entertainment report for the world's largest newsgathering organization. Previously, as the AP's music editor, she interviewed everyone from Beyoncé to Prince to Taylor Swift to Kanye West. She was the first to report the news of Whitney Houston's death, and the first person to get official confirmation of the passing of Prince. She was also the first to report the recent death of Chris Cornell.

JESSICA CARE MOORE. jessica Care moore is the executive producer and founder of Black Women Rock!, a thirteen-year-old rock-and-roll concert and education series dedicated to Betty Davis and supporting independent black women artists who play rock and roll. An internationally renowned poet, playwright, performance artist, and producer, she is a distinguished 2016 Kresge Arts Fellow, a 2017 Knight Arts Foundation winner, and the 2013 Alain Locke Award Recipient from the Detroit Institute of Arts. moore is the author of *The Words Don't Fit in My Mouth*, *The Alphabet Verses*, *The Ghetto*, *God Is Not an American*, *Sunlight through Bullet*

Holes, and the forthcoming collection *We Want Our Bodies Back*. moore is a signed recording artist for Talib Kweli's Javotti Media label, which released her first album, *Black Tea: The Legend of Jessi James*. She also has recorded with José James, Nas, Jeezy, Karriem Riggins, and the Last Poets. Born in Detroit, moore first came to national prominence when she won the legendary *It's Showtime at the Apollo* televised competition a record-breaking five times in a row.

PEACHES: An iconic feminist musician, producer, director, and performance artist, Peaches has spent nearly two decades pushing boundaries and wielding influence over mainstream pop culture from outside of its confines. She's collaborated with everyone from Iggy Pop and Daft Punk to Kim Gordon and Major Lazer; had her music featured in cultural watermarks like *Lost in Translation*, *The Handmaid's Tale*, and *Broad City*; and seen her work studied at universities around the world. Dubbed a "genuine heroine" by the *New York Times*, Peaches has released five critically acclaimed studio albums blending electronic music, hip-hop, and punk rock while tackling gender politics, sexual identity, ageism, and the patriarchy. Uncut has raved that her work brought together "high art, low humour and deluxe filth [in] a

hugely seductive combination," while *Rolling Stone* called her "surreally funny [and] nasty." Peaches has directed over twenty of her own videos, designed one of the most raw and creative stage shows in popular music, and has appeared at modern art's most prestigious gatherings, from Art Basel Miami Beach to the Venice Biennale. She mounted a one-woman production of *Jesus Christ Superstar*—redubbed *Peaches Christ Superstar*—which earned international raves, composed and performed the electro-rock opera *Peaches Does Herself*, which premiered at the Toronto International Film Festival, and sang the title role in a production of Monteverdi's epic seventeenth-century opera *L'Orfeo* in Berlin. It's all documented beautifully in the book *What Else Is in the Teaches of Peaches*, a collection of Holger Talinski's photos accompanied by text from Yoko Ono, Ellen Page, and Michael Stipe, among others. Her latest album, *Rub*, is her most audacious and unequivocal work to date, and she continues to tour behind it relentlessly, spreading joy and empowerment as she mixes the profane and the political in the singular way that only Peaches can.

JENN PELLY. Jenn Pelly is a contributing editor at Pitchfork. She is the author of a 33⅓ book on feminist punk band the Raincoats, and her writing has appeared in *Rolling Stone*, *Spin*, and the *Wire*.

LIZ PELLY. Liz Pelly is a music and culture journalist in New York. Her byline has appeared at the *Baffler*, the *Guardian*, *Rolling Stone*, the late *Boston Phoenix*, and elsewhere. Since 2013, she has co-edited the Media, a digital newspaper covering the intersections of art and activism.

STEPHANIE PHILLIPS. Stephanie Phillips is a London-based arts and culture journalist. She is also a member of the black feminist punk band Big Joanie. Her work has been featured in outlets such as Noisey, Bandcamp, and Alternative Press. She contributed an essay to the 2017 anthology *Under My Thumb: Songs That Hate Women and the Women Who Love Them*, edited by Rhian E. Jones and Eli Davies.

ANN POWERS. Ann Powers is a music critic and correspondent for NPR and the author of several books, most recently *Good Booty: Love and Sex, Black and White, Body and Soul in American Music* (Dey Street Books, 2017). She lives in Nashville with her family.

SHANA L. REDMOND. Shana L. Redmond is the author of *Anthem: Social Movements and the Sound of Solidarity in the African Diaspora*

(New York University Press, 2014) and the forthcoming *Everything Man: The Form and Function of Paul Robeson*. Her work has appeared in numerous media and literary outlets including NPR, *Huffington Post*, the Feminist Wire, and *Brick*. She teaches in the Herb Alpert School of Music at UCLA.

CARYN ROSE. Caryn Rose is a New York City–based writer and photographer who documents rock and roll and urban life. She is the author of two novels (*B-Sides and Broken Hearts* and *A Whole New Ballgame*) and three nonfiction books (including *Raise Your Hand*, a document of Bruce Springsteen's 2012 European tour). She is a contributor to Pitchfork, *MTV News*, Salon, *Billboard*, the *Village Voice*, Vulture, the *Guardian*, and NPR, among others.

SOLVEJ SCHOU. Solvej Schou is a Southern California–based writer and musician. Solvej's articles have been published by the Associated Press, the *New York Times*, the *Los Angeles Times*, *Billboard*, and other outlets, and she is a former AP staff writer and *Entertainment Weekly* senior staff writer. Her AP first-person story about auditioning for *American Idol* was published in the Da Capo book *Best Music Writing 2008*. She's interviewed artists including Aretha Franklin, Brian Wilson, Ringo Starr, Karen

O, Flea, Tyga, Katy Perry, Chrissie Hynde, and Patti Smith. Solvej has a bachelor's degree from Barnard College, Columbia University, and a master's degree in journalism from the University of Southern California.

MICHELLE THREADGOULD. Michelle Threadgould is an Oakland-based Chicana journalist. She covers music, politics, news, arts and culture, Latinx issues, and the poetry of resistance. She has written for CNN, *Pacific Standard*, KQED, Remezcla, Good, and the *New York Observer*.

SALAMISHAH TILLET. Salamishah Tillet is an associate professor of English and Africana studies at the University of Pennsylvania. In 2003, Salamishah and her sister, Scheherazade Tillet, co-founded A Long Walk Home, Inc., a Chicago-based nonprofit that uses art to empower young people and end violence against girls and women. She is the author of *Sites of Slavery: Citizenship and Racial Democracy in the Post–Civil Rights Imagination* (Duke University Press, 2012) and is currently working on a critical memoir on Nina Simone. She wrote the liner notes for John Legend and the Roots' Grammy-winning album *Wake Up!* in 2011 and for the vinyl reissue of *Nina Simone Sings the Blues* in 2016. She has appeared on the BBC, CNN, MSNBC, and NPR and in *Ebony* and *Essence,* published articles with TheAtlantic.com, the *Chicago Tribune,* the *Guardian,* the *Nation,* and Time.com and regularly contributes to *Elle* and the *New York Times.*

KATHERINE TURMAN. Katherine Turman is a music journalist, radio producer, and author. A Los Angeles native currently living in New York City, she co-authored the critically acclaimed 2013 oral history of heavy metal, *Louder than Hell* (Harper Collins), and has written for the *Village Voice,* the *Los Angeles Times, Rolling Stone, Billboard, Variety,* and numerous other outlets. She was editor of *RIP* magazine and the *LA Alternative Press,* and currently produces the syndicated classic rock radio show *Nights with Alice Cooper.*

GAYLE WALD. Gayle Wald is a professor of English and American studies at George Washington University, where she teaches courses on popular music and culture. She is author of three books, including *Shout, Sister, Shout!,* a biography of Rosetta Tharpe, and *It's Been Beautiful,* about *Soul!,* a pioneering TV showcase of the politics and culture of Black Power.

ALLISON WOLFE. Allison Wolfe was raised in an all-female, single-parent household by a lesbian feminist mother who started the first women's health clinic in Olympia, Washington. While attending university, she co-founded a punk feminist fanzine, *Girl Germs,* an all-girl band, Bratmobile, and the third-wave feminist punk movement Riot Grrrl. Allison also initiated the nonprofit feminist music festival Ladyfest. She lives in Los Angeles, where she got her master's degree in arts journalism from the USC Annenberg School for Communication and Journalism. Allison produces a monthly podcast for Tidal called *I'm in the Band,* sings in the band Ex Stains, and is working on an oral history of Riot Grrrl book and audio archive.

ANNIE ZALESKI. Annie Zaleski is a freelance journalist, editor, and critic based in Cleveland, Ohio. Previously, she was on staff as an editor at the *Riverfront Times* and *Alternative Press;* currently, she's a contributing writer at the A.V. Club and a columnist at Salon. Her profiles, interviews, and criticism have appeared in publications such as *Rolling Stone, Spin, Vulture,* RBMA, Stereogum, *Billboard,* the *Village Voice,* the *Cleveland Plain Dealer,* and *Las Vegas Weekly.* More recently she wrote the liner notes for the deluxe edition of R.E.M.'s *Out of Time* and was part of the team that helped relaunch the Rock and Roll Hall of Fame's website.

ABOUT THE ILLUSTRATORS

LINDSEY BAILEY. Lindsey Bailey is an artist and illustrator based in Memphis, Tennessee. She has worked on children's books, editorial illustration, commissioned portraits, and digital graphics. Her work can be seen at www.lindseyswop.com.

WINNIE T. FRICK. Winnie T. Frick is a comic artist and illustrator currently based in Brooklyn. Her visual interests include crosshatching, architecture, and doppelgängers.

ANNE MUNTGES. Anne Muntges is an artist who makes highly detailed drawings, prints, and installation art based on concepts of the home. Born in Denver and based in Brooklyn, her work was recently on view in the exhibition Drawn In, at the Children's Museum of the Arts in New York City. Her work has been exhibited in New York at the New York Foundation for the Arts, International Print Center, and Lilac Museum Steamship; in Chicago at the Ukrainian Institute of Modern Art; and in Buffalo at the Burchfield Penney Art Center. She received a BFA from the Kansas City Art Institute and an MFA from the University at Buffalo. Muntges has had fellowships to Anchor Graphics, Bemis Center for Contemporary Arts, Vermont Studio Center, and Ox-Bow School of Art and Artists' Residency, and she received a New York Foundation for the Arts Fellowship in Printmaking/Drawing/Artist Books in 2014. In 2017, Muntges was awarded fellowships at BRIC in New York, Guttenberg Arts in New Jersey, and the Roswell Artist-in-Residence Program in New Mexico.

JULIE WINEGARD. Julie Winegard is a designer and illustrator whose work focuses on pop culture and current events. She grew up in the hills of West Virginia and moved to New York City after graduating with a BFA in graphic design from West Virginia University. She will graduate with an MS in strategic communication from Columbia University in 2019.

ARTIST INDEX

ARTIST INDEX, continued

AUTHOR INDEX

ILLUSTRATOR INDEX

Black Dog & Leventhal Publishers
Hachette Book Group
1290 Avenue of the Americas
New York, NY 10104
www.hachettebookgroup.com
www.blackdogandleventhal.com

First Edition: October 2018

Black Dog & Leventhal Publishers is an imprint of Running Press, a division of Hachette Book Group. The Black Dog & Leventhal Publishers name and logo are trademarks of Hachette Book Group, Inc.

The publisher is not responsible for websites (or their content) that are not owned by the publisher.

The Hachette Speakers Bureau provides a wide range of authors for speaking events. To find out more, go to www.HachetteSpeakersBureau.com or call (866) 376-6591.

Print book interior design by Elizabeth Van Itallic

Library of Congress Cataloging-in-Publication Data
Names: McDonnell, Evelyn, editor.
Title: Women who rock : Bessie to Beyonce. Girl groups to riot grrrl /
[edited by] Evelyn McDonnell.
Description: First edition. | New York, NY : Black Dog & Leventhal, 2018.
Identifiers: LCCN 2018000198| ISBN 9780316558877 (hardcover) | ISBN
9780316558860 (ebook)
Subjects: LCSH: Women musicians—Biography. | Women singers—Biography. |
Women rock musicians—Biography. | Musicians—Biography.
Classification: LCC ML82 .W688 2018 | DDC 782.42164092/52 [B]—dc23
LC record available at https://lccn.loc.gov/2018000198

ISBNs: 978-0-316-55887-7 (hardcover); 978-0-316-55886-0 (ebook)

Printed in China

Imago

10 9 8 7 6 5 4 3 2 1